Instructor's Manual
to Accompany

Legal Research, Analysis, and Writing

WILLIAM H. PUTMAN

THOMSON

DELMAR LEARNING

Australia Canada Mexico Singapore Spain United Kingdom United States

WEST LEGAL STUDIES

Instructor's Manual to Accompany
Legal Research, Analysis, and Writing
by William H. Putman

Printed in the United States
  3 4 5 XXX 07 06 05

For more information contact Delmar Learning,
5 Maxwell Drive, Clifton Park, NY 12065-2919

Or find us on the World Wide Web at
www.delmarlearning.com or
www.westlegalstudies.com

For permission to use material from this text or product, contact us by
Tel   (800) 730-2214
Fax   (800) 730-2215
www.thomsonrights.com

Library of Congress Cataloging-in-Publication Data
ISBN: 0-7668-5456-6
Catalog Card Number: 2003009183

NOTICE TO THE READER

Publisher does not warrant or guarantee any of the products described herein or perform any independent analysis in connection with any of the product information contained herein. Publisher does not assume, and expressly disclaims, any obligation to obtain and include information other than that provided to it by the manufacturer.

The reader is notified that this text is an education tool, not a practice book. Since the law is in constant change, no rule or statement of law in this book should be relied upon for any service to any client. The reader should always refer to standard legal sources for the current rule or law. If legal advice or other expert assistance is required, the services of the appropriate professional should be sought.

The Publisher makes no representation or warranties of any kind, including but not limited to, the warranties of fitness for particular purpose or merchantability, nor are any such representations implied with respect to the material set forth herein, and the publisher takes no responsibility with respect to such material. The publisher shall not be liable for any special, consequential, or exemplary damages resulting, in whole or part, from the readers' use of, or reliance upon, this material.

THOMSON

DELMAR LEARNING

Instructor's Manual to Accompany

LEGAL
RESEARCH,
ANALYSIS,
and
WRITING

WILLIAM H. PUTMAN

CONTENTS

PREFACE

Legal Research, Analysis, and Writing is designed to be used as a main text for legal research, writing, and analysis courses. It can be useful in schools that have separate research and writing courses, where the first course focuses primarily on research with an introduction to writing, and the second course focuses on writing with research as a secondary component. For the research course the instructor would use Chapters 1 through 13. For the writing course instructors would use Chapters 9 through 19. Where both research and writing are combined in one course, instructors can select the chapters deemed appropriate for such a combined course.

The text is designed to cover the topics of legal research, analysis, and writing in general. It is organized in a manner to provide students with comprehensive information regarding the difficult areas of research, analysis, and writing. Each chapter begins with a hypothetical which raises a question or questions involving the subject matter of the chapter. Following the hypothetical is a presentation of the principles, concepts, guidelines, and information concerning the subject matter. Next, the principles and information discussed in the chapter are applied to answer the questions raised in the hypothetical. The answer to the hypothetical towards the end of the chapter allows the student to see how the subject matter ties together and is applied.

The text is divided into the following four parts:

PART I—INTRODUCTION TO RESEARCH ANALYTICAL PRINCIPLES AND THE LEGAL PROCESS

Part I is composed of two introductory chapters. The first chapter presents an overview of the legal system and the legal process and a summary of the basic legal principles involved in the process, such as authority, precedent, stare decisis, and so on. The second chapter introduces legal analysis and the IRAC analytical process.

PART II—LEGAL RESEARCH

Part II consists of six chapters that provide in-depth coverage of legal research and the research process. It begins with two chapters on primary authority—chapters on statutory and case law. Next are two chapters on secondary authority. Then is a chapter on computers and legal research followed by a chapter on legal citation.

PART III—LEGAL ANALYSIS

Part III covers matters essential to the analysis of a legal problem. It begins with a chapter on a principal component of a legal question (legal issue), the Key Facts—facts critical to the outcome of the case. Next are chapters on identifying and writing legal issues and a concluding two chapters on topics fundamental to legal analysis: Case Law Application and Counteranalysis.

PART IV—LEGAL WRITING

The focus of Part IV is on legal writing and the legal writing process. It covers the application of the principles presented in the previous chapters to the drafting of legal research memoranda, court briefs, and legal correspondence.

At the end of each chapter are assignments which require the student to perform research, analysis, or writing tasks. Additional assignments are included in the Online Resource that accompanies the text. The assignments range in difficulty and require the student to apply the principles and techniques presented in the text. The assignments are based on the facts and law presented in the assignment and the court opinions included in the text, Appendix A, or the Online Resource. The answers to the assignments are included in this manual. In addition, true/false and multiple choice questions for each chapter are included in the manual.

Finally, I welcome your comments and input. Any recommendations or information regarding teaching approaches you have found effective are appreciated. I can be reached as follows:

William Putman
Telephone: 970-240-8907
Email: putman@montrose.net

CHAPTER 1

Introduction to Legal Principles and Authorities

TEXT ASSIGNMENT ANSWERS

Instructor's note: The purpose of the first chapter is to provide students with a basic familiarity with the sources of law, hierarchy of the law, federal and state court systems, and fundamental concepts involved in legal analysis, such as precedent and authority. The material in the chapter may be covered in greater depth in other courses. It is presented here to ensure that basic information and concepts related to legal analysis and writing are covered and available to students in the text. Even if there is repetition of material presented in other courses, the information is important and bears repetition.

The exercises are designed to allow students the opportunity to apply the concepts presented in the chapter.

ASSIGNMENT 1

Instructor's note: This assignment requires students to research their states' statutes. Since most states have more than one court of limited jurisdiction, such as municipal, probate, and county courts, the assignment may be expanded to require students to name and describe the jurisdiction of more than one limited jurisdiction court.

ASSIGNMENT 2

Instructor's note: This assignment may be expanded to require students to describe the jurisdictional differences between the state's court of appeals and supreme court.

A trial court is where the evidence is presented, testimony is taken, and a decision is reached. It is where the matter is heard and decided. It differs from a court of appeals in that it is not the role of a trial court to review the decision of another court.

The primary function of a court of appeals is to review the decision of a trial court to determine and correct any error that may have been made. A court of appeals differs from a trial court in that it does not hear the matter, that is, it does not hear testimony, try the case, or hear the evidence.

ASSIGNMENT 3

A court opinion becomes a precedent when the facts and issues of an opinion are identical or similar to the facts and issues in the case before the court.

ASSIGNMENT 4

Instructor's note: Assignment 1 involves the following authority that is listed here for quick reference:

1. State A's Uniform Commercial Code statute.
2. State A's Consumer Credit Act.
3. State B's Uniform Commercial Code statute.
4. Federal statute—Consumer Credit Act.
5. *Iron v. Supply Co.*—Decision of highest court in State A.

6. *Milk v. Best Buy Inc.*—Decision of highest court in State B.
7. *Control Co. v. Martin*—Decision of intermediary court of appeals in State A.
8. *Lesley v. Karl Co.*—Decision of trial court in State A.
9. *Irene v. City Co.*—Federal case involving the federal Consumer Credit Act.
10. Regulations adopted by State A's corporation commission that apply to consumer credit and the sale of goods.
11. Restatements of the law defining sales, consumer credit, and other terms related to the problem.
12. An A.L.R. reference that directly addresses the issues in the case.

ASSIGNMENT 4A

Primary authority is defined as the law itself. It is composed of the enacted law (constitutional, legislative, regulatory, etc.) and the common/case law (court-made law). Secondary authority is any source a court may rely on that is not the law and that is not primary authority. With these definitions in mind, numbers 1 through 10 of the above listed authorities are primary authority.

a. Numbers 1 through 4 are laws passed by state or federal legislative bodies.
b. Numbers 5 through 9 are court decisions which present common or court-made law.
c. Number 10 is an administrative law. The regulation adopted by the state's corporation commission has the force of law.
d. Numbers 11 and 12 are secondary authority. They are reference sources that are not the law. Restatements of the Law are formulations of what the law should be and comments and discussions on why the formulations are recommended. A.L.R. references are notes and comments on the law, not the actual law.

ASSIGNMENT 4B

PART 1. Mandatory authority is any primary authority a court must rely on when reaching a decision. In this assignment, since the problem involves the sale of goods in State A, the mandatory authority is the authority that the courts in State A must apply when reaching a decision. Of the 12 sources of authority listed in the assignment, the following may be mandatory authority for State A courts:

a. **Number 4, the federal Consumer Credit Act.** The federal Consumer Credit Act may be mandatory authority for a State A court. The act may be mandatory authority if, by terms of the statute, it applies to govern the particular sale-of-goods question being addressed by the State A court.
b. **Numbers 1, 2, and 10, State A's Uniform Commercial Code, Consumer Credit Act, and corporation commission regulations.** These may be mandatory authority because they are enactments of State A's legislature and an administrative agency that are the laws of State A. The state courts must follow the laws enacted by the state legislative body and administrative agencies unless the laws violate the constitution.
c. **Numbers 5 and 7, *Iron v. Supply Co.* and *Control Co. v. Martin.*** These court opinions are decisions of the highest court and intermediary court of appeals in State A. The decisions of these courts establish the law in State A and must be followed by the courts in State A.
d. **Number 9, *Irene v. City Co.*** This federal court decision can be mandatory authority because, if the federal Consumer Credit Act (Number 4) applies, the federal court's interpretation of that law must be followed by State A courts.
e. **Number 8, *Lesley v. Karl Co.*** Trial court decisions in a state normally are not mandatory authority. Usually only the opinions of a state's highest court and intermediary courts of appeal are mandatory authority that other courts in the state must follow. This may vary from state to state.

PART 2. Not all of the primary authority will be mandatory authority for State A courts. Certain conditions must be present for primary authority to be mandatory authority.

a. **No. 4, the federal Consumer Credit Act.** In order for the federal statute to be mandatory authority, the provisions of the act must apply to govern the question being addressed by the court. In addition, a federal law will not apply if its application is deemed to violate the United States Constitution.

b. **Nos. 1, and 2, State A's Uniform Commercial Code and Consumer Credit Act.** State statutes are mandatory authority when:
   1. their provisions apply to govern the facts of the case (use the three-step process discussed in the ROLE OF AUTHORITY, MANDATORY AUTHORITY, Enacted Law subsection of the chapter),
   2. their application does not conflict with a federal law that governs the area, and
   3. their application does not violate the state or federal constitution.
c. **No. 10, regulations adopted by State A's corporation commission.** Regulations adopted by a State A administrative body can be mandatory authority when:
   1. their provisions apply to govern the facts of the case (use the three-step process discussed in the ROLE OF AUTHORITY, MANDATORY AUTHORITY, Enacted Law subsection of the chapter),
   2. their application does not conflict with a federal or state law that governs the area, and
   3. their application does not violate the state or federal constitution.
d. **No. 9, *Irene v. City Co.*** In order for the federal court decision to be mandatory authority:
   1. the federal statute (No. 4, the federal Consumer Credit Act in this case) must apply to govern the question,
   2. the case must be on point; that is, it is sufficiently similar to the facts of the case for the decision to apply as precedent (see Chapter 12), and
   3. the decision must not have been superseded by a higher federal court decision.
e. **No. 5, *Iron v. Supply Co.*** Under the doctrine of stare decisis, the decision of the highest court in State A is mandatory authority and must be followed by the lower courts in State A. The prerequisites are that the decision is on point (see Chapter 12) and its application does not violate either the state or federal constitution.
f. **No. 7, *Control Co. v. Martin.*** Under the doctrine of stare decisis, the decision of the intermediary court of appeals is mandatory authority and must be followed by the lower courts in State A. The prerequisites are that the decision is on point, its application does not violate either the state or federal constitution, and its application does not conflict with a higher court decision in State A (the state supreme court).

Also, under the doctrine of stare decisis, the intermediary court of appeals in State A will follow an earlier decision of a State A intermediary court of appeals if the earlier decision is on point. A later court of appeals, however, is not absolutely bound to follow an earlier court of appeals decision. It is free to amend or overrule the decision if it finds the earlier decision was in error or no longer reflects current public policy or current legal thinking.

ASSIGNMENT 4C

Persuasive authority is authority a court may rely on and follow but is not bound to rely on or follow. It can be either primary or secondary authority. In certain situations, all of the 12 listed sources of authority could be persuasive authority.

a. **Nos. 3 and 6, State B's Uniform Commercial Code statute and *Milk v. Best Buy Inc.*** The statutes and case law of State B cannot be mandatory authority in State A. A state is not required to follow the law of other states. But, in the absence of mandatory authority in State A, State A courts may consider, adopt, or follow State B law and court decisions.

   In order for a court decision to be considered persuasive authority, the decision must be on point. That is, the key facts and applicable law of the court opinion must be sufficiently similar to the key facts and applicable law of the case being heard by the court, before the opinion may provide guidance to the court in deciding an issue (see Chapter 12).
b. **Nos. 11 and 12, Restatements of the Law defining sales, consumer credit, and other terms related to the problem and an A.L.R. reference that directly addresses the issues in the case.** Restatements of the Law and A.L.R. references are secondary authority and therefore are not mandatory authority. In the absence of mandatory authority, a court may look to and adopt secondary authority if it so chooses. The usual prerequisite is that the secondary authority is on point; that is, it addresses legal questions and applies laws or legal principles that are sufficiently similar to the questions and laws being applied in the case before the court.
c. **No. 8, *Lesley v. Karl Co.*** A decision of a state trial court is not mandatory authority for other trial or higher courts in the state. The other courts, including the higher state courts, may consider, adopt, or follow a decision of a trial court.

d. **Nos. 5, 7, and 9, *Iron v. Supply Co., Control Co. v. Martin,* and *Irene v. City Co.*** When the decision of a federal court or a higher state court is not mandatory authority (see the previous discussion in Assignment 4B), the reasoning or holding may still be persuasive precedent and considered, adopted, or followed in whole or in part. An opinion may not be mandatory authority but a court may consider it persuasive authority when:
   - it is not on point, but the court refers to the reasoning or analysis in the decision for general guidance in interpreting the statute (see Chapter 12);
   - the decision has been superseded by a higher state court or later court of appeals decision in State A, yet the reasoning or analysis in the decision is persuasive to a subsequent court. The court may refer to the prior reasoning or analysis unless it was rejected by the subsequent ruling;
   - the question is governed by a federal statute but there is no federal case law interpreting the statute, leaving the state case as guidance; or
   - the question is governed by a state statute, but there is no state case law interpreting the statute; then a federal case law may be referred to for guidance.

e. **Nos. 1, 2, 3, 4, and 10, State A's Uniform Commercial Code statute, State A's Consumer Credit Act, State B's Uniform Commercial Code statute, federal Consumer Credit Act, and regulations adopted by State A's corporation commission which apply to consumer credit and the sale of goods.** A statute or regulation may not be mandatory authority because the elements of the law do not apply to govern the facts of the case. When a statute or regulation does not apply, a court may still look to the statute or regulation for guidance when interpreting another law that has similar provisions.

FOR EXAMPLE   A term defined in Act A may not be defined in Act B, the act that governs the problem being addressed by the court. In this situation, the definition in Act A may be relied on by the court, guide it in its interpretation of the term in Act B, and be adopted in whole or in part. In such a situation, Act A can be persuasive authority.

ASSIGNMENT 4D

In general the hierarchy of primary authority within each jurisdiction is the constitution (the highest authority), followed by the enacted law (legislative and administrative), then the common or court-made law. Where state and federal law both apply, the federal law takes precedence over state law. When there is primary mandatory authority and primary persuasive authority, the primary mandatory authority takes precedence over the primary persuasive authority. With these guidelines in mind, the hierarchy of the primary authority listed in the assignment is as follows (the highest primary authority is listed first followed by the next highest, etc.):

No. 4 Consumer Credit Act—the federal statute.

Nos. 1 State A's Uniform Commercial Code statute, and
   2 State A's Consumer Credit Act. The more specific statute generally has the greater authority value.

No. 10 Regulations adopted by State A's corporation commission, which apply to consumer credit and the sale of goods.

No. 9 *Irene v. City Co.*—Federal case involving the federal Consumer Credit Act.

No. 5 *Iron v. Supply Co.*—Decision of highest court in State A.

No. 7 *Control Co. v. Martin*—Decision of intermediary court of appeals in State A.

No. 8 *Lesley v. Karl Co.*—Decision of trial court in State A. As mentioned in Assignment 4C, the decisions of state trial courts do not usually have authoritative value. If in State A certain trial court decisions have authoritative value, that value is mandatory authority only for any courts lower than the trial court in that jurisdiction and takes precedence over persuasive authority, such as the persuasive authority listed below.

No. 3 State B's Uniform Commercial Code statute. State B's legislative enactments cannot be mandatory authority in State A. This statute's value as authority is subordinate to the authority listed above, all of which can be mandatory authority.

No. 6 *Milk v. Best Buy Inc.*—Decision of highest court in State B. Like No. 3 above, this is persuasive authority and is subordinate to the mandatory authority.

ASSIGNMENT 5

Assignment 5 involves the following authority, which is listed here for quick reference:

1. *Idle v. City Company*—A 1980 decision by the highest court of State A where the court created a cause of action in tort for the wrongful destruction of business records. The court ruled that a cause of action exists if the records were destroyed in anticipation of or while a worker's compensation claim is pending. The court also held that a cause of action exists if the destruction was intentional or negligent.
2. 1989 State A statute—The legislature of State A passed a law that created a cause of action in tort for the intentional destruction of business records. The statute provides that a cause of action exists if the destruction occurs in anticipation of or while a workmen's compensation claim is pending.
3. *Merrick v. Taylor*—A 1990 decision of the court of appeals of State A. The court of appeals is a lower court than the state's highest court. The court held that "intentional" within the meaning of the 1989 statute includes either the intentional destruction of records or the destruction of records as a result of gross negligence.
4. *Davees v. Contractor*—A decision of the highest court of State B interpreting a State B statute identical to the 1989 State A statute. The court held that "intentional" as used in the statute includes gross negligence only when the gross negligence is accompanied by a "reckless and wanton" disregard for the preservation of the business records.
5. 1991 federal statute—The statute is identical to the 1989 state statute. It only applies to contractors with federal contracts.
6. A.L.R. reference—An A.L.R. reference that addresses specific questions similar to those raised in the client's case.

ASSIGNMENT 5A

As discussed in Assignment 4A, primary authority is defined as the law itself. It is composed of the enacted law (constitutional, legislative, regulatory, etc.) and the common/case law (court made law). Secondary authority is any source a court may rely on that is not the law, that is not primary authority. Numbers 1 through 5 on this list are primary authority. Number 6, the A.L.R. reference, is secondary authority; it is not the law.

ASSIGNMENT 5B

a. Numbers 2, 3, and 5 can be mandatory authority. Numbers 2 and 5 are statutory law (enactments of legislative bodies), both of which could apply to govern the question of whether the destruction of business records constitutes a tort.

Number 2, the 1989 State A statute, is mandatory authority if the client pursues a tort claim against the employer for the destruction of the business records, the application of the statute is not preempted by the application of the federal statute, and the application of the statute does not conflict with the provisions of the state or federal constitution.

Number 3, *Merrick v. Taylor,* is a decision of the court of appeals of State A and can be mandatory authority for the lower courts in State A. *Merrick v. Taylor* can be mandatory authority if the case is on point, it has not been superseded by a higher state court decision, its application does not violate the state or federal constitution, and the question involves the interpretation of the 1989 State A statute.

Number 5, the 1991 federal statute, can be mandatory authority if the client's employer is a contractor with a federal contract and the application of the statute does not violate the United States Constitution.

b. Number 1, *Idle v. City Company,* is probably not mandatory authority because it has been superseded by the 1989 State A statute (No. 2). See the discussion of this case in Assignment 5D.

ASSIGNMENT 5C

As discussed in Assignment 4C, persuasive authority is authority a court may rely on and follow, but is not bound to rely on or follow. It can be either primary or secondary authority. In certain situations all of the six listed sources of authority could be persuasive authority with the possible exception of number 1, *Idle v. City Company*. If *Idle* has been superseded by the 1989 State A statute, it may not be authority at all. Refer to the discussion of this case in Assignment 5D.

a. **Number 2, 1989 State A statute.** The 1989 State A statute may be persuasive authority if the cause of action is based on another statute that has similar provisions to the 1989 statute, and the court looks to the statute for guidance when interpreting the similar provisions.

b. **Number 3, *Merrick v. Taylor*.** *Merrick* can be persuasive authority when:
   - it is not on point; a court may refer to the reasoning or analysis in the decision for general guidance in interpreting the statute (see Chapter 12);
   - the decision has been superseded by a higher state court or later court of appeals decision in State A, yet subsequent courts may find the reasoning or analysis in the decision to be persuasive. The court may refer to the prior reasoning or analysis unless it has been rejected by the subsequent ruling; or
   - the question is governed by a federal statute but there is no federal case law interpreting the statute, resulting in reliance on the state case for guidance. (This answer is similar to the answer in Assignment 4C d.)

c. **Number 4, *Davees v. Contractor*.** Decisions of other states may act as persuasive precedent. In the absence of mandatory authority in State A, State A courts may consider, adopt, or follow State B law and court decisions. In order for a court decision to be considered persuasive authority, the decision must be on point. That is, the key facts and applicable law of the court opinion must be sufficiently similar to the key facts and applicable law of the case being heard by the court before the opinion may provide guidance to the court in deciding an issue (see Chapter 12).

d. **Number 5, 1991 federal statute.** The federal statute may not be mandatory authority because the elements of the law do not apply to govern the facts of the case. When a statute does not apply, a court may still look to the statute or regulation for guidance when interpreting another law that has similar provisions. (This answer is similar to the answer in Assignment 4C e.)

e. **Number 6, A.L.R. reference.** An A.L.R. reference is not mandatory authority; it is secondary authority and therefore is persuasive authority by definition. In the absence of mandatory authority, a court may look to and adopt secondary authority if it so chooses. The usual prerequisite is that the secondary authority is on point; that is, it addresses legal questions and applies laws or legal principles that are sufficiently similar to the questions and laws being applied in the case before the court. (This answer is similar to the answer in Assignment 4C b.)

ASSIGNMENT 5D

Idle v. City Company is probably not mandatory authority because it has been superseded by the 1989 State A statute (No. 2). The 1989 State A statute was enacted subsequent to the *Idle* decision and creates a statutory cause of action in tort for the intentional destruction of business records.

Legislative bodies have the authority to modify or replace court decisions. This authority is only limited by the requirement that the legislative act may not violate the state or federal constitutions. In this instance, the *Idle* decision created a cause of action in tort for the intentional or negligent destruction of business records while a worker's compensation claim is pending. The subsequent State A legislative act replaces the court decision with a statute that limits the cause of action to the intentional destruction of business records.

By not including in the statute a cause of action for the negligent destruction of business records, that cause of action has been eliminated. The legislature is presumed to be aware of the law created by court decisions. By passing a statute that specifically addressed and narrowed a cause of action created by the court, it appears that the legislature intended to replace the decision of the court in *Idle v. City Company*. The statute, therefore, probably supersedes the court decision.

ASSIGNMENT 5E

If *Idle v. City Company* can be considered authority at all, it would only be authority for guidance in interpreting that portion of the cause of action that was not eliminated by the 1989 State A statute. The statute provides a cause of action for intentional destruction of business records. That part of the *Idle* decision which addressed the intentional destruction of business records may be considered authority. Any reasoning, rules, principles, or guidelines presented in the case concerning the intentional destruction of records may be considered authority by subsequent courts addressing issues involving the intentional destruction of business records.

ASSIGNMENT 5F

Merrick v. Taylor is a state court of appeals decision which interprets the "intentional destruction of business records" as used in the statute to include the destruction of records as a result of gross negligence. In effect, the decision expands the scope of the statute to include the negligent destruction of business records if the type of negligence is gross negligence. Courts have the authority to interpret statutes, and through the use of this authority courts have the power to expand or restrict the operation of a statute.

ASSIGNMENT 5G

Davees v. Contractor (No. 4), a State B court decision, cannot be mandatory authority in State A. State courts are never bound to follow the decisions of other states. The requirements for a court decision in another state to be persuasive authority are discussed in the answer to Assignment 5C.

In *Davees* the State B court interpreted a State B statute identical to the 1989 State A statute. The court interpreted the terms "intentional destruction of business records" to include grossly negligent acts only when the gross negligence was accompanied by a "reckless and wanton" disregard for the preservation of the records. If a State A court is addressing the question of what constitutes gross negligence as discussed in *Merrick v. Taylor,* it may look to the *Davees* decision for guidance if the question has not already been addressed by State A courts. In this situation the *Davees* decision would be considered persuasive authority.

ASSIGNMENT 5H

In general, the hierarchy of primary authority within each jurisdiction is the constitution (the highest authority), followed by the enacted law (legislative and administrative), then the common or court-made law. Where state and federal law both apply, the federal law takes precedence over state law. When there is primary mandatory authority and primary persuasive authority, the primary mandatory authority takes precedence over the primary persuasive authority. With these guidelines in mind the hierarchy of the primary authority listed in the assignment is as follows (the highest primary authority is listed first followed by the next highest, etc.). (Note that the introduction to this assignment is the same as the introduction to Assignment 4D; both assignments address the same question.)

    No. 5 1991 federal statute. If the federal law applies, it is higher authority than the state law.

    No. 2 1989 State A statute. The state law is subordinate to the federal law when the federal law applies. When the state law does apply, it is higher authority than case law.

    No. 3 *Merrick v. Taylor.* The decision of the State A court of appeals involving State A law is the next highest authority, unless there is a higher State A court decision on the subject. This assumes the *Idle v. City Company* decision is no longer authority because it has been replaced by the 1989 statute. If *Idle* is primary authority, it is higher authority than *Merrick* because it is a higher State A court than the court of appeals which decided the *Merrick* case.

    No. 4 *Davees v. Contractor.* The case law of State B cannot be mandatory authority in State A. A state is not required to follow the law of other states. At most the decisions of other states are persuasive authority. In the absence of mandatory authority in State A, State A courts may consider, adopt, or follow State B court decisions. The *Davees* decision has the least authoritative value of the primary authority presented in the assignment because Numbers 1, 2, 3, and 5, in certain situations, can be mandatory authority in State A, and mandatory authority is higher authority than persuasive authority.

SUGGESTED ASSIGNMENTS: The following are additional assignments related to the subject matter presented in this chapter:

1. Identify the sources of law in your state.

2. Describe the court system in your state. Include the role of each court (trial, appellate, etc.) and describe the jurisdiction of each court.
3. Discuss the hierarchy of authority of the sources of law in your state.

WEB ASSIGNMENT ANSWERS
ASSIGNMENT 1

Instructor's note: Most state supreme courts have Web sites. Many, but not all, courts of general jurisdiction also have Web sites. A general search, using the name of the court as the topic will usually find the court. For example: The search topic Texas Supreme Court will locate the Court's Web site. One of the best sites for finding state court sites is http://www.findlaw.com.

ASSIGNMENT 2

A state supreme court decision is mandatory precedent when the following requirements are met:

1. The court applying the law is a lower court in the same jurisdiction as the supreme court; and
2. The supreme court opinion is on point. That is, the supreme court opinion involves an identical or similar issue and identical or similar facts as the issue and facts before the lower court.

A state supreme court decision is persuasive precedent when it is not mandatory authority. This occurs in the following situations:

1. The court applying the supreme court decision is not a lower court in the same jurisdiction, such as when a court in another state refers to the supreme court decision or when the supreme court is referring to one of its own decisions; or
2. The decision is not on point. That is, the supreme court decision does not involve an issue or facts sufficiently similar to the issue or facts before the court to be considered on point. It may be used as persuasive precedent because the language or reasoning in the decision may be a valuable guide to the court in reaching its decision.

ASSIGNMENT 3

Assignment 3 involves the following authority, which is listed here for quick reference.

1. A 1998 State A statute that provides that a candidate for state supreme court judge must have resided in the state three years prior to the election.
2. A 2000 State B statute which states that individuals running for any county or municipal office must have resided in the county or municipality for six months.
3. *Garcia v. Municipality of Weston.* A 2001 State A court of appeals decision providing that a person running for state senate must reside within the senate district for a minimum of one year prior to the election.
4. *Reisin v. City.* A State B supreme court decision holding that a person running for any municipal position must reside in the municipality for three months.
5. *American Jurisprudence Second* section which provides that most states have a three-month residency requirement for the purposes of eligibility to run for municipal positions.

ANSWERS

PART A Primary authority is the law itself, such as constitutional, statutory, or case law. One and two are statutory law and therefore primary authority. Three and four are case law and therefore primary authority. Five is secondary authority.

PART B Mandatory authority is any source that a court must rely on when reaching a decision. Primary authority becomes mandatory authority only when it governs the legal question or issue being decided by the court. None of the authority is mandatory authority.

1. The 1998 State A statute does not apply to municipal elections, therefore it is not mandatory authority.
2. The 2000 State B statute is not a State A statute and State B law does not apply to State A matters, therefore it does not apply to State A elections.
3. *Garcia v. Municipality of Weston* does not apply to municipal elections; therefore it does not govern the issue of the residency requirement for those elections.
4. *Reisin v. City* is a State B court decision, and State B court decisions do not have to be followed in State A.
5. *American Jurisprudence Second* is secondary authority, and secondary authority is not the law and can never be mandatory authority.

PART C Persuasive authority is any authority a court is not bound to consider or follow but may consider or follow when reaching a decision. All of the authority listed may be persuasive authority because they may act as guidance for a court when deciding the question of residency requirements for municipal elections. The State A statute and court decision are State A law that establish the residency requirements for certain State A elections and may be considered when addressing questions concerning municipal elections. The State B statute and court decision provide guidance as to how another state has addressed residency requirements for municipal elections. The American Jurisprudence section provides guidance as to how most states have addressed the question.

ASSIGNMENT 4

The annotations to Colorado Statute 4-2-314 provide numerous examples of primary and secondary authority, a few of which are listed here.

Primary Authority

> *Palmer v. A. H. Robins Co., Inc.,* 595 F. Supp. 1290 (D. Colo. 1984)
> *Westric Battery Co. v. Standard Elec. Co.,* 482 F.2d 1307 (10th Cir. 1973)
> *Union Supply Co. v. Pust,* 196 Colo. 162, 583 P.2d 276 (1978)
> *Belle Bonfils Mem. Blood Bank v. Hansen,* 665 P.2d 118 (Colo. 1983)

Secondary Authority

> 67 Am. Jur.2d, Sales, §§ 743-690, 791-793
> 77 C.J.S. Sales, §§ 238, 252, 253, 271, 263, 266-270
> 47 U. Colo. L. Rev. 153 (1976) for article "The Enterprise Liability Theory of Torts"

ASSIGNMENT 5

The annotations to Article 2 section six of the Colorado state constitution provide numerous examples of primary and secondary authority. The first two case annotations and the first Am. Jur. 2d and C.J.S. annotations are listed here.

Cases

> *Goldberg. v. Musim,* 162 Colo. 461, 427 P.2d 698 (1967)
> *Simon v. State Compensation Ins. Auth.,* 903 P.2d 1139 (Colo. App. 1994)

Am. Jur. and C.J.S.

> 16B Am. Jur. 2d, Constitutional Law, § 620
> 16 C.J.S. Constitutional Law, § 153

TEST QUESTIONS AND ANSWERS

TRUE OR FALSE QUESTIONS

Please write a "T" or "F" to the left of each statement.

_____ 1. A constitution is not an example of enacted law.

_____ 2. Administrative law is usually more specific than statutory law.

_____ 3. Decisions of the highest court in a state are examples of common law.

_____ 4. The term *case law* does not encompass a broader range of law than the term *common law.*

_____ 5. Personal jurisdiction is the extent of a court's authority to hear and resolve specific disputes.

_____ 6. The United States District Court is the main trial court in the federal system.

_____ 7. A court of appeals may review new evidence when considering a matter on appeal.

_____ 8. The doctrine of stare decisis requires lower courts to follow the decision of a higher court in a jurisdiction in cases involving similar issues and facts.

_____ 9. If times have changed and there is good reason not to follow a prior decision of a higher court, a lower court may choose not to follow the precedent of a higher court in the jurisdiction.

_____10. Because of the doctrines of stare decisis and precedent, courts can be relied on to reach the same decision on an issue as earlier courts when the cases are sufficiently similar.

_____11. The United States Supreme Court may declare laws enacted by state legislatures unconstitutional.

_____12. Mandatory authority is a non–law source a court may rely on when reaching a decision.

_____13. A decision of a state court of appeals is an example of primary authority.

_____14. A restatement of the law is valuable as a research tool because is provides a comprehensive treatment of a specific area of the law.

_____15. A.L.R. is a series of books that contain the text of selected court opinions, along with scholarly commentaries on the opinions.

_____16. Legal dictionaries include definitions of legal terms and commentaries on the definitions.

_____17. Law reviews are usually published by law schools.

_____18. Secondary authority cannot be mandatory authority.

_____19. Not all primary authority is mandatory authority.

_____20. For a court opinion to be mandatory authority, it must be on point and it must be written by a higher court in the jurisdiction.

TRUE OR FALSE ANSWERS

Answer	Text Section	Answer	Text Section	Answer	Text Section
1. False	IIA	8. True	IIB3a	15. True	IVA
2. True	IIA3	9. False	IIB3b	16. False	IVA
3. True	IIB	10. True	IIB3b	17. True	IVA
4. False	IIB	11. True	IIB3b	18. True	IVB
5. False	IIB2a	12. False	IV	19. True	IVB
6. True	IIB2b	13. True	IVA	20. True	IVB
7. False	IIB2b	14. False	IVA		

MULTIPLE CHOICE QUESTIONS

Please circle the letter of the **most appropriate** answer.

1. As used in the text, enacted law includes:
    a. regulations adopted by administrative bodies.
    b. opinions of the United States Supreme Court.
    c. statutes.
    d. ordinances.
    e. all of the above
    f. a, b, and c
    g. a, c, and d

2. Constitutions:
    a. define the powers of the government.
    b. establish the structure of the government.
    c. define the rights of the people.
    d. all of the above
    e. a and c

3. In regard to subject matter jurisdiction, the basic types of courts are courts of:
    a. limited jurisdiction.
    b. personal jurisdiction.
    c. concurrent jurisdiction.
    d. general jurisdiction.
    e. all of the above
    f. a, c, and d
    g. a and d

4. Which of the following are courts of limited jurisdiction?
    a. United States Tax Court
    b. United States District Court
    c. a state small claims court
    d. all of the above
    e. a and b
    f. a and c

5. A court of appeals may:
    a. hear new testimony.
    b. retry the case.
    c. take new evidence.
    d. review the record of the trial court.
    e. all of the above

6. The basic principle that requires a court to follow a previous decision of a higher court when the current decision involves issues and facts similar to those involved in the prevision decision is the doctrine of:
    a. precedent.
    b. concurrent jurisdiction.
    c. subject matter jurisdiction.
    d. stare decisis.
    e. none of the above

7. The highest legal authority in a jurisdiction is the:
    a. decision of the state supreme court.
    b. decision of the United States Supreme Court.
    c. laws of the United States Congress.
    d. constitution.

8. Primary authority is:
    a. a non–law source a court may rely on when deciding an issue.
    b. authority a court must rely on when deciding an issue.
    c. authority a court may rely on when deciding an issue.
    d. the law itself.
    e. a, b, and c
    f. a and c

9. Examples of primary authority are:
    a. *American Law Reports*.
    b. ordinances.
    c. court opinions.
    d. treatises.
    e. all of the above
    f. a, b, and c
    g. b and c

10. The best source to obtain a general summary of the law is:
    a. a Restatement of the Law.
    b. a legal encyclopedia.
    c. a law review article.
    d. an A.L.R.

11. The best source to obtain a review of selected court opinions on specific topics and scholarly commentaries on the opinions is:
    a. a legal encyclopedia.
    b. a Restatement of the Law.
    c. a treatise.
    d. an A.L.R.
    e. all of the above

12. When a court in State A looks to a decision of a court in State B when deciding an issue, the decision in State B is:
    a. mandatory authority.
    b. concurrent jurisdiction.
    c. secondary authority.
    d. persuasive authority.
    e. none of the above

13. When the highest court in State A defines the term *malice,* all of the courts in State A are bound to follow the highest court's definition of the term. The State A definition is:
   a. primary authority.
   b. persuasive authority.
   c. secondary authority.
   d. mandatory authority.
   e. all of the above
   f. a and d
   g. b and d

14. The highest court in State B defines the term *malice.* The highest court in State A looks to the State B definition when defining the term. The State B definition is:
   a. primary authority.
   b. persuasive authority.
   c. secondary authority.
   d. mandatory authority.
   e. all of the above
   f. a and d
   g. a and b

15. The highest court in State A decides to adopt the Restatement of the Law definition of *malice*. Once adopted, the adopted definition is:
   a. secondary authority.
   b. persuasive authority.
   c. mandatory authority.
   d. all of the above
   e. a and b
   f. a and c

MULTIPLE CHOICE ANSWERS

Answer	Text Section	Answer	Text Section	Answer	Text Section
1. g	IIA	6. d	IIB3a	11. d	IVA
2. d	IIA1	7. d	III	12. d	IVB
3. g	IIB2d	8. d	IV	13. f	IVB
4. f	IIB2a	9. g	IVA	14. g	IVB
5. d	IIB2a	10. b	IV	15. c	IVB

CHAPTER 2

Introduction to Legal Research and Analysis

Instructor's note: The purpose of Chapter 2 is to provide students with an overview of legal analysis and the IRAC process. The assignments are designed to present students with problems that require them to apply the information and instructions presented in the chapter, that is, to conduct legal analysis and apply the steps of the IRAC process.

TEXT ASSIGNMENT ANSWERS

ASSIGNMENT 1

The following are the steps of the IRAC legal analysis process:

STEP 1. Identify the issue (the legal question) or issues raised by the facts of the client's case.

STEP 2. Identify the law that governs the issue. This may be enacted law, such as constitutional law, statutory law, etc. It may be common/case law or a combination of enacted law and common law.

STEP 3. Determine how the rule of law applies to the issue. This consists of three parts:

PART I—Identify the component parts (elements) of the rule of law. Identify what the rule of law requires.

PART II—Apply the facts of the client's case to the component parts of the rule of law, and determine how the rule applies. Match the facts of the client's case to the rule of law to determine how the rule of law applies.

PART III—Consider the possible counterarguments to the analysis of the issue.

STEP 4. Conclusion—summarize the results of the legal analysis.

ASSIGNMENT 2

STEP 1. IDENTIFY THE ISSUE. Under Section 30-236 of the state penal code, does forgery occur when an individual finds a check completely made out to cash, takes it to the bank, signs it on the back as instructed by the teller, and cashes it?

Instructor's note: This is a complete statement of the issue as covered in Chapters 10 and 11—that is, it includes the rule of law and detailed facts. Without having covered those chapters, students may state the issue more broadly, such as, "Does forgery occur when an individual cashes a check he or she found?"

STEP 2. IDENTIFY THE RULE OF LAW. The law is state penal code Section 30-236 and Section 45-3-109d.

STEP 3. DETERMINE HOW THE RULE OF LAW APPLIES TO THE ISSUE.

PART I—IDENTIFY THE COMPONENT PARTS (ELEMENTS) OF THE RULE OF LAW. Section 30-236 requires three elements:

1. falsely making or altering any signature, or any part of
2. any writing purporting to have any legal efficacy
3. with intent to injure or defraud.

Section 45-3-109d states that a check when made out to cash is a bearer instrument. A bearer instrument is payable to anyone possessing the instrument and is negotiable by transfer alone—it is the same as cash.

PART II—APPLY THE FACTS OF THE CLIENT'S CASE TO THE COMPONENT PARTS. The check was made out to cash and was completely filled out. According to Section 45-3-109d such an instrument is a bearer instrument, negotiable by transfer alone, and is the same as cash. Client merely went to the bank and changed the check into cash. Section 30-236 requires that for forgery to occur, there must be a false making or altering of any signature or any part of the writing. Here the client did not falsely sign a name or alter any signature; he signed his name on the back as instructed. Therefore, he did not commit the crime of forgery.

PART III—CONSIDER POSSIBLE COUNTERARGUMENTS TO THE ANALYSIS OF THE ISSUE. A possible counterargument is that the courts may interpret "false making" to include endorsements of bearer instruments by individuals who know they are not entitled to the money. A court may consider such signatures to be falsely made with the intent to defraud within the meaning of Section 30-236. Therefore, case law should be reviewed to address this possibility.

STEP 4. CONCLUSION. In summary, under Section 45-3-109d, the check the client signed, like cash, was a bearer instrument negotiable by transfer alone. Section 30-236 requires that for forgery to occur, there must be a false making or altering of any signature or any part of the writing. Here, the client did not falsely sign a name or alter any signature; he signed his name on the back as instructed. Therefore, he did not commit the crime of forgery. Case law should be reviewed to ensure that the courts have not interpreted "false making" to include an endorsement on the back of a check.

ASSIGNMENT 3

STEP 1. IDENTIFY THE ISSUE. Under Section 2397 of the state penal code, does a burglary occur when an individual enters a neighbor's garage by breaking a window, takes three cases of beer, and the garage is a separate building located about six feet from the dwelling?

Instructor's note: This is a complete statement of the issue as covered in Chapters 10 and 11—that is, it includes the rule of law and detailed facts. Without having covered those chapters, students may state the issue more broadly, such as, "Did a burglary occur when an individual breaks into a garage?"

STEP 2. IDENTIFY THE RULE OF LAW. The law defining burglary is state penal code Section 2397. The case of *State v. Nelson* interprets the term *dwelling* to include "outbuildings close to, but not physically connected with, a dwelling house, if such buildings are capable of being fenced in."

STEP 3. DETERMINE HOW THE RULE OF LAW APPLIES TO THE ISSUE.

PART I—IDENTIFY THE COMPONENT PARTS (ELEMENTS) OF THE RULE OF LAW. Section 2397 requires three elements:
1. breaking and entering
2. a dwelling house of another
3. with intent to commit a crime.

PART II—APPLY THE FACTS OF THE CLIENT'S CASE TO THE COMPONENT PARTS. The client's acts of breaking the window and entering the garage meet the first element. The garage belongs to another (a neighbor), and the court in *State v. Nelson* interpreted a dwelling to include an outbuilding close to the dwelling, if it is capable of being fenced in. The garage is probably capable of being fenced in, it is close to the house (six feet from the house), and it belongs to another; therefore, the second element is probably met. The act of taking the beer evidences a probable intent to commit a crime when he entered. Therefore, all the elements of the statute are met, and there is probably sufficient evidence to support a charge of burglary.

PART III—CONSIDER POSSIBLE COUNTERARGUMENTS TO THE ANALYSIS OF THE ISSUE.
Possible counterarguments may be raised based on the lack of facts. It is possible, but not likely, that the garage is not capable of being fenced in and, therefore, the fencing requirement stated in *Nelson* may not be met and the garage is not a dwelling within the meaning of the statute. It is also possible that the client did not intend to take anything when he entered the garage—he may just have been trying to find a place to keep warm and sleep. We need to determine his reason for breaking into the garage. Case law needs to be researched to determine if the entering with intent to commit crime requirement of the statute may be established by the conduct that takes place after entry.

STEP 4. CONCLUSION. Section 2397 of the state penal code defines burglary as "the breaking and entering of the dwelling house of another with the intent to commit a crime." In the case of *State v. Nelson,* the court held that a dwelling house includes buildings close to the house, if they are capable of being fenced in. There probably is enough evidence to support charges of burglary. The client apparently entered the garage with the intent to steal beer, and the garage will probably be considered a dwelling within the meaning of the statute. However, the matters raised in the counterargument need to be researched before a final conclusion can be reached.

ASSIGNMENT 4A

Prior to beginning the IRAC analytical process, gather all the information regarding the issue being addressed. Is the client's case file complete? Are there any documents missing from the file? Are all the relevant information and facts assembled? If a review of the file reveals that additional information is necessary, the researcher should contact the appropriate party and obtain the information before beginning.

It may be necessary as a preliminary step to do some basic research in the area(s) of law that govern the issue or issues. This may require reference to a legal encyclopedia or treatise, etc. Once the facts are gathered, the file complete, and a basic familiarity with the area of law acquired, the legal assistant should perform the four-step IRAC analytical process discussed in the chapter:

STEP 1. IDENTIFY THE ISSUE OR ISSUES RAISED BY THE FACTS OF THE CASE. Identifying and stating the issue are discussed in detail in Chapters 10 and 11. The issue may be identified in general terms initially.

Did the library violate the group's First Amendment rights?   **FOR EXAMPLE**

As more research is conducted, a complete statement of the issue in the context of the law and facts will be assembled.

In light of the provisions of the First Amendment, were the group's freedom of speech rights vi-   **FOR EXAMPLE**
olated by the library's refusal to include the organization's literature among its materials, while
accepting material from other groups such as the American Nazi Party?

When the analysis involves more than one issue, each issue should be analyzed and researched separately. Each issue should be researched and analyzed completely before proceeding to the next issue. In addition, the researcher should keep focused on the issue(s) of the case or the issue(s) assigned and avoid the temptation to address interesting or related questions that may arise as research is conducted.

STEP 2. FOR EACH ISSUE IDENTIFY THE RULE OF LAW THAT MAY GOVERN OR APPLY. The rule of law may be enacted law (constitutional, legislative) or court-made law (case law).

FOR EXAMPLE In this assignment it would be necessary to identify which constitutional rights or legislative acts (statutes) the library may have violated when it refused to accept the organization's literature.

This step should also include identifying all relevant case law that may be necessary to interpret the terms of the statute, or act as guidance in the determination of how the law applies to the issue being addressed. Relevant case law would consist of cases involving fact situations and issues similar to those being addressed in the client's case, wherein the court applied the same or a similar rule of law, and which show how the law applies.

STEP 3. ANALYZE THE LAW AND DETERMINE HOW THE LAW APPLIES TO THE ISSUE. This step involves three parts:

PART I—IDENTIFY THE ELEMENTS OF THE LAW. For each rule of law that may govern the question, what must be established under the rule for the rule to apply? What are the elements of the law?

FOR EXAMPLE In this assignment, the library may have violated the group's freedom of speech rights. The researcher must identify the conditions or elements that must be established in order for a violation of freedom of speech to occur.

These elements must be identified in order to determine if the library violated the group's freedom of speech rights.

PART II—APPLY THE ELEMENTS OR REQUIREMENTS OF THE RULE OF LAW TO THE ISSUE BEING ADDRESSED IN THE CLIENT'S FACTS. The elements or requirements of the rule of law must be applied to the facts of the client's case and a determination made about whether the library's refusal to accept the group's material violated their rights. If it is not clear from the rule of law how an element applies to the facts of the case, it may be necessary to refer to a court opinion which interprets the rule of law or provides guidance on how it applies in a fact situation similar to the client's case.

PART III—IDENTIFY AND EXPLORE ANY COUNTERARGUMENT OR COUNTERANALYSIS. Any counterargument the opposing side is likely to raise should be addressed.

FOR EXAMPLE The library may argue that the group's literature advocates acts of violence and is so inflammatory that it is similar to yelling "fire" in a crowded theater. Such literature is not protected by the freedom of speech provisions of the Constitution.

STEP 4. THE FINAL STEP IS THE CONCLUSION SUMMARIZING THE RESULTS OF THE ANALYTICAL PROCESS. The conclusion should include a summary of the law and analysis presented in the previous steps and a consideration of what action a court may take or how it may rule upon the issue. The conclusion may also include the identification of:

1. additional factual information that may be needed,
2. further research that may be required,
3. related issues or concerns.

ASSIGNMENT 4B

The steps discussed in the answer to Assignment 4A apply to each issue identified in Assignment 4B.

Step 1 requires the identification of each issue. In Assignment B, two possible causes of action are identified, one involving freedom of speech under the First Amendment and another involving equal protection under the Fourteenth Amendment. Each issue should be stated as specifically as possible in the context of the facts. See Chapters 9 and 10.

"Were the group's freedom of speech rights violated by the library's refusal to carry its   **FOR EXAMPLE**
literature?"

A final complete statement of the issue may not be possible until research and analysis are conducted.

Once the issues are identified as specifically as possible, the analysis steps should be separately followed for each issue.

One issue, such as the freedom of speech issue, should be analyzed completely. Steps 2, 3, and   **FOR EXAMPLE**
4 should be followed in regard to that issue. The analysis of the freedom of speech issue should
be entirely completed before the equal protection issue is addressed. Once the analysis of the
first issue is complete, steps 2, 3, and 4 should be followed in regard to the second issue.

In outline form, the process for analyzing the two issues presented in Assignment 4B would appear as follows:

1. **Step 1**—Identify each issue as completely as possible. Select one of the issues, and follow the remaining steps of the analytical process for that issue. Assume that the freedom of speech issue is selected first.
2. **Step 2**—Identify the specific rule of law concerning freedom of speech that applies to the question of a library's refusal to carry a group's material.
3. **Step 3**—Determine how the rule of law applies to the freedom of speech issue.
   Part I—Identify the component parts (elements) of the applicable freedom of speech rule of law.
   Part II—Apply the facts of the case to the elements of the rule of law.
   Part III—Consider and address the possible counterarguments.
4. **Step 4**—Prepare a conclusion: a recap of the analysis, a consideration of what action a court may take, and any recommendations.
5. Once Step 4 is completed for the freedom of speech issue, then Steps 2, 3, and 4 should be followed for the equal protection issue.

ASSIGNMENT 4C

The primary factors that may affect your objectivity are the preconceived notions, personal views, or emotional feelings the researcher may have toward the client or the extremist group the client heads. If the researcher is a follower of Islam, or has been subjected to anti-Islamic abuse or subjected to any prejudice in general, the researcher may be repulsed by what the group represents. Therefore, it may be very difficult for the researcher to approach the analysis of the legal issues objectively.

This can result in a failure to conduct an objective, critical analysis of the issues. The researcher may focus on that part of the research which indicates that freedom of speech and equal protection do not afford the group a remedy in this situation. The researcher may focus on that body of case law which indicates that the group's rights were not violated. The researcher may not conduct an objective analysis and fail to give equal credence to or vigorously pursue that line of authority which indicates that the group's freedom of speech and equal protection rights were violated.

If the researcher is a supporter of the group or its philosophy, then the opposite of the above may occur. The researcher may fail to vigorously pursue or consider that line of authority indicating that the group is not protected under freedom of speech or equal protection.

In both instances, the ability to objectively research and analyze the issues is compromised by the nature of the case and the personal views of the researcher. This can produce an incomplete analysis of the issues and the applicable law and result in an erroneous conclusion.

ASSIGNMENT 5A

The preliminary stages of this assignment, and all assignments involving the legal analysis of legal issues in a client's case, are the same as those mentioned in Assignment 4A. That is, prior to beginning the IRAC analytical process, the researcher should gather all the information regarding the issue being addressed. Is the client's case file complete? Are there any documents missing from the file? Are all the relevant information and facts assembled? If a review of the file reveals that additional information is necessary, the researcher should contact the appropriate party and obtain the information before beginning.

It may also be necessary as a preliminary step to do some basic research in the area(s) of law that govern the issue or issues. This may require reference to a legal encyclopedia or treatise, etc. Once the facts are gathered, the file complete, and a basic familiarity with the area of law acquired, the legal assistant should perform the four-step IRAC analytical process discussed in the chapter:

STEP 1. IDENTIFY THE ISSUE OR ISSUES RAISED BY THE FACTS OF THE CASE. The issue initially may be stated broadly, such as, "Did the client violate the state motor vehicle laws when he passed in a no-passing zone?" As the applicable law is identified and further research and analysis are conducted, the issue should be identified more precisely in the context of the law and facts.

 FOR EXAMPLE   Under the section of the motor vehicle code governing passing, § 293-301, is the statute violated when an individual began and ended a passing maneuver entirely in a no-passing zone, there was no oncoming traffic, and the maneuver was safely made?

STEP 2. IDENTIFY THE RULE OF LAW THAT GOVERNS THE ISSUE. After identifying the issue, the researcher would locate the law that governs the issue. In this case, Section 293-301 of the state motor vehicle code governs the question of passing maneuvers and no-passing zones. Thorough research should be conducted to ensure there are no additional applicable statutory sections.

This step should also include identifying all relevant case law that may be necessary to interpret the terms of the statute, or act as guidance in the determination of how the law applies to the issue being addressed. Relevant case law would consist of cases involving factual situations and issues similar to those being addressed in the client's case, wherein the court applied the same or a similar rule of law, and which show how the law applies. In this assignment the relevant case on the subject, *State v. Roth,* would be identified in Step 2.

STEP 3. ANALYZE THE LAW AND DETERMINE HOW THE LAW APPLIES TO THE ISSUE. As discussed in Assignments 4A and 4B, this step involves a three-part process of analyzing and applying the law that governs the issue.

PART I—IDENTIFY THE ELEMENTS OF THE LAW. This part requires the researcher to identify the elements of Section 293-301 of the motor vehicle code, which must be met for the section to apply. What are the elements of the section? The components or elements of Section 293-301 are easy to identify. The statute is violated when:

1. there is a passing maneuver
2. in a no-passing zone (a no-passing zone is defined as that portion of the road where the center of the road is marked with two solid stripes).

PART II—APPLY THE ELEMENTS OR REQUIREMENTS OF THE RULE OF LAW TO THE ISSUE BEING ADDRESSED (TO THE CLIENT'S FACTS). The elements or requirements of the rule of law must be applied to the facts of the client's case and a determination made whether the actions of the client violated the statute. It appears, from a literal reading of the section, that the client clearly violated the statute. The client:

1. admittedly performed a passing maneuver
2. in a no-passing zone (that is, the maneuver began and ended in the area where the center of the road was marked with two solid stripes).

PART III—IDENTIFY AND EXPLORE ANY COUNTERARGUMENT OR COUNTERANALYSIS. A possible counterargument that could be made to the analysis (probably a weak counterargument) is that a strict application of the statute is not appropriate since there were no oncoming vehicles and the passing maneuver was safely made.

Support of this counterargument could be based on the *State v. Roth* decision. In the case, the court ruled that a strict reading of the statute was not appropriate when the maneuver was safely made and the no-passing zone was not properly marked. The opinion, however, is probably not applicable because it is not on point. There are critical differences between the facts of *Roth* and the client's case.

In *Roth,* the passing maneuver began at the end of a no-passing zone that should have been marked as a passing zone. The pass was completed in a passing zone. In effect, the maneuver began and ended in a zone that should have been marked a passing zone. In the client's case the entire passing maneuver took place in a no-passing zone. There are no facts indicating that the no-passing zone was improperly marked.

It would be an absurd reading of *Roth* to argue that the opinion allows the avoidance of the clear application of the statute whenever a passing maneuver is safely made entirely within a no-passing zone. If that was the intent of the legislature, Section 293-301 would contain a provision excepting from the application of the section passes safely made in no-passing zones.

STEP 4. THE FINAL STEP IS THE CONCLUSION SUMMARIZING THE RESULTS OF THE ANALYTICAL PROCESS. The conclusion should include a summary of the law and analysis presented in the previous steps and a consideration of what action a court may take or how it may rule upon the issue. The conclusion may also include the identification of:

1. additional factual information that may be needed; in this case, whether the passing zone was properly marked,
2. further research that may be required; in this case, whether there are additional court opinions involving passes in a no-passing zone,
3. related issues or concerns.

Section 293-301 of the motor vehicle code prohibits passing in a no-passing zone. In our case, the passing maneuver was entirely conducted in a no-passing zone. Unless the no-passing zone was improperly marked as in the *Roth* case, it seems clear that the ticket will not be set aside. It is recommended that an investigation be conducted to determine if the passing zone was improperly marked. Also, it may be advisable to conduct further research to determine if there are additional cases addressing this issue. **FOR EXAMPLE**

ASSIGNMENT 5B

The preliminary stages (gathering the facts, reviewing the case file, etc.) and the four steps of the analytical process are the same in this assignment as in Assignment 5A. Presented below is a comparison between the performance of the steps of the analytical process in Assignment 5A and Assignment 5B.

STEP 1. IDENTIFY THE ISSUE OR ISSUES RAISED BY THE FACTS OF THE CASE. The approach to identifying the issue in this assignment is the same as in Assignment 5A. The difference is that the final statement of the issue is different because the key facts are somewhat different. In this assignment, the passing maneuver did not begin and end in the no-passing zone; the passing maneuver began approximately 20 feet from the end of the no-passing zone and was completed in a passing zone.

FOR EXAMPLE   Under the section of the motor vehicle code governing passing, §293-301, is the statute violated when an individual began a passing maneuver approximately 20 feet from the end of the no-passing zone and completed it in a passing zone, there was no oncoming traffic, and the maneuver was safely made?

STEP 2. IDENTIFY THE RULE OF LAW THAT GOVERNS THE ISSUE. The performance of Step 2 is the same for both Assignments 5A and 5B. Refer to the answer presented in Assignment 5A, Step 2.

STEP 3. ANALYZE THE LAW AND DETERMINE HOW THE LAW APPLIES TO THE ISSUE. Part I of this step is the same for both Assignments 5A and 5B; the major differences in the assignments are in Parts II and III, which are noted below.

PART I—IDENTIFY THE ELEMENTS OF THE LAW. As noted above, the performance of this part of Step 3 is the same as Part I in Assignment 5A. Refer to the answer presented in Assignment 5A, Step 3, Part I.

PART II—APPLY THE ELEMENTS OR REQUIREMENTS OF THE RULE OF LAW TO THE ISSUE BEING ADDRESSED (TO THE CLIENT'S FACTS). The elements or requirements of the rule of law must be applied to the facts of the client's case and a determination made whether the actions of the client violated the statute.

The performance of Part II is different in this assignment than in Assignment 5A. In this assignment it is unclear, based on the statutory and case law, whether the passing maneuver violates the law. An argument can be made either way. The statute provides that it is a violation of Section 293-301 to pass a vehicle in a no-passing zone. But, neither the section nor the relevant court decision, the *Roth* case, define what constitutes passing a vehicle in a no-passing zone. Is the statute violated only if the passing maneuver begins and ends in the no-passing zone, or is the statute also violated if the maneuver merely begins in the no-passing zone but does not end in the no-passing zone?

Neither the statute nor the *Roth* case address these questions. In *Roth,* the court stated that the purpose of the statute is to ensure safety on the public highways. The court ruled that a strict reading of the statute was not appropriate when the maneuver was safely made and the no-passing zone was not properly marked.

In the *Roth* case, the passing maneuver began in the last 30 feet of the no-passing zone, there was no oncoming traffic, and the maneuver was safely completed. The client's case is almost identical to the *Roth* case: the passing maneuver began in the last 30 feet of the passing zone, there was no oncoming traffic, and the maneuver was safely made. It could be argued that since the cases are almost identical, a strict reading of the statute is not appropriate and the statute should not apply, just as it did not apply in *Roth.* In our case, as in *Roth,* the purpose of ensuring safety on the public highways is not furthered by a strict reading of the statute.

A strong counterargument to this analysis is presented in Part III below. Without a determination of what constitutes passing a vehicle in a no-passing zone within the meaning of Section 293-301, it is unclear how a court may rule and which position will prevail.

PART III—IDENTIFY AND EXPLORE ANY COUNTERARGUMENT OR COUNTERANALYSIS. Any counterargument the opposing side is likely to raise should be addressed. A strong counterargument could be made that the *Roth* case does not apply, Section 293-301 should be strictly applied, and a passing maneuver that in any way begins in a no-passing zone violates the section.

In the *Roth* case, the court ruled that a strict reading of the statute was not appropriate when the maneuver was safely made and the no-passing zone was not properly marked. The opinion, however, is probably not applicable because it is not on point. There is a critical difference between the facts of *Roth* and the client's case.

In *Roth,* the passing maneuver began at the end of a no-passing zone that should have been marked as a passing zone. The pass was completed in a passing zone. In effect, the maneuver began and ended in a zone that should have been marked a passing zone. In the client's case, there are no facts indicating that the no-passing zone was improperly marked, therefore, the passing maneuver did not in effect begin in a passing zone and the case is not on point.

A determination of which analysis, the one presented in Part II or Part III, would most likely be adopted by the court cannot be made without an interpretation of what constitutes passing a vehicle in a no-passing zone. Further research needs to be conducted to determine whether the court will allow a less strict interpretation and application of the motor vehicle code only in situations where there is an error in marking the road such as occurred in *Roth.* Cases involving the improper marking of road signs or speed limits may provide guidance.

STEP 4. THE FINAL STEP IS THE CONCLUSION SUMMARIZING THE RESULTS OF THE ANALYTICAL PROCESS.
The conclusion should include a summary of the law and analysis presented in the previous steps and a consideration of what action a court may take or how it may rule upon the issue. The conclusion may also include the identification of:

1. additional factual information that may be needed; in this case, whether the no-passing zone was properly marked,
2. further research that may be required; in this case whether there are additional cases involving passes in a no-passing zone or cases involving improperly marked roads, such as cases involving signs or speed limits,
3. related issues or concerns.

Section 293-301 of the motor vehicle code prohibits passing in a no-passing zone. Neither the **FOR EXAMPLE** section nor the case law define what constitutes passing in a no-passing zone. It could be argued that the section should not apply because the facts of the client's case are almost identical to the *Roth* case, and the statute was not applied in *Roth.* It can also be argued that *Roth* does not apply because in *Roth* the no-passing zone was improperly marked, and in the client's case there is no indication that it was improperly marked.

A determination of which argument would most likely be adopted by the court cannot be made without an interpretation of what constitutes passing a vehicle in a no-passing zone. Further research needs to be conducted to determine whether the court will allow a less strict interpretation and application of the motor vehicle code only in situations where there is an error in marking the road such as occurred in *Roth.*

It is recommended that research be conducted to determine if the passing zone was improperly marked. Cases involving the improper marking of road signs or speed limits may provide guidance. It may be advisable to conduct further research to locate such cases, or determine if there are additional cases concerning this issue.

ASSIGNMENT 5C

The preliminary stages (gathering the facts, reviewing the case file, etc.) and the four steps of the analytical process are the same in this assignment as in Assignment 5A. Presented below is a comparison between the performance of the steps of the analytical process in Assignment 5A and Assignment 5C. Also, the answer to this assignment is very similar in part to Assignment 5B, but there are differences.

STEP 1. IDENTIFY THE ISSUE OR ISSUES RAISED BY THE FACTS OF THE CASE.
The approach to identifying the issue in this assignment is the same as in Assignment 5A. The difference is that the final statement of the issue is different because the key facts are somewhat different. In this assignment, the passing maneuver did not begin and end in the no-passing zone; the passing maneuver began in a passing zone and was completed in a no-passing zone.

FOR EXAMPLE   Under the section of the motor vehicle code governing passing, § 293-301, is the statute violated when an individual began a passing maneuver in a passing zone and completed it in a no-passing zone, there was no oncoming traffic, and the maneuver was safely made?

STEP 2. IDENTIFY THE RULE OF LAW THAT GOVERNS THE ISSUE. The performance of Step 2 is the same for both Assignments 5A and 5C. Refer to the answer presented in Assignment 5A, Step 2.

STEP 3. ANALYZE THE LAW AND DETERMINE HOW THE LAW APPLIES TO THE ISSUE. Part I of this step is the same for both assignments; the major differences are between Parts II and III which are noted below.

PART I—IDENTIFY THE ELEMENTS OF THE LAW.
The performance of this part of Step 3 is the same as Part I in Assignment 5A. Refer to the answer presented in Assignment 5A, Step 3, Part I.

PART II—APPLY THE ELEMENTS OR REQUIREMENTS OF THE RULE OF LAW TO THE ISSUE BEING ADDRESSED (TO THE CLIENT'S FACTS).
The elements or requirements of the rule of law must be applied to the facts of the client's case and a determination made whether the actions of the client violated the statute.

The performance of Part II is different in this assignment than in Assignment 5A. In this assignment, just as in Assignment 5B, it is unclear, based on the statutory and case law whether the passing maneuver violates the law. An argument can be made either way. The statute provides that it is a violation of Section 293-301 to pass a vehicle in a no-passing zone. But, neither the section nor the relevant court decision, the *Roth* case, define what constitutes passing a vehicle in a no-passing zone. Is the statute violated only if the passing maneuver begins and ends in the no-passing zone, or is the statute also violated if the maneuver begins in a passing zone and ends in the no-passing zone?

Neither the statute nor the *Roth* case address these questions. The court, in *Roth,* stated that the purpose of the statute is to ensure safety on the public highways. The court ruled that a strict reading of the statute was not appropriate when the maneuver was safely made and the no-passing zone was not properly marked.

In the *Roth* case, the passing maneuver began in the last 30 feet of the no-passing zone, there was no oncoming traffic, and the maneuver was safely completed. The client's case is somewhat similar to the *Roth* case: the passing was safely made and there was no oncoming traffic. It could be argued that, since the cases are similar, a strict reading of the statute is not appropriate and the statute should not apply, just as it did not apply in *Roth.* In our case, as in *Roth,* the purpose of ensuring safety on the public highways is not furthered by a strict reading of the statute.

A strong counterargument to this analysis is presented in Part III below. Without a determination of what constitutes passing a vehicle in a no-passing zone within the meaning of Section 293-301, it is unclear how a court may rule and which position will prevail.

PART III—IDENTIFY AND EXPLORE ANY COUNTERARGUMENT OR COUNTERANALYSIS.
Any counterargument the opposing side is likely to raise should be addressed. A strong counterargument could be made that the *Roth* case does not apply, Section 293-301 should be strictly applied, and a passing maneuver that in any way takes place in a no-passing zone violates the section.

In *Roth,* the court ruled that a strict reading of the statute was not appropriate when the maneuver was safely made and the no-passing zone was not properly marked. The opinion, however, is probably not applicable because it is not on point. There is a critical difference between the facts of *Roth* and the client's case. In *Roth,* the passing maneuver began at the end of a no-passing zone that should have been marked as a passing zone and ended in a passing zone. In effect, the maneuver began and ended in a zone that should have been marked a passing zone.

In the client's case, the pass was completed in a no-passing zone. There are no facts indicating that the no-passing zone was improperly marked; therefore, the passing maneuver did not in effect end in a passing zone like it did in *Roth* and the case is not on point.

A determination of which analysis, the one presented in Part II or Part III, would most likely be adopted by the court cannot be made without an interpretation of what constitutes passing a vehicle in a no-passing zone. Further research needs to be conducted to determine whether the court will allow a less strict interpretation and application of the motor vehicle code only in situations where there is an error in marking the road such as occurred in *Roth*. Cases involving the improper marking of road signs or speed limits may provide guidance.

STEP 4. THE FINAL STEP IS THE CONCLUSION SUMMARIZING THE RESULTS OF THE ANALYTICAL PROCESS. The conclusion should include a summary of the law and analysis presented in the previous steps and a consideration of what action a court may take or how it may rule upon the issue. The conclusion may also include the identification of:

a. additional factual information that may be needed; in this case, whether the no-passing zone was properly marked,
b. further research that may be required; in this case, whether there are additional cases involving passes in a no-passing zone,
c. related issues or concerns; none noted here.

ASSIGNMENT 5D

ASSIGNMENT 5A. There is probably sufficient information presented in the assignment for a complete analysis of the problem. It is always helpful, however, to have additional cases, and additional research would be advisable. A necessary fact, in light of the *Roth* decision, is whether the no-passing zone was properly marked.

ASSIGNMENT 5B. The additional factual information that may be needed in this assignment is whether the no-passing zone, where the passing maneuver was initiated, was properly marked. Further research may be required to identify whether there are additional cases involving passes in a no-passing zone or cases involving improperly marked roads such as cases involving signs or speed limits.

ASSIGNMENT 5C. Additional factual information that may be needed in this assignment is whether the no-passing zone, where the passing maneuver ended, was properly marked. The same additional case law research as mentioned in Assignment 5B above would be required.

SUGGESTED ASSIGNMENTS: For any of the legal memorandum assignments you intend to assign in the course, require students to describe the use of the steps of the IRAC process in the analysis of the problem presented in the assignment.

WEB ASSIGNMENT ANSWERS

ASSIGNMENT 1

The term *focus* means to keep the mind focused on the specific task assigned and not be sidetracked by other issues that may be raised by the facts of the case. Focus is important to the analytical process because a lack of focus may cause a researcher to get sidetracked on other issues and waste time researching and analyzing matters he or she is not assigned to work on.

The term *intellectual honesty* means to research and analyze a problem objectively, to not let emotions, personal views, or preconceived notions interfere with an objective analysis of the client's case. It is important because if personal views, prejudices, and so on, become part of the analysis, they may lead to a failure to conduct an objective, critical analysis of the case. The researcher may not vigorously pursue potential opposing arguments or may discount opposing authority.

ASSIGNMENT 2
PART A

STEP 1. IDENTIFY THE ISSUE. Under Section 24-457B of the state probate code, is a will revoked when the notation, "I hereby revoke this will and declare it to be void," (signed) is handwritten diagonally across the first paragraph of the will.

Instructor's note: This is a complete statement of the issue as covered in Chapters 10 and 11—that is, it includes the rule of law and detailed facts. Without having covered those chapters, students may state the issue more broadly, such as, "Is the will validly revoked by a notation across the first paragraph?"

STEP 2. IDENTIFY THE RULE OF LAW. The law governing revocation of wills is Section 24-457B of the state probate code. In the case of *Terrance v. Real,* the court interpreted the phrase "placed on the will or codicil" to require that the revocation language be so placed as to physically affect written words of the will.

STEP 3. DETERMINE HOW THE RULE OF LAW APPLIES TO THE ISSUE.

PART I—IDENTIFY THE COMPONENT PARTS (ELEMENTS) OF THE RULE OF LAW. Under Section 24-457B the following elements must be present for a will to be revoked:
1. a writing
2. declaring an intention to revoke the will
3. placed on the will
4. signed by the testator

PART II—APPLY THE FACTS OF THE CLIENT'S CASE TO THE COMPONENT PARTS. The writing requirement appears to be met—there is a handwritten notation and the statute does not require the writing to be typed. The second element appears to be met—the language "I hereby revoke this will and declare it to be void" clearly evidences an intent to revoke the will. The third element appears to be met—the notation is placed on the will. The case of *Terrance v. Real* requires that the revocation language must be placed to physically affect written words of the will. Here the notation is written diagonally across the first paragraph of the will where it clearly affects the will's written words. The final element is met—the testator signed it.

PART III—CONSIDER POSSIBLE COUNTERARGUMENTS TO THE ANALYSIS OF THE ISSUE. The only possible counterargument is that it must be typewritten. Here it was handwritten. The statute is silent on the question of whether the notation may be handwritten; therefore, case law should be referred to.

STEP 4. CONCLUSION. Section 24-457B of the state probate code provides that revocation language placed on a will and signed by the testator is sufficient to revoke a will. The case of *Terrance v. Real* requires that the revocation language must be placed to physically affect written words of the will. In this case, there was revocation language, written across the first paragraph of the will, and signed by the testator. All of the elements of the statute are met and the revocation appears to be valid under state law.

PART B

STEP 1. IDENTIFY THE ISSUE. Under Section 24-457B of the state probate code, is a will revoked when handwritten in the margins of the first page of the will is the notation, "I hereby revoke this will and declare it to be void," and the notation is signed by the deceased?

Instructor's note: This is a complete statement of the issue as covered in Chapters 10 and 11—that is, it includes the rule of law and detailed facts. Without having covered those chapters, students may state the issue more broadly, such as, "Is the will validly revoked by a notation in the margins of the first page of the will?"

STEP 2. IDENTIFY THE RULE OF LAW. The law governing revocation of wills is Section 24-457B of the state probate code. In the case of *Terrance v. Real,* the court interpreted the phrase "placed on the will or codicil" to require that the revocation language be so placed as to "physically affect written words of the will."

STEP 3. DETERMINE HOW THE RULE OF LAW APPLIES TO THE ISSUE.

PART I—IDENTIFY THE COMPONENT PARTS (ELEMENTS) OF THE RULE OF LAW. The relevant portions of Section 24-457B provide that the following elements must be present for a will to be revoked:

1.   a writing
2.   declaring an intention to revoke the will
3.   placed on the will
4.   signed by the testator

PART II—APPLY THE FACTS OF THE CLIENT'S CASE TO THE COMPONENT PARTS. The writing requirement appears to be met—there is a handwritten notation and the statute does not require the writing to be typed. The second element appears to be met—the language "I hereby revoke this will and declare it to be void" clearly evidences intent to revoke the will. The third element does not appear to be met. The case of *Terrance v. Real,* requires that the revocation language must be placed to physically affect written words of the will. Here the notation is written in the margins of the first paragraph of the will where it does not affect the written words. The final element is met—the testator signed it.

PART III—CONSIDER POSSIBLE COUNTERARGUMENTS TO THE ANALYSIS OF THE ISSUE. The only possible counterargument would be to study the revocation language to see if any of the revocation language is placed on any written words of the will.

STEP 4. CONCLUSION. Section 24-457B of the state probate code provides that revocation language placed on a will and signed by the testator is sufficient to revoke a will. The case of *Terrance v. Real* requires that the revocation language must be placed to physically affect written words of the will. In this case, there was revocation language, but it appears in the margins of the will, not physically affecting the will's written words. The third element is not met; therefore, the revocation is not valid.

PART C

STEP 1. IDENTIFY THE ISSUE. Under Section 24-457B of the state probate code, is a disposition to an individual in a will revoked when, handwritten diagonally across the first paragraph of the will is the following notation to the individual, "I hereby revoke and declare void all dispositions" and the notation is signed by the deceased?

Instructor's note: This is a complete statement of the issue as covered in Chapters 10 and 11—that is, it includes the rule of law and detailed facts. Without having covered those chapters, students may state the issue more broadly, such as, "Are the dispositions to the brother validly revoked by a notation across the first paragraph?"

STEP 2. IDENTIFY THE RULE OF LAW. The law governing revocation of wills is Section 24-457B of the state probate code. In the case of *Terrance v. Real,* the court interpreted the phrase "placed on the will or codicil" to require that the revocation language be so placed as to "physically affect written words of the will."

STEP 3. DETERMINE HOW THE RULE OF LAW APPLIES TO THE ISSUE.

PART I—IDENTIFY THE COMPONENT PARTS (ELEMENTS) OF THE RULE OF LAW. The relevant portions of Section 24-457B provide that the following elements must be present for a will to be revoked:

1.   a writing
2.   declaring of an intention to revoke the will

3. placed on the will
4. signed by the testator

PART II—APPLY THE FACTS OF THE CLIENT'S CASE TO THE COMPONENT PARTS. The key to this problem is whether the statute allows partial revocation. The statute reads "A will may be revoked . . ."; it doesn't read "a disposition within a will may be revoked." The statute doesn't appear to apply to partial revocation, although that may be the case. Before this question may be answered, research into case law must be conducted to determine if the courts have interpreted the statute to allow partial revocations. If so, then the analysis is similar to the analysis for Part A. It follows: The writing requirement appears to be met—there is a handwritten notation and the statute does not require the writing to be typed. The second element appears to be met—the language, "I hereby revoke and declare void all dispositions to my brother, Tom Harbin," clearly evidences intent to revoke the dispositions to Mr. Harbin. The third element appears to be met—the case of *Terrance v. Real* requires that the revocation language must be placed to physically affect written words of the will. Here the notation is written diagonally across the first paragraph of the will where it affects the written words. And the final element is met—the testator signed it.

PART III—CONSIDER POSSIBLE COUNTERARGUMENTS TO THE ANALYSIS OF THE ISSUE. In addition to the counterargument mentioned in Part II, the only other possible counterargument would be that it must be typewritten. Here it was handwritten. The statute is silent on the question of whether the notation may be handwritten therefore, case law should be referred to.

STEP 4. CONCLUSION. Section 24-457B of the state probate code provides that revocation language placed on a will and signed by the testator is sufficient to revoke a will. The case of *Terrance v. Real* requires that the revocation language must be placed to physically affect written words of the will. In this case, there was revocation of only a disposition within the will. The entire will was not revoked. If the statute allows partial revocation, then the disposition was revoked: there was revocation language, written across the first paragraph of the will, and signed by the testator. All of the elements of the statute were met and the revocation would appear to be valid under state law. Research must be conducted to determine if the statute allows partial revocation.

ASSIGNMENT 3
PART A

STEP 1. IDENTIFY THE ISSUE. In light of the provisions of Section 21-2-314 of the state commercial code, is there an implied warranty of merchantability for a toaster sold at a flea market booth that sells small appliances and is always open at the same location at the market?

Instructor's note: As with the other assignments, this is a complete statement of the issue(s) as covered in Chapters 10 and 11—that is, it includes the rule of law and detailed facts. Without having covered those chapters, students may state the issue more broadly, such as, "Is there a warranty of merchantability for goods sold at a flea market?"

STEP 2. IDENTIFY THE RULE OF LAW. The laws governing the sale of goods are Sections 21-2-314 and 21-1-101 of the state commercial code. Case law—*Dinelle v. Eldson*—where the court held that a flea market seller can be considered a merchant, within the meaning of the commercial code, if the seller sells the same products at the flea market on a continuous basis.

STEP 3. DETERMINE HOW THE RULE OF LAW APPLIES TO THE ISSUE.

PART I—IDENTIFY THE COMPONENT PARTS (ELEMENTS) OF THE RULE OF LAW. According to Section 21-2-314, for an implied warranty of merchantability to exist for the sale of goods, the following elements must be present:

1. sale
2. of goods
3. by a merchant with respect to goods of that kind

According to Section 21-1-101, a merchant is "one who is routinely engaged in the purchase and sale of the kind of goods involved in the sales contract."

PART II—APPLY THE FACTS OF THE CLIENT'S CASE TO THE COMPONENT PARTS. The first element is met because the transaction at the flea market was a sale. The second element is met because the sale was a sale of goods—the toaster. The third element also appears to be met. Section 21-1-101 defines a merchant as "one who is routinely engaged in the purchase and sale of the kinds of goods involved in the sales contract." According to the facts, small appliances are sold at the booth and it is always open at the same location at the flea market. So the seller appears to be routinely engaged in the purchase and sale of the kinds of goods involved. In addition, the court in *Dinelle v. Eldson* held that individuals who sell the same products at a flea market on a continuous basis can be considered merchants within the meaning of the commercial code. Since all three of the requirements of Section 21-2-314 appear to be met, it can be concluded that an implied warranty of merchantability exists for the sale of the goods. Since the toaster worked for only two days, it probably is not merchantable and, under Section 21-2-314, the seller must replace the goods or return the purchase price.

PART III—CONSIDER POSSIBLE COUNTERARGUMENTS TO THE ANALYSIS OF THE ISSUE. Possible counterarguments may be made based on missing facts. The seller sells small appliances, but does the seller routinely sell toasters? If the seller only occasionally sells toasters, then the seller may not be a merchant under 21-1-101 because the seller is not routinely engaged "in the sale of the kind of goods involved in the sales contract." Another missing fact that may give rise to a counterargument is how the client used the toaster. If the client abused the toaster and caused it to fail, then the toaster failure may not be due to its lack of merchantability.

STEP 4. CONCLUSION. Section 21-2-314 of the state commercial code provides that an implied warranty of merchantability exists for the sale of goods if the seller is a merchant of the type of goods involved in the sale. Section 21-1-101 of the commercial code defines a merchant as "one routinely engaged in the sale of the type of goods involved in the sale." The court in *Dinelle v. Eldson* held that individuals who sell the same products at a flea market, on a continuous basis, can be considered merchants within the meaning of the commercial code. Assuming there are no missing facts, all of the elements of the statute are met: there was a sale of goods by an individual who routinely sells those goods at the flea market. Under the statute, a warranty of merchantability is implied for the sale of the toaster and the client is entitled to either the return of her purchase price or a replacement toaster.

PART B

STEP 1. IDENTIFY THE ISSUE. In light of the provisions of Section 21-2-314 of the state commercial code, is there an implied warranty of merchantability for an item sold at a garage sale, and the seller has a garage sale every weekend at the same location?

Instructor's note: As with the other assignments, this is a complete statement of the issue as covered in Chapters 10 and 11—that is, it includes the rule of law and detailed facts. Without having covered those chapters, students may state the issue more broadly, such as, "Is there a warranty for goods sold at a garage sale?"

STEP 2. IDENTIFY THE RULE OF LAW. The laws governing the sale of goods are Sections 21-2-314 and 21-1-101 of the state commercial code. Case law—*Dinelle v. Eldson*—where the court held that a flea market seller can be considered a merchant within the meaning of the commercial code if the seller sells the same products at the flea market on a continuous basis.

STEP 3. DETERMINE HOW THE RULE OF LAW APPLIES TO THE ISSUE.

PART I—IDENTIFY THE COMPONENT PARTS (ELEMENTS) OF THE RULE OF LAW. According to Section 21-2-314, for an implied warranty of merchantability to exist for the sale of goods, the following elements must be present:
1. a sale
2. of goods
3. by a merchant with respect to goods of that kind.

According to Section 21-1-101, a merchant is "one who routinely is engaged in the purchase and sale of the kind of goods involved in the sales contract."

PART II—APPLY THE FACTS OF THE CLIENT'S CASE TO THE COMPONENT PARTS. The first element is met because the transaction was a sale. The second element is met because the sale was a sale of goods—the toaster. The third element may or may not be met depending on missing facts. Section 21-1-101 defines a merchant as "one who is routinely engaged in the purchase and sale of the kinds of goods involved in the sales contract." The facts do not tell us if toasters are routinely sold at the garage sale. Without this fact, we cannot determine whether the seller is a merchant as defined in 21-1-101 and, therefore, whether the third requirement of 21-2-314 is met.

If it is determined that the seller is "routinely engaged" in the sale of toasters at the garage sales, then the third element would be met. This would be the case, especially in light of the holding in *Dinelle v. Eldson,* where the court held that individuals who sell the same products at a flea market on a continuous basis can be considered merchants within the meaning of the commercial code. When garage sellers sell the same product on a continuous basis, it can be argued they are functionally the same as similar sellers at flea markets.

If the third element is met, then all three of the requirements of Section 21-2-314 are met, and it could be concluded that an implied warranty of merchantability exists for the sale of the toaster. Since the toaster worked for only two days, it probably is not merchantable, and under Section 21-2-314 the seller must replace the goods or return the purchase price.

PART III—CONSIDER POSSIBLE COUNTERARGUMENTS TO THE ANALYSIS OF THE ISSUE. Possible counterarguments may be made based on missing facts. The facts do not tell us if toasters are routinely sold at the garage sale. Without this fact, we cannot determine whether the seller is a merchant as defined in 21-1-101 and, therefore, whether the third requirement of 21-2-314 is met. If the seller only occasionally sells toasters, then the seller would not be a merchant under 21-1-101 because the seller is not routinely engaged "in the sale of the kind of goods involved in the sales contract." Another missing fact that may give rise to a counterargument is how the client used the toaster. If the client abused the toaster and caused it to fail, then the toaster failure may not have been due to its lack of merchantability.

STEP 4. CONCLUSION.
A conclusion cannot be reached because a key fact is missing: that is, whether the seller routinely sells toasters at the garage sale. If the seller does routinely sell toasters, then there probably is an implied warranty. Section 21-2-314 of the state commercial code provides that an implied warranty of merchantability exists for the sale of goods if the seller is a merchant of the type of goods involved in the sale. Section 21-1-101 of the commercial code defines a merchant as one routinely engaged in the sale of goods involved in the sale. The court in *Dinelle v. Eldson* held that sellers who sell the same products at a flea market on a continuous basis can be considered merchants within the meaning of the commercial code. In this situation it can be argued that garage sales are the functional equivalent of a flea market. Assuming there are no other missing facts, all of the elements of the statute are met: there was a sale of goods by an individual who routinely sells those goods at garage sales. Under the statute, a warranty of merchantability is implied for the sale of the toaster, and the client is entitled to either the return of her purchase price or a replacement toaster.

TEST QUESTIONS AND ANSWERS

TRUE OR FALSE QUESTIONS

Please write a "T" or "F" to the left of each statement.

_____ 1. One of the objects of legal analysis is to identify the issue raised by the facts of the client's case.

_____ 2. One of the objects of legal analysis is to determine how the law applies to the facts of the client's case.

_____ 3. The commonly used approach to legal analysis involves three steps.

_____ 4. The acronym used to refer to the analytical process is IRAC.

_____ 5. A properly stated issue requires the inclusion of the key and background facts.

_____ 6 The analysis/application step of the IRAC process cannot take place without the key facts.

_____ 7. The conclusion step of the analytical process presents the application of the law to the facts of the client's case.

_____ 8. Before the analysis process can begin, it may be necessary to conduct preliminary research in the area of law involved in the case.

_____ 9. Identification of the law governing the dispute is the first step of the analytical process.

_____10. The identification of the rule of law is probably the most important step in the analytical process.

_____11. When researching the law in a case that involves several issues, it is most efficient to research the law for all the issues at the same time.

_____12. Step 2 of the analytical process is usually composed of two parts.

_____13. The law that governs the issue(s) in a client's case may be either enacted law or common/case law.

_____14. When researching primary authority, the first step is to look for the case that is factually similar to the client's case.

_____15. If there is no constitutional or statutory law that applies to an issue in a client's case, the next step is to look to secondary authority.

_____16. Step 3 of the analytical process requires the identification of the elements of the law governing the issue.

_____17. Counteranalysis is part of Step 3 of the analytical process.

_____18. Step 4 of the analytical process includes the identification of additional facts or other information that may be necessary due to questions raised in the analysis of the problem.

_____19. Focus, as discussed in this chapter, applies to the first three steps of the IRAC process.

_____20. Rule 1.4 of the American Bar Association's Model Rules of Professional Conduct provides that a client must be represented competently.

TRUE OR FALSE ANSWERS

Answer	Text Section	Answer	Text Section	Answer	Text Section
1. True	I	8. True	IIIB	15. False	IIIC2
2. True	II	9. False	IIIC	16. True	IIIC2
3. False	III	10. False	IIIC	17. True	IIIC3
4. True	III	11. False	IIIC1	18. True	IIIC4
5. False	IIIA	12. True	IIIC2	19. True	IVA
6. True	IIIA	13. True	IIIC2	20. False	IVB
7. False	IIIA	14. False	IIIC2		

MULTIPLE CHOICE QUESTIONS

Please circle the letter of the **most appropriate** answer.

1. The object of legal analysis and legal research is to determine:
   a. the legal issue(s) raised by the facts.
   b. what law governs the legal issue(s).
   c. how the law applies to the facts.
   d. what legal remedy is available.
   e. all of the above
   f. a, b, and c

2. Before legal analysis can begin, the preliminary preparation that must take place includes:
   a. the identification of the issue.
   b. the gathering of the relevant facts.
   c. the acquisition of a basic familiarity with the area of law involved in the case.
   d. the identification of the legal remedy.
   e. all of the above
   f. a and b
   g. b and c

3. The preliminary process of gathering the facts includes:
   a. gathering all the relevant facts.
   b. organizing the facts.
   c. weighing the facts.
   d. identifying the key facts.
   e. all of the above
   f. a, b, and c

4. The legal research component of the legal analysis process is composed of the following parts:
   a. becoming familiar with the general area of law
   b. locating the law that governs the question
   c. determining how the law applies to the facts
   d. locating the law that interprets how the general law applies
   e. all of the above
   f. b, c, and d
   g. b and d

5. The law that applies to the issue(s) raised in a client's case may be:
   a. a municipal ordinance.
   b. a constitutional provision.
   c. an administrative agency rule.
   d. a rule of law established in a court opinion.
   e. all of the above
   f. a, b, and d

6. The reason(s) for locating constitutional or statutory law first when researching primary authority is (are):
   a. the constitutional or statutory provision may answer the question, and reference to other law is not required.
   b. the court opinion interpreting the law may be included with the constitutional or statutory provision.
   c. the annotations that follow the constitutional or statutory provision may refer to case law that interprets the law.
   d. all of the above
   e. a and b
   f. a and c

7. Which of the following are parts of Step 3 of the IRAC process?
   a. identification of the issue
   b. identification of the rule of law that governs the issue
   c. identification of the elements of the rule of law
   d. a summary of the law that applies
   e. all of the above
   f. none of the above

8. Which of the following are parts of Step 3 of the IRAC process?
   a. identification of the component parts of the rule of law
   b. application of the facts of the client's case to the component parts
   c. consideration of the possible counterarguments to the analysis of the issue
   d. all of the above
   e. a and b

9. Step 4 of the analytical process may include:
   a. a discussion of how the court may rule on the issue(s).
   b. identification of additional facts that may be necessary.
   c. identification of further research that may be necessary.
   d. identification of related issues or concerns.
   e. all of the above
   f. a, b, and c

10. As discussed in this chapter, *focus:*
   a. means to analyze only the issue(s) assigned.
   b. does not apply to Step 3 of the analytical process.
   c. means to keep focused on the client's facts and issue(s) being analyzed.
   d. does not apply to Step 2 of the analytical process.
   e. a, b, and c
   f. a and c

MULTIPLE CHOICE ANSWERS

Answer	Text Section	Answer	Text Section	Answer	Text Section
1. e	I	5. e	IIIC2	9. e	IIIC4
2. g	III	6. f	IIIC2	10. f	IVA
3. e	IIIA	7. c	IIIC3		
4. g	IIIC2	8. d	IIIC3		

CHAPTER 3

Constitutions, Statutes, Administrative Law, and Court Rules—Research and Analysis

TEXT ASSIGNMENT ANSWERS

ASSIGNMENT 1

The answer to this question depends on state law.

ASSIGNMENT 2

Fair Housing Act. 42 U.S.C. § 3601 et. seq. The easiest way to find this is through the popular name table under "Fair Housing Act."

ASSIGNMENT 3

17 U.S.C.A. § 1001. Under COPYRIGHTS—Digital audio recording device in U.S.C.A. index. Section 1001 (3):

> A 'digital audio recording device' is any machine or device of a type commonly distributed to individuals for use by individuals, whether or not included with or as part of some other machine or device, the digital recording function of which is designed or marketed for the primary purpose of, and that is capable of, making a digital audio copied recording for private use except for—
> (A) professional model products, and
> (B) dictation machines, answering machines, and other audio recording equipment that is designed and marketed primarily for the creation of sound recordings resulting from the fixation of nonmusical sounds.

ASSIGNMENT 4

Federal Home Loan Mortgage Corporation 12 U.S.C. § 4520. Under MINORITY BUSINESS ENTERPRISE—Federal Home Loan Mortgage Corporation.

ASSIGNMENT 5

18 U.S.C.A. § 3581. Under FELONIES—Definitions in U.S.C.A. index. Section 3581(b) provides that the authorized term if imprisonment for a Class A felony is "the duration of the defendant's life or any period or time."

ASSIGNMENT 6

Fifth Amendment headnote 18—Juveniles. *Application of Gault,* 387 U. S. 1, 87 S. Ct. 1428, 18 L. Ed2d 527 (1967).

ASSIGNMENT 7

Instructor's note: Students should not only copy the statute, they should identify in detail the components, such as the number, short title, definitions, substantive provisions, reference information, and so on.

ASSIGNMENT 8

PART A The elements of arson are the following:

1. A person must act knowingly—that is, intentionally
2. set fire to, burn, cause to be burned or by use of any explosive damage or destroy, or cause to be damaged or destroyed
3. any property
4. of another
5. without his consent.

PART B Tom has committed arson because all of the elements are met.

1. He acted knowingly—he did not accidentally blow up the barn.
2. By use of explosive he destroyed the barn.
3. He destroyed property—a barn is property.
4. The property belonged to another—a neighbor.
5. He acted without consent—assuming here the neighbor did not consent—there are no facts given concerning consent.

PART C

1. If the statute is strictly construed Lois has probably not committed arson because she did not "knowingly" set fire to the house. She accidentally set fire to the house. Case law should be consulted because the courts may have ruled that certain conduct, such as lighting a match to locate a safe after breaking into a house, is acting "knowingly" within the meaning of the statute. If that is the case, then Lois has committed arson because the remaining four elements are present.
2. She set fire to the house.
3. She set fire to property—a house is property.
4. The property belonged to another—assuming she did not break into her own house.
5. She acted without consent—assuming here the owner did not consent—there are no facts given concerning consent.

PART D Dai has committed arson because all of the elements are met.

1. She acted knowingly—she did not accidentally set the building on fire.
2. She set the building on fire.
3. She set fire to property—the diner is property.
4. The property belonged to another—the property did not belong entirely to her, for she owned the building with Steve. Steve owns an interest in the building. When she set fire to it, she set fire to the property of "another"—Steve's property interest in the building.
5. She acted without consent—assuming here that Steve did not consent—there are no facts given concerning consent.

ASSIGNMENT 9

The answer will be similar to the answer to Assignment 8, but may vary according to state law.

ASSIGNMENT 10

40 CFR 8. CFR Index. Under Environmental Impact Statements—Environmental Protection Statements-Antarctica, nongovernmental activities, environmental impact assessment.

ASSIGNMENT 11

Page 13274. Federal Register Index Vol. 66 January–April 2001. Under Drug Enforcement Administration—PROPOSED RULES.

ASSIGNMENT 12

ASSIGNMENT 12A

The statute applies to nuncupative wills. A nuncupative will is an oral will, a will that is not written.

Instructor's note: The instructor may require students to answer this question with a legal dictionary definition of *nuncupative.*

ASSIGNMENT 12B

The elements of the statute are as follows:

1. the testator must be in imminent peril of death,
2. the testator must have died as a result of the impending peril,
3. the testator must have declared the will to be his last will,
4. the testator must have made the declaration before two disinterested witnesses,
5. the will must be reduced to writing by or under the direction of one of the witnesses,
6. the reduction to writing must take place within 30 days after the declaration, and
7. the will must be submitted for probate within six months after the death of the testator.

ASSIGNMENT 12C

The statute does not apply to this situation. The statute applies to nuncupative (oral) wills. It does not apply to written wills. The facts in Part C involve a will written by the testator. This will would be governed by the statutes dealing with holographic wills (wills written by the testator, usually handwritten).

ASSIGNMENT 12D

QUESTION D1. There is insufficient information provided in the problem to determine if the will is valid under the statute. The following information is necessary:

1. It must be determined if Larry (the testator) was in imminent peril of death when he made the declaration. The statute requires that the testator be "in imminent peril of death. . . ." Even though the problem states that Larry is on his deathbed, the facts do not state that he was in imminent peril of death (although this probably can be assumed).

2. It must be determined if Larry died of the imminent peril. The statute requires that the testator must die "as a result of the impending peril. . . ." The facts do not state that Larry died as a result of the impending peril. Although the facts state Larry was on his deathbed and one would tend to assume he died as a result of the ailment, there is no direct statement to this effect in the facts. One must determine if Larry indeed died of the peril and not assume this is the case.

Instructor's note: Students should be advised to watch out for assumptions. A good rule to follow is do not assume anything, be sure. If necessary, gather more information or conduct additional research.

3. It must be determined if Larry's sister Mary and Tom are "disinterested witnesses" within the meaning of the statute. The statute requires that the testator's declaration be made before two disinterested witnesses. Beth is an interested witness because Larry leaves all his property to her. The other two witnesses are Tom and Mary. If Mary or Tom is determined to be an interested witness, then there are not two disinterested witnesses. The requirement that the declaration be witnessed by two disinterested witnesses would not be met, and the will would not be valid.

Even though Mary does not inherit under the declaration of the terms of the nuncupative will, she might still inherit a portion of the will pursuant to the provisions of subsection C of the statute. Therefore, she may be considered an interested party. The relevant statutory and case law must be researched to determine what constitutes an interested witness and if Mary is an interested witness.

It must also be determined if Tom, the next door neighbor, is an interested witness. Larry may have a written will in which Tom is named as a beneficiary. Under the provisions of subsection C of the statute, it is possible that Tom could inherit and, therefore, be considered an interested witness. As in Mary's case, the relevant statutory and case law must be researched to determine if Tom is an interested witness.

4. It must be determined if the declaration by Larry was made "before two disinterested witnesses." The question here is what constitutes "before." Tom heard the declaration, but he was not in the same room as Larry when the declaration was made. It must be determined if the statute requires that the witness be physically present in the same room as the testator when the declaration is made.

In order to answer this question, it will probably be necessary to research case law to determine what constitutes "before two disinterested witnesses." Although it is possible that another section of the probate code spells out what constitutes proper witnessing, it is more likely that this question is addressed by the courts.

QUESTION D2. According to subsection C of the statute, the nuncupative will does not revoke an existing written will. Under subsection C, the nuncupative will only changes the written will to the extent necessary to give effect to the nuncupative will. Subsection B further limits the effect of the nuncupative will. It provides that a nuncupative will may only dispose of personal property in an aggregate value not exceeding one thousand dollars.

The combined effect of these two sections is that Larry's nuncupative will disposes of Larry's personal property in an amount not exceeding one thousand dollars. His written will is affected only to this extent.

SUGGESTED ASSIGNMENT: Require the students to locate your state law governing nuncupative wills and perform the assignment using that law rather than the law presented in this assignment.

ASSIGNMENT 13

ASSIGNMENT 13A
Section 2-201 provides that a contract for the "sale of goods . . . is not enforceable . . . unless there is some writing. . . ." The statute does not refer to the lease of goods and, therefore, does not appear to apply to the lease of goods. Research should be conducted, however, to determine if "sale of goods" is interpreted to include the lease of goods. There may be a definition section of the Commercial Code Sales Act which defines "sale of goods." Also, there may be a court opinion that interprets what constitutes the "sale of goods."

ASSIGNMENT 13B
The required elements for a contract for the sale of goods of five hundred dollars or more to be enforceable are the following:

1. the contract must be in writing,
2. the writing must be sufficient to indicate that a contract for sale has been made between the parties, and
3. the contract must be signed by the party against whom enforcement is sought, i.e., the party being sued or that party's authorized agent or broker.

ASSIGNMENT 13C

QUESTION C1. The statute does not limit who can enforce the contract. It does, however, provide limits against whom enforcement may be sought. The statute limits enforcement to those contracts "signed by the party against whom enforcement is sought. . . ." In other words, a contract may only be enforced against a party who signed it. Since neither party signed the contract, it is not enforceable against either party.

QUESTION C2. The statute provides that a contract is not enforceable unless it is "signed by the party against whom enforcement is sought. . . ." If Mary is the only party who signed the contract, under the provisions of the statute, the contract can only be enforced against her. Therefore, only the seller can enforce the contract.

QUESTION C3. It must be assumed in answering Questions C3 and C4 that the written contract is "sufficient to indicate that a contract for sale has been made between the parties. . . ." Since the contract was signed by both parties, under the provisions of the statute, it is enforceable against both parties. The fact that the contract incorrectly provides for the sale of 9 tires, rather than the 10 the parties orally agreed on, does not render the contract unenforceable. The statute provides that a "writing is not insufficient because it omits or incorrectly states a term agreed upon. . . ."

Where, however, the contract incorrectly states a term, the statute provides that the contract is not enforceable "beyond" the quantity shown in the contract. In this case, the contract provides for the sale of 9 tires. Therefore, in light of the provisions of the statute, the contract is enforceable for the sale of up to 9 tires.

QUESTION C4. The answers to Questions C3 and C4 are very similar. Since the contract was signed by both parties, under the provisions of the statute it is enforceable against both parties. The fact that the contract incorrectly provides for the sale of 15 tires rather than the 10 tires the parties orally agreed on does not render the contract unenforceable. As noted in the answer to Question C3, the statute provides that a "writing is not insufficient because it omits or incorrectly states a term agreed upon. . . ."

As noted in the answer to Question C3, where the contract incorrectly states a term, the statute provides that the contract is not enforceable beyond the quantity shown in the contract. In this case, the contract provides for the sale of 15 tires. Therefore, in light of the provisions of the statute, the contract should be enforceable for the sale of up to 15 tires.

The statute, however, does not address a question that is implied in this problem. The statute only provides that the contract is not enforceable "beyond the quantity" stated in the contract. What if the contract incorrectly states a quantity in excess of the amount orally agreed upon by the parties and a party wants the contract enforced only in the amount of the oral agreement?

In this case, the oral agreement was for 10 tires and the writing provides for the sale of 15 tires. Is the contract enforceable for a quantity in excess of the amount orally agreed upon? A literal reading of the statute is yes; it is enforceable for a quantity of up to 15 tires even though the parties orally agreed only to 10. In this situation, it is advisable to research case law to determine if the courts have interpreted the statute to limit the enforcement of the quantity to the amount orally agreed upon by the parties—10 tires.

QUESTION C5. There is an enforceable contract under the provisions of the statute if the slip of paper is "sufficient to indicate that a contract for sale has been made between the parties. . . ." The statute does not provide any guidance as to what is sufficient; therefore, research would be necessary to determine if any other statute defines "sufficient" or if the courts have interpreted what constitutes a sufficient writing under the statute.

If research indicates that the writing is sufficient, then additional research would be necessary to determine to what extent the contract is enforceable. Since the writing does not include any of the terms of the agreement, such as quantity or price, the statute is of little guidance. Court cases involving similar fact situations would have to be researched to determine how and to what extent the courts have enforced similar contracts.

SUGGESTED ASSIGNMENT: Require the students to locate the statute of frauds section of your state's commercial code and perform the assignment using that law rather than the law presented in this assignment.

ASSIGNMENT 14

Instructor's note: The statutory section in this assignment involves privileged communications between spouses. Often there are other state statutes which limit this privilege. For example, some states have statutes which provide that the privilege does not apply in cases involving child neglect and abuse. Therefore, students should be advised that they should always conduct thorough research into all related statutes.

ASSIGNMENT 14A

The statutory elements of Section 35-1-4 are as follows:

1. A husband and wife may testify for or against each other in all actions with the following exception:
2. A husband and wife may not testify
   a. as to any communication or admission
   b. made by either of them to the other
   c. during the marriage.

   This prohibition does not apply in actions:

   a. between the husband and wife, and
   b. where the custody, support, health, or welfare of their children or children in either spouse's custody or control is directly in issue.

ASSIGNMENT 14B

As indicated in Assignment 14A above, a husband and wife may testify for or against each other in all actions unless the testimony involves "any communication or admission" made by them to each other during the marriage. In addition, they may testify for or against each other concerning communications or admissions made during the marriage when the action is between the husband and wife, and directly in issue is the custody, etc., of their children, or children in either spouse's custody or control.

Except in the situation mentioned in the previous paragraph, a husband and wife are prohibited from testifying either for or against each other in all actions in regard to communications or admissions made to each other during the marriage.

ASSIGNMENT 14C

QUESTION C1. It is assumed that husband and wife were married when husband admitted he knew that he ran the stop sign because he was drunk. Since the conversation took place during the marriage, and the lawsuit does not involve an action between husband and wife, wife cannot be compelled to testify concerning husband's admission. The statute provides that "neither may testify" concerning such conversations made during the marriage. There is no provision in the statute that allows a spouse to be compelled to testify in this situation.

QUESTION C2. The answer to this question is essentially the same as the answer to question C1. Since the conversation took place during the marriage, and the lawsuit does not involve an action between husband and wife, wife cannot voluntarily testify concerning husband's admission. The statute provides that "neither may testify" concerning such conversations. There is no provision in the statute that allows one spouse to waive the privilege.

QUESTION C3. This question can be interpreted in two ways. Can wife voluntarily testify concerning the conversation if husband and wife are legally separated at the time the testimony is offered? The answer to this question is addressed in the answer to C4 below.

This question can also be interpreted as follows: Can wife voluntarily testify concerning the conversation if husband and wife are legally separated at the time the conversation took place? The answer to this question depends on how "during the marriage" is interpreted. The statute provides that neither may testify as to any communication made "during the marriage." If the conversation took place while the parties were legally separated, was it made "during the marriage" within the meaning of the statute? Does a legal separation terminate the privilege? Are the parties no longer married for the purposes of this statute when they are legally separated?

The statutes must be reviewed to determine if there is a definition or other section that defines "during the marriage." In the absence of an applicable statutory section, the case law must be researched for a court opinion which discusses whether a conversation that takes place between a husband and wife while they are legally separated is made "during the marriage" and therefore privileged under Section 35-1-4. In the absence of statutory or case law, it would be necessary to refer to secondary authority such as a legal encyclopedia.

QUESTION C4. It is assumed here that the conversation took place during the marriage. The question then is whether the statute only applies while the parties are married. In other words, if the parties are no longer married, may they testify about conversations that took place during the marriage?

The statute states that neither party may testify as to conversations between them during the marriage. The statute does not have a section that provides that the privilege only applies while the parties are married; the statute does not specifically require that the parties be married at the time the testimony takes place. Therefore, the privilege probably applies even when the parties are no longer married.

It is, however, possible that the statute has been interpreted differently. Therefore, the student should always conduct research to determine if the legislature or the courts have interpreted the statute differently.

QUESTION C5. The answer to this question depends upon what constitutes a marriage in the state. The statute prohibits testimony as to communications or admissions made "during the marriage." If the state laws recognize common law marriages, and husband and wife having lived together for 20 years constitutes a valid common law marriage, then they are married and the statute applies. It would be necessary to determine the answer to the following questions:

1. Does the state recognize common law marriages?
2. What is required for a common law marriage?
3. In addition to living together as husband and wife, have the parties met all the requirements for a valid common law marriage?

QUESTION C6. More information is needed to answer this question. The statute provides that a husband or wife may testify concerning conversations made during the marriage in actions between the husband and wife where the custody, support, health, or welfare of their children or children in either spouses's custody or control is directly in issue. Therefore, it is necessary to determine what is in issue in the divorce action in order to answer this question. If the custody, etc., of the children is directly in issue, then the conversation is admissible.

SUGGESTED ASSIGNMENT: Require the students to locate your state law governing privileged spousal communications and perform the assignment using that law rather than the law presented in this assignment.

WEB ASSIGNMENT ANSWERS

ASSIGNMENT 1

The answer to this question depends on state law.

ASSIGNMENT 2

Truth in Lending Act 15 U.S.C.A. § 1601 et seq.

ASSIGNMENT 3

20 U.S.C.A. § 1070D-31 et seq. Found in the U.S.C.A. index under COLLEGES AND UNIVERSITIES—Robert C. Byrd Honors Scholarship Program.

ASSIGNMENT 4

18 U.S.C.A. § 3584 establishes limitations on consecutive sentences. Found in the U.S.C.A. index under CRIMES AND OFFENSES—Consecutive sentences, limitations.

ASSIGNMENT 5

Instructor's note: In order to properly perform Assignment 5, students should look up the term *holographic* in a law dictionary.

PART A
The statute applies to written wills including holographic wills—wills handwritten by the testator.

PART B
The witnessing requirements are set out in § 15-11-502(1)(c). The section provides that two individuals must sign the will prior to or after the testator's death. They must sign within a reasonable time after they witness, in the conscious presence of the testator, either the signing of the will or the testator's acknowledgement of his signature or acknowledgment of the will. Section 15-11-1-502(2) provides that a holographic will does not have to be witnessed.

PART C
A holographic will is valid if the signature and material portions of the will are in the testator's handwriting.

PART D–1
In order to determine if the will is valid under subsection (1) of the statute, additional information is necessary. Subsection (1)(c) provides that the witnesses must sign within a reasonable time after they witness, in the conscious presence of the testator, the testator sign the will or **the testator's acknowledgment of that signature or acknowledgment of the will.** The witnesses did not see Joan sign the will; they witnessed it the next day. However, the testator may have acknowledged her signature or acknowledged the will the next day when the witnesses witnessed it. If this occurred, then under subsection (1)(c) the will would be validly witnessed. Therefore, this additional information is necessary to determine whether the will is valid.

PART D–2
We need additional facts to answer this question. The facts state that Joan wrote and signed the will. Did she hand write it or type it? A holographic will is a will written by the testator in his or her own hand. Assuming the signature and material portions of the will are written in Joan's handwriting, then it is valid under subsection (2) of the statute. The section does not require witnessing.

ASSIGNMENT 6

Perform Assignment 5 using your state statute governing wills.

ASSIGNMENT 7
PART A

Section 18-732, Burglary—Elements
1. A person must act knowingly—that is, intentionally
2. enter unlawfully or remain unlawfully after a lawful or unlawful entry
3. in a building or occupied structure
4. with intent to commit a crime in the building or structure
5. against another person or property.

Section 18-760, Robbery—Elements
1. A person must act knowingly—that is, intentionally
2. take anything of value
3. from the person or presence of another
4. by use of force, threats, or intimidation.

Section 18-773, Larceny—Elements

1. A person must wrongfully take, obtain, or withhold, by any means
2. from the possession of the owner or any other person
3. money, personal property or article of value
4. with intent to permanently deprive another person of the use and benefit of the property.

PART B

Larry has committed larceny because all of the elements of the statute are met:

1. A person must wrongfully take, obtain, or withhold, by any means—when Larry absconded with Denise's shopping bag he wrongfully took or obtained it.
2. From the possession of the owner or any other person—he took or obtained it from the owner, Denise.
3. Money, personal property or article of value—it must be assumed that the bag itself was, or contained, "personal property or an article of value."
4. With intent to permanently deprive another person of the use and benefit of the property—it must be assumed that when Larry absconded with the bag he intended to keep it.

Larry has not committed burglary because there is no unlawful entry of a building with the intent to commit a crime. He has not committed robbery because he did not use force, threats, or intimidation.

PART C

Larry has committed both robbery and larceny because the elements of both statutes have been met:

Robbery—Elements

1. A person must act knowingly—that is, intentionally—Larry intentionally grabbed the lady's handbag and struggled with her.
2. Take anything of value—a handbag is something of value.
3. From the person or presence of another—he took it from another person, the lady who owned it.
4. By use of force, threats, or intimidation—he used force when he struggled with the lady for the bag.

Larceny—Elements

1. A person must wrongfully take, obtain, or withhold, by any means—Larry wrongfully took the handbag when he grabbed it as he ran by.
2. From the possession of the owner or any other person—he took it from the possession of the owner.
3. Money, personal property or article of value—a handbag is personal property.
4. With intent to permanently deprive another person of the use and benefit of the property—it must be assumed that when Larry absconded with the bag he intended to keep it.

Larry has not committed burglary because there is no unlawful entry of a building with the intent to commit a crime.

PART D

Depending on the court's interpretation of the statute, Mike has probably committed larceny. Note the discussion of the fourth element below.

1. A person must wrongfully take, obtain, or withhold, by any means—when Mike refused to pay the bill he acted wrongfully by withholding from the bartender money due for the tab.
2. From the possession of the owner or any other person—he withheld payment from the bartender, the person who was the owner or other person entitled to the tab.
3. Money, personal property or article of value—it must be assumed that the tab is money.
4. With intent to permanently deprive another person of the use and benefit of the property—it must be assumed that when Mike refused to pay the tab and left he intended to never pay it. If he intended to pay the tab the next day, then it is not so clear. If that were the case, then case law would need to be consulted to determine how the

courts interpret the statute. The courts may interpret "permanently deprive" to mean that one intends to permanently deprive another person when he or she refuses to pay when payment is demanded. In that case Mike, even if he intended to pay the next day, would still have "permanently deprived" the bartender of the money due.

Mike has not committed burglary because there is no unlawful entry of a building with the intent to commit a crime. He has not committed robbery because he did not take anything of value from the bartender by use of force, threats, or intimidation, he simply withheld something of value—he refused to pay. His threats to the bartender do not turn his refusal to pay into the crime of robbery.

PART E
Depending on the interpretation of the statute, Don has probably committed burglary and larceny.

Burglary—Elements

1. A person must act knowingly—that is, intentionally—Don intentionally entered the school bus.
2. Enter unlawfully or remain unlawfully after a lawful or unlawful entry—it must be assumed Don entered unlawfully since he entered the bus when the family was away and there are no facts indicating that he was invited into the bus.
3. In a building or occupied structure—the bus was occupied by the family. The statute does not require that the intruder know the structure is occupied. If the statute were interpreted by the courts to require that the individual knew the structure was occupied, and Don did not know it was occupied when he entered, then he did not commit burglary.
4. With intent to commit a crime in the building or structure—we must assume that he went into the bus searching for food that he intended to take. Although he may not have thought taking food is a crime, taking food, like taking anything else of value in this situation, is a crime.
5. Against another person or property—he took property (the food) belonging to the family.

Larceny—Elements

1. A person must wrongfully take, obtain, or withhold, by any means—Don wrongfully took the food.
2. From the possession of the owner or any other person—he took it from the possession of the owner.
3. Money, personal property or article of value—food is personal property.
4. With intent to permanently deprive another person of the use and benefit of the property—it must be assumed that when Don took the food he did not intend to give it back.

Don has not committed robbery; he did not use force, threats, or intimidation.

TEST QUESTIONS AND ANSWERS
TRUE OR FALSE QUESTIONS
Please write a "T" or "F" to the left of each statement.

_____ 1. Most criminal law is governed by statutory law rather than by common law.
_____ 2. All statutes have definition sections that define the key terms used in the statute.
_____ 3. The scope section includes the short title and what is specifically covered in the statute.
_____ 4. Some statutes provide that the statute is cumulative to the common law.
_____ 5. Annotations often include cross references to other statutes.
_____ 6. Slip laws are published by the *United States Code Congressional and Administrative News Service*.
_____ 7. The *United States Code Annotated* is the official code of the laws of the Untied States.
_____ 8. The *United States Code* is annotated.
_____ 9. Most state laws are initially published in pamphlets similar to the federal slip laws.
_____10. The most common approach for locating a statute is to refer to the table of contents.

_____11. Administrative law is primary authority and consists of the rules and regulations of administrative agencies and the court opinions interpreting them.

_____12. Federal administrative regulations are published by the Government Printing Office in the *United States Code*.

_____13. Federal regulations may be located in the *Code of Federal Regulations* by consulting the index or table of contents.

_____14. The *Code of Federal Regulations* and the *Federal Register* are available on both Westlaw and LEXIS.

_____15. The Federal Rules of Criminal Procedure are included in the *United States Code*.

_____16. The first step of the statutory analysis process is divided into three parts.

_____17. The first step of the statutory analysis process requires both the location of all applicable law and a determination of which statute applies.

_____18. The second step of the statutory analysis process is divided into two parts.

_____19. If the term *or* is used in a statute, both of the conditions or listed items are required.

_____20. Before a statute may be applied to the facts of a client's case, the elements of the statute must be identified.

TRUE OR FALSE ANSWERS

Answer	Text Section	Answer	Text Section	Answer	Text Section
1. True	II	8. False	IIIA1	15. True	V
2. False	II	9. True	IIIB	16. False	VIA
3. False	II	10. False	IIIC1	17. True	VIA
4. True	IIG	11. True	IVA	18. True	VIB
5. True	IIH	12. False	IVA	19. False	VIB
6. False	IIIA1	13. True	IVA2	20. True	VIB
7. False	IIIA1	14. True	IVA2		

MULTIPLE CHOICE QUESTIONS

Please circle the letter of the **most appropriate** answer.

1. Laws passed by local governing bodies such as a city council are usually referred to as:
   a. legislative acts.
   b. codes.
   c. statutes.
   d. ordinances.
   e. b and c

2. Some statutes do not have:
   a. numbers assigned for each section.
   b. definition sections.
   c. scope sections.
   d. substantive sections.
   e. all of the above
   f. b and c
   g. a and c

3. Statutory annotations usually include:
   a. a history section.
   b. official comments on the section.
   c. research guides.
   d. notes to decisions.
   e. all of the above
   f. b, c, and d

4. The laws of the United States are published in the:
   a. *United States Statutes at Large*.
   b. *United States Code*.
   c. *United States Code Annotated*.
   d. *United States Code Service*.
   e. all of the above
   f. a and b

5. The *United States Code Annotated:*
   a. has a general index.
   b. is published by the United States Government Printing Office.
   c. does not come with a conversion table.
   d. is updated with pocket parts.
   e. all of the above
   f. a and d

6. Statutes may be located through the use of:
   a. the general index.
   b. the table of contents.
   c. the popular name table.
   d. pocket parts.
   e. all of the above
   f. a, b, and c

7. Federal administrative law is published in the:
   a. *Federal Register.*
   b. *United States Code.*
   c. *Code of Federal Regulations.*
   d. *United States Code Annotated.*
   e. all of the above
   f. a, b, and c
   g. a and c

8. To locate state administrative law refer to:
   a. *Code of Federal Regulations.*
   b. *United States Code Service.*
   c. the state agency.
   d. *United States Code Annotated.*
   e. all of the above
   f. a and c

9. Usually court rules are divided into the following categories:
   a. civil procedure
   b. administrative procedure
   c. criminal procedure
   d. trial procedure
   e. a, b, and c
   f. a and c
   g. a, c, and g

10. The first step in the statutory analysis process requires:
    a. the identification of the statutory elements.
    b. a determination of which statute applies.
    c. a determination of how the statute applies.
    d. all of the above
    e. a and b

11. The second step of the statutory analysis process requires:
    a. a careful reading of the statute.
    b. a determination of whether the statute provides more than one rule or test.
    c. a review of all the sections of the statute.
    d. identification of the statutory elements.
    e. all of the above
    f. a, b, and d

12. "Wills are valid if they are in the handwriting of the testator and signed by the testator." The use of "and" means that:
    a. either condition may be present for a will to be valid.
    b. both conditions must be met for a will to be valid.
    c. the use of "and" makes both requirements mandatory for a will to be valid.
    d. only one of the conditions must be met for a will to be valid.
    e. a and d
    f. b and c

13. The final step of the statutory analysis process requires:
    a. the application of the elements to the facts of the client's case.
    b. a determination of what the statute declares, requires, or prohibits.
    c. a determination of whether the statute requires more than one rule or test.
    d. the location of the applicable statute.
    e. none of the above

14. Which of the following are steps in the statutory analysis process?
    a. a determination if the statute applies to the legal problem
    b. the location of the case law that interprets the statute
    c. the identification of the statutory elements
    d. the application of the statute to the legal problem
    e. all of the above
    f. a, c, and d
    g. b, c, and d

15. Which of the following formats are presented in the text for use when applying a statute to a legal problem?
    a. table format
    b. chart format
    c. narrative summary format
    d. brief format
    e. all of the above
    f. a, b and c
    g. b and c

MULTIPLE CHOICE ANSWERS

Answer	Text Section	Answer	Text Section	Answer	Text Section
1. d	I	6. f	IIIC1	11. d	VIB
2. f	II	7. g	IVA	12. f	VIB
3. e	II	8. c	IVB	13. a	VIC
4. e	IIIA1	9. f	V	14. f	VI
5. f	IIIA1	10. b	VIA	15. g	VI

CHAPTER 4

Case Law—Research and Briefing

TEXT ASSIGNMENT ANSWERS

ASSIGNMENT 1

Instructor's note: As discussed in the text, there is no standard form for a brief of a court opinion, nor are there any hard and fast rules governing format. It is important to emphasize to students that there are various different styles and formats for case briefs that they may encounter. The format presented in the text should be viewed as a basic outline of the essential parts of a case brief; it can be adapted as necessary to meet your needs.

The elements of a case brief are the following:

Citation
Parties
Facts
Prior Proceedings
Issue
Holding
Reasoning
Disposition
Comments

The following is a description of the elements of a case brief:

1. **CITATION** The citation includes the name of the parties, where the case can be found, the court that issued the opinion, and the year of the opinion.
2. **PARTIES** The names and legal status of the parties.
   The caption at the beginning of the opinion gives the full name of the parties.
   The legal status refers to the litigation status of the parties. This includes the status at the trial and appellate levels. The status is usually indicated in the caption. The plaintiff is the party who filed the lawsuit; the defendant is the party against whom the suit is brought.
   The appeal status of the parties immediately follows the trial court status in the caption.
3. **FACTS** The fact section of a case brief includes a summary of those facts which describe the history of the events that gave rise to the litigation. The fact section should include key and background facts.
   Key Facts. The key facts are those facts in the opinion to which the law applies and that are essential to the decision reached by the court. They are those facts upon which the outcome of the case is determined. If the key facts were different, the outcome of the case would probably be different.
   Background Facts. Background facts are those facts that put the key facts in context. They are facts necessary to make sense of the story, and, thereby, provide the reader with an overall context within which the key facts occur, an overall picture of the events of the case.
4. **PRIOR PROCEEDINGS/PROCEDURAL HISTORY** Prior proceedings are those events that occurred in each court before the case reached the court whose opinion you are briefing. Most opinions are not written by trial courts; they are written by courts of appeals:
   • either an intermediary court of appeals, such as the U.S. Circuit Court of Appeals, or,
   • the highest court of the jurisdiction, such as the U.S. Supreme Court.

Therefore, there are usually prior proceedings. If you are briefing an opinion of a trial court, there may be no prior proceedings because the trial court was the first court to hear the case.

The prior proceedings should include:
a. the party initiating the proceeding and the cause of action,
b. the court before which the proceeding was brought,
c. the result of the proceeding,
d. the party appealing, and
e. what is being appealed.

5. **ISSUE/ISSUES** The issue is the legal question addressed and answered by the court. It is the precise legal question raised by the specific facts of the case. The issue should be stated as narrowly and concisely as possible in the context of the facts of the case. A court opinion may contain several issues. Each issue should be separately identified in the case brief unless you are instructed to brief only one or fewer than all of the issues.

6. **HOLDING** The holding is the court's resolution of the issue. It is the decision of the court, the answer to the issue. There should be a separate holding for each issue identified in the issue section of the case brief. Some texts prefer that the holding be a simple one-word "yes" or "no" response to the issue. It is recommended in the text that the holding be presented as a complete response to the issue. This means that the holding should include all the elements of the issue, presented in the form of a statement.

7. **REASONING** Usually the largest part of an opinion is the court's presentation of the reasons in support of the holding. Just as for each issue there is a holding, for each holding there should be reasons explaining why the holding was reached.

The reasoning portion of an opinion usually consists of two parts:
a. The rule of law that governs and applies to the facts of the dispute. It may be constitutional, legislative, or case law, and consist of any legal principle, doctrine, or rule of law that applies to the issue in the case.
b. The court's application of the rule to the facts of the case.

The Reasoning section of the case brief should include the rule of law and a summary of the court's application of the rule of law to the facts—how the rule of law applies to the facts of the case. Lengthy quotes from the case should be avoided. The reasoning should be summarized.

The reasoning section should include a summary of the reasoning of any concurring opinion.

8. **DISPOSITION** In this section, include the relief granted by the court, which is the order entered by the court. This is usually located at the very end of the opinion.

9. **COMMENTS** Include here any observations you may have concerning the court opinion. This could include any of the following:
a. why you agree or disagree with the decision;
b. a summary of any dissenting opinions;
c. why the case may or may not be on point;
d. references to the opinion in subsequent cases or secondary sources such as a law review article;
e. any information updating the case, that is, information concerning whether the case is still good law.

ASSIGNMENT 2

Court opinions are important primarily because they constitute the largest body of the law, far larger in volume than constitutional or statutory law. In the broadest sense, it is essential to acquire a general familiarity with this body of law since it represents such a large portion of the law. In a narrower sense, one must study case law because so many areas of law are governed by case law.

There are numerous additional reasons why reading and analyzing court opinions and studying case law are important. Overall, the major reasons are the following:

1. To learn the common law. As mentioned above, much of the law is court-made. Case law must be referred to in order to learn the elements of a court-made law. A client's fact situation may be governed by case law, and to determine what law applies and the probable outcome of its application, case law must be analyzed.

2. To interpret constitutional or statutory law. Court opinions often announce rules of law that govern how a statu-

tory or constitutional term or provision is to be interpreted or applied. Therefore, case law must be consulted to understand how to interpret or apply a statute or constitutional provision.

3. To help understand the litigation process. Court opinions often address legal questions which arise in the context of the litigation process, either before, during, or after trial. Court opinions give insight into the process by explaining what conduct is appropriate, which arguments are successful, where errors are made, how procedural rules apply, how trials and motion hearings should proceed, etc.

4. To gain insight into legal analysis. In a court opinion, the court often analyzes the law. The court discusses what law applies, how it applies, the reasons for its application, and how the reasons operate to govern the application of the law to the facts of the case. By studying court opinions, one learns how to assemble a legal argument, how to determine if a law applies, and how to support a legal argument.

5. To develop legal writing skills. Judges are usually experienced in legal writing, and most opinions are well written. One may read opinions with an eye as to how sentences and paragraphs are structured, how case law and statutory law are referred to and incorporated into legal writing, how transitions are accomplished, etc. If one encounters difficulty with how to put some aspect of research into writing, an opinion can be referred to for guidance on how a court handled a similar matter.

ASSIGNMENT 3

A. *Essex Ins. Co. v. Davidson,* 248 F.3d 716 (8th Cir. 2001).
B. Battery requires intent to cause the offensive or harmful contact; it does not require intent to injure.
C. *Com. v. Hager,* 41 S.W.3d 828 (Ky. 2001).
D. Arson, key 28 Evidence, Admissibility in general.
E. 137 F. Supp. 2d 1054; United States District Court for the Southern District of Ohio; Civil Rights key 373, Federal Courts key 18 and Limitation of Actions key 104.5

ASSIGNMENT 4

The answer will vary according to state law.

ASSIGNMENT 5

A. 68 A.L.R.4th 507
B. *McLaugthlin v. U.S.,* 476 U.S. 16, 106 S. Ct. 1677, 90 L. Ed. 2d 15 (1986)
C. *U.S. v. Garrett,* 3 F.3d 390 (11th Cir. 1993)

ASSIGNMENT 6

The answer will vary according to state law.

ASSIGNMENT 7

The process of briefing a case serves several useful purposes and functions:

1. **Analysis/Learning.** Writing a summary of the essential elements of an opinion in an organized format leads to better understanding of the case and the reasoning of the court. Opinions are often complex, and the reasoning is hard to identify, difficult to follow, or spread throughout the opinion. The preparation of a case brief requires study of the opinion, identification of what is essential, and elimination of the nonessential. This process of studying a case and analyzing it piecemeal helps the reader gain a better understanding of it. The analytical process of focusing on the structure of the case helps you gain an understanding of the reasoning, thereby assisting your analysis of the law.

2. **Research/Reference.** A case brief is a time-saving research tool. It provides a summary of the essentials of a case that can be quickly referred to when reviewing the case. This saves the time that would be involved in having to reread and reanalyze the entire case in order to remember what the court decided and why. When working

on a complex legal problem involving several court opinions or when time has passed since a case was read, the availability of case briefs can result in a considerable savings of time because it is often difficult to remember which opinion said what.

A case brief is a valuable tool for the attorney assigned to the case. The attorney may not need to read all the cases related to an issue. The attorney can read the case briefs prepared by the researcher and save time by quickly weeding out those cases that are not key and identifying and focusing on the cases that should be read.

3. **Writing.** The process of briefing a case serves as a valuable writing tool. It provides you with an exercise in which you learn to sift through a court opinion, identify the essential elements, and assemble your analysis into a concise written summary.

ASSIGNMENT 8

CITATION: *Morgan v. Greenwaldt,* 786 So.2d 1037 (Miss. 2001). Genia A. Morgan, Plaintiff-Appellant; Brtenda Greenwaldt, Susan Brotherton, Melinda Leah Lewis and St. Dominic-Jackson Memorial Hospital. Defendants-Appellees.

HOLDING: Plaintiff's consent to treatment included placement in a secure environment thus precluding her false imprisonment claim. Defendant presented no evidence to support either an assault or battery claim. Defendant did not show the necessary intent, or gross negligence conduct required for damages can be assessed for intentional infliction or emotional distress.

DISPOSITION: The trial court's granting a directed verdict on the issues of false imprisonment, assault and battery, gross negligence, and intentional infliction of emotional distress was affirmed.

ASSIGNMENT 9

CITATION: *People v. Sanders,* 99 Ill.2d 262, 457 N.E.2d 1241 (1983)

PARTIES:
    State of Illinois, Plaintiff, Appellant
    Robert Sanders, Defendant, Appellee

HOLDING: The court held that a conversation between a husband and wife was not protected by the statutory spousal privilege when the conversation took place in the presence of their children, age thirteen, ten, and eight, at least one of whom was old enough to understand the conversation.

DISPOSITION: The court reversed the judgment of the appellate court and remanded the case to that court.

CITATION: *United States v. Martinez-Jimenez,* 864 F.2d 664 (9th Cir. 1898)

PARTIES:
    United States of America, Plaintiff, Appellee
    Gilbert Martinez-Jimenez, Defendant, Appellant

HOLDING: The court held that a toy gun that appeared to be a genuine weapon to individuals present at the scene of the crime, or individuals responding to the crime, fell within the meaning of a "dangerous weapon" under 18 U.S.C. § 2113(d).

DISPOSITION: The conviction of the defendant for armed bank robbery was affirmed.

ASSIGNMENT 10
PART A

CASE BRIEF United States v. Leon

CITATION: *United States v. Leon,* 468 U.S. 897 (1984)

PARTIES:
> United States, Petitioner
> Alberto Antonio Leon et al., Respondents

FACTS: A police investigation commenced on information provided by an informant who did not have a proven, reliable track record. Based on tips from the informant and investigative results, an experienced police narcotics investigator prepared an application for a warrant to search certain residences. The application was reviewed by several deputy district attorneys and submitted to a state superior court judge, who issued the warrant. Upon execution of the warrant, drugs were found. The defendants were indicted on drug charges in the District Court for the Central District of California. The evidence seized from the warrant was used to substantiate drug-related charges against several respondents in this case.

PRIOR PROCEEDINGS: The respondents moved to suppress the evidence yielded by the search, claiming the search violated the Fourth Amendment. Motions to suppress were granted by the district court. The court concluded that the affidavit in support of the warrant was insufficient to establish probable cause. The court stated that the police officer had acted in good faith in preparing the application for the warrant, but rejected the government's suggestion that the Fourth Amendment exclusionary rule should not apply where evidence is seized in reasonable, good-faith reliance on a search warrant. The government appealed to the 9th Circuit Court of Appeals. The court of appeals affirmed the ruling of the district court.

ISSUE: In light of the provisions of the Fourth Amendment exclusionary rule, must evidence be suppressed when it is seized pursuant to the execution of a search warrant that is invalid due to magistrate error, and the officers executing the warrant acted in the good-faith belief in the validity of the warrant?

HOLDING: No. The Fourth Amendment exclusionary rule does not require the suppression of evidence when it is seized by officers acting in the good-faith belief in the validity of a search warrant and the warrant is invalid due to magistrate error.

REASONING: The court concluded that in the Fourth Amendment context, the exclusionary rule can be modified somewhat without jeopardizing its intended function. The Fourth Amendment has never proscribed the introduction of illegally seized evidence in all proceedings and does not expressly preclude the use of evidence obtained in violation of its commands. The exclusionary rule is not intended or able to provide a cure for the invasion of a defendant's rights which has already taken place. It is designed to deter police misconduct, rather than to punish the errors of judges and magistrates. There is no evidence that judges will ignore the Fourth Amendment. There is no basis for believing that the exclusion of evidence seized pursuant to a warrant will have a deterrent effect on the issuing judge.

Therefore, the exclusion of evidence when the officer's conduct is based upon a good-faith belief in the validity of a warrant will not further the ends of the exclusionary rule.

DISPOSITION: Judgment of the Court of Appeals was reversed.

PART B

CASE BRIEF Acacia Mutual v. American General

CITATION: *Acacia Mutual Life Insurance Company v. American General Life Insurance Company,* 111 N.M. 106, 802 P.2d 11 (1990)

PARTIES:
    Aaron D. Silver, Defendant, Appellant
    John Clark, Receiver, Appellee

FACTS: A limited partnership was dissolved due to insolvency. Silver was the general partner in the partnership. Clark was appointed by the district court as the receiver. Clark arrived at a global settlement agreement that allowed creditors to be paid and the receivership terminated.

    The limited partnership agreement contained a provision which provided that the partnership "shall indemnify" the general partners against all claims incurred by them in connection with their activities on behalf of the partnership. Silver objected to the settlement agreement claiming this clause allowed him to be reimbursed by the partnership for partnership debts he paid. Silver's interpretation of the agreement would require additional contributions by the limited partners.

PRIOR PROCEEDINGS: The district court held that Silver's claim was untimely and approved the settlement agreement. Silver appealed.

ISSUE: Under the New Mexico Limited Partnership Act, NMSA 1978, Section 54-2-23 (Repl. Pamp. 1988), is an interpretation of an indemnification provision of a limited partnership agreement enforceable when the interpretation would require additional contributions by the limited partners to pay off the general partner?

HOLDING: No. Under the New Mexico Limited Partnership Act, an interpretation of an indemnification provision of a limited partnership agreement is not enforceable when the interpretation would require additional contributions by the limited partners to pay off the general partner.

REASONING: Section 54-2-23 of the New Mexico Limited Partnership Act governs the distribution of assets upon the dissolution of a limited partnership. In setting out the order of priority for the distribution of assets, the act provides that limited partners are paid before general partners. The interpretation of the indemnification clause argued by Silver would have the general partners paid off by the limited partners. Since there were no assets left in the partnership, Silver's interpretation would clearly violate the statutorily mandated order of priority of distribution.

DISPOSITION: The Supreme Court affirmed the district court holding.

COMMENT: The basis of the decision was the statutory order of priority of distribution. Justice Ransom, specially concurring, found no conflict between the indemnification agreement and the statutory order of priority relied on.

PART C

CASE BRIEF Commonwealth v. Shea

CITATION: *Commonwealth v. John J. Shea,* 38 Mass. App. Ct. 7, 644 N.E.2d 244 (1995)

PARTIES:
    John J. Shea, Defendant, Appellant
    Commonwealth of Massachusetts, Plaintiff, Appellee

FACTS: Defendant and a friend invited two women for a ride on defendant's boat; they accepted. About five miles offshore defendant threw both women overboard when they rejected his sexual advances and requested that he return them to shore. The water was fifty-two degrees with waves one to two feet high. Defendant knew of the water conditions because at one point he jumped in the water himself to hold one of the women underwater for an unspecified length of time. Both women told defendant that they couldn't swim before he threw them into the water. Defendant drove away and left them in the water. At this time no other boats were in sight.

PRIOR PROCEEDINGS: The Commonwealth of Massachusetts charged defendant with kidnapping, attempted murder, assault and battery with a dangerous weapon, and indecent assault and battery against the two women. After a jury trial in the Plymouth Superior Court, defendant was convicted of all charges. Defendant appealed.

ISSUE: For purposes of Massachusetts criminal law, Mass. Gen. Laws ch. 265, § 15A, can the ocean be considered a dangerous weapon when known nonswimmers are forced into cold and choppy waters five miles from shore and abandoned?

HOLDING: No. The ocean in its natural state cannot be considered a dangerous weapon because it is not subject to human control.

REASONING: Massachusetts General Laws ch. 265, § 15A provides that "Whoever commits assault and battery upon another by means of a dangerous weapon shall be punished. . . ." The Appeals Court of Massachusetts found the terms "objects" or "instrumentalities" consistently present in court opinions where dangerous weapons issues were decided under Mass. Gen. Laws ch. 265, § 15A. The court noted that a dangerous weapon, as an object or instrumentality, must be subject to the control of the batterer either by possession or by authority. The court found that the ocean in this case was not subject to human control and, therefore, was not a dangerous weapon within the meaning of the statute.

DISPOSITION: The convictions on the charges of assault and battery by means of a dangerous weapon were reversed.

COMMENTS: The opinion goes on to state that it may be possible for a "force of nature" to be used as a dangerous weapon. The court does not clarify the point any further though, and what is necessary for a natural force to become a dangerous weapon is not clear in the opinion.

PART D

CASE BRIEF Atlantic Beach Casino, Inc. v. Morenzoni

CITATION: *Atlantic Beach Casino, Inc. v. Morenzoni,* 749 F.Supp 38 (D. R.I. 1990)

PARTIES:
  Atlantic Beach Casino, Inc., et al., Plaintiffs
  Edward T. Morenzoni, et al., Defendants

FACTS: Plaintiffs scheduled a performance by the music group "2 Live Crew." The Westerly Town Council scheduled a show cause hearing concerning the revocation of plaintiffs' entertainment license. The plaintiffs moved for a temporary restraining order prohibiting the defendants from holding the hearing, revoking plaintiffs' entertainment license, and prohibiting the scheduled 2 Live Crew Concert. The Westerly Town Council was acting under the authority of Westerly Code of Ordinances 17-84 and 17-87. Ordinance 17-87 provided that "Any license granted under Section 17-84 and 17-88 may be revoked by the Town Council after public hearing for cause shown."

PRIOR PROCEEDINGS: There are no prior proceedings in this case. The court rendering the opinion, the U.S. District Court, is the trial court.

ISSUE: In light of the freedom of speech provisions of the First Amendment, are municipal ordinances constitutional when the ordinances provide that "Any license granted under Section 17-84 and 17-88 may be revoked by the Town Council after public hearing for cause shown"?

HOLDING: No. The ordinances as written are unconstitutional because they completely lack any standards justifying prior restraint of speech.

REASONING: The First Amendment guarantees freedom of speech. The actions of the town council constitute prior restraint. The court, referring to *Shuttlesworth v. Birmingham,* 394 U.S. 147, 150-151 (1969), stated that in order to survive constitutional scrutiny, a licensing scheme involving prior restraint must contain "narrow, objective and definite standards to guide the licensing authority." The court noted that the Westerly ordinance left the issuance and revocation of licenses to the unbridled discretion of the town council. The court stated that the Westerly ordinances did not even approach the necessary level of specificity constitutionally mandated.

DISPOSITION: The court enjoined the defendants from holding the hearing, revoking the plaintiffs' license, or prohibiting the scheduled concert.

PART E

CASE BRIEF Cardwell v. Gwaltney

CITATION: *Cardwell v. Gwaltney,* 556 N.E.2d 953 (Ind. Ct. App. 1990)

PARTIES:
   Donna Gayle Gwaltney Cardwell, Appellant
   Kenneth Wayne Gwaltney, Appellee

FACTS: After the divorce of Cardwell and Gwaltney, an order for child support was entered. Gwaltney petitioned to modify the order after he spent a year in jail. He sought to be absolved from paying the support obligations that had accrued while he was in jail and that were delinquent. Cardwell and Gwaltney reached an agreement which released Gwaltney from the delinquency.

PRIOR PROCEEDINGS: The trial court upheld the agreement. The county prosecuting attorney objected because Cardwell was a recipient of AFDC funds and had assigned her support rights to the state. The trial court would not set aside the agreement.

ISSUE: Pursuant to the child support provisions set out in Indiana Code Section 31-2-11-12, can an order entered for child support payments be modified to retroactively release an obligor from an accrued amount that became due while the obligor was in prison?

HOLDING: No. An order entered for child support payments in the state of Indiana may not be modified to retroactively release an obligor from paying an accrued amount.

REASONING: Indiana Code Section 31-2-11-12 provides that "a court may not retroactively modify an obligor's duty to pay a delinquent support payment." The Court of Appeals noted that the law requires that any modification of a support order must act prospectively. The court referred to Ind. Child Support Guideline 2 which provides "An obligor cannot be held in contempt for failure to pay support when he does not have the means to pay, but the obligation accrues and serves as a reimbursement to the custodial parent, or, more likely, to the welfare department if he later acquires the ability to meet his obligation."

DISPOSITION: The appellate court reversed the trial court and remanded the matter to the trial court for further action.

COMMENT: A court may modify a support order prospectively when an obligor's income changes.

PART F

CASE BRIEF State v. Benner

CITATION: *State v. Benner,* 654 A.2d 435 (Me.1995)

PARTIES:

State of Maine, Plaintiff-Appellee

David Benner, Defendant-Appellant

FACTS: The defendant's girlfriend originally complained to police that he hit her. At trial she stated that the defendant did not hit her, but rather she hurt herself while drunk. The responding officer testified that on the night of the complaint he observed the victim to be sober, frightened, and nervous and her hand was swollen. He also observed that the defendant was drunk. Appellant was charged with assault under 17-A Me. Rev. Stat. Ann. § 207(1) (1983 & Supp. 1994).

PRIOR PROCEEDINGS: The defendant was convicted of assault in the Maine superior court (the trial court). The jury found that the circumstantial evidence was sufficient to meet the elements of assault. Defendant appealed.

ISSUE: In light of the provisions of the criminal assault statute, 17-A. Me. Rev. Stat. Ann. § 207(1) (1983 & Supp. 1994), is there sufficient evidence to support an assault conviction when the evidence includes the following:

1. the victim was home alone with the defendant;
2. the two were having an argument;
3. the victim made a complaint;
4. the victim appeared to the responding officer to be distraught, scared, and nervous;
5. the victim's hand was swollen;
6. the defendant was intoxicated; and
7. the victim was sober?

HOLDING: Yes. The circumstantial evidence listed in the issue is sufficient to uphold a conviction for assault.

REASONING: Maine Revised Statutes Annotated Title 17-A, § 207 (1) provides that "[a] person is guilty of assault if he intentionally, knowingly, or recklessly causes bodily injury or offensive physical contact to another." The Maine Supreme Judicial Court, in finding that the elements of assault were met in accordance with the provisions of statute, referred to controlling case law. The court, relying on *State v. Ingalls,* 544 A.2d 1272, 1276 (Me.1988), noted that a conviction may be grounded on circumstantial evidence. The court held that, viewing the evidence in the light most favorable to the state, there was sufficient circumstantial evidence to support the jury verdict.

DISPOSITION: The Maine Supreme Judicial Court affirmed the trial court judgment.

PART G

CASE BRIEF McClain v. Adams

CITATION: *McClain v. Adams,* 146 S.W.2d 373 (Tex. Civ. App. 1941)

PARTIES:

Eliza McClain et al., Plaintiffs, Appellees

Willie Adams, Defendant, Appellant

In re: Douglass' Estate

FACTS: Annie Douglass, the alleged testator, died on September 8, 1934. A witness alleged that the deceased stated from her bed on September 6, 1934, that she knew she would die and she wanted all her money and property left to the defendant. Other witnesses were present. On the morning of her death, Ms. Douglas went on errands. Shortly after returning home, she became sick and died later that evening. One of the witnesses to the September 6, 1934, statement put it in writing, which the defendant submitted as a nuncupative will to the probate court. Plaintiffs contested the probate of the writing as an invalid nuncupative will.

PRIOR PROCEEDINGS: The Jefferson County probate court (trial court) held for the plaintiffs and denied probate of the alleged nuncupative will. Defendant appealed to the county district court, where the writing was admitted for probate. Plaintiffs next appealed to the Texas Court of Civil Appeals, which affirmed the district court. Plaintiffs appealed again to the Commission of Appeals of Texas, Section A.

ISSUE: Under Texas Probate Code, Tex. Rev. Civ. Stat. art. 3346 (1925), can an alleged nuncupative will be admitted for probate when it has been established that the words which constitute the nuncupative will were spoken by the deceased two days before she died, and on the day of her death she left her home to run errands?

HOLDING: No. Where the deceased had time to run errands subsequent to the time the words were spoken which constitute the alleged nuncupative will, the will is not eligible for probate as a nuncupative will.

REASONING: The requisites of a nuncupative will are established in Tex. Rev. Civ. Stat. art. 3346 (1925). The section provides that the nuncupative will must be "made in the time of the last sickness of the deceased." In discussing what constitutes a "last sickness" the court referred to the case of *Prince v. Hazleton,* 20 Johns., N.Y., 502, 11 Am. Dec. 307, which established the in extremis rule. The rule provides that a nuncupative will is not valid unless it is made by the testator when the testator is in extremis, or overtaken by sudden and violent sickness, and does not have the time or opportunity to make a written will.

The evidence in this case showed that two days after making the statements which constitute the nuncupative will, the deceased walked to a neighbor's house and went with the neighbor to a store. The deceased had the time, ability, and opportunity to prepare a will. The activity of the deceased showed that she did not meet the elements required for an extremis state, rendering the nuncupative will inadmissible for probate.

DISPOSITION: The judgments of the district court and the court of civil appeals were reversed, and judgment was entered denying probate of the will.

PART H

CASE BRIEF Cooper v. Austin

CITATION: *Cooper v. Austin,* 837 S.W.2d 606 (Tenn. Ct. App. 1992)

PARTIES:
   Phillip J. Cooper, Plaintiff-Appellant
   Charles Austin, Defendant-Appellee

FACTS: Testator requested two friends to witness and sign a document. They witnessed the testator's signature and then signed the document themselves. All signatures were executed in the presence of a notary, who then signed and notarized the document. During that time, the testator did not inform the witnesses or the notary that the document was a codicil to his will, although testator did inform one witness earlier that the document was a codicil. The codicil was submitted for probate as the will of the deceased.

PRIOR PROCEEDINGS: The admission of the codicil as the last will was contested in the probate court on the grounds that the codicil had not been properly executed or witnessed. The probate court certified the contest to the circuit court. A jury trial was held, and the circuit court granted a motion for directed verdict and directed a verdict denying the admission of the codicil as the last will. The court ruled that the proponent of the admission of the codicil had not met the burden of proof regarding the manner in which a will must be executed. The plaintiff appealed.

ISSUE: Under the statute governing the execution of a will, Tenn. Code Ann. § 32-1-104 (1984), may a codicil be admitted for probate when the testator did not signify, to at least one of the attesting witnesses, that the instrument was his will?

HOLDING: No. In Tennessee, a codicil cannot be admitted to probate as a valid will when the testator does not signify to all of the attesting witnesses that the instrument is his will.

REASONING: The rule of law governing the execution of wills is Tenn. Code Ann. § 32-1-104 (1984). The statute provides that the testator "shall signify to the attesting witnesses that the instrument is his will. . . ." In this case, one witness testified that he had been told by the testator prior to the signing that the document was a codicil to his will. Another witness testified that testator told him it was a codicil, and he also testified that he didn't know it was a codicil; this contradiction effectively eliminated his testimony. The notary public testified that testator signified to her that she was to notarize a paper, but did not refer to it as a will or codicil. In the absence of conclusive testimony showing that the testator signified to all witnesses that the document was a will or codicil, the court found that the statutory requirement was not met.

DISPOSITION: Judgment of the trial court was affirmed.

SUGGESTED ASSIGNMENTS: When students are assigned the task of preparing a legal memorandum, require that a case brief be submitted for each court opinion involved in the assignment.

WEB ASSIGNMENT ANSWERS

ASSIGNMENT 1

No. *People v. Gaul-Alexander,* 38 Cal. Rptr. 2d 176 (Cal. App. 5 Dist., 1995). Located under bigamy key number 1. The case may be located using the California, Pacific, or General digest.

ASSIGNMENT 2

No. *United States v. Romero,* 897 F2d 47 (2nd Cir. 1990). Located in annotations to 18 U.S.C.A. 1117.

ASSIGNMENT 3

Maloof v. Bonser, 769 A2d 339 (N.H. 2000). Located in Atlantic Digest or General Digest key 115 Damages k 117.

ASSIGNMENT 4

Akerman v. Oryx Communications, Inc., 810 F.2d 336 (7th Cir. 1987). Consult the 10th Decennial Digest table of cases.

ASSIGNMENT 5

CASE BRIEF *Hershley v. Brown*

CITATION: *Hershley v. Brown,* 655 S.W.2D 671 (Mo.App. 1983)

PARTIES: Shelley Hershley and Roy Hershley, Plaintiffs, Appellants
              Merlin D. Brown, Defendant, Appellee

FACTS: In 1977 Dr. Merlin Brown (Brown) informed Shelley Hershley and her husband, Roy Hershley, that he would perform a bilateral tubal ligation on Mrs. Hershley by burning, cauterizing, or otherwise removing portions of her fallopian tubes. In December of 1977, Dr. Brown performed a surgical sterilization procedure on Mrs. Hershley. In October of 1980 Mrs. Hershley conceived a child. The Hershleys claimed that not until after Mrs. Hershley had conceived did they become aware of the fact that Dr. Brown had performed the sterilization procedure by inserting a Wolfe tubal ring instrument rather than by burning, cauterizing, or otherwise removing portions of Mrs. Hershley's tubes. The Wolfe tubal ring was manufactured by Richard Wolfe Medical Instruments. The Hershleys filed suit against Dr. Brown and Richard Wolfe Medical Instruments alleging strict liability, negligent installation of a foreign object, and fraudulent misrepresentation and concealment of a battery.

PRIOR PROCEEDINGS: The defendants moved to dismiss the complaint on the ground that it failed to state a claim and the claim was barred by the statute of limitations. The trial court granted the motions. The Hershleys appealed. At oral argument they dismissed their appeal against Richard Wolfe Medical Instruments.

ISSUE I: Under Missouri tort law, may a physician be held strictly liable for performing an allegedly defective sterilization procedure?

ISSUE II: In light of the provisions of the statute of limitations in § 516.105, is the performance of a surgical procedure subject to the two-year limitations period when the claim is that a physician negligently implanted a Wolfe ring rather than negligently permitting it to remain in the body?

HOLDING ISSUE I: No. The doctrine of strict liability does not apply to physicians, therefore, a physician may not be held strictly liable for performing an allegedly defective sterilization procedure.

HOLDING ISSUE II: Yes. Where the claim is that a physician negligently implanted a Wolfe ring rather than negligently permitting it to remain in the body, the two-year limitations period applies.

REASONING ISSUE I: The court stated that no Missouri case had addressed the issue and noted that leading cases from other jurisdictions had held that physicians may not be held liable under a theory of strict liability. The court quoted the reasoning of the Wisconsin court in *Hoven v. Kelble,* 79 Wis.2d 444, 256 N.W.2d 397 (1977) where the court stated:

> Medical services are an absolute necessity to society, and they must be readily available to the people. It is said that strict liability will inevitably increase the cost for medical services, which might make them beyond the means of many consumers, and that imposition of strict liability might hamper progress in developing new medicines and medical techniques. 256 N.W.2d at 391

Hershley at 675. The court also referred to the reasoning in *Carmichael v. Reitz,* 17 Cal.App.3d 958, 95 Cal.Rptr. 381 (1970) and stated that if there is injury but "no negligence or fault is shown, liability without fault may not be imposed to find the medical doctor liable." *Hershley* at 675. The court agreed with the reasoning of these courts and refused to apply the strict liability doctrine to physicians.

REASONING ISSUE II: Claims of negligence and malpractice are governed by Missouri statute § 516.105, which provides that all such actions must "be brought within two years from the date of the occurrence of the act of neglect complained of." The act includes an exception which provides that when the act of neglect "is introducing and negligently permitting any foreign object to remain within the body of a living person, the action shall be brought within two years from the date of the discovery of the alleged negligence. . . ." The court stated that "To fall within this tolling provision, the petition must allege that the object was introduced and negligently permitted to remain in the body." *Hershley* at 675. The court ruled that the exception did not apply because the allegation was that Dr. Brown negligently performed the procedure, rather than negligently permitting the object to remain in the body.

DISPOSITION: The trial properly dismissed the strict liability claim, and the court was correct in applying the two-year statute of limitations.

COMMENTS: Note that there were other issues addressed by the court and the case was remanded for further proceedings on some of those issues.

ASSIGNMENT 6

Instructor's note: The Sixth Amendment to the Constitution guarantees a defendant the right to effective assistance of counsel. The court does not mention the Sixth Amendment in the decision, therefore it is not included in the brief.

CASE BRIEF *State v. Wong*

CITATION: *State v. Wong,* 97 Ohio App.3d 244, 646 N.E.2d 538 (1994)

PARTIES: State of Ohio, Plaintiff, Appellee
              Carrie Wong, Defendant, Appellant

FACTS: In October of 1991 Carrie Wong fired several shots from her home at police officers. She had recently had a miscarriage and was taking medication to control pain and uterine contractions. She was under the influence of alcohol at the time of the shootings. She was charged with six counts of felonious assault. At trial her attorney abandoned a possible defense of not guilty by reason of insanity when neither of the court-appointed psychologists would testify that she was insane under Ohio law. At trial the prosecution unsuccessfully attempted to introduce into evidence a letter allegedly written by Ms. Wong just prior to the shooting. The letter was damaging to her, and because both psychologists relied on the letter when assessing her condition, allowing them to testify would have possibly opened the door to the admission of the letter.

PRIOR PROCEEDINGS: Ms. Wong was convicted by a jury on all counts. She appealed and the court of appeals denied her appeal. Ms. Wong filed a motion for reconsideration under Ohio App. R. 26.

ISSUE: Under Ohio law regarding the right to counsel, is a defendant denied effective assistance of counsel when the trial counsel abandons a defense of insanity because neither of the court-appointed psychologists would testify that the defendant was insane and their testimony might result in the admission of damaging evidence?

HOLDING: No. A defendant is not denied effective assistance of counsel when the trial counsel abandons a defense of insanity because neither of the court-appointed psychologist would testify that the defendant was insane and their testimony might result in the admission of damaging evidence.

REASONING: The court stated, " To establish a claim for ineffective assistance of counsel, the trial lawyer's conduct must be so deficient as to deprive the defendant of a fair trial, meaning that there exists a reasonable *probability* that, were it not for counsel's errors, the result of the trial would have been different." *Wong,* 646 N.E.2d at 540 referring to *State v. Bradley* (1989), 42 Ohio St.3d 136, 538 N.E.2d 373. The court noted that on appeal it held that the trial counsel's actions were not deficient because an attorney might reasonably decide not to risk losing credibility with the jurors by having his own witnesses on cross-examination state that the appellant was actually sane. The court also noted that allowing the psychologists to testify would have possibly opened the door to the letter. The court rejected Ms. Wong's argument that trial counsel had a duty to argue the insanity defense because it was her only hope of acquittal. The court stated, "We know of no law, and do not wish to create one, which would require every criminal defense attorney to plead the insanity defense just because it was the defendant's only chance to escape a conviction." *Wong,* 646 N.E.2d at 540.

DISPOSITION: The court denied Ms. Wong's motion for reconsideration.

COMMENTS: None.

ASSIGNMENT 7

CASE BRIEF *Melia v. Dillon Companies, Inc.*

CITATION: *Melia v. Dillon Companies, Inc.,* 18 Kan. App. 2d 5, 846 P.2d 257 (1993).

PARTIES: Martin Melia, Plaintiff, Appellee
Dillon Companies, Inc., Defendant, Appellant

FACTS: Randy Atkin (Atkin), the head of security for a store owned by Dillon Companies, Inc. (Dillon), saw Martin Melia (Melia) leave the store without paying for a pouch of tobacco. Melia was stopped in the parking lot where he said that he had forgotten to pay for the tobacco. He agreed to reenter the store where he stated he unintentionally left the store without paying. Melia thought he would be allowed to pay for the tobacco, but Atkin informed him that the matter would be treated as a shoplifting offense. Atkin informed him that, pursuant to store policy, the police would be called and a complaint filed. He was detained approximately one hour until the police arrived. After the police arrived and investigated the incident, a notice to appear in municipal court on a charge of theft was issued. Melia was then allowed to leave. Later, he was found not guilty of theft. He sued the store for false imprisonment and malicious prosecution.

PRIOR PROCEEDINGS: After a trial in the district court the jury returned a verdict in favor of Melia. Dillon appealed the verdict arguing that the trial court erred when it failed to grant its motion for directed verdict.

ISSUE: In light of the provisions of Kan. Stat. Ann. § 21-3424, Criminal Restraint, does false imprisonment occur when an individual is detained for investigation of shoplifting based on the store security officer's observation that the individual put an item in his pocket and left the store and the individual claimed he forgot to pay for the item?

HOLDING: No. The officer had probable cause to believe Melia stole the tobacco and the merchant's defense under § 21-3424(3) allows detention for the purpose of investigation by a law enforcement officer.

REASONING: The Kansas statute governing unlawful restraint, Kan. Stat. Ann. § 21-3424, provides that "(1) Unlawful restraint is knowingly and without legal authority restraining another so as to interfere substantially with his liberty." Section (3) of the statute establishes that detention by a merchant for shoplifting does not constitute unlawful restraint when a store employee has probable cause to believe that a person has actual possession of and has wrongfully taken merchandise. The detention must be in a reasonable manner and for a reasonable period of time.

   In addressing the detention, the court noted that "probable cause such as may justify a detention exists where the facts and circumstances within the knowledge of the one who is detaining are sufficient to warrant a person of reasonable caution to believe that the person detained has committed an offense." *Melia,* 846 P.2d at 260. The court noted that Melia concealed the tobacco from view by placing it in his pocket and left the store without paying. Based on Atkin's observations of these acts, Atkin had probable cause to believe Melia had wrongfully removed the tobacco. In holding that the trial court erred in denying the store's motion for a directed verdict on the false imprisonment claim, the court stated, "once probable cause exists, the merchant's defense under 21-3424(3) includes the right to reasonably detain a suspected shoplifter for the sole purpose of investigation by a law enforcement officer." *Id* at 260.

DISPOSITION: The trial court erred in denying Dillon's motion for directed verdict and the judgment of the trial court was reversed.

COMMENTS: None.

TEST QUESTIONS AND ANSWERS
TRUE OR FALSE QUESTIONS

Please write a "T" or "F" to the left of each statement.

_____ 1. Common law may be created when a court decision makes new law.

_____ 2. A court opinion usually includes a statement of facts, points of law, rationale, and a dissenting opinion.

_____ 3. Case law is far larger in volume than either constitutional or statutory law.

_____ 4. One of the major reasons to read case law is to gain insight into the litigation process.

_____ 5. Most court opinions have at least one dissenting opinion.

_____ 6. A case citation includes the volume number, page number, and name of the reporter(s) where the court opinion may be found.

_____ 7. Court decisions available through court Web sites are referred to as parallel citations.

_____ 8. The syllabus is usually included in the body of a court opinion.

_____ 9. Most of the court opinions in the United States, both federal and state, are published by West Group.

_____10. Most federal and state court decisions are not published.

_____11. Most court opinions, when published, are published in three formats.

_____12. The page and volume number of a decision in an advance sheet is usually not the same as the page and volume number of the bound volume.

_____13. The decisions of the United States Supreme Court are published in the *Federal Reporter.*

_____14. The official reporter for the decisions of the United States Supreme Court is the *Supreme Court Reporter.*

_____15. The decisions of the United States District Courts are published in the *Federal Supplement.*

_____16. *United States Supreme Court Reports, Lawyers' Edition* is an unofficial publication of United States Supreme Court decisions published by LexisNexis.

_____17. Selected decisions of state appellate courts are published in the regional reporters.

_____18. Some opinions are difficult to read because the subject matter is complex or the court may have incorrectly interpreted the law.

_____19. In a case brief, it is not necessary to include background facts.

_____20. The primary source to determine if an opinion has been reversed is a *Shepard's* citator.

TRUE OR FALSE ANSWERS

Answer	Text Section	Answer	Text Section	Answer	Text Section
1. True	II	8. False	IVA3	15. True	VA4
2. False	II	9. True	IVA	16. True	VA4
3. True	III	10. True	VA	17. True	VA5
4. True	III	11. True	VA	18. True	VIC
5. False	IVA	12. False	VA2	19. False	VID
6. True	IVA1	13. False	VA4	20. True	VE
7. False	IVA1	14. False	VA4		

MULTIPLE CHOICE QUESTIONS

Please circle the letter of the **most appropriate** answer.

1. Common law is often referred to as:
   a. case law.
   b. court opinions.
   c. judicial decisions.
   d. judge-made law.
   e. all of the above
   f. a and c
   g. a and d

2. A court, when addressing the issue of what the term *publication* means when used in a specific statute, is:
   a. establishing law through interpreting existing law.
   b. exercising a function not delegated to a court.
   c. establishing common law through creating new law.
   d. creating substantive sections.
   e. all of the above
   f. a and c

3. Which of the following are *not* mentioned in the text as reason(s) for reading and analyzing court opinions?
   a. to interpret constitutional and statutory law
   b. to locate additional primary and secondary authority
   c. to understand the litigation process
   d. to gain insight into legal analysis

4. A case citation may include:
   a. a parallel citation.
   b. the reporter volume number.
   c. the reporter page number.
   d. the reporter name.
   e. all of the above
   f. b, c, and d

5. The following are included in the body of a court opinion:
   a. the facts of the case
   b. headnotes
   c. prior proceedings
   d. the court's reasoning
   e. all of the above
   f. a, b, and d
   g. a, c, and d

6. In a published court opinion, the following elements are written by the publisher:
   a. the syllabus
   b. the headnotes
   c. the key numbers
   d. all of the above
   e. a and c

7. Most court opinions are published in:
   a. the *National Register.*
   b. *State Registers.*
   c. advance sheets.
   d. the *Federal Register.*
   e. all of the above
   f. a, b, and c

8. Most reporter volumes include a:
   a. table of cases.
   b. table of statutes.
   c. table of words and phrases.
   d. key number digest.
   e. all of the above
   f. a, c, and d

9. The decisions of the United States Supreme Court are published in the following sets:
   a. *Supreme Court Reporter*
   b. *Federal Reporter*
   c. *United States Supreme Court Reports, Lawyers' Edition*
   d. *United States Reports*
   e. all of the above
   f. a ,b, and d
   g. a, c, and d

10. The decisions of the United States District Courts are published in the:
    a. *Federal Reporter.*
    b. *United States Reports.*
    c. *United States Federal Reports.*
    d. *Federal Supplement.*
    e. all of the above
    f. a and b

11. Which of the following are specialized federal reporters?
    a. *Federal Rules Decisions*
    b. *West's Bankruptcy Reporter*
    c. *United States Claims Court Reporter*
    d. all of the above
    e. a, b, and c

12. Reporters that publish selected state court decisions are the:
    a. *South Eastern Reporter.*
    b. *Southern.*
    c. *Pacific Reporter.*
    d. *North Eastern Reporter.*
    e. all of the above
    f. b, c, and d

13. The main ways to locate case law are:
    a. look to the statutory annotations, if the research involves interpreting a statute.
    b. refer to a digest.
    c. refer to Westlaw or LEXIS.
    d. refer to a secondary source.
    e. all of the above
    f. b, c, and d

14. Case briefs usually include the following elements:
    a. facts
    b. prior proceedings
    c. body of the opinion
    d. issue(s)
    e. all of the above
    f. a, b, and d

15. Online sources that may be used to determine if a case is still good law are:
    a. LexCite.
    b. Key Cite.
    c. AllCite.
    d. *Shepard's Citation Services.*
    e. a, b, and c
    f. a, b, and d

MULTIPLE CHOICE ANSWERS

Answer	Text Section	Answer	Text Section	Answer	Text Section
1. g	II	6. d	IVA	11. d	VA4d
2. a	II	7. c	IVA2	12. e	VA5
3. b	III	8. e	VA3	13. e	VB
4. e	IVA1	9. g	VA4	14. f	VID
5. g	IVA	10. d	VA4	15. f	VIE

CHAPTER 5

Secondary Authority—Encyclopedias, Treatises, Annotated Law Reports, Digests, Shepard's

TEXT ASSIGNMENT ANSWERS

ASSIGNMENT 1

To obtain a background or overall understanding of a specific area of the law if you are unfamiliar with an area of law.

To locate primary authority (the law) on a question being researched.

To be relied upon by the court when reaching a decision.

ASSIGNMENT 2

Corp § 767, 768, 1018, 2766-2768. Under "Corporations" in the general index—oppression by majority.

ASSIGNMENT 3

Bribery § 4; Federal Courts § 2239; and United States § 17; Found in the Table of Statutes.

ASSIGNMENT 4

Dead Bodies § 43. Found in general index under "dead bodies—viewing of body prevented."

ASSIGNMENT 5

Names § 2. Found in general index under "names—definition." "A name is a word or words, designation, or appellation used to distinguish a person or thing or class from others."

ASSIGNMENT 6

Chapter 40 Ultra Vires. The term for the action of a corporation that exceed its power is "ultra vires." The term is defined in section 3399.

ASSIGNMENT 7

A.L.R. index under "brainwashing." 40 A.L.R 1062 § 3 et seq.

ASSIGNMENT 8

Yes. 129 A.L.R. Federal 273. Check the annotation history table.

ASSIGNMENT 9

19 Am. Jur Proof of Facts 2d 1, Defense of Paternity Charges. Located in the A.L.R.3d, A.L.R.4th, A.L.R.5th, A.L.R. Fed Digest, under the topic "abortion."

The Nebraska case is *Carhart v. Stenberg,* 192 F.3d. 1142, (8th Cir. 1999)—Located in the 2001 Supplement to the A.L.R.3d, A.L.R.4th, A.L.R.5th, and A.L.R. Fed Digest under the topic "abortion."

ASSIGNMENT 10

14 A.L.R. Fed. 664 § 32. Located in the A.L.R. Table of Laws, Rules, and Regulations to A.L.R.3d, A.L.R.4th, A.L.R.5th, and A.L.R. Fed.

ASSIGNMENT 11

Topic/subtopic/key—"Assault and battery"; Hus & W 209(5). Found in the descriptive word index—97 *Federal Practice Digest 4th.*

ASSIGNMENT 12

Davis v. State, 881 P2d 657, 110 Nev. 1107 (1994). Found in the *Tenth Decennial Digest* 1991–1996 Vol. 4— Topic—"kidnapping," subtopic—"defenses."

ASSIGNMENT 13

Topics/key numbers—Civil R 148, 153; Damag 50.10; Estop 85. Found in the table of cases of the *Federal Practice Digest 4th.*

ASSIGNMENT 14

Held unconstitutional in part in 390 US 570. Sixth Circuit cases: 185 F2d 807, 394 F2d 823, and 474 F2d 1248. Second Circuit case: 243 F3d 642. Found in *Shepard's Federal Statute Citations, United States Code,* 1988–1994 edition and the Cumulative Supplement Sept. 2001.

ASSIGNMENT 15

United States v. Butler. Found in *Shepard's Federal Citations,* 1995 Vol.

WEB ASSIGNMENT ANSWERS

ASSIGNMENT 1

A. 74 Am. Jur. 2d *Torts* § 34. Found in the index under "torts, property rights, interference with."
B. *Kolin v. Rosel Well Perforators Inc.,* 241 Kan. 206, 734 P2d 1177 (1987). Found in the 2001 Cumulative Supplement to 74 Am. Jur.2d *Torts* § 34.
C. J. W. McElhaney, "Spoliation Stinks: Destruction of Evidence Calls for a Strong Response," 86 ABA J. 70 (June 2000). Found in the Sept 1999–Aug. 2000 volume of the *Index to Legal Periodicals and Books,* under "spoliation of Evidence."

ASSIGNMENT 2

No. There must be an arrest, indictment, or information. *The Law of Torts,* § 431. "Malicious prosecution—instigating or continuing the prosecution or proceeding." This can be located in the index under "malicious prosecution, instigation of proceeding requirement."

ASSIGNMENT 3

Section 238, note 34. This is located by referring to the case name in the table of cases.

ASSIGNMENT 4

Thomas G. Fischer, *Intentional Spoliation of Evidence, Interfering with Prospective Civil Action, as Actionable,* 70 A.L.R.4th 984 (1989). It is located in the *A.L.R. Quick Index* under "spoliation."

ASSIGNMENT 5

Answer: Arizona does not recognize spoliation of evidence as a separate tort. See *Tobel v. Travelers Ins. Co.,* 988 P.2d 148 (Ariz. App. 1999). The answer is located in the supplement to 70 A.L.R. 4th 984 under "§ 2.5 [New] Action not recognized."

ASSIGNMENT 6

13 A.L.R. Fed 369, supp, § 9 and 118 A.L.R. Fed. 473, § 27. Located in *Cases Cited in A.L.R Federal.*

ASSIGNMENT 7

A. *Americans with Disabilities Act* § 1. Located by referring to the Am. Jur. 2d Table of Statutes, Rules, and Regulations cited.
B. The act has the purpose of:
   (1) providing a clear and comprehensive national mandate for the elimination of discrimination against individuals with disabilities;
   (2) providing clear, strong, consistent, enforceable standards addressing discrimination against individuals with disabilities;
   (3) ensuring that the federal government plays a central role in enforcing the standards established in the ADA on behalf of individuals with disabilities; and
   (4) invoking the sweep of congressional authority, including the power to enforce the Fourteenth Amendment and to regulate commerce, in order to address the major areas of discrimination faced day-to-day by people with disabilities.

ASSIGNMENT 8

Torts Key Number 13—Obstruction of or interference with legal remedies. Located in the *10th Decennial Digest,* Part 2, Volume 59, word index under "spoliation." The title of the section, "Obstruction of or Interference with Legal Remedies," is located by referring to Torts Key Number 13 in volume 53.

ASSIGNMENT 9

Crim Law 1134(10); Hab Corp 701, 811; Sent & Pun 1378, 1380(2), 1381(5). Located in the Table of Cases, Vol 14 (2002), *General Digest 10th Series.*

ASSIGNMENT 10

156 F3d 977. The answer is in *Shepard's Federal Citations, Federal Reporter Third Series Volumes 110–172,* Supplement 1995–1999, Vol 7.

ASSIGNMENT 11

87 A.L.R. 5th 698 n. Located in *Shepard's Pacific Reporter Citations,* Annual Cumulative Supplement, Vol. 95, March 2002, No. 3.

TEST QUESTIONS AND ANSWERS

TRUE OR FALSE QUESTIONS

Please write a "T" or "F" to the left of each statement.

_____ 1. Secondary authority is a source a court may rely on that is not the law.

_____ 2. Although secondary authority is persuasive authority, it may not be mandatory authority.

_____ 3. A legal encyclopedia provides a summary, critique, and analysis of the law.

_____ 4. *Corpus Juris Secundum* is more selective in its inclusion of cases than *American Jurisprudence 2d*.

_____ 5. Both *Corpus Juris Secundum* and *American Jurisprudence 2d* are available on Westlaw and LEXIS.

_____ 6. A treatise is valuable as a research tool when you are seeking a more detailed treatment of the law than that provided by a legal encyclopedia.

_____ 7. Treatises may consist of a single volume or multiple volumes.

_____ 8. Most single volume treatises are not updated with pocket parts.

_____ 9. Most treatises are available on Westlaw and LEXIS.

_____10. *American Law Reports* are similar to treatises in that they provide a comprehensive analysis of a single area of law such as the law of torts.

_____11. A.L.R. annotations include a survey of the cases from every jurisdiction that have addressed the issue(s) discussed in the annotation.

_____12. A.L.R. are available on both Westlaw and LEXIS.

_____13. A digest provides a very detailed discussion of a specific area of law.

_____14. In the West Digest system each legal topic is divided into subtopics, and each subtopic is assigned a key number.

_____15. The *United States Reports Digest* includes the decisions of the United States Supreme Court.

_____16. The Key Number digests are available on Westlaw and LEXIS.

_____17. *Shepard's Citations* are similar to digests in that they provide a brief summary of all court opinions on a specific topic.

_____18. There are *Shepard's* for both statutory and case law.

_____19. *Shepardizing* refers to the process used to determine the current validity of an authority.

_____20. *Shepard's Citations* are available on both Westlaw and LEXIS.

TRUE OR FALSE ANSWERS

Answer	Text Section	Answer	Text Section	Answer	Text Section
1. True	I	8. True	IIIA	15. False	VC2
2. True	II	9. False	IIIB3	16. False	VD3
3. False	II	10. False	IV	17. False	VI
4. False	IIA1	11. True	IV	18. True	VI
5. False	IIA3	12. False	IVB3	19. True	VI
6. True	IIIB1	13. False	V	20. False	VIA
7. True	IIIA	14. True	VA		

MULTIPLE CHOICE QUESTIONS

Please circle the letter of the **most appropriate** answer.

1. Which of the following are legal encyclopedias?
   a. Am. Jur. 2d
   b. A.L.R.
   c. *American Law Summaries*
   d. *Shepard's Law Summaries*
   e. all of the above
   f. a, b, and c

2. *Corpus Juris Secundum* and *American Jurisprudence 2d* are similar in that in both sets:
   a. topics are arranged alphabetically.
   b. there is a general index.
   c. at the beginning of each topic is a topic summary.
   d. there are table of statutes, rules, and regulations.
   e. all of the above
   f. a , b, and c

3. *Corpus Juris Secundum* and *American Jurisprudence 2d* differ in that:
   a. *Corpus Juris Secundum* is more selective in its inclusion of cases.
   b. *Corpus Juris Secundum* emphasizes state law more than does *American Jurisprudence 2d.*
   c. *American Jurisprudence 2d* has more volumes than does *Corpus Juris Secundum.*
   d. *Corpus Juris Secundum* includes a new topic service.
   e. all of the above
   f. none of the above
   g. a, b, and c

4. Topics may be located in both *Corpus Juris Secundum* and *American Jurisprudence 2d* by consulting:
   a. the general index.
   b. the table of contents.
   c. the table of statutes, rules, and regulations.
   d. Westlaw and LEXIS.
   e. all of the above
   f. a, b, and c

5. Most treatises have the following features:
   a. a new topic service
   b. a narrative presentation of the subject matter
   c. a table of cases
   d. a table of regulations
   e. all of the above
   f. a, b, and c
   g. b and c

6. Techniques for locating a specific topic in a treatise include reference:
   a. from another source such as a legal encyclopedia.
   b. to the table of contents.
   c. to the table of cases.
   d. to the general index.
   e. all of the above
   f. b, c, and d

7. A.L.R. annotations include:
   a. the text of leading state and federal court opinions.
   b. an analysis of specific issues raised in leading opinions.
   c. the text and analysis of specific federal statutes.
   d. research references.
   e. all of the above
   f. a, b, and c
   g. a, b, and d

8. A.L.R. annotations include the following components:
   a. a prefatory statement
   b. a jurisdictional index
   c. a scope section
   d. research references
   e. all of the above
   f. b, c, and d

9. To locate specific A.L.R. annotations you may consult the:
   a. A.L.R. New Topic Service.
   b. A.L.R. Digest.
   c. Index to Annotations.
   d. Table of Laws and Rules Cited.
   e. a, b, and c
   f. b, c, and d
   g. a and d

10. In regard to the West Digest system:
   a. each legal topic is divided into subtopics and assigned a key number.
   b. subtopics are referred to by both topic and key number.
   c. there are specific digests for state and federal statutes.
   d. there are both state and regional digests.
   e. all of the above
   f. a, b, and d

11. Each digest set includes:
    a. a descriptive word index.
    b. a table of cases.
    c. a table of statutes.
    d. an outline of the laws and list of topics at the beginning of each volume.
    e. all of the above
    f. a, b, and d

12. Technique(s) that may be used to locate specific cases in a digest are:
    a. to consult the descriptive word index.
    b. to consult the topic outline.
    c. to consult the table of cases.
    d. if you already know of a case that is related to the issue being researched, refer to the topic and key number of the relevant headnote.
    e. all of the above
    f. a, b, and c

13. *Shepard's* case law citators include the following features:
    a. parallel citations
    b. a brief summary of the court opinion

    c. later case treatment
    d. reference to secondary sources
    e. all of the above
    f. a, c, and d

14. There are *Shepard's Citations* for:
    a. case law.
    b. statutory law.
    c. constitutional law.
    d. federal regulations.
    e. all of the above
    f. a, b, and c

15. *Shepard's* statutory law citators include the following features:
    a. a brief summary of the statute
    b. history
    c. case treatment of the statute
    d. reference to secondary authority
    e. all of the above
    f. a, b, and c
    g. b, c, and d

MULTIPLE CHOICE ANSWERS

Answer	Text Section	Answer	Text Section	Answer	Text Section
1. a	IIA	6. e	IIIB2	11. f	VB
2. e	IIA1	7. g	IV	12. e	VD
3. f	IIA1	8. e	IVA	13. f	VIA
4. f	IIA2	9. f	IVB	14. e	VIB
5. g	III	10. f	V	15. g	VI

CHAPTER 6

Secondary Authority—Periodicals, Restatements, Uniform Laws, Dictionaries, Legislative History, and Other Secondary Authorities

TEXT ASSIGNMENT ANSWERS

ASSIGNMENT 1

D. Orentlicher. 1998, no. 3, *U. Ill. L. Rev.* 837-57 1998. Found in the subject author index under "assisted suicide."

ASSIGNMENT 2

"Online patent searching: a good news story, but not the whole story." By James F. Cottone. *79 Journal of the Patent and Trademark Office Society,* 233-240, April '97. Found in the subject index under "online searching."

ASSIGNMENT 3

"Mastering the obvious: the open and obvious doctrine in Illinois." *85 Illinois Bar Journal 28(4)* Jan '97. Found in the *Current Law Index* table of cases.

ASSIGNMENT 4

False Imprisonment § 35. Found in the index under "False imprisonment." Under § 35, the elements of false imprisonment are the following:

(a) (the actor) acts intending to confine the other or a third person within boundaries fixed by the actor, and

(b) his act directly or indirectly results in such a confinement of the other, and

(c) the other is conscious of the confinement or is harmed by it.

According to § 35 (2) "(a)n act which is not done with the intention stated in Subsection (1,a) does not make the actor liable to the other for a merely transitory or otherwise harmless confinement, although the act involves an unreasonable risk of imposing it and therefore would be negligent or reckless if the risk threatened bodily harm." Under the "Comment to Subsection (2)" If the actor knows or should know that the confinement may involve an unreasonable risk to the victim, the actor may be subject to liability.

Section 37 addresses confinement caused indirectly by the institution of criminal proceedings. Found in comment c in the "Comment on Subsection (1)".

ASSIGNMENT 5

Appropriation of Trade Values § 39 Definition of Trade Secret. Found in the index to *Restatement (Third) of Unfair Competition* under "trade secrets—definition of."

Section 39 Definition of Trade Secret: A trade secret is any information that can be used in the operation of a business or other enterprise and that is sufficiently valuable and secret to afford an actual or potential economic advantage over others.

The reason for providing protection to trade secrets to protect the plaintiff from unfair competition and deprive the defendant of unjust enrichment attributable to bad faith. The protection encourages investment in research by providing an opportunity to capture the returns from successful innovations. The protection also promotes the efficient exploitation of knowledge by discouraging the unproductive hoarding of useful information and facilitating disclosure to employees, agents, licensees, and others who can assist in its productive use. The protection also furthers the interest in personal privacy. Found in Comment A to § 39.

Rhode Island Law—R.I. G.L.A. § 6-41-1 et seq. Found in references under § 39.

Flotec, Inc. v. Southern Research, Inc., 16 F. Supp 2d 992 (S.D. Ind. 1998)—Restatement Case Citations Supplement.

ASSIGNMENT 6

Uniform Commercial Code § 2-206—Found in U.L.A. U.C.C. index under "sales—offer, acceptance, or definitions." C.J.S. Sales §§ 24 to 34—Found in the "Library References" section of the annotations under § 2-206.

Central Illinois Public Serviced Co. v. Atlas Minerals, Inc., 146 F.3d 448 (7th Cir. 1998)—Found in the Supplement's "Notes to Decisions" section of the annotations under § 2-206.

ASSIGNMENT 7

Online Child Protection Commission, 114 Stat. 464; 114 Stat. 2763, Leg. Hist. 2459. Located in the index to the *United States Code Congressional and Administrative News Service,* Vol. 5, 106th Cong., under topic "children and minors"; subtopic "abuse."

ASSIGNMENT 8

Form: Autos 516—parents of minor driver, complaint against. Located in the index (2001 Vol. A–C) to *Am. Jur. Pleading and Practice Forms* under the topic "automobiles and highway traffic"; subtopic "negligent entrustment/pedestrians."

WEB ASSIGNMENT ANSWERS

ASSIGNMENT 1

Carole Cox-Korn, *Computer Animation: The Litigator's Legal Ally.* 5 no. 2 Ga. B.J. 28 (Oct. 1999). Found in the Sept 1999–Aug. 2000 volume of the *Index to Legal Periodicals and Books,* under "Cox-Korn, Carole."

ASSIGNMENT 2

A *Restatement (Second) of Torts* § 316 (Duty of Parent to Control Conduct of Child). It may be located by referring to the *Restatement (Second) of Torts,* table of contents.

B. Section 316 provides that:

A parent is under a duty to exercise reasonable care so to control his minor child as to prevent it from intentionally harming others or from so conducting itself as to create an unreasonable risk of bodily harm to them if the parent
(a) knows or has reason to know that he has the ability to control his child, and
(b) knows or should know of the necessity and opportunity for exercising such control.

C. *Dinsmore-Poff v. Alvord,* 972 P.2d 978 (Alaska 1999). The case is in the 2001 Cumulative Pocket Part in § 316.

ASSIGNMENT 3

A. Section 210.2 Murder. It may be located by referring to the Part II "Definition of Specific Crimes" section of the table of contents of the Model Penal Code.

B. Section 210.2 (2) provides that the offense is a first degree felony.

C. *Commonwealth v. Laudenburger,* 715 A.2d 1156 (Pa. Super 1998). The case is located in note 23, Accomplices, felony murder of the "Notes to Decisions" annotation to § 210.2.

ASSIGNMENT 4

The act is presented in "114 Stat. 1381." The answer is found in the Index and Popular Names Acts to the *United States Code and Administrative News,* Vol. 5, 106th Congress—Second Session 2000.

ASSIGNMENT 5

The purpose "is to promote the transfer and commercialization of the technology created in our Nation's system of over 700 federal laboratories, thereby increasing scientific collaboration between federal laboratories and private industry. Specifically, the bill would improve and streamline the ability of federal agencies to license government-owned inventions." Located in the Index and Popular Names Acts to the *United States Code and Administrative News,* Vol. 5, 106th Congress—Second Session 2000. The index refers to "Leg. Hist. 1799." The purpose is located on page 1799.

TEST QUESTIONS AND ANSWERS

TRUE OR FALSE QUESTIONS

Please write a "T" or "F" to the left of each statement.

_____ 1. A law review article usually provides an analysis and critique of a legal topic that is the same or less in depth than a treatise.

_____ 2. Law review articles may be authored by both law professors and law students.

_____ 3. Commercial publications such as *Legal Assistant Today* are considered one of the categories of legal periodicals.

_____ 4. The *Index to Legal Periodicals* includes a subject/author index and a table of cases.

_____ 5. The *Index to Legal Periodicals* and the *Current Law Index* are available on Westlaw and LEXIS.

_____ 6. Restatements are frequently cited by courts and are not accorded a recognition greater than that accorded to treatises.

_____ 7. There is currently a Restatement for security law.

_____ 8. Included with each Restatement of the law is a digest.

_____ 9. Beginning with the *Restatement Second,* there are cumulative appendix volumes.

_____10. Restatements are available on both Westlaw and LEXIS.

_____11. "Model acts" are drafted for those situations where a state does not intend to adopt an entire law but rather intends to modify a uniform law to meet the state's requirements.

_____12. A uniform law is secondary authority source that may become primary authority if adopted by a state legislature.

_____13. Uniform laws are available on Westlaw but not on LEXIS.

_____14. *Black's Law Dictionary* is available on Westlaw and LEXIS.

_____15. *Words and Phrases* includes only terms that have been defined in federal and state court opinions.

_____16. Legislative history is primary authority.

_____17. One source for obtaining legislative history is the *Congressional Information Service.*

_____18. The *Congressional Information Service* is available on Westlaw and LEXIS.

_____19. If you want to determine what your state requires to establish a negligence claim, you can consult the state's approved jury instructions.

_____20. Looseleaf services are publications that focus on a specific area of law and include primary authority such as statutes, regulations, and summaries of court and administrative decisions.

TRUE OR FALSE ANSWERS

Answer	Text Section	Answer	Text Section	Answer	Text Section
1. False	I	8. False	IIIA	15. True	V
2. True	II	9. False	IIIA	16. False	VI
3. True	IIA	10. True	IIIA2	17. True	VIB
4. True	IIB2	11. True	IV	18. False	VIB2
5. True	IIB3	12. True	IV	19. True	VIIA
6. False	III	13. False	IVB3	20. True	VIIC
7. True	III	14. False	V		

MULTIPLE CHOICE QUESTIONS

Please circle the letter of the **most appropriate** answer.

1. To obtain an in-depth analysis and critique of a specific legal topic refer to a:
   a. Restatement of the Law.
   b. legal encyclopedia.
   c. law review article.
   d. digest

2. Which of the following are categories of legal periodicals?
   a. legal newsletters
   b. law reviews
   c. legal association publications
   d. legal newspaper
   e. all of the above
   f. b and c

3. Law reviews usually include:
   a. a digest.
   b. notes and comments.
   c. books reviews.
   d. a table of statutes.
   e. all of the above
   f. b, c, and d
   g. b and c

4. Which of the following are research tools designed to help a researcher locate specific articles?
   a. *Current Law Index*
   b. *American Legal Periodical Review*
   c. *Index to Legal Periodicals*
   d. *Index to Foreign Legal Periodicals*
   e. all of the above
   f. b, c, and d

5. To locate a standardized definition or statement of the law and reasons in support of the definition or statement, refer to:
   a. a Restatement of the Law.
   b. an A.L.R.

c. A.C.J.S.
   d. a legal dictionary.

6. Restatements of the Law have the following features:
   a. comments
   b. reporters' notes
   c. cross references
   d. all of the above
   e. a and b
   f. a and c

7. To locate a specific Restatement topic consult the:
   a. alphabetical index.
   b. table of contents.
   c. appendix volume.
   d. Restatement topic digest.
   e. all of the above
   f. a, b, and c
   g. a and b

8. *Uniform Laws Annotated* have the following features:
   a. a table of cases
   b. a digest of court opinions interpreting the uniform law
   c. commissioner's notes
   d. a new topic service
   e. all of the above
   f. none of the above

9. Uniform laws may be located through the use of:
   a. *West Uniform Laws Digest.*
   b. *Uniform Laws Annotated, Master Edition.*
   c. reference from another source such as a court opinion.
   d. the *Uniform Laws Annotated Research Guide.*
   e. all of the above
   f. b and c

10. To locate a model text from which a law may be crafted consult:
    a. a treatise.
    b. an A.L.R.
    c. a legal dictionary.
    d. a uniform law.

11. To obtain the legal meaning of a term used in the law, consult a:
    a. Restatement of the Law.
    b. law review article.
    c. legal dictionary.
    d. uniform law.

12. Legislative history is composed of:
    a. committee reports.
    b. transcripts of hearings.
    c. statements of legislators concerning the legislation.
    d. other materials published for use in regard to the specific law.
    e. all of the above
    f. a, b, and c

13. The main sources of legislative history mentioned in the text are:
    a. congressional bills.
    b. committee hearings.
    c. committee reports.
    d. congressional debates.
    e. all of the above
    f. b, c, and d

14. Which of the following are sources for locating and compiling federal legislative history?
    a. *United States Code Congressional and Administrative News Service*
    b. *Congressional Information Service*
    c. *Sources of Compiled Legislative Histories*
    d. congressional record
    e. all of the above
    f. a, b, and c

15. If you want to determine the elements of a specific cause of action in a state, consult:
    a. an A.L.R.
    b. a Restatement of the Law.
    c. a legal encyclopedia.
    d. the state's jury instruction on the cause of action.
    e. all of the above
    f. none of the above

MULTIPLE CHOICE ANSWERS

Answer	Text Section	Answer	Text Section	Answer	Text Section
1. c	II	6. d	III	11. c	V
2. e	IIA	7. f	IIIB2	12. e	VI
3. g	II	8. c	IVA	13. e	VIA
4. f	IIB2	9. f	IVB	14. e	VIB
5. a	III	10. d	IV	15. d	VIIA

CHAPTER 7

Computers and Legal Research

TEXT ASSIGNMENT ANSWERS

Instructor's note: For assignments 1–7 use Westlaw.

ASSIGNMENT 1

Ohio Rev. Code Ann. § SECT; 1701.78. Section (D)provides that the agreement shall be approved by the shareholders of each corporation. Section (F) provides that approval requires the affirmative vote of two-thirds of the shareholders entitled to vote.

To locate: Click on the "U.S. State Materials" database, then select "Ohio," then "Statutes & Legislative Materials," then "Statutes Annotated." In the Terms and Connectors search box, type the search terms "corporations & merger & shareholder approval."

ASSIGNMENT 2

To locate: Click on the "U.S. State Materials" database, then select your state, then "Statutes & Legislative Materials," then "Statutes Annotated." In the Terms and Connectors search box, type the search terms "corporations & merger & shareholder approval."

ASSIGNMENT 3

Campbell v. State, 300 Ark. 570, 781 S.W. 2d 14 (1989). A public official becomes subject to removal when convicted by a plea of guilty or a verdict of guilty at the conclusion of trial, not when all appeals have been exhausted. To locate: Click on the "U.S. State Materials" database, then select "Arkansas," then "Cases," then "State Court." In the Terms and Connectors box, type the search terms "judge & vote buying & removal."

ASSIGNMENT 4

10 A.L.R. 663 (1993). To locate: Click on the "KeyCite, ALR and American Jurisprudence" database, then select "American Law Reports." Select "Natural Language" and in the Natural Language box, type "Admissibility of evidence of polygraph results in an action for malicious prosecution."

ASSIGNMENT 5

Colbert v. State, 736 So.2d 682 (Ala.Cr.App. 1998); defendant was convicted of attempted possession of a controlled substance and his probation was revoked; the case was remanded because in the order revoking probation, the trial court did not sufficiently state the evidence relied upon and the reasons for revoking probation. To locate: Click on "Find" at the top of the Welcome page, then select "Find by Title," then type in "Colbert" in the Party box and select "Alabama" under "State" at the bottom of the page, and click "Go."

ASSIGNMENT 6

Infants Key 68.3; *State v. Brammeier,* 1 Or. App. 612, 464 P.2d 717 (1970). On the drop-down menu on the Welcome page expand the "Infants" key, then expand the "Crimes" key under "Infants," then expand the "Rights and Privileges as to Prosecution" key under "Crimes" then select "Arrest and Detention," and click "Go." On the Search page select "Oregon" at the lower left of the page and click "Search." The difficult part of this assignment is determining that "Juveniles" is categorized under "Infants." This may take some trial and error by students or they may check any West's Digest index.

ASSIGNMENT 7

U.S. v. Hamrick, 43 F.3d 877 (4th Cir. 1995) and *U.S. v. Perry,* 991 F.2d 304 (6th Cir. 1993). To locate: Click "KeyCite" at the top of the Welcome page, then enter "43 R.3d 877" in the Enter Citation box. On the Results page click the "KC Citing Ref" tab at the top left of the page.

Instructor's note: For assignments 8–14 use LEXIS.

ASSIGNMENT 8

Roman v. Carrol, 127 Ariz 398, 821 P.2d 307 (Ariz., App. 1980). To locate: select the "States Legal—U.S." database, then click on "Arizona Cases & Court Rules," select "Option 2. By Court," then click on "Az Supreme Court, Court of Appeals & Tax Court." In the Terms and Connectors box, type the search terms "damages & emotional distress & pet."

ASSIGNMENT 9

Restatement of the Law, Second, Torts § 441 Intervening Force Defined. "(1) An intervening force is one which actively operates in producing harm to another after the actor's negligent act or omission has been committed."
Restatement of the Law, Second, Torts § 440 Superseding Cause. "A superseding cause is an act of a third person or other force which by its intervention prevents the actor from being liable for harm to another which his antecedent negligence is a substantial factor in bringing about."

    To locate: Click on the "Secondary Legal" database, then select "ALI Restatements of Law," then select "Torts," then select "Rules, Comments & Notes." In the Terms and Connectors box, type the search terms "intervening force defined." This search locates § 441. The search terms "superceding cause defined" locate § 440.

ASSIGNMENT 10

Geo. Code Ann. § 19-5-3. Grounds for total divorce. Section (6) provides that adultery by either of the parties after marriage is grounds for divorce. *Survey of Domestic Relations Cases from June 1977 through May 1978,* 30 Mercer L. Rev. 59 (1978). To locate: Click on the "States Legal—U.S. Database," then select "Georgia," then "Statutes & Legislative Materials," then "GA—Official Code of Georgia Annotated," then expand "Domestic Relations," and expand "Chapter 5. Divorce." Click on "19-5-3."

ASSIGNMENT 11

Follow the same procedure used in Assignment 10 using your state rather than Georgia.

ASSIGNMENT 12

46 A.L.R. 3d 964. "Anti-Hitchhiking Laws: Their Construction and Effect in Action for Injury to Hitchhiker," by Robert A. Brazner. *Libertine v. Aetna Ins. Co.* (1985, La. App. 3d Cir.) 477 So. 2d 1286. To locate: Click on the "Secondary Legal" database, then select "American Law Reports (ALR2d, ALR3d, ALR4th, ALR5th, ALR FED, & L.Ed2d)." In the Terms and Connector box, type "hitchhiker injury."

ASSIGNMENT 13

At the time of publication of this text 10 citing decisions are listed. No negative history. 10 A.L.R. 5th 337. To locate: Click the "*Shepard's* Check a Citation" box at the top of the page and enter "607 NE 2d 15."

ASSIGNMENT 14

18 US.C.S. 1111. Section (b)Whoever is guilty of murder in the first degree shall be punished by death or by imprisonment for life. *Woollard v. United States,* 416 F2d. 50 (19689 CA 5 Ga.) To locate: Click on the "Federal Legal—U.S." database, then select "United States Code Service (USCS) Materials," then "United States Code Service—Titles 1 through 50," then expand "Title 18. Crimes and Criminal Procedure," then expand "Part I Crimes," then expand "Chapter 51. Homicide," then select "§ 1111 Murder."

ASSIGNMENT 15

Click on your state, then locate the criminal code, then the statute for murder or homicide. If a search function is available, locate your state code, then search for murder or homicide.

WEB ASSIGNMENT ANSWERS

Instructor's note: For assignments 1–6 use Westlaw.

ASSIGNMENT 1

Tennessee v. Garner, 471 U.S. 1, 105 S. Ct. 1694, 85 L.Ed.2d 1 (1985). In regard to deadly force the Court stated "[w]here the officer has probable cause to believe that the suspect poses a threat of serious physical harm, either to the officer or to others, it is not unconstitutionally unreasonable to prevent escape by using deadly force." *Id.* at 11. To locate the case, click on the "U.S. Federal Materials" database, then the "Cases and Judicial Materials" database, then "Supreme Ct. Cases after 1944," then using the Terms and Connectors box, search terms "deadly force & police."

ASSIGNMENT 2

Boyd v. Baeppler, 215 F.3d 594 (6th Cir. 2000). To locate the case, click on "KeyCite" and type in "471 U.S. 1" in the "Enter Citation" box. The case is located in the left-hand column.

ASSIGNMENT 3

James O. Pearson, Jr., *Modern Status: Right of Peace Officer to Use Deadly Force in Attempting to Arrest Fleeing Felon,* 83 A.L.R. 3d 174 (1978). To locate: Click on the "KeyCite, ALR and American Jurisprudence" database, then click on "American Law Reports." Click on "Field Restrictions" and next to the title field restriction "TI" type in "deadly force"—Ti(deadly force)—and click "Go."

ASSIGNMENT 4

5 Am. Jur. 2d *Arrest* §§ 112-114. To locate: Click on the "KeyCite, ALR and American Jurisprudence" database, then click on "American Jurisprudence," then click on "American Jurisprudence 2d," then in the Terms and Connectors box, type in "deadly force & felony."

ASSIGNMENT 5

Michael R. Smith, *Police Use of Deadly Force: How Courts and Policy-Makers Have Misapplied Tennessee v. Garner,* 7 Kan. J.L. & Pub. Pol'y 100 (1998).

To locate: Click on the "Law Reviews, Bar Journals & Legal Periodicals" database, then click on "Journals & Law Reviews Combined." In the terms and connectors field, click on "Field Restrictions," and next to the title field restriction "TI" type in "police & deadly force"—TI (police & deadly force)—and click "Go."

ASSIGNMENT 6

Depends on state. To locate: Click on the "U.S. State Materials" database, then click on your state, then click on "Cases," then "State Courts." In the terms and connectors box, type "deadly force & police."

Instructor's note: For assignments 7–12 use LEXIS.

ASSIGNMENT 7

Bleich v. Florence Crittenton Services of Baltimore, Inc., 98 Md. App.123, 632 A.2d 463 (1993). To locate: Click on the "States Legal-U.S." database, then click "Maryland," then "Cases and Court Rules," then Option 2 "By Court," then "Md Federal and State Cases." In the terms and connectors box, type "child care and contract and interference."

ASSIGNMENT 8

Thomas G. Fischer, Annotation, *Liability of Corporate Director, Officer, or Employee for Tortious Interference with Corporation's Contract with Another,* 72 A.L.R.4th 492 (1989). To locate: Click on the "Secondary Legal" database, then click "American Law Reports (ALR2d, ALR3d, ALR4th, ALR5th, ALR FED, & L.Ed2d)." In the terms and connectors box, type "corporate director and interference with contract."

ASSIGNMENT 9

Susan M. Gilles, *Promises Betrayed: Breach of Confidence as a Remedy for Invasions of Privacy,* 43 Buff. L. Rev. 1 (1995). To locate: Click on the "Secondary Legal" database, then click "Law Review, Combined." In the terms and connectors box, type "corporate director and invasions of privacy and breach of contract."

ASSIGNMENT 10

Restatement (Second) of Torts § 652H. To locate: Click on the "Secondary Legal" database, then click "ALI Restatements of Law," then click on "Torts," then "Table of Contents," then "Division 6—Injurious Falsehood," then "Chapter 28 An invasion of Privacy," then click on "§ 652 H Damages."

ASSIGNMENT 11

Public information, agency rules, opinions, orders, records, and proceedings. To locate: Click on the "Federal Legal U.S." database, then click on "United States Code Service (USCS) Materials," then "USCS-Popular Name Table." Then go to the letter F and locate the Freedom of Information Act of 1986. The citation "5 USCS § 552" will appear. Return to the Home page and click "Get a Document" at the top of the page, and in the Get by Citation box type "5 USCS 552."

ASSIGNMENT 12

United States v. Swiss Am. Bank. Ltd., 274 F.3d 610 (1st Cir. 2001). To locate: Click the *"Shepard's* Check a Citation" box at the top of the page and enter "471 US 462."

TEST QUESTIONS AND ANSWERS

TRUE OR FALSE QUESTIONS

Please write a "T" or "F" to the left of each statement.

_____ 1. The most frequently used electronic fee-based databases are Westlaw and LEXIS.

_____ 2. Westlaw is available directly on the Internet and through a software package called WestMate.

_____ 3. In Westlaw, if the search query is "bank & robber," the search is a Terms and Connectors search.

_____ 4. In a Westlaw search where the search query is "bank & robber," the search will retrieve all documents that contain either search term.

_____ 5. A natural language search is often referred to as a Boolean search.

_____ 6. In a Westlaw terms and connectors search, if you wish to exclude a term from a search query, place @ before the term.

_____ 7. A disadvantage of a natural language search is that you are unable to tailor the search.

_____ 8. In a Westlaw search you may locate a case through a table of contents search.

_____ 9. A field restriction allows you to limit your search to specific portions of a document.

_____10. KeyCite, like *Shepard's Citations,* allows you to update primary authority.

_____11. In Westlaw, status flags are used to inform the researcher of the current status of a case.

_____12. In a LEXIS search where the search query is "bank and robber," the search will retrieve all documents that contain both terms.

_____13. In a LEXIS terms and connectors search, a space between words means that the search will locate documents where the terms appear in the same order.

_____14. The "Segments" option in LEXIS allows you to limit your search to specific portions of documents, such as the headnotes of a case or the title of a statute.

_____15. When viewing a LEXIS search result, select "KWIC" if you want to view the complete text of a document.

_____16. Westlaw lists the steps of your search after the word "Source" near the top of every search page.

_____17. You may update a LEXIS search through the use of LEXIS's *Shepard's Citations Service.*

_____18. In LEXIS, a signal such as a stop sign is used as an indication of the current status of a case.

_____19. The databases of LOIS and VersusLaw are less extensive than Westlaw and LEXIS.

_____20. Findlaw is one of the most comprehensive non fee-based Web sites.

TRUE OR FALSE ANSWERS

Answer	Text Section	Answer	Text Section	Answer	Text Section
1. True	I	8. False	IIB2	15. False	IIIB4
2. True	II	9. True	IIB3	16. False	IIIB5
3. True	IIB	10. True	IIB5	17. True	IIIB5
4. False	IIB1	11. True	IIB5	18. True	IIIB6
5. False	IIB1	12. True	IIIB1	19. True	IV
6. False	IIB	13. True	IIIB1	20. True	IVA
7. True	IIB1	14. True	IIIB3		

MULTIPLE CHOICE QUESTIONS

Please circle the letter of the **most appropriate** answer.

1. It is important to know how to research using print resources for the following reasons:
   a. A familiarity with print sources makes it easier to understand the structure of electronic databases.
   b. The research material may not be on an electronic database.
   c. Access to an electronic database may not be available.
   d. It is economical.
   e. all of the above
   f. a, c, and d

2. In regard to Westlaw, you may find statutory law through a search by:
   a. statutory title.
   b. citation.
   c. issue.
   d. table of contents.
   e. all of the above
   f. a, b, and c
   g. b, c, and d

3. If a Westlaw terms and connectors search is for documents that contain all the search terms, use which of the following connector(s):
   a. a space between the terms
   b. /s
   c. &
   d. " "
   e. none of the above

4. If a Westlaw terms and connectors search is for documents that contain either of the search terms, use which of the following connector(s):
   a. %
   b. /s
   c. &
   d. " "
   e. none of the above

5. If a Westlaw terms and connectors search is for documents that contain both of the search terms in the same sentence, use which of the following connector(s):
   a. a space between the terms
   b. /s
   c. &
   d. " "
   e. none of the above

6. If a Westlaw terms and connectors search is for documents where the search terms appear in the same order as they appear in the query, use which of the following connector(s):
   a. a space between the terms
   b. /s
   c. &
   d. " "
   e. none of the above

7. In a Westlaw search you may find case law through a search by:
   a. citation.
   b. issue.
   c. case name.
   d. digest.
   e. all of the above
   f. a, b, and c

8. When updating case law research in Westlaw, the indication that a case has been criticized but not reversed in indicated through the use of a:
   a. red stop sign.
   b. green flag.
   c. yellow flag.
   d. yellow stop sign.
   e. none of the above

9. If a LEXIS terms and connectors search is for documents that contain either of the search terms, use which of the following connector(s):
   a. a space between the terms
   b. or
   c. and
   d. s/
   e. none of the above

10. In regard to a LEXIS terms and connectors search, if you want to exclude a term from the search query, use which of the following connector(s):
    a. /n
    b. %
    c. pre/n
    d. and not
    e. none of the above

11. In regard to LEXIS, you may find statutory law through a search by:
    a. citation.
    b. issue.
    c. table of contents.
    d. statutory segment.
    e. all of the above
    f. a, b, and c

12. When updating case law research in LEXIS, the indication that a case has been criticized but not reversed is indicated through the use of a:
    a. red stop sign.
    b. red flag.
    c. yellow flag.
    d. yellow triangle.
    e. none of the above

13. To perform a LEXIS search for secondary authority, perform the following steps:
    a. State the issue or research question as specifically as possible in the context of the facts.
    b. Formulate the terms and connectors or natural language search query.

    c. Locate the appropriate database.
    d. Perform the search.
    e. all of the above
    f. a, and c

14. Which of the following are commercial Web-based research services?
    a. Westlaw.
    b. Findlaw.
    c. LOIS.
    d. VersusLaw.
    e. all of the above
    f. a, b, and c
    g. a, c, and d

15. In a LEXIS search you may find case law through a search by:
    a. case name.
    b. docket number.
    c. issue.
    d. digest.
    e. all of the above
    f. a, b, and c
    g. a and c

MULTIPLE CHOICE ANSWERS

Answer	Text Section	Answer	Text Section	Answer	Text Section
1. e	I	6. d	IIB1	11. f	IIIB2
2. g	IIB	7. e	IIB2	12. d	IIIB6
3. c	IIB1	8. c	IIB5	13. e	IIIC
4. e	IIB1	9. b	IIIB1	14. g	IV
5. b	IIB1	10. d	IIIB1	15. f	IIIB2

CHAPTER 8

Legal Citation

TEXT ASSIGNMENT ANSWERS

Instructor's note: For the following exercises use either the *Bluebook* or the *ALWD Citation Manual.*

ASSIGNMENT 1

The United States of America v. Thomas Terry
Answer: *Bluebook—United States v. Terry; ALWD—U.S. v. Terry.*
Mary Kay Kraft, Mark Johnson, and Vanessa Hays v. Joseph Beazley and the City of Chicago.
Answer: *Kraft v. Beazley*
Kerry Handle et al. v. The Jamestown Cooperative
Answer: *Handle v. Jamestown Cooperative*
Kalley Institute v. Carrington Insurance Company, Incorporated
Answer: *Kalley Inst. v. Carrington Ins. Co.*
The American Civil Liberties Union v. Micron Management Corporation dba Taylor Management
Answer: *ACLU v. Micron Mgt. Corp.*

ASSIGNMENT 2

Bluebook—United States v. Matlock, 415 U.S. 164, 94 S. Ct. 988, 39 L. Ed. 2d 242 (1974). *ALWD—U.S. v. Matlock,* 415 U.S. 164, 94 S. Ct. 988, 39 L. Ed. 2d 242 (1974).

ASSIGNMENT 3

Give the correct citation for the following case; include the parallel citations. Douglas D. Robberts versus Carroll E. Swain, volume 487 South Eastern Reporter page 760, North Carolina Appeals Court 1997. The citation is to page 766.
Answer: *Roberts v. Swain,* 487 S.E. 2d 760, 766 (N.C. App.1997)

ASSIGNMENT 4

Nguyen v. Fasano, 84 F. Supp. 2d 1099 (S.D. Cal. 2000)

ASSIGNMENT 5

Herndon v. Barrell, 101 N.C. App. 636, 639, 400 S.E.2d 769 (1991)

ASSIGNMENT 6

18 U.S.C. § 1112 (1994)
18 U.S.C.A. § 1112 (West 1996)   United States Code Annotated
18 U.S.C.S. § 1112 (LexisNexis 2000)   United States Code Service

ASSIGNMENT 7

U.S. Const. amend V; U.S. Const. art. IV, § 3

ASSIGNMENT 8

26 U.S.C. § 112; U.S. Const. amend. IV

ASSIGNMENT 9

6 Am. Jur. 2d *Assault and Battery* § 2 (1999)

ASSIGNMENT 10

Dan B. Dobbs, *The Law of Torts* § 40 (West Group 2000)

ASSIGNMENT 11

Douglas J. Gunn, *Torts—Negligence—The Sudden Emergency Doctrine Is Abolished in Mississippi,* 51 Miss. L.J. 301 (1980)—Short citation: Gunn, 51 Miss. L.J. 301.

ASSIGNMENT 12

Bluebook—Restatement (Third) of Torts: Apportionment of Lia. §§ 8 to 10 (1999); **In *ALWD* the title is italicized**—*Restatement (Third) of Torts: Apportionment of Lia.* §§ 8 to 10 (1999);

ASSIGNMENT 13

Bluebook—Jason H. Eaton, Annotation, *Effect of Use, or Alleged Use, of Internet on Personal Jurisdiction in, or Venue of, Federal Court Case,* 155 A.L.R. Fed. 535 (1999). **In *ALWD* the citation does not include "Annotation"**—Jason H. Eaton, *Effect of Use, or Alleged Use, of Internet on Personal Jurisdiction in, or Venue of, Federal Court Case,* 155 A.L.R. Fed. 535 (1999).

ASSIGNMENT 14

Restatement (Third) of Torts: Apportionment of Lia. §§ 21 to 10 and Eaton, 155 A.L.R. Fed. 535. **In *ALWD* the Restatement title is italicized**—*Restatement (Third) of Torts: Apportionment of Lia.* §§ 21 to 10 and Eaton.

WEB ASSIGNMENT ANSWERS

Instructor's note: For the following exercises use either the *Bluebook* or the *ALWD Citation Manual.* The assignments are included here followed by the answers.

ASSIGNMENT 1—CASE CITATIONS

a. Dickerson v. the U.S. is reported at volume 530 of the *United States Reports* at page 428. It was decided in 2000.

b. California v. Beheler is reported at volume 463 of the *United States Reports* at page 1121; it is also reported in the *Supreme Court Reporter* at volume 103, page 3517, and in volume 77 of the *Lawyer's Edition 2d* at page 1275. It was decided in 1983.

c. U.S. v. Galindo-Gallegos is a 2001 decision of the Ninth Circuit Court of Appeals. It is reported in the 255 volume of the *Federal Reporter* third series at page 1154.

d. Lamaster v. Chicago North Eastern Illinois District Council is a 1991 decision of the United States District Court for the Northern District of Illinois. It is reported in volume 766 of the *Federal Supplement* at page 1497.

e. State v. Loo is a 2000 decision of the Hawaii Supreme Court reported in volume 10 of the *Pacific Reporter* third series at page 728.

f. Valentine, L.L.C. v. Flexible Business Solutions, L.L.C., is a 2000 decision of the Connecticut Superior Court reported at 2000 Westlaw at 960901.

g. State v. Outagamie County Board of Adjustment, is a 2001 decision of the Wisconsin Supreme Court reported in volume 244 of the *Wisconsin Reports* second series at page 613 and volume 628 of the *North Western Reporter* second series at page 376.

h. Dsuban v. Union Township Board of Zoning Appeals, is a 2000 decision of the Ohio Court of Appeals reported in the second series of the *North Eastern Reporter* at volume 748, page 597.

Answers:

a. ***Bluebook***—*Dickerson v. United States,* 530 U.S. 428 (2000). ***ALWD***—*Dickerson v. U.S.,* 530 U.S. 428 (2000).

b. *California v. Beheler,* 463 U.S. 1121, 103 S. Ct. 3517, 77 L. Ed. 2d 1275 (1983).

c. ***Bluebook***—*United States v. Galindo-Gallegos,* 255 F.3d 1154 (9th Cir. 2001). ***ALWD***—*U. S. v. Galindo-Gallegos,* 255 F.3d 1154 (9th Cir. 2001).

d. *Lamaster v. Chicago N.E. Ill. Dist. Council,* 766 F. Supp. 1497 (N.D. Ill. 1991).

e. *State v. Loo,* 10 P.3d 728 (Haw. 2000).

f. *Valentine, L.L.C. v. Flexible Bus. Solutions, L.L.C.,* 2000 WL 960901 (Conn. Super. Ct. 2000).

g. *State v. Outagamie County Bd. of Adjustment,* 244 Wis. 2d 613, 628 N.W.2d 376 (Wis. 2001).

h. *Dsuban v. Union Township Bd. of Zoning Appeals,* 748 N.E. 2d 597 (Ohio Ct. App. 2000).

ASSIGNMENT 2—STATUTORY AND CONSTITUTIONAL CITATIONS

a. Article 4, section 2 of the United States Constitution.

b. Title 18 section 3182 of the United States Code (2000), the Federal Extradition Act.

c. Title 42 sections 12101, 12105 and 12121 of the United States Code (1994).

d. The Uniform Criminal Extradition Act, 11 Uniform Laws Annotated 97 (1995), sections 1 through 31.

Answers:

a. U.S. Const. art. IV, § 2.

b. ***Bluebook***—Federal Extradition Act 18 U.S.C. § 3182 (2000). ***ALWD***—**the name of the act is italicized**—*Federal Extradition Act,* 18 U.S.C. § 3182 (2000).

c. ***Bluebook***—Americans with Disabilities Act, 42 U.S.C. §§ 12101, 12105, 12121. (1994). ***ALWD***—**the name of the act is italicized**—*Americans with Disabilities Act,* 42 U.S.C. §§ 12101, 12105, 12121 (1994).

d. Uniform Criminal Extradition Act §§ 1-31, 11 U.L.A. 97 (1995).

ASSIGNMENT 3—SECONDARY AUTHORITY

a. American Jurispurdence Second volume 25 Elections, section 94, 1985.

b. Volume 99 sections 214, 215, and 229 of Worker's Compensation, Corpus Juris Secundum, 1992.

c. *Intoxication Test Evidence: Criminal and Civil,* a treatise by E. Fitzgerald and D. Hume, section 2:30; published by Lawyers Co-op in 1987.

d. The treatise, *Weinstein's Federal Evidence,* section 607.03 by Jack B. Weinstein & Margaret A. Berger; taken from the second edition published in 2001.

e. The Note "Why Superseding Cause Analysis Should Be Abandoned," by Terry Christlieb, published 1993 in Volume 72 of the Texas Law Review at page 166.

f. The article "Statutes as Sources of Law Beyond Their Terms in Common Law Cases," by Robert F. Williams, published in 1982 in Volume 50 of the George Washington Law Review at page 554.

g. The Second Restatement of Torts section 6, 1965.

h. The Second Restatement of Agency sections 343 through 346, 1958.

i. The annotation by Thomas G. Fischer "Liability of Corporate Director, Officer, or Employee for Tortious Interference with Corporation's Contract with Another," published in 1989 in volume 72 of the American Law Reports fourth series at page 492.

j. The annotation by P.A. Agabin "Duty and Liability of Closely Held Corporation, Its Directors, Officers or Majority Stockholders, in Acquiring Stock of Minority Shareholder," published in 1966 in volume 7 of the American Law Reports third series at page 500.

Answers:

a. 25 Am. Jur. 2d, *Elections* § 94 (1985).

b. 99 C.J.S. *Workers' Compensation* §§ 214, 215, 229 (1992).

c. E. Fitzgerald & D. Hume, *Intoxication Test Evidence: Criminal and Civil* § 2:30 (Lawyers Co-op 1987). **Note that the *Bluebook* does not require the name of the publisher.**

d. Jack B. Weinstein & Margaret A. Berger, *Weinstein's Federal Evidence* § 607.03 (2d ed. 2001). **Note that the *ALWD* requires the name of the publisher.**

e. Terry Christlieb, Note, *Why Superseding Cause Analysis Should Be Abandoned,* 72 Tex. L. Rev. 166 (1993).

f. Robert F. Williams, *Statutes as Sources of Law Beyond Their Terms in Common Law Cases,* 50 Geo. Wash. L. Rev. 554 (1982).

g. *Bluebook*—Restatement (Second)of Torts § 6 (1965). **In the *ALWD* the title is italicized—***Restatement (Second) of Torts* § 6 (1965).

h. *Bluebook*—Restatement (Second) of Agency §§ 343-346 (1958). **In the *ALWD* the title is italicized—***Restatement (Second) of Agency* §§ 343-346 (1958).

i. Thomas G. Fischer, Annotation, *Liability of Corporate Director, Officer, or Employee for Tortious Interference with Corporation's Contract with Another,* 72 A.L.R.4th 492 (1989). **Note that *ALWD* does not require the use of the word "Annotation."**

j. P.A. Agabin, Annotation, *Duty and Liability of Closely Held Corporation, Its Directors, Officers or Majority Stockholders, in Acquiring Stock of Minority Shareholder,* 7 A.L.R.3d 500 (1966). **Note that *ALWD* does not require the use of the word "Annotation."**

TEST QUESTIONS AND ANSWERS

TRUE OR FALSE QUESTIONS

Please write a "T" or "F" to the left of each statement.

_____ 1. If research sources are incorrectly cited, opposing counsel may be less inclined to settle a case.

_____ 2. The main source of authority on legal citation for the past seventy-five years is *ALWD Citation Manual: A Professional System of Citation.*

_____ 3. The *Bluebook* and *ALWD* are the primary sources for rules on citation used by both law and paralegal schools.

_____ 4. In the *Bluebook,* there are some differences between the citation format used when citing authorities in court documents and legal memoranda and the citation format used in scholarly pieces such as law review articles.

_____ 5. Most of the examples provided in the white pages of the *Bluebook* are for citation format to be used when drafting court documents.

_____ 6. Most states have adopted some citation rules that differ from the *Bluebook.*

_____ 7. Case names should be italicized or underscored.

_____ 8. For capitalization of words other than those mentioned in the *Bluebook* and *ALWD,* both books refer to the *Chicago Manual of Style.*

_____ 9. Quotations of fifty words or more are set off from the rest of the text by a fives-pace indentation (one tab) from the left and right margins and are single-spaced.

_____10. The use of string citations in court documents and legal memoranda is generally disfavored, but their use is not prohibited.

_____11. Citations to both state and federal case citations include the subsequent history, if any.

_____12. Case names may be either italicized or underscored.

_____13. If there are multiple plaintiffs or defendants in a case name, use *"et al."* or *"et ux."* after the first named party.

_____14. When the United States is a party, both the *Bluebook* and *ALWD* require that "United States" be spelled out.

_____15. When citing the United States Constitution, the term "Article" is capitalized and abbreviated.

_____16. If the cited material is taken from the main text of a statute, the year of the volume of the text is not required in the citation.

_____17. The *Bluebook* rules governing citations to evidentiary and procedural rules differ from the *ALWD* rules.

_____18. In an A.L.R. citation, the *ALWD* omits the use of "Annotation" following the author name.

_____19. When a citation is to a legal dictionary, only the *ALWD* requires the inclusion of the name of the editor in the citation.

_____20. If a citation is to the main text of a Restatement, the year of the publication is not required.

TRUE OR FALSE ANSWERS

Answer	Text Section	Answer	Text Section	Answer	Text Section
1. True	IA	8. False	IIE	15. False	IIIB
2. False	IB	9. True	IIF	16. False	IIIC1
3. True	IB	10. True	IIH	17. True	IIID
4. True	IB	11. True	IIIA1	18. True	IVA
5. False	IB	12. True	IIIA2	19. True	IVB
6. True	IB	13. False	IIIA2	20. False	IVE
7. True	IIB	14. False	IIIA2		

MULTIPLE CHOICE QUESTIONS

Please circle the letter of the **most appropriate** answer

1. It is important that citations be correct for the following reasons:
   a. A citation that is incorrect in form or content sends the message that the drafter is either not careful or lacks education
   b. Errors in documents submitted to a court may cause the judge to question the competence of the attorney and the quality and content of the research and analysis
   c. Opposing counsel may question the ability of the attorney to mount an effective opposition and be less inclined to settle a case
   d. The writer's research and analysis skills may become suspect if research sources are not properly presented
   e. all of the above
   f. a, b, and d

2. The *ALWD Citation Manual:*
   a. has fewer pages than the *Bluebook.*
   b. begins with citation to primary authority.
   c. has blue pages for citations to be used in court documents.
   d. has blue pages for citations to be used in law reviews.
   e. a, b, and c
   f. none of the above

3. Items that should be italicized or underscored are:
   a. reporter abbreviations.
   b. case names.
   c. names of Internet sites.
   d. internal cross references such as supra.
   e. all of the above
   f. a, b, and c
   g. b, c, and d

4. Block quotations:
   a. are set off from the rest of the text by a ten space indentation from the left margin only.
   b. consist of quotations of fifty or more words.
   c. are single spaced.
   d. are set off from the rest of the text by a double space.
   e. all of the above
   f. a, b, and c
   g. b, c, and d

5. Ellipses are used to indicate:
   a. omission of material from the beginning of a quote.
   b. omission of material from the end of a quote.
   c. omission of material from the middle of a quote.
   d. omission of one or more paragraphs from a block quote.
   e. all of the above
   f. b, c, and d

6. The reference to the exact page or location of quoted material is referred to as a:
   a. key page citation.
   b. pinpoint cite.
   c. jump citation.
   d. parallel citation.
   e. none of the above
   f. b and c
   g. a, b, and c

7. Short citations:
   a. are used primarily because they save space and are less disruptive to the flow of the text.
   b. often include *id.*
   c. often include *supra.*
   d. often include *hereinafter.*
   e. all of the above
   f. a, b, and c

8. Which of the following are examples of signals?
   a. *Id.*
   b. *Supra.*
   c. *Hereinafter.*
   d. *See.*
   e. all of the above
   f. a, b, and c

9. In regard to the use of section and paragraph symbols:
   a. do not use "at" when referring to a paragraph or section.
   b. insert a space before but not after the symbol.
   c. when citing consecutive sections, include the first and last sections, and separate the sections with a dash.
   d. when citing multiple sections or paragraphs that are not consecutive, place a comma between the sections or paragraphs, and do not place "and" or an ampersand (&) before the final section or paragraph.
   e. all of the above
   f. a, c, and d
   g. b, c, and d

10. A case citation includes the following:
    a. case name
    b. parallel citation, if any
    c. abbreviation for the court issuing the opinion, unless the issuing court is included in the reporter abbreviation
    d. year of the citation
    e. all of the above
    f. a, b, and d

11. In regard to citing case law:
    a. pinpoint citations follow the initial page reference.
    b. the page number on which the case begins follows the reporter abbreviation.
    c. when there is a parallel citation, the pinpoint citation is required for the state reporter only.
    d. the page number on which the case ends is included following the reporter abbreviation.
    e. a, b, and c
    f. a and b

12. According to the *Bluebook,* the citation format for a citation to a constitution consists of the:
    a. abbreviated name of the constitution.
    b. article or amendment number.
    c. section number.
    d. all of the above
    e. a and b

13. Which of the following are components of a citation to a federal statute?
    a. code abbreviation
    b. section symbol (§)
    c. the year of the publication or supplement
    d. publisher, if it is a commercial publication—in parentheses
    e. all of the above
    f. a, b, and c

14. Which of the following are components of a citation to an A.L.R. annotation?
    a. full name of the author
    b. page number where the annotation begins and ends
    c. title of the annotation
    d. abbreviated name of the publication
    e. all of the above
    f. a and c
    g. a, c, and d

15. Which of the following are components of a law review citation?
    a. full name of the author
    b. title of the article
    c. page where the article begins
    d. abbreviated title of the law review
    e. all of the above
    f. a, b, and c
    g. b, c, and d

MULTIPLE CHOICE ANSWERS

Answer	Text Section	Answer	Text Section	Answer	Text Section
1. e	I	6. f	IIG	11. f	IIIA3
2. f	I	7. e	II-I	12. d	IIIB
3. g	IIB	8. d	IIK	13. e	IIIC
4. g	IIF2	9. f	IIL	14. g	IVA
5. f	IIF6	10. e	IIIA1	15. e	IVD

CHAPTER 9

Legal Analysis—Key Facts

TEXT ASSIGNMENT ANSWERS

Instructor's note: In all of the assignments in this chapter, the student must identify key facts. As noted in the chapter, key facts are the legally significant facts of a case that raise the question of how or whether the law governing the dispute applies. They are those facts upon which the outcome of the case is determined: the facts that establish or satisfy the elements of a cause of action and are necessary to prove or disprove a claim. The test the student should use in determining whether a fact is key is "If this fact is changed, would the outcome of the application of the law be affected or changed?" This test should be used when performing the following assignments.

ASSIGNMENT 1

STEP 1. **Identify each cause of action possibly raised by the facts.** This step involves determining the possible cause or causes of action raised by the facts.

STEP 2. **Determine the elements of each cause of action identified in Step 1.** This step usually requires some research. Research may be necessary either to determine the elements of the possible causes of action or to ensure that the law has not changed since the last time research was conducted.

STEP 3. **List all the facts possibly related to the elements of the causes of action identified in Step 2.** List all the facts possibly related to the elements of each cause of action. This includes gathering the facts from the client interview and any interviews that have been conducted with witnesses, and reviewing any documents in the case file that may contain factual information.

STEP 4. **Determine which of the client's facts apply to establish or satisfy the elements of each cause of action—the key facts.** Step 4 primarily is the process of eliminating those facts listed in Step 3 that are not essential or key facts. This is accomplished by taking each element of each cause of action and determining which fact or facts are essential in establishing or satisfying that element. It may be that additional potential causes of action are identified as research and investigation take place. Each step should be applied to each cause of action identified.

ASSIGNMENT 2

STEP 1. **Read the entire case with the following general question in mind, "What was decided about which facts?"** Read the entire case in order to determine the legal question addressed and the decision reached by the court. While reading the case, keep in mind the question, "What was decided about which facts in this case?"

STEP 2. **Look to the holding.** The holding is the court's application of the rule of law to the legal question raised by the facts of the case. It is the court's answer to the legal question. Ask the following questions to help identify the holding:

"What is the court's answer to the legal question?"
"How does the court apply the rule of law to the legal question raised?"

STEP 3. **Identify the facts necessary to the holding—the key facts.** This step is composed of two parts:

1. List all facts related to the holding. List all the facts presented in the case related to the holding. This may require going through the case and listing all the facts presented by the court.
2. Determine the key facts. From the facts listed, determine the key facts by identifying those facts necessary or essential to the decision reached. Which facts determine the outcome of the case? There are several ways to identify these facts:
   a. One test is to ask yourself whether the decision would have been the same if a fact had not occurred or if the fact had occurred differently. If the answer is yes, the fact is not a key fact. Apply this test to each fact listed.
   b. If no single fact, when changed or omitted, would affect or change the decision, ask whether the decision was governed by the court's consideration of the facts as a group, rather than as individual facts.
   c. Where the court lists in its reasoning the elements of a cause of action, ask yourself which of the facts apply to establish the elements. These are key facts.
   d. Ask yourself whether the court indicates that a certain fact is a key fact.
   e. Ask yourself if the key facts are identified in concurring or dissenting opinions.

ASSIGNMENT 3

Flowers v. Campbell. Plaintiff accused defendant of charging him $12.99 for a lock that had been advertised for $9.97. Plaintiff became involved in a verbal exchange with defendant immediately before the fight. Defendant was an employee of Montgomery Ward & Company.

United States v. Leon. Most of the facts presented in the first two pages of the case are irrelevant. The background facts are the following: A police investigation commenced on information provided by an informant who did not have a proven, reliable track record. Based on tips from the informant and investigative results, an experienced police narcotics investigator prepared an application for a warrant to search certain residences. The application was reviewed by several deputy district attorneys and submitted to a state superior court judge, who issued the warrant. Upon execution of the warrant, drugs were found. The defendants were indicted on drug charges in the District Court for the Central District of California. The evidence seized from the warrant was used to substantiate drug-related charges against several respondents in this case.

ASSIGNMENT 4

PART 1. **Key facts in Assignment 5, Chapter 10.** Assignment 5 has two parts.

PART A. **Key Facts:** The broad statement of the issue is whether Beth was a guest and, therefore, barred by the guest statute from suing Allen for his negligence when he wrecked the car in which Beth was a passenger. The key facts are the following:

1. Beth was a passenger in the car.
2. Allen was the driver of the car.
3. Beth had loaned Allen money.
4. Allen told her he would give her free rides to help repay the loan.
5. Allen lost control and wrecked the car.

PART B. **Key Facts:** The broad statement of the issue is whether Tom committed a battery while making a citizen's arrest. The key facts are the following:

1. Alex broke Tom's property (lawn furniture).
2. Tom and his sons made a citizen's arrest of Alex.
3. Alex was subdued during the arrest.
4. Alex was hit and kicked after he was subdued.

PART 2. **Key Facts in Assignment 6, Chapter 10.**

PART A.   **Key Facts** *Dean v. Dickey*

1. The instrument was typed wholly by the testator.
2. The instrument was intended by the testator to be his last will and testament.
3. The instrument was signed by the testator and one witness.

PART B.   **Key Facts** *United States v. Martinez-Jiminez*

1. The defendant was engaged in a bank robbery.
2. The weapon was a toy gun.
3. The toy gun was held at the defendant's side and not aimed at the customers.
4. Witnesses believed the toy gun was real.

PART C.   **Key Facts** *Wolcott v. Wolcott*

1. Husband made a voluntary career change.
2. The voluntary career change resulted in a major reduction in the husband's income.
3. Husband unilaterally reduced his combined child support payment without judicial approval or forewarning his former spouse.
4. He failed to make a full disclosure of his income.
5. He engaged in a self-indulgent lifestyle without regard to the necessities of his children.

PART D.   **Key Facts** *People v. Sanders*

1. The conversations were between the husband and wife.
2. The conversations took place while they were married.
3. The conversations took place in the presence of some or all the children, ages 13, 10, and 8.

ASSIGNMENT 5

CHAPTER 10 HYPOTHETICAL—KEY FACTS As stated in the Application section of Chapter 10, the issue in the hypothetical is "Under the state tort law, does intentional infliction of emotional distress occur when a person suffers severe insomnia and anxiety as a result of witnessing a friend's child being injured by a vehicle that is out of control due to being driven at a high rate of speed through a school zone?" The key facts are the following:

1. Ida saw a vehicle traveling at a high rate of speed, jump a curb in a school zone, crash through a fence surrounding the playground, and hit a seesaw.
2. She saw that two children were injured and one of the children was the son of her friend Karen.
3. She became extremely upset and has suffered severe insomnia and extreme anxiety since the wreck.
4. She has received medical treatment for the insomnia and anxiety.

CHAPTER 11 HYPOTHETICAL—KEY FACTS The broad issue is whether evidence seized by the state police during the execution of a search warrant can be suppressed. The key facts are the following:

1. Evidence was seized by state police.
2. The police seized the evidence during the execution of a search warrant.
3. The warrant was improperly issued by a state court judge.
4. The warrant was defective because there was not sufficient probable cause to justify the search.
5. The police did not know the warrant was defective and executed it in the good faith belief it was valid.

CHAPTER 12 HYPOTHETICAL—KEY FACTS The broad issue is whether a majority shareholder acted improperly in refusing to issue dividends to the minority shareholders. The following are the key facts:

1. Steve is the majority shareholder of a closely held corporation; he owns 52 percentage of the stock.
2. Don and David, the minority shareholders, each own 24 percentage of the stock.
3. Steve manages the business and refuses to issue stock dividends.
4. Steve has given himself three large salary increases and several cash bonuses.
5. The corporation has an accumulated cash surplus of $500,000.

ASSIGNMENT 6
ASSIGNMENT 10A, CHAPTER 4, *UNITED STATES V. LEON*—KEY FACTS

1. Law enforcement officers seized evidence pursuant to the execution of a search warrant.
2. The officers executed the warrant in the good-faith belief that the warrant was valid.
3. The warrant was defective due to magistrate error (there was insufficient probable cause to issue the warrant).

ASSIGNMENT 10B, CHAPTER 4, *ACACIA MUTUAL V. AMERICAN GENERAL*—KEY FACTS

1. The limited partnership was being dissolved.
2. The partnership agreement had an indemnification clause which required the partners to indemnify the general partner against all claims incurred by him in connection with his activities on behalf of the partnership.
3. Silver, the general partner, demanded indemnification pursuant to the indemnification provision.
4. There were no assets in the partnership from which to make the indemnification.
5. The demanded indemnification would require additional contributions by the limited partners.

ASSIGNMENT 10C, CHAPTER 4, *COMMONWEALTH V. SHEA*—KEY FACTS

1. Defendant's boat was on the ocean approximately five miles from the shore.
2. Defendant threw the women overboard.
3. Defendant drove away and left the women in the ocean.

ASSIGNMENT 10E, CHAPTER 4, *CARDWELL V. GWALTNEY*—KEY FACTS

1. Father was ordered to pay child support under the provisions of the divorce decree.
2. Father failed to make child support payments during the year he was incarcerated.
3. The mother reached an agreement with the father that he did not have to pay the child support payments during the year he was incarcerated.

ASSIGNMENT 7
ASSIGNMENT 5, CHAPTER 17—KEY FACTS

1. The first half of the will was in the handwriting of Mr. Dixon, the testator.
2. The second half of the will was typewritten at his direction by his neighbor.
3. The will was signed by Mr. Dixon.
4. The will was not witnessed.
5. The will had a self-proving affidavit that met the requirements of the statute.

ASSIGNMENT 6, CHAPTER 17—KEY FACTS

1. Mr. Eldridge was ordered to make child support payments in the divorce decree.
2. Mr. Eldridge failed to make child support payments for a 10-month period during which he was unemployed.
3. Upon Mr. Eldridge's petition, the trial court excused Mr. Eldridge from paying one-half of the child support obligation that had accrued during the 10 months. Note: The ruling of the trial court is a key fact because the issue involves a determination whether the trial court acted properly.

ASSIGNMENT 7, CHAPTER 17—KEY FACTS

1. Mr. Jones and Ms. Steward live in a cottage located on a bluff overlooking the ocean.
2. Mr. Jones tied Ms. Steward to a lightning rod attached to the cottage.
3. This took place during an electrical storm.

ASSIGNMENT 8

As discussed in the chapter, a key fact is an individual key fact if the fact, when changed, would affect or change the outcome of the case. There are situations where no individual fact standing alone is a key fact; that is, no single fact is so significant or critical that, if changed, it would change or affect the outcome of the case. There are situations, however, where the individual facts, when considered as a group or as a whole, may determine or affect the outcome of the case. In these situations, individual facts become key facts only when they are considered as a group; that is, when they are considered and weighed together rather then individually.

In this assignment, the question is whether the conduct of the bill collector was sufficient to constitute infliction of emotional distress. Was the conduct "extreme or **outrageous conduct?"**

Instructor's note: This assignment illustrates the difference between individual key facts and groups of key facts, and the student should point out that difference in the answer.

The bill collector engaged in the following conduct:

1. Every other evening for the past two weeks he has called the client at home.
2. Each call took place after 8:30 P.M.
3. During each call he threatened to call the client's employer and inform him that she refuses to pay her bills.
4. On every Monday, Wednesday, and Friday during the past two weeks he has called the client at work.
5. The calls continued despite her request that he quit calling her at work.
6. On two Saturdays he has come to her home and threatened to sue her and throw her in jail.

It is possible that no single act of the listed acts is sufficient to constitute "extreme or outrageous conduct" under the law of infliction of emotional distress. For example, the fact that he threatened to sue her when he came to her home may not, by itself, constitute "extreme or outrageous conduct." It is possible, therefore, that no single fact of the listed facts, if changed, would change a determination of whether infliction of emotional distress has taken place.

It is likely, however, that when all of these facts are considered together, when they are taken as a whole, they may constitute "extreme or outrageous conduct" and give rise to a cause of action for infliction of emotional distress. Each act taken individually may not be sufficiently egregious to constitute "extreme or outrageous conduct." The accumulated impact of all the acts when considered as a group, however, may be sufficiently extreme or outrageous to cause severe emotional distress and constitute infliction of emotional distress.

SUGGESTED ASSIGNMENTS: For any interoffice memorandum assignment you assign, require the students to apply the four-step process for identifying the key facts in a client's case. As part of the assignment, the student should describe the application of the four steps.

For any case brief assignment, require students to apply the three-step process for identifying the key facts in a court opinion. As part of the assignment, the student should describe the application of the three steps.

WEB ASSIGNMENT ANSWERS

ASSIGNMENT 1

Instructor's note: When performing this assignment, students should use the three-step process for identifying key facts presented in the "Key Facts Identification—Case Law" section of Chapter 9.

STEP 1.   READ THE ENTIRE CASE. Read the case with the question in mind, "What was decided about which facts?"

STEP 2. LOOK TO THE HOLDING. The court held that the doctrine of strict liability does not apply to physicians. A physician, therefore, may not be held strictly liable for performing an allegedly defective sterilization procedure.

STEP 3. IDENTIFY THE KEY FACTS.

PART I—LIST ALL THE FACTS THAT MAY BE RELATED TO THE HOLDING. In 1977, Dr. Merlin Brown (Brown) informed Shelley Hershley and her husband, Roy Hershley, that he would perform a bilateral tubal ligation on Mrs. Hershley by burning, cauterizing, or otherwise removing portions of her fallopian tubes.

In December of 1977, Dr. Brown performed a surgical sterilization procedure on Mrs. Hershley by inserting a Wolfe tubal ring instrument, manufactured by Richard Wolfe Medical Instruments, rather than by burning, cauterizing, or otherwise removing portions of Mrs. Hershley's tubes.

In October of 1980, Mrs. Hershley conceived a child.

The Hershleys claimed that not until after Mrs. Hershley had conceived did they become aware of the fact that Dr. Brown had performed the sterilization procedure by inserting the Wolfe tubal ring instrument.

PART II—IDENTIFY WHICH OF THE LISTED FACTS ARE KEY FACTS. Generally, strict liability is liability for a result, even if there is no fault or impropriety in causing the result. Whether strict liability applies is a question of law to be decided by the court. The key facts are only those facts that are the basis for the cause of action. Here those facts are that Dr. Brown inserted a Wolfe tubal ring instrument and Mrs. Hershley subsequently conceived a child. Had these facts not occurred, there would not have been a strict liability claim.

ASSIGNMENT 2

Instructor's note: When performing this assignment, students should use the three-step process for identifying key facts presented in the "Key Facts Identification—Case Law" section of Chapter 9.

STEP 1. READ THE ENTIRE CASE. Read the case with the question in mind, "What was decided about which facts?"

STEP 2. LOOK TO THE HOLDING. A defendant is not denied effective assistance of counsel when the trial counsel abandons a defense of insanity because neither of the court-appointed psychologists would testify that the defendant was insane, and their testimony might result in the admission of damaging evidence.

STEP 3. IDENTIFY THE KEY FACTS.

PART I—LIST ALL THE FACTS THAT MAY BE RELATED TO THE HOLDING. In October of 1991, Carrie Wong fired several shots from her home at police officers. She had recently had a miscarriage and was taking medication to control pain and uterine contractions. She was under the influence of alcohol at the time of the shootings; she was charged with six counts of felonious assault. At trial her attorney abandoned a possible defense of not guilty by reason of insanity when neither of the court-appointed psychologists would testify that she was insane under Ohio law. At trial the prosecution unsuccessfully attempted to introduce into evidence a letter allegedly written by the appellant just prior to the shooting. The letter was damaging to the appellant and because both psychologists relied on the letter when assessing her condition, allowing them to testify would have possibly opened the door to the letter.

PART II—IDENTIFY WHICH OF THE LISTED FACTS ARE KEY FACTS. The key facts are the following:

At trial her attorney abandoned a possible defense of not guilty, by reason of insanity, when neither of the court-appointed psychologists would testify that she was insane under Ohio law.

At trial the prosecution unsuccessfully attempted to introduce into evidence a letter allegedly written by the appellant just prior to the shooting.

The letter was damaging to the appellant and because both psychologists relied on the letter when assessing her condition, allowing them to testify would have possibly opened the door to the letter.

These facts are key because they are the facts which gave rise to the attorney's decision to abandon the defense of insanity. Were these facts changed, the attorney may have raised the defense, and the claim of ineffective assistance of counsel may not have been raised.

ASSIGNMENT 3

Instructor's note: When performing this assignment, students should use the four-step process for identifying key facts presented in the "Key Facts Identification—Client's Case" section of Chapter 9.

STEP 1. IDENTIFY EACH CAUSE OF ACTION. The question is, "what is Mr. Roberts entitlement under the provisions of the will and Section 2253?"

STEP 2. DETERMINE THE ELEMENTS. Tom's claim to the $25 and the family allowance is based on Section 2253. Therefore, the elements in this assignment are the elements of Section 2253.

1. A decedent's surviving spouse is entitled to a family allowance of forty thousand dollars ($40,000).
2. Family allowance is in addition to any share passing to the surviving spouse by the decedent's will.
3. Unless otherwise provided by the decedent in the will or other governing instruments.

STEP 3. LIST ALL FACTS RELATED TO THE ELEMENTS. All the facts presented in the fact section are possibly related to the elements of the cause of action identified in Step 2, with the exception of the following facts: Tom Roberts was a compulsive gambler with debts, and they had been married for 10 years.

STEP 4. DETERMINE WHICH FACTS APPLY—THE KEY FACTS.

1. A decedent's surviving spouse is entitled to a family allowance of forty thousand dollars ($40,000)—Tom is the surviving spouse.
2. The family allowance is in addition to any share passing to the surviving spouse by the decedent's will—the share passing to Tom by the will is $25.
3. Unless otherwise provided by the decedent in the will or other governing instrument, the will devises a total of $25 to Tom Roberts, "said sum to constitute his entire gift from my estate." The will further directed that, "My husband, Tom Roberts, shall not receive, nor be entitled to, any family allowance or personal property allowance from my estate as provided by state law."

TEST QUESTIONS AND ANSWERS

TRUE OR FALSE QUESTIONS

Please write a "T" or "F" to the left of each statement.

_____ 1. A failure to conduct a proper interview may result in an ethical violation.
_____ 2. Key facts are the facts that give rise to the legal dispute.
_____ 3. In a lawsuit, a fact is information present in a case concerning someone's interpretation of what took place.
_____ 4. A rule of law prescribes or directs action or forbearance.
_____ 5. The rule of law and facts of a case are *equally* important in a legal dispute.
_____ 6. The determination of whether a court opinion is on point is completely governed by the similarity between the facts of the opinion and the facts of the client's case.
_____ 7. The outcome of the application of the law to the elements of a cause of action depends on the facts.
_____ 8. In the text, background facts are referred to as those facts that are coincidental to the event but are not of significant legal importance in the case.
_____ 9. Background facts may also be irrelevant facts.
_____10. In the text, irrelevant facts are referred to as those facts that give an overview of the factual event and provide the reader with the overall context within which the key facts occurred.
_____11. Key facts are often referred to as ultimate facts.

_____12. A test to identify a key fact is to ask the question: "If this fact is changed, would the outcome of the application of the law be affected or changed?"

_____13. There are three categories of key facts mentioned in the text.

_____14 When a single fact is so significant that if it were changed the outcome of the case would change, it is referred to as a primary key fact.

_____15. The text recommends a five-step process for identifying key facts in a client's case.

_____16. When determining the key facts in a client's case, it is necessary to determine the elements of the cause of action because the plaintiff must present facts that establish or prove the existence of *each* element.

_____17. When determining the key facts in a client's case, list all the facts that may possibly be related to the cause of action, and if necessary err on the side of listing too many facts.

_____18. The text recommends a four-step process for identifying the key facts in a court opinion.

_____19. When determining the key facts in a court opinion, it is necessary to list all the facts possibly related or necessary to the holding.

_____20. The third step of the process for identifying the key facts in a court opinion is composed of three parts.

TRUE OR FALSE ANSWERS

Answer	Text Section	Answer	Text Section	Answer	Text Section
1. True	I	8. False	IVA	15. False	VI
2. True	I	9. True	IVB	16. True	VIB
3. False	II	10. False	IVB	17. True	VIC
4. True	II	11. True	IVC	18. False	VII
5. True	III	12. True	V	19. True	VIIC
6. False	III	13. False	VB	20. False	VIIC
7. True	III	14. False	VB1		

MULTIPLE CHOICE QUESTIONS

Please circle the letter of the **most appropriate** answer.

1. Key facts are often referred to as:
   a. material facts.
   b. primary facts.
   c. significant facts.
   d. universal facts.
   e. all of the above
   f. a, b, and c
   g. a and c

2. A fact may be:
   a. a thing.
   b. an action.
   c. an event.
   d. a circumstance.
   e. all of the above
   f. a, b, and c
   g. b, c, and d

3. Facts are important in a lawsuit because:
   a. the determination of how the law applies often depends on the presence of certain facts.
   b. facts are an essential element of the issue.
   c. the outcome of the application of the law depends on the existence or absence of facts.
   d. the determination of whether a case is on point is completely governed by the facts.
   e. all of the above
   f. a, b, and c

4. Facts that are coincidental to the event but not of legal significance in the case are referred to as:
   a. key facts.
   b. ultimate facts.
   c. secondary facts.
   d. irrelevant facts.
   e. all of the above
   f. c and d

5. Facts that provide the overall context within which the event occurred are referred to as:
   a. key facts.
   b. ultimate facts.
   c. secondary facts.
   d. background facts.
   e. all of the above
   f. c and d

6. Facts critical to the outcome of the case are referred to as:
   a. primary facts.
   b. key facts.
   c. universal facts.
   d. background facts.
   e. all of the above
   f. a and b

7. Which of the following are categories of key facts?
   a. ultimate key facts.
   b. individual key facts.
   c. groups of facts.
   d. background facts.
   e. all of the above
   f. a, b, and c
   g. b and c

8. When a single fact is so significant that if it were changed the outcome of the case would change, it is referred to as:
   a. a primary key fact.
   b. an universal key fact.
   c. an individual key fact.
   d. a secondary key fact.
   e. all of the above
   f. a, b, and c

9. When several facts, considered together, may determine the outcome of a case, they are referred to as:
   a. primary key facts.
   b. universal key facts.
   c. groups of facts.
   d. secondary key facts.
   e. all of the above
   f. a, b, and c

10. Which of the following are steps used to determine which of the facts in a client's case are key facts?
    a. Identify each cause of action possibly raised by the facts.
    b. Identify the facts necessary to the holding.
    c. List all the facts possibly related to the elements of the causes of action.
    d. Determine which of the facts apply to establish or satisfy the elements of each cause of action.
    e. all of the above
    f. a, c, and d

11. When identifying the key facts in a client's case:
    a. research may not be required to identify the possible causes of action.
    b. list all the facts possibly related to the elements of the possible causes of action.

c. identify all the elements of each possible cause of action.
    d. the facts that establish or satisfy the elements of each cause of action. are the key facts.
    e. all of the above
    f. b, c, and d

12. Which of the following are steps used to determine the key facts in a court opinion?
    a. Read the entire case.
    b. Determine the elements of each cause of action.
    c. List all the facts possibly related to the elements of the causes of action.
    d. Determine which of the facts apply to establish or satisfy the elements of each cause of action.
    e. all of the above
    f. b, c, and d

13. When identifying the key facts in a court opinion:
    a. when reading the opinion, keep in mind the question, "What was decided about which facts?"
    b. list all possible facts related to the decision reached.
    c. look to the holding.
    d. all of the above
    e. a and b

14. Which of the following are ways to identify the key facts in a court opinion?
    a. Ask yourself whether the decision would have been the same if a fact had not occurred.
    b. Ask yourself whether the court indicates that a certain fact is a key fact.
    c. Ask yourself if the key facts are identified in concurring or dissenting opinions.
    d. Look to other court opinions that have discussed the case.
    e. all of the above
    f. a, b, and c
    g. a, c, and d

15. It is a sunny day and Tom is stopped at a light at a four-way intersection in the city, waiting for the light to change. Mary, stopped behind him, accidentally lets her foot slip off the brake, and her vehicle bumps into Tom's vehicle. The fact that it is a clear day is most likely a:
    a. key fact.
    b. background fact.
    c. secondary fact.
    d. primary fact.
    e. none of the above
    f. b and c
    g. a and c

MULTIPLE CHOICE ANSWERS

Answer	Text Section	Answer	Text Section	Answer	Text Section
1. g	I	6. b	IVC	11. e	VI
2. e	II	7. g	VB	12. a	VII
3. f	IV	8. c	VB1	13. d	VII
4. d	IVA	9. c	VB2	14. f	VIIC
5. d	IVB	10. f	VI	15. b	III

CHAPTER 10

Legal Analysis—Issue Identification

TEXT ASSIGNMENT ANSWERS

Instructor's note: The format for the presentation of the issues in the following assignments is the format presented in this chapter and Chapter 11: Law + Legal Question + Key Facts. The purpose of the assignments is to require the student to identify the issue in both a client's case and a court opinion.

In answering the questions, the student should use the steps presented in the chapter for issue identification. The steps are reprinted here as an aid to the instructor.

Issue Identification—Client's Case

Step 1. Identify each type of cause of action and area of law possibly involved.
Step 2. Determine the elements of each cause of action identified in Step 1.
Step 3. Determine which of the facts of the client's case apply to establish or satisfy the elements of each cause of action—the key facts.
Step 4. Assemble the issue from the law and key facts identified in Steps 2 and 3.

Issue Identification—Case Law

Step 1. General question.
Step 2. Look to the holding.
Step 3. Assemble the issue.

Instructor's note: In all the assignments, people and events should not be identified by specific name in the statement of the issue. For example, in the statement of the issue in the fifth assignment, Beth is identified as a passenger and Allen is identified as the driver. The reasons for this are discussed in the "General Considerations" section of Chapter 11.

ASSIGNMENT 1

STEP 1. IDENTIFY EACH TYPE OF CAUSE OF ACTION AND AREA OF LAW POSSIBLY IN-VOLVED. The first step is the identification of the potential cause or causes of action and area(s) of law raised by the client's fact situation. This includes a broad identification of potential issues, the general areas of law, and the client's facts related to each area of law. This preliminary identification is based upon education and experience and usually does not require any research.

STEP 2. DETERMINE THE ELEMENTS OF EACH CAUSE OF ACTION IDENTIFIED IN STEP 1. Steps 2, 3, and 4 should be applied separately to each potential issue or cause of action identified in Step 1. Step 2 requires researching the area of law to determine the elements necessary to establish a cause of action. Once the elements are identified, proceed to Step 3.

STEP 3. DETERMINE WHICH OF THE FACTS OF THE CLIENT'S CASE APPLY TO ESTABLISH OR SATISFY THE ELEMENTS OF EACH CAUSE OF ACTION—THE KEY FACTS. Every issue is a question of how the law applies to the facts of the client's case. Steps 1 and 2 identify the law that must be included in the issue; Step 3 identifies the facts that must be included in the issue. These facts are called the key facts.

The key facts are identified by determining which facts of the client's case apply to establish or satisfy the requirements of each element of the cause of action. This step is necessary because, in order to state a claim, and thereby obtain relief, facts must be presented which establish or satisfy the requirements of each element. Once Step 3 is completed, all of the elements necessary to identify the issue are in place. You may not be certain whether a fact meets the standard established for an element. Often that determination may not take place until trial. Just make sure there is some fact that *arguably* meets the requirements of each of the elements of the cause of action.

STEP 4. ASSEMBLE THE ISSUE. Gather and assemble the elements of the issue.

As mentioned in Step 2, Steps 2 through 4 are applied to each of the issues broadly identified in Step 1. Identify and address each issue separately and completely before proceeding to the next issue. It may be that certain issues are eliminated as the other steps are followed, such as when research reveals that there are not sufficient facts present to support a cause of action. It may be that additional issues are identified as research takes place.

ASSIGNMENT 2

STEP 1. GENERAL QUESTION. The first part of this step is to read the entire court opinion before attempting to identify the issue. Important information concerning an issue may be scattered throughout the opinion. An initial reading of the entire opinion provides the researcher with an overview of the case and an awareness of where information is located in the opinion. This is helpful when you begin to analyze specific portions of the opinion. While reading the case, keep in mind the question, "What was decided about which facts in this case?"

STEP 2. LOOK TO THE HOLDING. Often the fastest way to track down the issue is to focus on the holding and ask the following questions:

1. "What was decided in the holding?" In other words, "What legal question or issue was addressed and answered by the holding?" This identifies the second element of the issue, the legal question addressed by the court.
2. "What statute, rule of law, principle, etc., was applied by the court to reach this holding?" This question helps identify the relevant rule of law, the first element of the issue.
3. "Which of the facts presented in this case are related and necessary to the determination of the question addressed in the holding?" or "Which of the facts, if changed, would change the outcome of the holding?" These questions help identify the third element of the issue, the key facts.

STEP 3. ASSEMBLE THE ISSUE. Assemble the identified elements in the question format presented in Chapter 11.

ASSIGNMENT 3

STEP 1. IDENTIFY EACH TYPE OF CAUSE OF ACTION AND AREA OF LAW POSSIBLY INVOLVED. The possible causes of action are robbery and larceny.

STEP 2. DETERMINE THE ELEMENTS OF EACH CAUSE OF ACTION IDENTIFIED IN STEP 1.

Section 18-760, Robbery—Elements

1. A person must act knowingly—that is, intentionally
2. Take anything of value
3. From the person or presence of another
4. By use of force, threats, or intimidation.

Section 18-773, Larceny—Elements

1. A person must wrongfully take, obtain, or withhold, by any means
2. From the possession of the owner or any other person
3. Money, personal property or article of value
4. With intent to permanently deprive another person of the use and benefit of the property.

STEP 3. DETERMINE WHICH OF THE FACTS OF THE CLIENT'S CASE APPLY TO ESTABLISH OR SATISFY THE ELEMENTS OF EACH CAUSE OF ACTION—THE KEY FACTS.

Section 18-760, Robbery—Elements

1. A person must act knowingly—that is intentionally. Larry intentionally borrowed the drill.
2. Take anything of value. The drill is something of value.
3. From the person or presence of another. The drill belonged to his neighbor.
4. By use of force, threats, or intimidation. He threatened to beat up the neighbor if he came to get the drill or file charges.

Section 18-773, Larceny—Elements

1. A person must wrongfully take, obtain, or withhold, by any means. Larry refused to return the drill after his neighbor asked him to return it.
2. From the possession of the owner or any other person. The neighbor owns the drill.
3. Money, personal property or article of value. The drill is personal property.
4. With intent to permanently deprive another person of the use and benefit of the property. Larry said he was keeping the drill.

STEP 4. ASSEMBLE THE ISSUE FROM THE LAW AND KEY FACTS IDENTIFIED IN STEPS 2 AND 3.
Under criminal code §18-760, does robbery occur when a person refuses to return a borrowed drill and tells the owner he will beat him up if he tries "to come get it?" In light of the provisions of criminal code §18-773, does larceny occur when an individual borrows a drill, refuses to return it to the owner, and states that he is keeping it?

ASSIGNMENT 4

Instructor's note: The answer to this assignment is similar to the answer in Assignment 3. The answer will be different according to the differences between your state's statutes and statutes in the assignment.

ASSIGNMENT 5

This assignment requires the identification of the issue in two client cases; therefore, the four-step issue identification process presented above should be followed by the student.

PART A
STEP 1. CAUSE OF ACTION AND AREA OF LAW INVOLVED. Beth wishes to sue Allen for the injuries sustained when Allen lost control of the car he was driving. Although the problem does not state the basis of her claim, Beth will probably sue under the law of negligence. The facts do not indicate that Allen intentionally wrecked the car; therefore, negligence is the most likely cause of action. The statute presented in the facts which may bar the use of negligence as a cause of action is the guest statute.

STEP 2. ELEMENTS OF THE CAUSE OF ACTION IDENTIFIED IN STEP 1. The issue in this problem does not involve the elements of negligence; therefore, it is not necessary to identify those elements. The issue is whether the guest statute bars Beth's negligence claim. Therefore, the elements of the guest statute are critical in this case. As presented in the fact situation, the elements of the guest statute are the following:

The statute bars suits against drivers by automobile guests, except when:

a. the passenger confers a substantial benefit on the driver, and
b. that is the reason the driver provided the ride.

STEP 3. THE KEY FACTS RELEVANT TO THE ELEMENTS OF THE APPLICABLE LAW:

1. Allen was the driver of the car,
2. Beth was a passenger in Allen's car,
3. Beth loaned Allen money,
4. Allen told her he would give her three free rides to the city to help repay the loan,
5. the wreck took place during one of the rides.

STEP 4. ASSEMBLE THE ISSUE FROM THE LAW AND KEY FACTS IDENTIFIED IN THE PREVIOUS STEPS.

1. The applicable law is the guest statute.
2. The question is whether the negligence suit is barred by the guest statute.
3. The key facts are Beth was a passenger in Allen's car and the wreck took place during a ride Allen was giving Beth to help repay a loan.
4. Putting these elements of the issue together, the issue is as follows: **In light of the provisions of the guest statute, is a negligence suit barred when a passenger is injured in a wreck that took place during a ride the driver was providing the passenger to help repay a loan from the passenger?**

PART B
STEP 1. CAUSE OF ACTION AND AREA OF LAW INVOLVED. There are two possible causes of action that Alex may pursue—common law battery and unauthorized citizen's arrest; therefore, there are two possible issues in the problem. Although Alex could possibly also sue for intentional infliction of emotional distress, the only laws presented in the problem are common law battery and unauthorized citizen's arrest. Therefore, it is assumed that for the purposes of this assignment the causes of action in question are battery and unauthorized citizen's arrest.

STEP 2. ELEMENTS OF THE POSSIBLE CAUSES OF ACTION IDENTIFIED IN STEP 1.

Battery—unauthorized, harmful contact

Citizen's Arrest—Although the problem does not define what constitutes an unauthorized citizen's arrest, it does present when a citizen's arrest is allowed. A citizen's arrest is allowed when the purpose is to prevent destruction of property.

STEP 3. THE KEY FACTS RELEVANT TO THE ELEMENTS OF THE APPLICABLE LAW. The key facts relevant to the battery issue are as follows:

1. Tom is making a citizen's arrest,
2. Tom's sons help Tom,
3. Alex is subdued,
4. after Alex is subdued, Tom and his sons continued to hit and kick him.

The key facts relevant to the citizen's arrest issue are the following:

1. Alex breaks Tom's lawn chair, and
2. Tom arrests Alex as Alex begins to break more lawn furniture.

STEP 4. ASSEMBLE THE ISSUE FROM THE LAW AND KEY FACTS IDENTIFIED IN THE PREVIOUS STEPS.

Battery Issue

1. The applicable law is the state's common law of battery.
2. The question is whether a battery occurred.
3. The key facts are Tom and his sons are making a citizen's arrest; Alex is subdued; after Alex is subdued Tom and his sons continue to kick and hit him.

Putting these elements of the issue together, the battery issue is as follows: **Under the (name of state) common law of battery, does a battery occur when individuals, while making a citizen's arrest, continue to hit and kick the party being arrested after the party is subdued?**

Citizen's Arrest Issue

1. The applicable law is the state's common law allowing citizen's arrest.
2. The question is whether citizen's arrest was lawful.
3. The key facts are Alex breaks Tom's lawn chair, and Tom arrests Alex as Alex begins to break more lawn furniture.

Putting these elements of the issue together, the citizen's arrest issue is as follows: **Under the (name of state) common law of citizen's arrest, is a citizen's arrest lawful when the arrest takes place after the party being arrested breaks the arresting party's lawn chair and begins to break more lawn furniture?**

ASSIGNMENT 6

Instructor's note: Each part of Assignment 6 requires the student to identify a specific issue in a court opinion. The three-step process for identifying an issue in a court opinion should be used by the student and included in the answer. Emphasize to the student the importance of keeping in mind one of the following questions when reading the case as required in Step 1:

"What was decided about which facts in this case?" or in other words, "What question concerning which law and key facts was decided by the court?"

PART A

Identify the validity of the will issue in *Dean v. Dickey*. In this case, the court presents a fairly complete statement of the issue in the first sentence of the opinion. The student still should use the three-step process to become familiar with the process and to obtain a more complete statement of the issue.

STEP 1. GENERAL QUESTION. A general reading of the entire opinion reveals that the case involves a question of whether an instrument typed by the deceased is entitled to probate as a holographic will under Texas law.

STEP 2. LOOK TO THE HOLDING. The court upheld the trial court's affirmation of the order of the county court which denied the probate of the instrument. When performing Step 2, the student should answer the following three questions presented in the chapter. The answers to these questions help identify and provide the elements of the issue.

"**What was decided in the holding?**" In this case, the court answered the question of whether the instrument was entitled to probate as the holographic will of the deceased.

"**What statute, rule of law, or principle was applied by the court to reach this holding?** "The statutes interpreted and applied in the case are Texas probate code Articles 8283, 8284, and 3344.

"**Which of the facts presented in this case are related and necessary to the determination of the question addressed in the holding?**" In other words, what are the key facts? In this case the facts relevant to the holding are that the testamentary instrument was typewritten wholly by the deceased, intended by him to be his last will and testament, and signed by him and one witness.

STEP 3. ASSEMBLE THE ISSUE. The governing law is presented in Articles 8283, 8284, and 3344 of the Texas Probate Code.

The question is whether the instrument is entitled to probate as the holographic will of the deceased.

The key facts are the instrument was typed wholly by the deceased, intended by him as his last will and testament, and signed by him and witnessed by one witness.

The issue when assembled is as follows: **In light of the provisions of Texas Probate Code sections 8283, 8284, and 3344 is an instrument entitled to probate as the holographic will of the deceased when it is typed wholly by the deceased, intended by him as his last will and testament, and signed by him and witnessed by one witness?**

PART B

Identify the issue concerning whether the weapon was a "dangerous weapon" in the case of *United States v. Martinez-Jimenez.*

STEP 1. GENERAL QUESTION. A general reading of the opinion reveals that the case involves a question of whether a toy replica of a firearm used in a bank robbery can be **considered a "dangerous weapon" under the federal bank robbery statue.**

STEP 2. LOOK TO THE HOLDING. In the opinion the court stated that a toy replica of a firearm did fall within the meaning of a "dangerous weapon" under the statute. In the conclusion of the opinion, the court stated that a robber's use of a replica of a weapon, that appears to be genuine, carries the same penalty as the use of a genuine weapon.

> **"What was decided in the holding?"** In this case the court decided that a toy replica of a firearm did fall within the meaning of a "dangerous weapon" under the applicable federal statute.
>
> **"What statute, rule of law, or principle was applied by the court to reach this holding?"** The applicable law is 18 U.S.C. § 2113(d).
>
> **"Which of the facts presented in this case are related and necessary to the determination of the question addressed in the holding?"** What are the key facts? In this case, the facts relevant to the holding are that the defendant robbed a bank with the display of what witnesses believed was a real handgun, and the gun was a toy gun that simulated the appearance of a real firearm.

STEP 3. ASSEMBLE THE ISSUE. The applicable law is 18 U.S.C. § 2113(d).

The question is whether a toy replica of a firearm is a "dangerous weapon" within the meaning of the statute.

The key facts are the defendant displayed a toy replica of a firearm when he robbed a bank, the replica simulated the appearance of a real firearm, and witnesses believed the weapon was a real firearm.

The issue when assembled is as follows: **Under the provisions of the federal bank robbery statute, 18 U.S.C. § 2113(d), is a toy replica of a firearm a "dangerous weapon" when the defendant robs a bank through the display of the replica, the replica simulated the appearance of a real firearm, and the witnesses believed the replica was a real firearm?**

PART C

In the case of *Wolcott v. Wolcott,* identify the issue concerning the modification of child support due to a change of financial circumstances.

STEP 1. GENERAL QUESTION. A reading of the entire opinion reveals that the case involves a question of under what circumstances a trial court may modify or abate a child support obligation when a parent makes a voluntary change of employment that reduces his income. *Note that the procedural issue is whether the trial court erred when it refused to grant husband's motion to reduce or abate his support obligation. The trial court denied the motion on the basis that the husband's voluntary career change was made in bad faith.* The factual issue is, under what circumstances may a court grant or refuse a request for a reduction or abatement in child support due to a voluntary career change?

STEP 2. LOOK TO THE HOLDING. The appeals court upheld the trial court's denial of the husband's motion for reduction or abatement of his child support obligation on the basis that he had not acted in good faith in regard to his support obligations when he changed employment.

> **"What was decided in the holding?"** In this case, the court held that a voluntary change of employment that results in a major reduction in income does not justify a reduction or abatement of a child support obligation when the change is not made in good faith.
>
> **"What statute, rule of law, or principle was applied by the court to reach this holding?"** The court does not include in the opinion the state statute that governs the modification of child support orders. The court does refer to several out of state decisions which hold that, where a career change is not made in good faith, a reduction in a support obligation will not be warranted.

"**Which of the facts presented in this case are related and necessary to the determination of the question addressed in the holding?**" What are the key facts? In this case, the facts relevant to the holding are that the husband made a voluntary career change, and the change resulted in a major reduction in his income. There was evidence that the husband's career change was made in bad faith. For example, there was evidence that the husband planned to make the career change but did not so advise his wife prior to entering the marital settlement agreement. There was evidence of the husband's disregard for several financial obligations undertaken by him in the marital settlement agreement; of his failure or inability to make a full disclosure of his income and assets to wife and the court; and of his self-indulgence with regard to his own lifestyle and personal necessities, without regard to the necessities of his children and his former spouse.

STEP 3. ASSEMBLE THE ISSUE. The applicable law is not stated; therefore, reference should be made to the relevant law in general terms.

The question is whether a modification of a child support obligation is proper when there is a voluntary career change.

The key facts are the career change was voluntary, the change resulted in a major reduction in income, and there is evidence the change was made in bad faith.

The issue when assembled is as follows: **Under New Mexico's law governing modification of child support orders, does a voluntary career change justify a reduction or abatement of a child support obligation when the career change results in a major reduction in income and there is evidence the change was not made in good faith?**

PART D

In the case of *People v. Sanders,* identify the issue concerning the existence of spousal privilege for communications made in the presence of children. In this case, as in the assignment in Part A, the court actually presents a fairly complete statement of the issue in the second sentence of the opinion. The student should still follow the three-step issue identification process to become familiar with the process and to obtain a more complete statement of the issue.

STEP 1. GENERAL QUESTION. A general reading of the entire opinion reveals that the case involves a question of the admissibility of interspousal communications and whether the spousal privilege is destroyed when conversations take place in the presence of the children of the spouses.

STEP 2. LOOK TO THE HOLDING. The court held that the presence of the 13-year-old child rendered the conversation ineligible for the protection of the statutory privilege.

"**What was decided in the holding?**" In this case, the court held that the presence of the 13-year-old during the conversation rendered the conversation ineligible for protection under the statute.

"**What statute, rule of law, or principle was applied by the court to reach this holding?**" The court interpreted and applied the Illinois statute governing privileged spousal communications, Ill. Rev. Stat. 1981, ch 38, para. 155-1.

"**Which of the facts presented in this case are related and necessary to the determination of the question addressed in the holding?**" What are the key facts? In this case, the conversation took place between the husband and wife in the presence of the wife's sons ages 13, 10, and 8. No evidence was presented that the oldest child was either too young or insufficiently bright to understand the conversation.

STEP 3. ASSEMBLE THE ISSUE. The applicable law is the Illinois statute governing privileged spousal communications, Ill. Rev. Stat. 1981, ch 38, para. 155-1.

The question is whether the spousal communication is a privileged communication.

The key facts are that the conversation was between the spouses and took place in the presence of the wife's sons, ages 13, 10, and 8. No evidence was presented that the oldest child was either too young or insufficiently bright to understand the conversation.

The issue when assembled is as follows: **Under the statute governing spousal communications, Ill. Rev. Stat. 1981, ch 38, para. 155-1, is a communication between spouses privileged when the communication takes place in the presence of the spouses' sons and at least one of the sons is old enough to understand the conversation?**

ASSIGNMENT 7

STEP 1. GENERAL QUESTION. A reading of the opinion reveals that the case involves a question of whether a law firm should be disqualified from representing Metropolitan Life Insurance Company because of its prior representation of Gene Phillips of Syntek in a divorce matter. Note that the procedural issue is whether the trial court properly denied Syntek's motion for disqualification of counsel.

STEP 2. LOOK TO THE HOLDING. The court upheld the trial court's denial of Syntek's motion to disqualify Metropolitan's counsel. The court reversed the court of appeal's ruling that the trial court abused its discretion when it denied Syntek's motion.

> **"What was decided in the holding?"** The court decided that the trial court did not abuse its discretion when it concluded that the law firm's representation of Gene Phillips (of Syntek), in a prior divorce action, was not substantially related to its representation of Metropolitan. The factual issue involves the question of whether the relationship between the two matters was sufficient to require the disqualification of the firm to act as counsel for Metropolitan.
>
> **"What statute, rule of law, or principle was applied by the court to reach this holding?"** The court applied Rule 1.09 of the Texas Disciplinary Rules of Professional Conduct.
>
> **"Which of the facts presented in this case are related and necessary to the determination of the question addressed in the holding?"** In other words, what are the key facts? In this case, the facts relevant to the holding are that the law firm represented Gene Phillips of Syntex in a prior divorce matter. There was evidence that the firm's representation of Metropolitan involved the use of information available to the public, and the information was not obtained as a result of the firm's representation Syntax in the divorce case.

STEP 3. ASSEMBLE THE ISSUE. The applicable law is Rule 1.09 of the Texas Disciplinary Rules of Professional Conduct.

The question is whether the law firm should be disqualified from representing a party in a lawsuit.

The key facts are the law firm represented the opposing party in a previous action. Information used by the law firm in the present lawsuit was available to the public and was not obtained as a result of the firm's representation in the divorce case.

The issue when assembled is as follows: **In light of the provisions of Rule 1.09 of the Texas Disciplinary Rules of Professional Conduct, should a law firm be disqualified from representing a party in a lawsuit when the firm, in a previous suit, represented an individual who owned a controlling interest in the opposing party and the present action involves information available to the public and not obtained as a result of the firm's representation in the previous suit?**

ASSIGNMENT 8

Read *Morgan v. Greenwaldt* presented in the following text. What is the substantive false imprisonment issue raised by the facts of the case?

STEP 1. GENERAL QUESTION. A general reading of the opinion reveals that the case involves a question of whether the plaintiff was falsely imprisoned. Note that the procedural issue is whether the trial court properly granted a directed verdict on the false imprisonment claim.

STEP 2. LOOK TO THE HOLDING. In the holding, the court ruled that the trial court properly directed a verdict on the issue of false imprisonment.

"What was decided in the holding?" In essence the court held there was sufficient evidence for the trial court to determine that the plaintiff was not falsely imprisoned.

"What statute, rule of law, or principle was applied by the court to reach this holding?" The court applied the state's common law definition of false imprisonment.

"Which of the facts presented in this case are related and necessary to the determination of the question addressed in the holding?" What are the key facts? In this case, the facts relevant to the holding are that the plaintiff voluntarily consented to treatment at the hospital, there was testimony that she exhibited out-of-control behavior and was posing a threat to herself and to others, and she was then placed in a secure environment for over two hours.

STEP 3. ASSEMBLE THE ISSUE. The applicable law is Mississippi's common law definition of false imprisonment.

The question is whether the plaintiff was falsely imprisoned.

The key facts are that plaintiff voluntarily consented to treatment at the hospital, she exhibited out of control behavior and was posing a threat to herself and to others, and she was placed in a secure environment for over two hours.

The issue when assembled is as follows: **Under Mississippi's common law definition of false imprisonment, is an individual falsely imprisoned when she voluntarily consents to treatment at a hospital and is placed in a secure environment for two hours after exhibiting out-of-control behavior which posed a threat to herself and others?**

WEB ASSIGNMENT ANSWERS

ASSIGNMENT 1

Instructor's note: In answering the questions in these assignments students should use the steps presented in the chapter for issue identification.

STEP 1. IDENTIFY EACH TYPE OF CAUSE OF ACTION AND AREA OF LAW POSSIBLY INVOLVED. The question is what Mr. Roberts is entitled to under the provisions of the will and section 2253. Tom disputes the administrator's determination that Tom is only entitled to $25 of his wife's estate.

STEP 2. DETERMINE THE ELEMENTS OF EACH CAUSE OF ACTION IDENTIFIED IN STEP 1. Tom's claim is based on section 2253. The elements of the statute are the following:

1. A decedent's surviving spouse is entitled to a family allowance of forty thousand dollars ($40,000)
2. The family allowance is in addition to any share passing to the surviving spouse by the decedent's will
3. Unless otherwise provided by the decedent in the will or other governing instruments.

STEP 3. DETERMINE WHICH OF THE FACTS OF THE CLIENT'S CASE APPLY TO ESTABLISH OR SATISFY THE ELEMENTS OF EACH CAUSE OF ACTION—THE KEY FACTS.

1. A decedent's surviving spouse is entitled to a family allowance of forty thousand dollars ($40,000)—Tom is the surviving spouse.
2. Family allowance is in addition to any share passing to the surviving spouse by the decedent's will—The share passing to Tom by the will is $25.
3. Unless otherwise provided by the decedent in the will or other governing instrument—The will devises a total of $25.00 to Tom Roberts, "said sum to constitute his entire gift from my estate." The will further directed that, "My husband, Tom Roberts, shall not receive nor be entitled to any family allowance or personal property allowance from my estate as provided by state law."

STEP 4. ASSEMBLE THE ISSUE FROM THE LAW AND KEY FACTS IDENTIFIED IN STEPS 2 AND 3. Under the provisions of probate code § 2253, "is a decedent's surviving spouse entitled to a family allowance when the will devises $25.00 to the spouse and provides the spouse 'shall not receive nor be entitled to any family allowance or personal property allowance from my estate as provided by state law'"?

ASSIGNMENT 2

STEP 1. IDENTIFY EACH TYPE OF CAUSE OF ACTION AND AREA OF LAW POSSIBLY INVOLVED. The cause of action is the validity of a will under § 15-11-502.

STEP 2. DETERMINE THE ELEMENTS OF EACH CAUSE OF ACTION IDENTIFIED IN STEP 1. The following are the elements of the relevant sections of the statute.

1. The will must be in writing
2. Signed by the testator, or in the testators name by some other individual in the testator's conscious presence and by the testator's direction
3. Signed by at least two individuals either prior to or after testator's death
   a. Signed within a reasonable time after he or she witnessed,
   b. In the conscious presence of the testator,
   c. The signing as described in 2 above or the testator's acknowledgment of that signature or acknowledgment of the will.

STEP 3. DETERMINE WHICH OF THE FACTS OF THE CLIENT'S CASE APPLY TO ESTABLISH OR SATISFY THE ELEMENTS OF EACH CAUSE OF ACTION—THE KEY FACTS.

1. The will must be in writing—the attorney drafted it, so obviously it was in writing.
2. Signed by the testator, or in the testator's name by some other individual in the testator's conscious presence and by the testator's direction—Lisa directed Beth to sign the will for her. Before Beth signed, Lisa passed out.
3. Signed by at least two individuals either prior to or after testator's death—there were two witnesses; the witnessing took place prior to Lisa's death.
   a. Signed within a reasonable time after he or she witnessed—The two witnesses saw Beth sign the will, then signed it themselves after Lisa regained consciousness.
   b. In the conscious presence of the testator—Lisa was not conscious when Beth signed the will.
   c. The signing as described in 2 above or the testator's acknowledgment of that signature or acknowledgment of the will—The witnesses saw Beth sign the will, then they witnessed it after Lisa regained consciousness.

STEP 4. ASSEMBLE THE ISSUE FROM THE LAW AND KEY FACTS IDENTIFIED IN STEPS 2 AND 3. In light of the provisions of Colorado probate code § 15-11-502, is a will valid when

1. The testator directed another to sign for her,
2. The testator was unconscious when the person signed,
3. Two witnesses saw the person sign for the testator, and
4. The witnesses witnessed the will after the testator regained consciousness?

ASSIGNMENT 3

Instructor's note: The answer to this assignment is similar to the answer in Assignment 2. The answer will be different according to the differences between your state's statute and Colorado's.

ASSIGNMENT 4

STEP 1. GENERAL QUESTION. The student should read the entire court opinion and keep in mind the question, "What was decided about which facts in the case?"

STEP 2. LOOK TO THE HOLDING.

1. What was decided in the holding? The court concluded that Bratz's actions did not support a first-degree robbery conviction.
2. What statute did the court apply to reach the holding? RCW § 9A.56.190.

3. Which of the facts presented in the case are related and necessary to the determination of the question addressed in the holding? Bratz entered a bank, approached a teller, and stated "I have nitroglycerin in my coat and I need you to give me money or I'll blow up the bank." He did not show nitroglycerin to anyone, nor was any nitroglycerin found on him when he was arrested and searched by the police.

STEP 3. ASSEMBLE THE ISSUE. Under RCW § 9A.56.190 is there sufficient evidence to support charges of first-degree robbery when an individual approaches a bankteller, states, "I have nitroglycerin in my coat and I need you to give me money or I'll blow up the bank," and does not physically display the nitroglycerin?

TEST QUESTIONS AND ANSWERS
TRUE OR FALSE QUESTIONS

Please write a "T" or "F" to the left of each statement.

_____ 1. The most difficult task a researcher faces when engaging in legal analysis is to correctly identify the key facts.

_____ 2. The identification of the issue determines which direction the research will take.

_____ 3. If the issue is misidentified, malpractice may result because the client is billed for a service not requested.

_____ 4. In the broadest sense, the issue is the precise legal question raised by the specific facts of the dispute.

_____ 5. "Does state code § 231 govern garage sales held on private property?" is an example of a question of how the law applies.

_____ 6. The issue is composed of three parts.

_____ 7. The law component of an issue may be a constitutional provision or a common law doctrine.

_____ 8. The facts component of an issue is composed of the key facts and sufficient background facts to identify the context of the dispute.

_____ 9. "Under the holographic will statute, § 3951, is a will valid if it is handwritten by a neighbor at the testator's direction?" is an example of a narrow statement of an issue.

_____10. A narrow statement of the issue fails to inform the researcher of the specific factual context of the dispute.

_____11. A broad statement of the issue fails to inform the researcher of the specific factual context of the dispute.

_____12. The identification of the legal question(s) or issue(s) in a client's case is a four-step process.

_____13. One of the steps in the process of identifying the issue(s) in a client's case is to keep in mind the question: "What was decided about which facts in this opinion?"

_____14. When dealing with multiple issues in a client's case, address each issue separately and completely before proceeding to the next issue.

_____15. One of the steps in the process of identifying the issue(s) in a client's case is the identification of the key and background facts.

_____16. "The issue in this case is whether the trial court erred when it denied the motion to dismiss" is an example of an issue stated in the procedural context.

_____17. The goal when reading a case is to identify the substantive rather than the procedural issue(s).

_____18. The identification of the issue(s) in a court opinion is a four-step process.

_____19. The fastest way to locate the issue(s) in a case is to focus on the key facts.

_____20. The issue(s) may be set out more clearly in a dissenting opinion than in the majority opinion.

TRUE OR FALSE ANSWERS

Answer	Text Section	Answer	Text Section	Answer	Text Section
1. False	I	8. False	IIIC	15. False	IVC
2. True	I	9. True	IIIB	16. True	V
3. True	I	10. False	IIID	17. True	V
4. False	II	11. True	III	18. False	V
5. False	II	12. True	IV	19. False	VB
6. True	III	13. False	IVA	20. True	VB
7. True	IIIA	14. True	IVD		

Note: Number 5 is an example of a question of whether the law applies.

MULTIPLE CHOICE QUESTIONS

Please circle the letter of the **most appropriate** answer.

1. The identification of the issue:
   a. is the first step of the legal analysis process.
   b. is the most important task a researcher faces when engaging in legal analysis.
   c. determines the direction research will take.
   d. may result in malpractice if it is misidentified.
   e. all of the above
   f. a, b, and c
   g. a and b

2. Issues may be broken down into which of the following categories?
   a. a question of how the facts apply
   b. a question of how the law applies
   c. a question of constitutional interpretation
   d. a question of the interpretation of statutory law
   e. all of the above
   f. a and b

3. "Under the provisions of the battery statute, is a battery committed when an individual merely encourages the batterer?" is a question of:
   a. when the law applies.
   b. which law applies.
   c. whether the law applies at all.
   d. how the law applies.
   e. all of the above
   f. none of the above

4. The issue in a client's case is composed of which of the following parts?
   a. sufficient background facts to identify the context of the dispute
   b. key facts
   c. the legal question
   d. the applicable law
   e. all of the above
   f. b, c, and d

5. The law component of an issue may be a:
   a. constitutional provision.
   b. state statute.
   c. municipal ordinance.
   d. common-law doctrine.
   e. all of the above
   f. a, b, and c
   g. a, b, and d

6. "Does state statute § 4599 permit the installation of a sidewalk one foot from the curb?" is an example of a:
   a. narrow statement of the issue.
   b. question of which law applies.
   c. question of when the law applies.
   d. broad statement of the issue.
   e. all of the above
   f. a and b

7. A narrow statement of the issue:
   a. fails to inform the researcher of the specific factual context of the dispute.
   b. fails to inform the researcher of the precise law involved in the dispute.
   c. fails to inform the researcher of the specific law involved in the dispute.
   d. helps the researcher determine which direction research will take.
   e. none of the above
   f. a, b, and c

8. Which of the following are steps in the process of identifying the issue(s) in a client's case?
   a. Focus on the holding.
   b. Determine which of the facts apply to establish or satisfy the elements of each cause of action—the key facts.

c. Determine the elements of each cause of action identified in Step 1.

d. Assemble the issue from the law and key facts identified in Steps 2 and 3.

e. All of the above

f. b and c

g. b, c, and d

9. The identification of the issue(s) in a client's case requires the:

a. identification of the general areas of law involved.

b. identification of the elements of the cause(s) of action.

c. identification of the key and background facts.

d. assembly of the issue.

e. all of the above

f. a, b, and d

g. b and d

10. Which of the following are steps in the process of identifying the issue(s) in a court opinion?

a. Focus on the holding.

b. Determine which of the facts apply to establish or satisfy the elements of each cause of action— the key facts.

c. Determine the elements of each cause of action identified in Step 1.

d. Assemble the issue from the law and key facts identified in Steps 2 and 3.

e. all of the above

f. b, c, and d

11. In regard to the identification of the issue(s) in a court opinion:

a. when the case has more than one issue, follow the steps separately and completely for one issue before proceeding to identify the next issue.

b. the issue may be stated more clearly in a concurring opinion.

c. the issue may be stated more clearly in a dissenting opinion.

d. look to the holding.

e. all of the above

f. a, b, and d

12. The issue in a court opinion is composed of which of the following parts?

a. sufficient background facts to identify the context of the dispute

b. key facts

c. the legal question

d. the applicable law

e. all of the above

f. b, c, and d

MULTIPLE CHOICE ANSWERS

Answer	Text Section	Answer	Text Section	Answer	Text Section
1. e	I	5. e	IIIA	9. f	IV
2. b	II	6. a	IIID	10. a	V
3. d	II	7. d	I & IIID	11. e	V
4. f	III	8. g	IV	12. f	III

CHAPTER 11

Legal Analysis—Stating the Issue

TEXT ASSIGNMENT ANSWERS

Instructor's note: The format students should follow for the presentation of the issue in the following assignments is the format presented in this chapter, that is, Law + Legal Question + Key Facts.

In addition, note that there may be several correct ways to draft the comprehensive/narrow statement of the issue called for in the assignments. It is important that any formulation of the issue presented by the students should follow the Law + Legal Question + Key Facts format and include:

1. a complete statement of the law and
2. all the key facts presented in the model answers below.

ASSIGNMENT 1

A broad or shorthand formulation of the issue is a simple statement of the issue that does not include a reference to the specific facts or the law. A broad formulation of the issue is appropriate when the participants in the conversation are familiar with the facts and know the law that applies to the issue. A narrow or comprehensive formulation of the issue is more complete than a broad statement of the issue. It conveys in one sentence the specific law, legal question, and the key facts of the issue.

The elements of a narrow statement of an issue are the following:

1. The applicable law. The specific law or rule that controls the dispute.
2. The legal question. The legal question that is raised by the facts of the dispute.
3. The key facts. The key or legally significant facts that determine whether or how the law or rule applies.

It is important to phrase the issue narrowly when engaged in legal writing for the following reasons:

1. It directs the researcher to the specific area of the law that controls the question raised by the facts involved in the dispute. This saves research time; the researcher is directed immediately to the specific area of law in question and less time is spent looking for the specific law that governs the issue.
2. In an interoffice memo or a court brief, a comprehensive or narrow formulation of the issue sets the scope of the memo by informing the reader at the outset precisely what is in dispute. The reader is not forced to try to determine the question from the analysis section. The reader, therefore, is less likely to misunderstand what is in dispute.
3. A narrowly framed issue saves time in the law office. Future researchers, by reading the issue, know precisely what law and facts are covered in the memo. They are not forced to read the analysis section to determine if the memo is related or applies to the case they are working on.

ASSIGNMENT 2

PART A

"Under the provisions of the California code governing the grounds for dissolution of a corporation . . ."

PART B
"Under the provisions of the California code governing the dissolution of a corporation, Cal. Corp. Code § 1800, grounds, . . ."

PART C
"Under the provisions of the California code governing the dissolution of a corporation in the event of shareholder deadlock, . . ."

PART D
"Under the provisions of the California code governing the dissolution of a corporation in the event of shareholder deadlock, Cal. Corp. Code § 1800, . . ."

SUGGESTED ASSIGNMENTS: For Parts A through D of Assignment 2, have the students locate your state statute governing the dissolution of corporations, and answer the questions using that law rather than the law presented in the assignment.

ASSIGNMENT 3
PART A
"In light of the provisions of Georgia Code Ann. § 11-2-314, Implied warranty: merchantability, is there an implied warranty of merchantability for a new toaster purchased at a flea market booth, when the market is open year round and the same products are always sold at the booth?"

PART B
"Under Georgia Code Ann. § 11-2-314, Implied warranty: merchantability, is there an implied warranty of merchantability for a new toaster purchased at a garage sale?"

PART C
"In light of the provisions of Georgia Code Ann. § 11-2-314, Implied warranty: merchantability, is there an implied warranty of merchantability for a soft drink purchased at a local fast food restaurant?"

PART D
"According to the provisions of Georgia Code Ann. § 11-2-314, Implied warranty: merchantability, is there an implied warranty of merchantability for a soft drink purchased from a vendor at a flea market?"

ASSIGNMENT 4
PART A
"In light of the provisions of the law governing the warranty of merchantability, Georgia Code Ann. § 11-2-314, is there an implied warranty of merchantability for a new toaster purchased at a flea market booth, when the market is open year round and the same products are always sold at the booth?"

PART B
"Under the Georgia statute governing the warranty of merchantability, Georgia Code Ann. § 11-2-314, is there an implied warranty of merchantability for a new toaster purchased at a garage sale?"

PART C
"In light of the provisions of the law governing the warranty of merchantability, Georgia Code Ann. § 11-2-314, is there an implied warranty of merchantability for a soft drink purchased at a local fast food restaurant?"

PART D
"According to the provisions of the law governing the warranty of merchantability, Georgia Code Ann. § 11-2-314, is there an implied warranty of merchantability for a soft drink purchased from a vendor at a flea market?"

ASSIGNMENT 5

Instructor's note: The answers to Assignment 5 will differ from the answers to Assignment 3 only in the statute number and description. The assignment will require students to research the local statutes.

ASSIGNMENT 6
PART A
Shorthand/broad statement of the issue:
    "Is a will, half-written by a witness, valid?"

Instructor's note: There are several ways this issue may be broadly stated; only one is presented above. The simplest broad statement of the issue would be, "Is the will valid?"

Comprehensive/narrow statement of the issue:
"In light of the provisions of the New Washington probate code governing holographic wills, is a will valid when it is properly witnessed, and one-half of the will is in the testator's handwriting, and one-half is in the handwriting of a witness?"

    "In light of the provisions of the New Washington probate code governing holographic wills, New Wash. Prob. Code § 60, is a will valid when it is properly witnessed, and one-half of the will is in the testator's handwriting, and one-half is in the handwriting of a witness?" (Statement of issue including statutory citation)

PART B
Shorthand/broad statement of the issue:
"Is a will which is half-written by a witness and witnessed by two interested witnesses, valid?"

Instructor's note: Just as in Part A of this assignment, there are several ways this issue may be broadly stated; only one is presented above. The simplest broad statement of the issue would be "Is the will valid?"

Comprehensive/narrow statement of the issue:
"In light of the provisions of the New Washington probate code governing holographic wills, is a will valid when it is witnessed by three witnesses, two of whom will inherit under the will; and one-half of the will is in the testator's handwriting, and one-half is in the handwriting of a witness?"

    "In light of the provisions of the New Washington probate code governing holographic wills, New Wash. Prob. Code § 60, is a will valid when it is witnessed by three witnesses, two of whom will inherit under the will; and one-half of the will is in the testator's handwriting, and one-half is in the handwriting of a witness?" (**Statement of issue including statutory citation**)

PART C
Shorthand/broad statement of the issue:
"Is a will valid which is half-written by a witness and signed by a witness?"

Instructor's note: As in Parts A, there are several ways this issue may be broadly stated; only one is presented above. The simplest broad statement of the issue would be "Is the will valid?"

Comprehensive/narrow statement of the issue:
"In light of the provisions of the New Washington probate code governing holographic wills, is a will valid when it is properly witnessed, signed by a witness at the direction of the testator, and one-half of the will is in the testator's handwriting, and one-half is in the handwriting of a witness?"

    "In light of the provisions of the New Washington probate code governing holographic wills, New Wash. Prob. Code § 60, is a will valid when it is properly witnessed, signed by a witness at the direction of the testator, and one-half of the will is in the testator's handwriting, and one-half is in the handwriting of a witness?" (**Statement of issue including statutory citation**)

ASSIGNMENT 7
PART A
Shorthand/broad statement of the issue:
"Is the statement `concerning' the plaintiff?"

Instructor's note: There are several ways this issue may be broadly stated; only one is presented above. The simplest broad statement of the issue is presented above. Another broad statement would be: "Is the statement 'concerning' the plaintiff according to the law of slander?"

Comprehensive/narrow statement of the issue:
"According to the State's (name of state) law of slander, is a statement `concerning' the plaintiff when an individual on a radio talk show states that all the town's psychiatrists are frauds?"

PART B
Shorthand/broad statement of the issue:
"Is the statement `concerning' the plaintiff?"

Instructor's note: As in Part A, there are several ways this issue may be broadly stated; only one is presented above. The simplest broad statement of the issue is presented above. Another broad statement would be: "Is the statement 'concerning' the plaintiff under the law of slander when there is only one psychiatrist in town?"

Comprehensive/narrow statement of the issue:
"According to the State's (name of state) law of slander, is a statement 'concerning' the plaintiff when an individual on a radio talk show states that all the town's psychiatrists are frauds, and there is only one psychiatrist in the town?"

SUGGESTED ASSIGNMENT: For Parts A and B of Assignment 7 have the students locate and answer the questions using the law of your state governing slander.

ASSIGNMENT 8
PART A
"In light of Ohio's law governing the infliction of emotional distress, can a bystander recover for negligent infliction of emotional distress when the bystander witnesses the death of a victim from three blocks away?"

PART B
"According to the provisions of the Texas Corporation Code governing oppressive conduct, does oppressive conduct occur when a majority shareholder refuses to issue dividends, triples his salary, and grants himself excessive bonuses?"

PART C
"In light of Florida's tort law governing libel, is libel committed when a newspaper publishes an article indicating that an individual has criminal connections?"

PART D
"Under the State's (name of state) battery law is a battery committed when law enforcement officers, while making a lawful arrest, encounter resistance, use force to overcome that resistance, and continue to use force after the resistance has ceased?"

SUGGESTED ASSIGNMENT: For Parts A through D of Assignment 8 have the students locate and answer the questions using your state law governing the area of law involved in each part.

WEB ASSIGNMENT ANSWERS

ASSIGNMENT 1

PART A

"In light of the provisions of Colo. Rev. Stat. Ann. § 19-2-511, Statements, is a statement made by a juvenile, without the presence of a parent, guardian, or legal custodian and without advisement of the juvenile's rights, admissible when the juvenile appears to be eighteen years old and told the police she was eighteen?"

PART B

"Under the provisions of Colo. Rev. Stat. Ann. § 19-2-511, Statements, is a statement made by a juvenile, without the presence of a parent, guardian, or legal custodian and without advisement of the juvenile's rights, admissible when the principal and the school's security officer interrogated the juvenile about his part in a theft that took place at the school?"

PART C

"According to Colo. Rev. Stat. Ann. § 19-2-511, Statements, is a statement made by a juvenile, without the presence of a parent, guardian, or legal custodian and without advisement of the juvenile's rights, admissible when the juvenile, while stopped for speeding, is interrogated by an officer concerning the speeding offense?"

PART D

"Under the provisions of Colo. Rev. Stat. Ann. § 19-2-511, Statements, is a statement made by a juvenile, without the presence of a parent, guardian, or legal custodian and without advisement of the juvenile's rights, admissible when the juvenile, after being arrested for curfew violation, confesses to a police officer on the way to the police station that she was drunk, without the officer asking the juvenile any questions?"

ASSIGNMENT 2

PART A

"In light of the provisions of the statute governing statements by juveniles, Colo. Rev. Stat. Ann. § 19-2-511, is a statement made by a juvenile, without the presence of a parent, guardian, or legal custodian and without advisement of the juvenile's rights, admissible when the juvenile appears to be eighteen years old and told the police she was eighteen?"

PART B

"Under the provisions of the statute governing statements by juveniles, Colo. Rev. Stat. Ann. § 19-2-511, is a statement made by a juvenile, without the presence of a parent, guardian, or legal custodian and without advisement of the juvenile's rights, admissible when the principal and the school's security officer interrogated the juvenile about his part in a theft that took place at the school?"

PART C

"According to the statute governing statements by juveniles, Colo. Rev. Stat. Ann. § 19-2-511, is a statement made by a juvenile, without the presence of a parent, guardian, or legal custodian and without advisement of the juvenile's rights, admissible when the juvenile, while stopped for speeding, is interrogated by an officer concerning the speeding offense?"

PART D

"Under the provisions of the law governing statements by juveniles, Colo. Rev. Stat. Ann. § 19-2-511, is a statement made by a juvenile, without the presence of a parent, guardian, or legal custodian and without advisement of the juvenile's rights, admissible when the juvenile, after being arrested for curfew violation, confessed to a police officer on the way to the police station that she was drunk, without the officer asking the juvenile any questions?"

ASSIGNMENT 3
PART A
"In light of the provisions of Tex. Penal Code Ann. § 28.02, Arson, is arson committed when an individual sets his neighbor's field on fire?"

PART B
"Under Texas statute § 28.02, Arson, does arson take place when an individual sets a shed on fire, falsely believing the shed belongs to him and is on his property?"

PART C
"According to Texas statute § 28.02, Arson, is arson committed when an individual sets a large pile of weeds on fire on a windy day, the fire sets a neighbor's house on fire, and the individual knew he should wait to burn the weeds?"

PART D
"Under Tex. Penal Code Ann. § 28.02, Arson, does arson take place when an individual, driving under the influence of alcohol, loses control of his vehicle, hits a neighbor's car, and sets it on fire?"

ASSIGNMENT 4

Instructor's note: The answers to Assignment 4 will differ from the answers to Assignments 1 and 3 only in the statute numbers and descriptions. The assignment will require students to research the local statutes.

TEST QUESTIONS AND ANSWERS
TRUE OR FALSE QUESTIONS

Please write a "T" or "F" to the left of each statement.

_____ 1. A test to determine if an issue is complete is whether the reader, when reading the issue, knows the specific legal question, the law, and the facts of the dispute.

_____ 2. A broad statement of the issue includes the law and the specific facts.

_____ 3. A broad statement of the issue is appropriate in communications when the participants are familiar with the facts and law of the case.

_____ 4. A narrow statement of the issue does not guide the reader to the specific law in question.

_____ 5. The most effective formulation is a broad statement of the issue.

_____ 6. A broad statement of the issue states the scope of a memo by informing the reader at the outset what is precisely in dispute.

_____ 7. The text recommends that an issue should be composed of four elements.

_____ 8. The format for presenting the issue recommended in the text follows the standard legal analysis format.

_____ 9. The format for presenting the issue is the rule of law followed by the legal question and the facts.

_____ 10. The law component of the issue may be presented in either a broad or narrow context.

_____ 11. When an issue is based on the common law, the case citation should be referred to.

_____ 12. The text recommends the inclusion of the citation in the issue when the rule of law is enacted law.

_____ 13. It is not appropriate to use only a citation in the issue when the rule of law is enacted law.

_____ 14. The question component of the issue must relate to or concern the specific law included in the law component.

_____ 15. The facts component of the issue should include the key facts and sufficient background facts to inform the reader of the context of the dispute.

_____ 16. When there are multiple facts, it is appropriate to condense the facts when stating the issue.

_____ 17. An issue should be stated objectively when presented to a court.

_____ 18. An issue not stated objectively may cause the reader to question the ability of the author and discount the legal argument that follows.

_____19 It is not appropriate to list key facts when stating the issue.
_____20. When stating the issue, identify people and events specifically by name.

TRUE OR FALSE ANSWERS

Answer	Text Section		Answer	Text Section		Answer	Text Section
1. True	I		8. True	III		15. False	VI
2. False	II		9. True	III		16. True	VI
3. True	II		10. True	IV		17. True	VII
4. False	II		11. False	IVA		18. True	VII
5. False	III		12. True	IVB1		19. False	VI
6. False	III		13. True	IVB1		20. False	VIII
7. False	III		14. True	V			

MULTIPLE CHOICE QUESTIONS

Please circle the letter of the **most appropriate** answer.

1. The issue should include:
   a. sufficient background facts to place the key facts in context.
   b. the key facts.
   c. the applicable law.
   d. the legal question.
   e. all of the above
   f. a, b, and c
   g. b, c, and d

2. "Can Mr. Jones recover damages for negligence?" is an example of a:
   a. a narrow statement of the issue.
   b. a complete statement of the issue.
   c. a broad statement of the issue.
   d. a comprehensive statement of the issue.
   e. all of the above
   f. a, b, and c

3. The most effective formulation of the issue is a:
   a. comprehensive statement.
   b. broad statement.
   c. narrow statement.
   d. shorthand statement.
   e. all of the above
   f. a and c
   g. a, c, and d

4. When an issue is stated correctly it:
   a. informs the reader of sufficient background facts to understand the context of the key facts.
   b. directs the reader to the specific area to law involved in the dispute.
   c. sets the scope of the memo in a legal memorandum.
   d. saves researchers time.

   e. all of the above
   f. a, b, and c
   g. b, c, and d

5. Which of the following formats is recommended for presenting the elements of the issue?
   a. the facts followed by the legal question and the law
   b. the law followed by the facts, and then the legal question
   c. the legal question followed by the law and the facts
   d. the law followed by the legal question and the facts

6. The reasons in support of the recommended format for presenting the issue are:
   a. it follows the standard legal analysis format.
   b. the rule should be presented first for readability purposes.
   c. it is usually easier to write the issue following this format.
   d. it is a most-effective tool when confronting the complex challenges presented by multiple fact issues.
   e. all of the above
   f. a, b, and c

7. The law component of an issue based on enacted law may include the:
   a. title.
   b. citation.
   c. title paraphrased.
   d. description.
   e. all of the above
   f. a, b, and c

8. In "Under the New Washington kidnapping statute, which includes intent to confine as an element of kidnapping, . . ." the presentation of the enacted law includes the:
    a. citation.
    b. title.
    c. title paraphrased.
    d. description.
    e. all of the above
    f. b and d
    g. c and d

9. In "According to N. Wash. Code § 20-40-1, kidnapping . . ." the presentation of the enacted law includes the:
    a. citation.
    b. title.
    c. title paraphrased.
    d. description.
    e. all of the above
    f. a and b
    g. a and c

10. The question component of the issue must:
    a. relate to or concern the specific law included in the law component.
    b. present the specific legal question raised by the facts.
    c. link the law with the facts.
    d. all of the above
    e. a and b

11. The facts component of the issue must:
    a. be readable.
    b. include key facts.
    c. include sufficient background facts to provide the context of the key facts.
    d. set the factual scope of the legal question.
    e. all of the above
    f. a, b, and c
    g. a, b, and d

12. When drafting the fact component of the issue:
    a. all the key facts must be included.
    b. the key facts may be categorized.
    c. the key facts may be condensed.
    d. the key facts may be listed.
    e. all of the above
    f. b, c, and d
    g. b and d

13. In "Under Indiana corporation law, does oppressive conduct occur when a majority shareholder engages in several actions that are beneficial solely to the majority shareholder and detrimental to the interests of the minority shareholders?":
    a. all the key facts are included.
    b. the key facts are categorized.
    c. the key facts are condensed.
    d. the key facts are listed.
    e. none of the above
    f. a and c

14. An issue may:
    a. be constructed in a manner that favors an outcome.
    b. include the specific names of people.
    c. include the specific names of events.
    d. not list the facts.
    e. all of the above
    f. b and c
    g. none of the above

15. A properly constructed issue may:
    a. include a statutory title without a citation.
    b. be stated objectively.
    c. not include a list of key facts.
    d. be stated broadly.
    e. all of the above
    f. a and b

MULTIPLE CHOICE ANSWERS

Answer	Text Section	Answer	Text Section	Answer	Text Section
1. g	I	6. e	III	11. g	VI
2. c	II	7. e	IVB	12. f	VI
3. f	III	8. g	IVB	13. b	VI
4. g	III	9. f	IVB	14. g	VIII
5. d	III	10. d	V	15. f	Entire Chapter

CHAPTER 12

Case Law Analysis—Is a Case On Point?

TEXT ASSIGNMENT ANSWERS

ASSIGNMENT 1

The term *on point* means that a case can apply as precedent to the client's case. A case is on point when there is a sufficient similarity between the key facts and rule of law/legal principle of the court opinion and the client's case for the court opinion to govern or provide guidance to a later court in deciding the outcome of the client's case. In other words, when a court opinion is on point it may govern or guide a subsequent court in the resolution of an issue in a case before that court.

ASSIGNMENT 2

Instructor's note: It should be emphasized to the student that the determination of whether a case is on point is a two-step process; the requirements of both steps must be met before a case can be considered to be on point and apply as precedent.

The two-step process for determining when a case is on point is as follows:

STEP 1. ARE THE KEY FACTS SUFFICIENTLY SIMILAR FOR THE COURT OPINION TO APPLY AS PRECEDENT? The first step is to determine if the significant or key facts in the court opinion are sufficiently similar to the key facts in the client's case, so that the court opinion may apply as precedent. This is accomplished by comparing the key facts of the court opinion with the key facts of the client's case.

Once the key facts are compared, the court opinion may apply as precedent if the key facts are identical or sufficiently similar to those of the client's case. If there are differences, the differences must not be of such a significant degree that the opinion cannot apply as precedent.

STEP 2. ARE THE RULES/PRINCIPLES OF LAW SUFFICIENTLY SIMILAR FOR THE COURT OPINION TO APPLY AS PRECEDENT? The second step is to determine whether the rule of law or legal principle applied in the court opinion is the same rule of law or legal principle that applies in the client's case. If it is not the same rule of law or principle, is it sufficiently similar to the rule/principle that applies in the client's case for the opinion to still apply as precedent? Where a different rule or principle was applied in the court opinion, the opinion may still be on point when the court's interpretation of the rule or principle is so broad in scope that it applies to the different law or rule that governs the client's case.

ASSIGNMENT 3

The three-part process for determining if a case is on point when there are different key facts is as follows:

PART 1. IDENTIFY THE SIMILARITIES BETWEEN THE KEY FACTS. This part involves identifying and comparing the key facts. The key facts that are similar in the court opinion and the client's case should be listed.

PART 2. IDENTIFY THE DIFFERENCES BETWEEN THE KEY FACTS. Like Part 1, this part involves identifying and comparing the key facts. The key facts that are different in the court opinion, and the client's case, should be listed.

PART 3. DETERMINE IF THE DIFFERENCES ARE OF SUCH A SIGNIFICANT DEGREE THAT THE OPINION CANNOT APPLY AS PRECEDENT. This part consists of comparing and analyzing the differences between the key facts identified in Part 2. The significance of the differences is determined by substituting the client's key facts for those of the court opinion. If the substitution of the key facts would result in changing the outcome of the court opinion, the opinion cannot be used as precedent.

The text discusses four variations that may be encountered when dealing with different key facts. These variations should be considered when there are differences between the key facts of the court opinion and the key facts of the client's case. The different key fact variations are listed below:

1. minor difference in key facts
2. major difference in key facts—case is not on point
3. major difference in key facts—case is on point
4. major difference in key facts—case is on point, broad legal principle

Instructor's note: For the answer to this assignment to be complete, the four different key fact variations presented in the preceding paragraph should be included.

ASSIGNMENT 4

Instructor's note: In order to answer this question the student must combine the requirements presented in the discussion in the text entitled "Different Rule or Principle." This section discusses when a case may be on point when the legislative act or common law rule/principle applied in the court opinion is different from the act or rule/principle that applies in the client's case. The requirements that must be met for a court opinion to be on point and apply as precedent in such situations are presented in the chapter in Figures 12-4 and 12-5. The requirements are essentially the same for both legislative acts and common-law rules or principles.

The instructor should emphasize that the entire discussion of the requirements or steps that must be followed involves only those situations where there is no court opinion in the jurisdiction that directly interprets the legislative act or common-law rule/principle that applies in the client's case. The instructor should also emphasize that the student must keep in mind that, since the act or rule/principle applied in the court opinion is different from that which applies in the client's case, the court opinion is persuasive precedent. The court hearing the client's case does not have to follow it; it is not mandatory precedent. The court has discretion and must be persuaded.

Both of the steps or requirements listed below must be met before the court opinion may be considered on point and apply as persuasive precedent. The two requirements that must be met when the doctrine/rule applied by the court is different from the doctrine/rule that applies in the client's case are as follows:

1. There is a similarity in language between the legislative acts or common-law rules/principles, and
2. There is a similarity in function between the legislative acts or common-law rules/principles.

The acts or common-law rules/principles involved in the court opinion and the client's case must be similar in language. That is, they must both deal with the same term.

If the question in the client's case involves what constitutes residency, the act or rule/principle **FOR EXAMPLE** applied in the court opinion must involve the term residency.

The acts or common-law rules/principles that apply in the court opinion and the client's case must be similar in function. That is, they must both involve a similar function.

FOR EXAMPLE If the issue in the client's case involves residency requirements for the purpose of running for the office of county sheriff, and the act or rule that applies does not define the residency requirements, the act or rule applied in the court opinion should involve residency requirements and elective office. Both acts or rules are similar in function; they both involve elective office.

If the issue in the client's case involves residency requirements for the purpose of filing a divorce, and the applicable act or rule does not define residency, an act or rule applied in a court opinion involving residency requirements for elective office involves a different function and is not similar in function.

ASSIGNMENT 5

The determination of whether a case is on point is important for the following reasons:

1. The determination of whether a case is on point must be made before the case may apply as precedent and be used and relied on by a court in its determination of how an issue will be decided. Note that the court may be unaware of the case, and it may be necessary to bring it to the court's attention.

2. In as much as the court will consider precedent in reaching its decision, cases that are on point need to be found to provide guidance to the attorney as to how the issue in the client's case may be decided. Cases that are on point must be located and analyzed to determine what impact they may have on the decision in the client's case. If the case that is on point indicates that the decision will most likely be against the client, then it may be appropriate to pursue settlement or other options.

ASSIGNMENT 6

EXAMPLE 1

The case is on point because the requirements of the two-step process are met.

STEP 1. ARE THE KEY FACTS SUFFICIENTLY SIMILAR FOR THE COURT OPINION TO APPLY AS PRECEDENT? Although there are differences, the client's key facts are sufficiently similar to the key facts in *Karl v. Herald* for the case to be on point. Both cases involve small corporations where the majority shareholder controlled the corporation. In both cases the majority shareholder was paid a lucrative salary. In both cases the corporation was in a position to pay dividends. In both cases the majority shareholder was in control of the board of directors and refused to issue dividends.

The major fact difference is that in the client's case the majority shareholder claims that the cash surplus is necessary for emergencies and no emergency has occurred in the last five years that would require more than $50,000. There was no such claim in *Karl*. This difference does not keep the case from being on point; it just affects how the opinion applies, not whether it applies. This is discussed in Step 2.

STEP 2. ARE THE RULES OF LAW SUFFICIENTLY SIMILAR FOR THE COURT OPINION TO APPLY AS PRECEDENT? Both cases involve the same statute, section 96-25-16 of the Business Corporation Act. In both cases the parties seek redress for the failure of the other party to issue dividends. In essence, in both cases the same question is raised: "Did the majority shareholder unfairly or wrongly withhold dividends?" Therefore, there is little question that *Karl* is on point in regard to Step 2.

In the client's case the majority shareholder claims the cash surplus is necessary for emergencies. This fact difference in the client's case affects how the opinion applies, not whether it applies. In *Karl* the court defined oppressive conduct as "any unfair or fraudulent act by a majority shareholder that inures to the benefit of the majority and to the detriment of the minority." This definition will be applied to determine whether the majority shareholder's statement that the dividends were withheld because the cash surplus was necessary for emergencies is a defense to the claim that her actions were unfair or fraudulent.

EXAMPLE 2

The case is on point because the requirements of the two-step process are met.

STEP 1. ARE THE KEY FACTS SUFFICIENTLY SIMILAR FOR THE COURT OPINION TO APPLY AS PRECEDENT?

Although there are differences, the client's key facts are sufficiently similar to the key facts in *Karl v. Herald* for the case to be on point. Both cases involve small corporations where the majority shareholder controlled the corporations. In both cases the majority shareholder was paid a lucrative salary. In both cases the corporation was in a position to pay dividends. In both cases the majority shareholder was in control of the board of directors and refused to issue dividends.

The major fact difference is that in the client's case the majority shareholder claims that the client's dividend is her job. There was no such statement in *Karl*. This difference does not keep the case from being on point; it just affects how the opinion applies, not whether it applies. This is discussed in Step 2.

STEP 2. ARE THE RULES OF LAW SUFFICIENTLY SIMILAR FOR THE COURT OPINION TO APPLY AS PRECEDENT?

Both cases involve the same statute, section 96-25-16 of the Business Corporation Act. In both cases the parties seek redress for the failure of the other party to issue dividends. In essence, in both cases the same question is raised: "Did the majority shareholder unfairly or wrongly withhold dividends?" Therefore, there is little question that *Karl* is on point in regard to Step 2.

In the client's case the majority shareholder claims that the client's dividend is her job. This fact difference in the client's case affects how the opinion applies, not whether it applies. In *Karl* the court defined oppressive conduct as "any unfair or fraudulent act by a majority shareholder that inures to the benefit of the majority and to the detriment of the minority." This definition will be applied to determine whether the majority shareholder's claim that the client's dividend is her job is a defense to the claim that her actions were unfair or fraudulent.

EXAMPLE 3

The case is not on point because the requirements of the two-step process are not met.

STEP 1. ARE THE KEY FACTS SUFFICIENTLY SIMILAR FOR THE COURT OPINION TO APPLY AS PRECEDENT?

The key facts of the client's case are not sufficiently similar to the key facts in *Karl v. Herald* for the opinion to be on point. Both cases involve small businesses where one person is in control of the business. In both cases the person in control of the business benefits from the business and the other person does not.

The major fact difference that keeps *Karl* from being on point is that in *Karl* the business is a corporation and in the client's case the business is a partnership. This is a critical difference. Partnerships do not share profits by issuing stocks. The considerations involved in profit sharing by partnerships are entirely different from those of a corporation.

STEP 2. ARE THE RULES OF LAW SUFFICIENTLY SIMILAR FOR THE COURT OPINION TO APPLY AS PRECEDENT?

Karl is not on point in regard to Step 2 because different laws and issues are involved. In *Karl* the court applied corporation law, and the issue involved the question of whether stock dividends were improperly withheld. The client's case will be governed by a partnership statute and will not involve a question involving stock dividends. In *Karl* questions involving partnership profits and salaries were not addressed. Therefore the case is not on point.

ASSIGNMENT 7

Instructor's note: In several of the parts of this assignment, additional factual information is required to completely answer the question. This is intentional. It emphasizes to the student the importance of obtaining all the relevant information before beginning to analyze a problem. In addition, the problems allow the student to engage in the process of identifying missing critical information and to analyze problems when information is missing. In the answers the student should identify the missing information and analyze the problems even though information is missing.

SUGGESTED ASSIGNMENTS: For Parts A through D of Assignment 7, have the students locate your state law governing applications for general relief and service of process and answer the questions using that law rather than the law presented in the assignment. Use the court opinions presented in the assignments.

PART A
1. **Fact similarities and differences between the court opinion and the client's situation.**

Similarities

- Both cases involve an application for general relief funds.
- In both cases it was determined that the applicant's income exceeded the maximum allowable income and the application was denied.
- In both cases the applicant was denied an appeal hearing.

Differences

- In the client's case the income determination was based on income from the client's part-time job and support from his parents. In the court opinion the income was based upon income from Mr. Jones's two part-time jobs.
- In the court opinion Mr. Jones is a first-time applicant. In the client's case there is no indication of whether the client is a first-time applicant.
- In the client's case Tom lives at home with his parents and does not pay rent and utilities. In the court opinion there is no indication where Mr. Jones lives or whether he pays rent and utilities.
- In the court opinion Mr. Jones demanded an appeal hearing to explain his special circumstances. In the client's case there is no indication that Tom is alleging special circumstances.

2. **Is the court opinion on point? Why or why not?**

The case is probably on point because the requirements of the two-step process are met.

Step 1. Are the key facts sufficiently similar for the court opinion to apply as precedent? Both the court opinion and the client's case involve an application for general relief funds, a denial of the application, and denial of an appeal hearing. Therefore, the key facts are sufficiently similar for the case to apply as precedent.

The fact that the client lives at home and part of the income determination was based upon the support from his parents is not significant. The regulation provides that the determination may be based upon financial support as well as the applicant's income.

The other differences, whether the client is a first-time applicant and whether the client alleges special circumstances affect how the court opinion applies, not whether it applies. This is discussed below in the answer to the third question.

Step 2. Are the rules of law sufficiently similar for the court opinion to apply as precedent? Both the court opinion and the client's case involve the same agency regulation and the same question involving the regulation: "Is the individual entitled to an appeal hearing?" Therefore, the requirements of Step 2 are met.

3. **If the court opinion is on point, what will the probable decision be in regard to the question raised by the client's facts?**

Assuming the case is on point, because of the differences between the court opinion and the client's case, the probable outcome cannot be determined without further information or without assuming further information.

The court opinion held that a first-time applicant for general relief funds is entitled to a hearing when special circumstances are alleged. Is the client a first-time applicant? If it is determined that he is a first-time applicant, he may be entitled to a hearing because the opinion entitles a first-time applicant to a hearing under some circumstances.

If Tom is not a first-time applicant, he may still be entitled to a hearing depending on how the opinion is interpreted. Does the holding only apply to first-time applicants or did the court refer to first-time applicants only because Mr. Jones was a first-time applicant? Is the language and reasoning of the opinion so broadly written that it can be argued that the holding also applies to applicants who are not first-time applicants? If that is the case, then the client may be entitled to a hearing under the holding.

Another element in the court opinion is that special circumstances must be alleged. Did the client's application for an appeal hearing allege special circumstances? The facts do not provide this information, and this fact must be determined.

If it is determined that the client is a first-time applicant or that the opinion applies to other than first-time applicants, and it is determined that special circumstances were alleged by the client, then the client would be entitled to a hearing according to the holding of the opinion.

PART B

1. **Fact similarities and differences between the court opinion and the client's situation.**

Similarities

- Both cases involve an application for general relief funds.
- In both cases the applicant is a first-time applicant.
- In both cases the application was denied based upon information contained in the application.
- In both cases the applicant was denied an appeal hearing.
- In both cases the applicant alleges special circumstances that entitle him to benefits. Although the facts in the client's case do not specifically mention that the request for an appeal hearing alleged special circumstances, this can be assumed because the facts state that the client believed he had special circumstances entitling him to relief.

Differences

- In the court case the reason the application was denied was stated in the opinion. In the client's case the reason for the denial is not stated.
- In the client's case there is reference to legislation which prohibits an appeal hearing when the denial of the application for general relief is based on information provided in the application.

2. **Is the court opinion on point? Why or why not?**

The court opinion is probably on point. The requirements of both Steps 1 and 2 appear to be met.

Step 1. Are the key facts sufficiently similar for the court opinion to apply as precedent? Both the court opinion and the client's case involve an application for general relief funds, a denial of the application based upon information contained in the application, and denial of an appeal hearing. Therefore, the key facts are sufficiently similar for the case to apply as precedent.

The fact that the reason for the denial of the application in the client's case is not presented is probably not significant. The assumption is that the denial was because the client's income was above the threshold maximum.

Research would have to be conducted to determine if this assumption is correct. If the denial was based on other reasons, such as the application was not completely filled out or the client lied on the application, the court opinion may not apply because the holding grants the right to a hearing when special circumstances are alleged (assuming the special circumstances refer to financial circumstances). The holding does not appear to apply to other special circumstances. Additional research would have to be conducted to determine whether one is entitled to a hearing when the special circumstances involve other matters, such as an incomplete application.

The other factual difference is that in the client's case there is reference to legislation which prohibits an appeal hearing when the denial of the application for general relief is based on information provided in the application. This fact affects how the opinion applies, not whether it applies, and is addressed in the third question below.

Step 2. Are the rules of law sufficiently similar for the court opinion to apply as precedent? Both the court opinion and the client's case involve the same agency regulation, and the same question involving the regulation: "Is the individual entitled to an appeal hearing?" Therefore, the requirements of Step 2 are met. The question of the impact of the legislation affects how the opinion applies, not whether the case is on point. This is discussed below in the answer to the third question.

3. **If the court opinion is on point, what will the probable decision be in regard to the question raised by the client's facts?**

Assuming the case is on point, the probable outcome cannot be absolutely determined without further information or without assuming further information. It probably can be concluded, however, that the holding presented in the opinion applies and the client is entitled to an appeal hearing. The client, just as Mr. Jones in the court opinion, was a first-time applicant who was denied general relief funds. He alleges special circumstances and according to the opinion is entitled to an appeal hearing.

Was the legislation mentioned in the client's facts passed prior to the court opinion and discussed in the opinion? If so, in light of the holding which granted a hearing, the legislation probably does not apply and the client is entitled to a hearing.

Even if the legislation was passed subsequent to the court opinion, the legislation probably does not apply or is unconstitutional because it takes away a right to a hearing which the court held an applicant is entitled to under the state constitution. As discussed in Chapter 1, state legislation which conflicts with the state constitution is unconstitutional and unenforceable.

PART C

1. **Fact similarities and differences between the court opinion and the client's situation.**

Similarities

- Both cases involve general relief funds.
- In both cases, the applicant was denied an appeal hearing.

Differences

- The court opinion involves a first-time application for general relief funds. The client's case involves a termination of general relief funds that the client was already receiving.

2. **Is the court opinion on point? Why or why not?**

The case is probably not on point because the requirements of the two-step process are not met.

Step 1. Are the key facts sufficiently similar for the court opinion to apply as precedent? Both the court opinion and the client's case involve general relief funds and the denial of an appeal hearing.

The court opinion and the client's case are significantly different. The court opinion involved a first-time application for general relief funds. In the client's case, the client is already receiving the funds; his initial application for relief funds was granted. The client's case does not involve a denial of an application for funds; it involves a termination of relief. The court opinion does not address the issue of the denial of a hearing when relief is being terminated, which involves different considerations. The key facts are so significantly different that the opinion probably does not apply as precedent.

Step 2. Are the rules of law sufficiently similar for the court opinion to apply as precedent? The court opinion involves an agency regulation which refers to an applicant and the denial of general relief funds. The regulation, as presented in the facts, does not address termination of relief already granted. Even if other provisions of the regulation do address the termination of relief already granted, the court opinion only refers to that portion of the regulation involving the denial of the application for benefits, not the termination of benefits. Therefore, it appears that the rule of law that applies in the opinion and the client's case are different, and the requirements of Step 2 are not met.

3. **If the court opinion is on point, what will the probable decision be in regard to the question raised by the client's facts?**

As discussed above, the court opinion is probably not on point. The facts and the rule of law are different. One could argue, however, that regardless of the differences, the general constitutional principle applied in the opinion should apply in the client's case. That is, the due process clause of the state constitution should entitle an individual to a hearing when the funds are denied or terminated. It is questionable whether this argument would succeed.

Additional research would be needed to determine the scope of the constitutional right to a hearing, and a court opinion that is more on point should be located.

PART D

1. **Fact similarities and differences between the court opinion and the client's situation.**

Similarities

- Both cases involve a landlord, tenant, and a notice of default that was improperly delivered.
- In the court opinion the tenant received the notice the next day. In the client's case the notice was received the next day.

Differences

- In the court opinion notice of default was placed in the tenant's mailbox. In the client's case the landlord told the client's daughter to inform the tenant that he was in default.

2. **Is the court opinion on point? Why or why not?**

   The case is probably on point because the requirements of the two-step process are met.

   Step 1. Are the key facts sufficiently similar for the court opinion to apply as precedent? The court opinion and the client's case are sufficiently similar for the case to apply as precedent. Both cases involve a landlord, tenant, and a notice of default. In both cases, the notice of default was received the next day.

   The differences are probably not significant because in both the court opinion and the client's case the method of delivery of the notice of default was not in compliance with the requirements of the statute.

   Step 2. Are the rules of law sufficiently similar for the court opinion to apply as precedent? The court opinion and the client's case involve the same statute and involve the same question under the statute: "Was the notice of default effective when it was improperly delivered, the client received actual notice, and the client was not prejudiced by the improper notice?"

3. **If the court opinion is on point, what will the probable decision be in regard to the question raised by the client's facts?**

   Assuming the case is on point, the probable decision will be that the notice of default is effective. Regardless of how the notice of default was delivered, in both the court opinion and the client's case the notice was received the next day. The court ruled that although the method of delivery did not comply with the statute, the intent of the act is accomplished if the tenant receives actual notice and is not prejudiced by the improper notice. Just as in the court opinion, the client received the notice the next day, and there are no facts presented that he was prejudiced by the improper notice.

   Note that the tenant was not prejudiced in both the court opinion and the client's case because the notice was received within the thirty-day notice of default period. The client had an opportunity to respond within the thirty days and, therefore, was not subject to eviction for failure to respond within the thirty days.

4. **Would it make any difference if the daughter informed the tenant after thirty days but before the eviction suit was filed?**

   This is a change in the key facts which does not affect a determination of whether the case is on point, but which does affect how the opinion applies. The case is still on point because it involves the same rule of law, and the same basic facts: landlord and tenant, notice of default, and the improper delivery of a notice of default. The ruling applies, but a different result could be reached. The court ruled that the notice of default was effective if the tenant received actual notice and was not prejudiced by the improper notice.

   The outcome of the application of the court's holding would depend upon additional facts. Was the client prejudiced by the delivery after thirty days but before the filing of the eviction suit? If the client was prejudiced, then the notice of default was improper. The client could have been prejudiced because he did not have an opportunity to respond within the thirty days and, therefore, was subject to eviction for failure to respond within the thirty days.

PART E

1. **Fact similarities and differences between the court opinion and the client's situation.**

Similarities

- Both cases involve a landlord, tenant, and a notice of default.

Differences

- In the court opinion, notice of default was placed in the tenant's mailbox. In the client's case, the notice of default was posted on the front door.
- In the court opinion, the tenant retrieved the notice the next day. In the client's case, the notice was received after the thirty-day default period had passed.

2. **Is the court opinion on point? Why or why not?**

Without additional information relevant to Step 1, it cannot be determined if the case is on point. This is discussed in Step 1 below.

Step 1. Are the key facts sufficiently similar for the court opinion to apply as precedent? A determination of whether the requirements of Step 1 are met is dependent upon the acquisition of an additional key fact. The notice of default was posted on the client's front door. It must be determined if the client's front door is the "most public part of the residence." The statute provides that notice of default may be accomplished by "posting at the most public part of the residence."

If the client's front door is the "most public part of the residence," then the service of process was proper under the statute. This is a critical difference between the key facts of the court opinion and the client's case that could render the court opinion not on point and therefore not usable as precedent.

The court opinion addresses situations where the method of delivery of the notice of default does not comply with the statute, but the tenant receives actual notice and is not prejudiced by the improper notice. The court opinion does not address situations where the method of delivery of the notice is in compliance with the statute. It does not apply in such situations and, therefore, cannot be precedent in such cases.

If, however, the front door is not the "most public part of the residence," the method of delivery was not in compliance with the statute and the requirements of Step 1 are met: Both cases involve a landlord, tenant, and a notice of default that was improperly delivered. The difference in when the notice of default was received affects how the opinion applies, not whether it applies.

Step 2. Are the rules of law sufficiently similar for the court opinion to apply as precedent? If the front door is the "most public part of the residence," then the client's case does not involve the same rule of law as the court opinion, and the requirements of this step are not met. The question in this situation involves the late receipt of notice properly delivered and involves a different rule of law or statute.

If the front door is not the "most public part of the residence," then the client's case does involve the same rule of law as the court opinion, and the requirements of this step are met. Both the court opinion and the client's case involve the same statute.

3. **If the court opinion is on point, what will the probable decision be in regard to the question raised by the client's facts?**

Assuming the case is on point, that is, the method of delivery of the notice was in violation of the statute, the probable decision will be that the notice of default was not effective. In the court opinion, the court held that even if the method of delivery of the notice did not comply with the statute, if the tenant had actual notice and was not prejudiced, the notice was effective.

In the client's case, the client did not receive notice within the thirty days and, therefore, could be prejudiced by the improper notice. The client could be prejudiced because the court could enter an order of eviction for failure to respond to the notice of default within thirty days. Therefore, under the holding of the court opinion, the notice of default was not effective.

PART F

Instructor's note: The answer to this assignment is essentially the same as the answer to the first part of Part D.

1. Fact similarities and differences between the court opinion and the client's situation.

Similarities

- Both cases involve a landlord, tenant, and a notice of default that was improperly delivered.
- In the court opinion, the tenant received the notice the next day. In the client's case, the notice was received the next day.

Differences

- In the court opinion notice of default was placed in the tenant's mailbox. In the client's case the notice was delivered by regular mail.

2. Is the court opinion on point? Why or why not?

The case is probably on point because the requirements of the two-step process are met.

Step 1. Are the key facts sufficiently similar for the court opinion to apply as precedent? The court opinion and the client's case are sufficiently similar for the court opinion to apply as precedent. Both cases involve a landlord, tenant, and a notice of default that was improperly delivered. In both cases, the notice of default was received the next day.

The differences are probably not significant because in both the court opinion and the client's case the method of delivery of the notice of default was not in compliance with the requirements of the statute.

Step 2. Are the rules of law sufficiently similar for the court opinion to apply as precedent? The court opinion and the client's case involve the same statute and involve the same question under the statute: "Was the notice of default effective when it was improperly delivered, the client received actual notice, and was not prejudiced by the improper notice?"

3. If the court opinion is on point, what will the probable decision be in regard to the question raised by the client's facts?

Assuming the case is on point, the probable decision will be that the notice of default is effective. Regardless of how the notice of default was delivered, in both the court opinion and the client's case the notice was received the next day. The court ruled that although the method of delivery did not comply with the statute, the intent of the act was accomplished if the tenant received actual notice and was not prejudiced by the improper notice. Note that the tenant was not prejudiced in both the court opinion and the client's case because the notice was received within the thirty-day notice of default period. The client had an opportunity to respond within the thirty days and, therefore, was not subject to eviction for failure to respond within the thirty days.

Just as in the court opinion, the client received the notice the next day, and there are no additional facts presented which indicate that the client was prejudiced by the improper notice.

PART G

Instructor's note: Note that the answer to this assignment is similar to the answer to Part E. In both cases the method of the delivery of the notice of default was in compliance with the statute.

1. Fact similarities and differences between the court opinion and the client's situation.

Similarities

- Both cases involve a landlord, tenant, and a notice of default.

Differences

- In the court opinion, notice of default was placed in the tenant's mailbox. In the client's case, the notice of default was delivered by certified mail.

- In the court opinion, the tenant retrieved the notice the next day. In the client's case, the client refused to accept the notice.

2. **Is the court opinion on point? Why or why not?**

The court opinion is probably not on point because the requirements of Steps 1 and 2 are not met.

Step 1. Are the key facts sufficiently similar for the court opinion to apply as precedent? There is a critical difference between the key facts of the court opinion and the client's case that renders the court opinion not on point and therefore not usable as precedent. The statute provides that the "notice of default may be accomplished by delivery by certified mail, . . ." In the client's case, this method was adopted by the landlord; therefore, the method of delivery was proper. There is no requirement in the statute that the delivery be accepted. Therefore, in the client's case the method of delivery was proper, while in the court opinion the method of delivery was improper.

The court opinion addresses situations where the method of delivery of the notice of default does not comply with the statute, but the tenant receives actual notice and is not prejudiced by the improperly delivered notice. The court opinion does not address situations where the method of delivery of the notice is in compliance with the statute. It does not apply to situations such as the client's where the method of delivery is proper, and the opinion, therefore, cannot be precedent in such cases.

Step 2. Are the rules of law sufficiently similar for the court opinion to apply as precedent? The client's case does not involve the same rule of law as the court opinion; therefore, requirements of this step are not met. The question in this situation involves the refusal to accept a properly delivered notice of default and a different rule of law or statute applies.

3. **If the court opinion is on point, what will the probable decision be in regard to the question raised by the client's facts?**

Assuming the case is on point, that is, the method of delivery of the notice was in violation of the statute for some reason, it is difficult to determine what the probable decision would be. In the court opinion, the court held that even if the method of delivery of the notice did not comply with the statute, if the tenant had actual notice and was not prejudiced, the notice was effective.

In the client's case, the client did not receive actual notice because the client refused to accept it. Any prejudice that may have occurred was due to the act of the client. The court could rule that the prejudice was due to the client's actions and hold that the notice was, therefore, effective.

WEB ASSIGNMENT ANSWERS

ASSIGNMENT 1

EXAMPLE 1

The case is probably not on point because the requirements of the two-step process are not met.

STEP 1. ARE THE KEY FACTS SUFFICIENTLY SIMILAR FOR THE COURT OPINION TO APPLY AS PRECEDENT? There are few similarities between the court opinion and the client's case. Both the court opinion and the client's case involved false information that was defamatory and communicated to third persons. In *Cox v. Redd* the communication to third persons was unintentional; in the client's case it is not clear whether the conduct was unintentional. Although the client pulled the person to the side, he spoke loudly enough that others heard the communication. This may have been intentional.

The key fact difference that keeps the case from being on point is that in *Cox v. Redd* the information was written, not oral as in the client's case. This is a critical difference because the law governing written defamation may differ from the law governing oral defamation.

Although these fact differences may prevent the case from being on point, if the law governing written and oral defamation is substantially the same the court may look to *Cox* for guidance even though it is not directly on point. This is discussed in Step 2.

STEP 2. ARE THE RULES OF LAW SUFFICIENTLY SIMILAR FOR THE COURT OPINION TO APPLY AS PRECEDENT?

The statute that was applied and interpreted in *Cox* was a libel statute. The statute governs written defamation. The client's case involves oral defamation (slander). The state probably has a separate oral defamation statute. If that is the case, a different law applies and the case is **not on point.**

If the state has no case on point interpreting the slander statute and the slander statute is similar to the libel statute, then a court may look to *Cox* for guidance. This is especially so in light of the court's interpretation of "intentional publication" to mean "either the actual intent to publish or, where there is no intent to publish, reckless or grossly negligent conduct that results in publication." The client may have acted with gross negligence when he pulled the person to the side and spoke loudly enough for others to hear.

EXAMPLE 2

The case is on point because the requirements of the two-step process are met.

STEP 1. ARE THE KEY FACTS SUFFICIENTLY SIMILAR FOR THE COURT OPINION TO APPLY AS PRECEDENT?

The client's key facts are sufficiently similar to the key facts in *Cox v. Redd* for the case to be on point. Both cases involve defamatory statements that were written in a letter. In both cases the contents of the letter were communicated to a third person as a result of negligence. The fact that in one case the letter was unintentionally mailed and in the other case it was left on a dining room table is not a significant difference. The means by which third parties had access to the letter is not a key fact. The key fact is the nature of the conduct that caused the letter to fall into the hands of a third party.

The fact that the letter was published in a newspaper in the client's case is not a significant difference. The communication took place when it was delivered to the newspaper. The newspaper republished it. That republication may give rise to another lawsuit against the paper, but it does not affect the question of whether the client committed libel.

It could be argued that a key difference is that in *Cox* the conduct was gross negligence and in the client's case it was simple negligence. This difference does not keep the case from being on point; it just affects how the opinion applies, not whether it applies. This is discussed in Step 2.

STEP 2. ARE THE RULES OF LAW SUFFICIENTLY SIMILAR FOR THE COURT OPINION TO APPLY AS PRECEDENT?

Both *Cox* and the client's case involve the same statute and the same question: "Is a defamatory writing, communicated to a third person as a result of negligence, 'intentional publication' within the meaning of the statute?" The definition of "intentional publication" is at issue in both cases. Therefore, there is little question that *Cox* is on point in regard to Step 2. In the client's case the outcome may be different than that reached in *Cox* if the court determines that the client's conduct was not grossly negligent.

EXAMPLE 3

The case is on point because the requirements of the-two step process are met.

STEP 1. ARE THE KEY FACTS SUFFICIENTLY SIMILAR FOR THE COURT OPINION TO APPLY AS PRECEDENT.

The client's key facts are sufficiently similar to the key facts in *Cox v. Redd* for the case to be on point. Both cases involve defamatory statements that were written in a letter. In both cases the contents of the letter were communicated to a third person as the apparent result of negligence. The fact that in one case the letter was mailed and opened by the wrong party and in the other case it was left on a dining room table is not a significant difference. The means by which the third party had access to the letter is not a key fact. The key fact is the nature of the conduct that caused the letter to fall into the hands of a third party.

It could be argued that a key difference is that in *Cox* the conduct was gross negligence and in the client's case it was simple negligence. This difference does not keep the case from being on point; it just affects how the opinion applies, not whether it applies. This is discussed in Step 2. It could also be argued that the client was grossly negligent in mailing the letter to Alice when he knew her boyfriend occasionally opened Alice's mail. If that is the situation then the case is exactly like *Cox:* both cases involve grossly negligent conduct.

STEP 2. ARE THE RULES OF LAW SUFFICIENTLY SIMILAR FOR THE COURT OPINION TO APPLY AS PRECEDENT? Both *Cox* and the client's case involve the same statute and the same question: "Is a defamatory writing, communicated to a third person as a result of negligence, 'intentional publication' within the meaning of the statute?" The definition of "intentional publication" is at issue in both cases. Therefore, there is little question that *Cox* is on point in regard to Step 2. In the client's case the outcome may be different than that reached in *Cox* if the court determines that the client conduct was not grossly negligent.

ASSIGNMENT 2
EXAMPLE 1
The case is on point because the requirements of the two-step process are met.

STEP 1. ARE THE KEY FACTS SUFFICIENTLY SIMILAR FOR THE COURT OPINION TO APPLY AS PRECEDENT? The client's key facts are sufficiently similar to the key facts in *Melia v. Dillon Companies, Inc.* for the case to be on point. The facts in the client's case and *Melia* are almost identical. Both cases involve alleged shoplifting in a store. In both cases a customer left the store without paying for merchandise. In both cases a security person saw the customer leave without paying and stopped the person. In both cases the individuals stated that they intended to pay but forgot to pay for the merchandise. In both cases the person was held for shoplifting.

STEP 2. ARE THE RULES OF LAW SUFFICIENTLY SIMILAR FOR THE COURT OPINION TO APPLY AS PRECEDENT? Both cases involve the right of a merchant to detain a customer suspected of shoplifting. Both cases involve the question of whether false imprisonment occurs when a customer is detained to allow an investigation for shoplifting when the store has probable cause to believe that shoplifting has occurred. Therefore, there is little question that *Melia* is on point in regard to Step 2.

EXAMPLE 2
The case is on point because the requirements of the two-step process are met.

STEP 1. ARE THE KEY FACTS SUFFICIENTLY SIMILAR FOR THE COURT OPINION TO APPLY AS PRECEDENT? Although there are differences, the client's key facts are sufficiently similar to the key facts in *Melia v. Dillon Companies, Inc.* for the case to be on point. Both cases involve alleged shoplifting in a store. In both cases a security person saw a customer put an item in his or her pocket. In both cases the security person believed the customer left the store without paying for merchandise and stopped the person. In both cases the customer was detained for the purpose of determining whether shoplifting had taken place.

The major difference is that in the client's case the client put the merchandise back and the security guard mistakenly believed the client left without paying for it. This difference does not keep the case from being on point; it just affects how the opinion applies, not whether it applies. This is discussed in Step 2

STEP 2. ARE THE RULES OF LAW SUFFICIENTLY SIMILAR FOR THE COURT OPINION TO APPLY AS PRECEDENT? Both cases involve the right of a merchant to detain a customer suspected of shoplifting. Both cases involve the question of whether false imprisonment occurs when a customer is detained to allow an investigation for shoplifting when the store has probable cause to believe that shoplifting has occurred. Therefore, there is little question that *Melia* is on point in regard to Step 2.

The principle discussed in *Melia* is a merchant's right to detain a customer if the merchant has probable cause to believe the customer has left the store without paying for merchandise. The fact that the store was mistaken in its belief that the client had taken the merchandise goes to the question of probable cause. This affects how the opinion applies, not whether it applies. If it is determined that the store security officer, in failing to notice that the client returned the merchandise, acted without probable cause, the principle stated in *Melia* still applies and the case is on point. This is, the merchant did not have a right to detain the client because the merchant did not have probable cause to believe that the client had left the store without paying for the merchandise.

EXAMPLE 3

The case is not on point because the requirements of the two-step process are not met.

STEP 1. ARE THE KEY FACTS SUFFICIENTLY SIMILAR FOR THE COURT OPINION TO APPLY AS PRECEDENT?

The key facts of the client's key facts are not sufficiently similar to the key facts in *Melia v. Dillon Companies, Inc.* for the case to be on point. In *Melia* the officer saw the customer put something in his pocket and leave the store without paying for it. Therefore the officer had probable cause to detain the customer. In the client's case there are no facts indicating that the officer had probable cause to believe that the client had left the store without paying for merchandise. In the client's case the client was detained for 30 minutes before he was searched. In *Melia* no such detention took place; Mr. Melia had the merchandise when he left the store, and he was not detained for a period of time before he was searched.

STEP 2. ARE THE RULES OF LAW SUFFICIENTLY SIMILAR FOR THE COURT OPINION TO APPLY AS PRECEDENT?

Melia is not on point in regard to Step 2 because different issues are involved. Both cases involve the question of alleged shoplifting and the right of a merchant to detain a customer suspected of shoplifting. They differ in that *Melia* involved the question of whether false imprisonment occurs when a customer is detained to allow an investigation for shoplifting when the store has probable cause to believe that shoplifting has occurred. In the client's case there was no probable cause.

In addition there is a question in the client's case that is not addressed in *Melia*. In the client's case, the client was detained for 30 minutes before he was searched. This raises a question of whether he was detained for a reasonable period of time for the purpose of investigating the circumstances of the shoplifting. This question was not addressed in *Melia*.

TEST QUESTIONS AND ANSWERS

TRUE OR FALSE QUESTIONS

Please write a "T" or "F" to the left of each statement.

_____ 1. Case law analysis is the process of determining if a court opinion governs or affects the outcome of a client's case.

_____ 2. A key criterion for a court opinion to be on point is that the key and background facts of the opinion are sufficiently similar to the key and background facts of the client's case.

_____ 3. The terms *precedent* and *on point* are often used interchangeably.

_____ 4. The determination of whether a case is on point is important because of the doctrines of precedent and stare decisis.

_____ 5. The doctrine of precedent is a basic principle of the common-law system that requires a court to follow a previous decision of that court or a higher court in the jurisdiction when the current decision involves issues and key facts similar to those involved in the previous decision.

_____ 6. Stare decisis is an earlier court decision on an issue that governs or guides a subsequent court in its determination of an identical or similar issue based on identical or similar key facts.

_____ 7. A case is precedent (on point) if there is a sufficient similarity between the key facts and rule of law or legal principle of the court opinion and the matter before the subsequent court.

_____ 8. Persuasive precedent must be followed by the lower courts in the jurisdiction.

_____ 9. A ruling of the highest court in state B may be mandatory precedent for the lower courts in state A.

_____10. The determination of whether a case is on point *must* be made before the case may apply as precedent.

_____11. A case that is on point should be analyzed to help the attorney determine what course of action to take.

_____12. In order for a case to be on point, three requirements must be met.

_____13. In order for a case to be on point, the key and background facts of the court opinion must be sufficiently similar to the key and background facts of the client's case.

_____14. The phrase "on all fours" is used to describe opinions where the facts of the opinion and those of the client's case and the rule of law that applies are identical or so similar that the court opinion is clearly on point.

_____15. When the key facts of the court opinion and the key facts of the client's case are not similar, the court opinion may still be on point.

_____16. When the key facts of the court opinion and the key facts of the client's case are not similar, if the substitution of the key facts would not result in changing the outcome of the case, the court opinion can be used as precedent.

_____17. When there is a *major* difference in the key facts of a court opinion and the key facts of the client's case, the opinion cannot be on point.

_____18. If the rule or principle applied in the court opinion is the same rule or principle that applies in the client's case, the opinion is on point.

_____19. If the law applied in the court opinion is different from that which applies to the client's case, the court opinion cannot be mandatory precedent.

_____20. A court opinion interpreting a common-law rule or principle may apply as precedent for a client's case that requires the application of a different common-law rule or principle.

TRUE OR FALSE ANSWERS

Answer	Text Section	Answer	Text Section	Answer	Text Section
1. True	I	8. False	IIIC	15. True	IVA2
2. False	II	9. False	IIIB	16. True	IVA2
3. True	II	10. True	III	17. False	IVA2
4. True	III	11. True	III	18. False	IVB
5. False	IIIA	12. False	IV	19. True	IVB2
6. False	IIID	13. False	IV	20. True	IVB2
7. True	IIIA	14. True	IVA1		

Note: Number 18 is false—the key facts must also be sufficiently similar.

MULTIPLE CHOICE QUESTIONS

Please circle the letter of the **most appropriate** answer.

1. If a court opinion governs or affects the outcome of a client's case, it is referred to as:
   a. a key case.
   b. the lead case.
   c. being on point.
   d. the primary case.
   e. all of the above
   f. none of the above

2. A case is on point if:
   a. the key facts are sufficiently similar to the key facts of the client's case.
   b. the key and background facts are sufficiently similar to the key and background facts of the client's case.
   c. the rule of law of the court opinion is sufficiently similar to the rule of law of the client's case.
   d. the legal questions are the same.

   e. all of the above
   f. a and d
   g. a and c

3. The determination of whether a case is on point is important because of the doctrine(s) of:
   a. res judicata.
   b. precedent.
   c. stare decisis.
   d. finality.
   e. all of the above
   f. a, b, and c
   g. b and c

4. A court opinion that a court looks to for guidance when reaching a decision, but is not bound to follow, is referred to as:
   a. mandatory precedent.
   b. persuasive precedent.

c. stare decisis.
d. on point.
e. all of the above

5. A court opinion that a court is bound to follow when reaching a decision is referred to as:
   a. mandatory precedent.
   b. persuasive precedent.
   c. stare decisis.
   d. primary authority.
   e. all of the above
   f. a, c, and d

6. Precedent is:
   a. an earlier court decision on an issue that governs or guides a subsequent court in its determination of an identical or similar issue based on identical or similar key facts.
   b. a decision from a higher court in a jurisdiction.
   c. a decision that a court may look to for guidance when reaching a decision but is not bound to follow.
   d. a basic principle of the common-law system that requires a court to follow a previous decision of that court or a higher court in the jurisdiction when the current decision involves issues and key facts similar to those involved in the previous decision.
   e. all of the above

7. Stare decisis is:
   a. an earlier court decision on an issue that governs or guides a subsequent court in its determination of an identical or similar issue based on identical or similar key facts.
   b. a decision from a higher court in a jurisdiction.
   c. a decision that a court may look to for guidance when reaching a decision, but is not bound to follow.
   d. a basic principle of the common-law system that requires a court to follow a previous decision of that court or a higher court in the jurisdiction when the current decision involves issues and key facts similar to those involved in the previous decision.
   e. all of the above

8. It is important to determine if a case is on point because:
   a. statutory law requires case law for interpretation.
   b. cases that are on point need to be found to provide guidance as to how a client's case may be decided.

c. the hierarchy of the law requires the identification of cases on point.
d. statutory law, standing alone, is not sufficient to answer most legal questions.
e. all of the above
f. a, b, and c

9. For a case to be on point and apply as precedent:
   a. the significant or key facts of the court opinion must be sufficiently similar to the key facts of the client's case.
   b. if the facts are not similar, the rule of law or legal principle applied in the court opinion must be so broad that it applies to many diverse fact situations.
   c. the rule of law or legal principle applied in the court opinion must be the same or sufficiently similar to the rule of law or legal principle that applies in the client's case.
   d. the background and key facts of the court opinion must be sufficiently similar to the background and key facts of the client's case.
   e. all of the above
   f. a, b, and c
   g. b, c, and d

10. When the key facts of the court opinion and the key facts of the client's case are not identical, which of the following are parts of the process for determining if the opinion is on point:
    a. identify the similarities between the key facts
    b. identify the differences between the key facts
    c. identify the differences between the key and background facts
    d. identify the similarities between the key and background facts
    e. a and b
    f. b and c

11. Which of the following are variations that may be encountered when dealing with key facts?
    a. minor difference in key facts—case on point
    b. major difference in key facts—case not on point
    c. major difference in key facts—case on point
    d. major difference in key facts—case on point, broad legal principle
    e. all of the above
    f. a, b, and c

12. If the law applied in the court opinion is different from the law that applies to the client's case, the opinion can be:
   a. persuasive precedent.
   b. mandatory precedent.
   c. mandatory precedent if the key facts are sufficiently similar.
   d. persuasive precedent only if the statutes are part of the same legislative act.
   e. all of the above

13. A court opinion interpreting one legislative act may be used as precedent for a client's case that involves the application of a different legislative act when:
   a. the statutes are part of the same legislative act.
   b. there is a similarity in language between the legislative acts.
   c. there is a similarity in function between the legislative acts.
   d. the key facts are identical or nearly identical.
   e. all of the above
   f. b and c
   g. a, b, and c

14. A court opinion that applies a common-law rule or principle different from that which applies to a client's case may apply as precedent to a client's case when:
   a. there is a similarity in language between the common-law rules or principles.
   b. there is a similarity in function between the common law rules or principles.
   c. the key facts are identical or nearly identical.
   d. the court opinion is from the same jurisdiction as the client's case.
   e. all of the above
   f. a and b
   g. a, b, and c

15. A court opinion may apply as precedent when:
   a. there is a major difference in the key facts.
   b. there is a minor difference in the key facts.
   c. the rule or principle applied in the court opinion is the same rule or principle that applies in the client's case.
   d. the rule or principle applied in the court opinion is different from the rule or principle that applies in the client's case.
   e. all of the above
   f. a, c, and d

MULTIPLE CHOICE ANSWERS

Answer	Text Section	Answer	Text Section	Answer	Text Section
1. c	I	6. a	IIIA	11. e	IVA2
2. g	II	7. d	IIID	12. a	IVB2
3. g	III	8. b	III	13. f	IVB2
4. b	IIIB	9. f	IV	14. f	IVB2
5. a	IIIB	10. e	IVA2	15. e	IV

CHAPTER 13

Counteranalysis

TEXT ASSIGNMENT ANSWERS

ASSIGNMENT 1

Counteranalysis is an exploration of how and why a specific law does or does not apply to the facts of a case. It is the process of discovering and considering the counterargument to a legal position or argument; it is the process of anticipating the argument the opponent is likely to raise in response to the analysis of an issue.

Counteranalysis should be employed whenever legal research is conducted or the strengths and weaknesses of a case are considered; in other words, always.

ASSIGNMENT 2

Counteranalysis is important for several reasons:

1. As an officer of the court, an attorney has an ethical duty to disclose legal authority adverse to the position of the client that is not disclosed by the opposing counsel. Therefore, a paralegal, to properly inform the attorney, must locate and provide the attorney with all relevant authority, including that which is adverse to the client.
2. Both the attorney and paralegal have an ethical duty to do a complete and competent job. Research and analysis are not complete unless all sides of an issue and all legal arguments have been considered. Failure to completely analyze a problem can constitute malpractice.
3. Counteranalysis aids in the proper evaluation of the merits of a case and can assist in the selection of the appropriate course of action to follow.
4. It is important to locate and disclose adverse authority in order to maintain credibility with your supervisor. You may not be considered reliable, and the credibility of your research may be questioned if you ignore or fail to identify and disclose adverse authority.
5. When a legal brief is submitted to a court, if you identify and address adverse authority in the brief, you have an opportunity to soften its impact by discrediting or distinguishing it. You have an opportunity to provide reasons why the adverse authority does not apply, and your credibility is enhanced. The reader is allowed to consider the adverse authority in the context of your response to it. This opportunity is missed if you fail to include the adverse authority.

ASSIGNMENT 3

The statute relied on as a guide does not apply. The duties of a city council member are much different than the duties of a state senator. A state senator is engaged with a wide range of issues involving the entire state. A three-year residency requirement may be necessary to ensure that a candidate for the Senate has a sufficient familiarity with the state to perform the duties of the position. The duties of a member of the city council involve fewer issues and are not statewide in scope. Therefore, the differences in the requirements of the positions render § 359-23A inappropriate for use as a guide when interpreting § 2231.

ASSIGNMENT 4

Reliance on the court opinion is misplaced—key fact difference. Reliance on the court opinion is misplaced because the key facts in the opinion and the key facts of the client's case are different to such a degree that they render the court opinion unusable as precedent. In *Baldonado v. State,* the court held that the arresting officer had reasonable suspicion to believe that a crime had been committed and, therefore, the detention of the defendant was lawful. There were several facts that supported the reasonable suspicion. The officer had a description of the plaintiff's vehicle from the dispatcher. The officer saw the plaintiff in the described car. At the scene, the spouse and a neighbor corroborated the dispatcher's information that a violent dispute had taken place. The plaintiff attempted to leave when requested to stay at the scene.

In the present case, there are insufficient facts to support a reasonable suspicion that a crime had been committed. In *Baldonado,* the neighbor and the plaintiff's spouse corroborated the dispatcher's information that a violent dispute had taken place. In the present case, there was less corroboration: a neighbor stated he thought a domestic dispute had taken place. In *Baldonado,* the officer saw the plaintiff in the described car at the scene, the plaintiff was requested to stay, the plaintiff attempted to leave, and the officer stopped him from leaving. In the present case, the officer did not know the plaintiff was the party involved in the dispute: there was no specific description of the vehicle by the dispatcher, the neighbor described it only as a "red vehicle," and the officer did not find the plaintiff at the scene. Also, in the present case, the plaintiff was not ordered to stay and then attempted to leave. The facts are so different from those in *Baldonado v. State* that the case cannot be relied on as precedent to support the position that the detention was proper.

ASSIGNMENT 5

Seven ways to challenge an argument based on an enacted law are the following:

1. The elements of the statute are not met.
2. The statute is sufficiently broad to permit a construction or application different from that urged by the opposition.
3. The statute has been misconstrued or does not apply.
4. The statute relied upon as a guide to interpret another statute does not apply and, therefore, cannot be used as a guide in interpreting the other statute.
5. The statute relied on has not been adopted in your jurisdiction.
6. The interpretation of the statute urged by the opposition is unconstitutional or violates another legislative act.
7. The statute relied on is unconstitutional.

ASSIGNMENT 6

Seven ways to challenge an argument based on a court opinion are the following:

1. Reliance on the court opinion is misplaced because the key facts in the opinion and the key facts of the client's case are different to such a nature or degree that they render the court opinion unusable as precedent.
2. Reliance on the court opinion is misplaced because the rule of law or legal principle applied in the court opinion does not apply.
3. The court opinion is subject to an interpretation different from that relied upon in support of a legal position.
4. The rule or principle adopted in the opinion relied on is not universally followed.
5. The opinion relied on presents several possible solutions to the problem, and the one urged by the opposition is not mandatory and is not the best choice.
6. The position relied on no longer represents sound public policy and should not be followed.
7. There are other equally relevant cases that do not support the position adopted in the case relied on.

Instructor's note: When students are assigned Assignments 7 or 8, they should be instructed to present all counter-arguments that reasonably can be argued given the information included in the assignment.

In Assignment 7 there is no counterargument that the statute relied on has not been adopted in your jurisdiction because the facts state that the applicable statute is Section 40-3-6-9A of the state criminal code.

The fact that an argument is not likely to succeed, however, does not make it unreasonable.
Also, point out to students that, were this a real case, each counterargument would have to be supported by research.

In Part A of Assignment 7, it can be argued that the elements of the statute are not met because the father's actions did not constitute malice or concealment within the meaning of the statute. In a real case, this counterargument would have to be supported with statutory or case law.

ASSIGNMENT 7

Counteranalysis of a legal position or argument based on a statute.

Instructor's note: Of the seven counterarguments or counteranalysis approaches to a legal position based on a statute listed in the text, no facts are presented in this assignment which indicate that the following counterarguments are available:

1. The statute is sufficiently broad to permit a construction or application different from that urged by the opposition. The arguments and facts presented in the problems in this assignment do not raise questions involving potential multiple interpretations of the statute.
2. The statute is unconstitutional or the interpretation of the statute is unconstitutional or violates another act. The arguments and facts included in the problems do not raise questions that the statute is unconstitutional or violates another statute.
3. The statute relied upon as a guide to interpret another statute does not apply and, therefore, cannot be used as a guide in interpreting the other statute. There is only one statute mentioned in the assignment.
4. The statute relied on has not been adopted in your jurisdiction. The assignment includes a statute that has been adopted in the jurisdiction.

PART A

ARGUMENT: Tom's actions of taking his son for two months in the summer and failing to inform Mary of the son's location, failing to allow her to communicate with him, and his statement to Mary before he left with the son, "I'm going to punish you for the way you've treated me" constitute concealment within the meaning of the statute.

COUNTERARGUMENTS:
1. **The elements of the statute are not met for the following reasons:**
   a. Tom's failure to tell Mary her son's location and to allow her to communicate with him does not constitute concealment within the meaning of the statute. As used in the statute, the term *conceals* requires further acts of concealment by Tom in addition to his failure to tell Mary her son's location or to allow her to communicate with him.
   b. The statute requires that the noncustodial parent must act with malice. Tom's actions of failing to tell Mary her son's location, failing to allow her to communicate with him, and his statement, "I'm going to punish you for the way you've treated me" do not constitute malice within the meaning of the statute. Malice requires more egregious conduct than that included in the facts.

2. **The statute has been misconstrued or does not apply.**
   a. The statute is designed to prohibit a noncustodial parent from improperly interfering with the custodial rights of the custodial parent. In this case, Tom had legal custody of his son during the time in question. He was the custodial parent and, therefore, the statute does not apply.
   b. The statute has been misconstrued because none of Tom's acts interfered with Mary's custodial rights. Tom's actions took place while he had legal custody and in no way affected Mary's custodial rights.

PART B

ARGUMENT: Tom's actions of taking his son for two months in the summer and failing to inform Mary of the son's location, failing to allow her to communicate with him, and his statement to Mary before he left with the son, "Since you wouldn't allow me to communicate with him when you had custody, I'm going to do the same" constitute concealment within the meaning of the statute.

COUNTERARGUMENTS: The only difference between Part B and Part A is the nature of Tom's statement to Mary when he left with the son. Essentially, the same counterarguments presented in Part A apply to Part B.

1. **The elements of the statute are not met for the following reasons:**
   a. Tom's failure to tell Mary her son's location and to allow her to communicate with him does not constitute concealment within the meaning of the statute. As used in the statute the term *conceals* requires further acts of concealment by Tom in addition to his failure to tell Mary her son's location or to allow her to communicate with him.
   b. The statute requires that the noncustodial parent act with malice. Tom's actions of failing to tell Mary her son's location, failing to allow her to communicate with him, and his statement, "Since you wouldn't allow me to communicate with him when you had custody, I'm going to do the same," do not constitute malice within the meaning of the statute. Malice requires more egregious conduct than that stated in the facts.
2. **The statute has been misconstrued or does not apply.**
   a. The statute is designed to prohibit a noncustodial parent from improperly interfering with the custodial rights of the custodial parent. In this case, Tom had legal custody of his son during the time in question. He was the custodial parent; therefore, the statute does not apply.
   b. The statute has been misconstrued because none of Tom's acts interfered with Mary's custodial rights. Tom's actions took place while he had legal custody and in no way affected Mary's custodial rights.

PART C

ARGUMENT: Tom's actions of taking his son for two months in the summer and failing to inform Mary of the son's location and failing to allow her to communicate with him constitute concealment within the meaning of the statute.

COUNTERARGUMENTS: The only difference between Part C and Part A is that Tom said nothing when he left with his son. The absence of this fact makes it even less likely that the statute applies. Counterarguments similar to those presented in Part A apply in Part C.

1. **The elements of the statute are not met for the following reasons:**
   a. Tom's failure to tell Mary her son's location and to allow her to communicate with him does not constitute concealment within the meaning of the statute. As used in the statute, the term *conceals* requires further acts of concealment by Tom in addition to his failure to tell Mary her son's location or to allow her to communicate with him.
   b. The statute requires that the noncustodial parent act with malice. Tom's actions of failing to tell Mary her son's location and failing to allow her to communicate with him do not constitute malice within the meaning of the statute. Malice requires more egregious conduct than that stated in the facts.

2. **The statute has been misconstrued or does not apply.**
   a. The statute is designed to prohibit a noncustodial parent from improperly interfering with the custodial rights of the custodial parent. In this case, Tom had legal custody of his son during the time in question. He was the custodial parent; therefore, the statute does not apply.
   b. The statute has been misconstrued because none of Tom's acts interfered with Mary's custodial rights. Tom's actions took place while he had legal custody and in no way affected Mary's custodial rights.

PART D

ARGUMENT: Tom's action of returning his son one day late, after a two-month visitation period, constitutes failure to return the child without good cause for a protracted period of time within the meaning of the statute.

COUNTERARGUMENTS:

1. **The elements of the statute are not met for the following reasons:**
   a. Tom's return of his son one day late after a two-month visitation period does not constitute a "protracted period of time" within the meaning of the statute. A "protracted period of time" as used in the statute is significantly longer than one day.
   b. The statute requires that the noncustodial parent act with malice. Tom's actions of failing to tell Mary her son's location and returning him one day late do not constitute malice within the meaning of the statute. Malice requires more egregious conduct than that stated in the facts.
2. **The statute has been misconstrued or does not apply.**
   a. The statute is designed to prohibit a noncustodial parent from improperly interfering with the custodial rights of the custodial parent. Tom's act of detaining his son one day longer than the allowed two-month visitation period was an improper extension of his visitation rights that took place while he was the custodial parent. The statute applies to detentions by noncustodial parents. This case involves a detention by a custodial parent; therefore, the statute does not apply.

PART E

ARGUMENT: Tom's action of returning his son two weeks late after a two-month visitation period constitutes failure to return the child without good cause for a protracted period of time within the meaning of the statute.

COUNTERARGUMENTS: The only difference between Part D and Part E is that Tom failed to return his son for a longer period of time. Counterarguments similar to those presented in Part D apply in Part E.

1. **The elements of the statute are not met for the following reasons:**
   a. Tom's return of his son two weeks late after a two-month visitation period does not constitute a "protracted period of time" within the meaning of the statute. A "protracted period of time" as used in the statute is longer than two weeks.

Instructor's note: Two weeks is much longer than one day and more likely to constitute a "protracted period" within the meaning of the statute. As in all the problems of this assignment, statutory or case law would be needed to support the argument that two weeks is not a "protracted period."

   b. The statute requires that the noncustodial parent act with malice. Tom's actions of failing to tell Mary her son's location and returning him two weeks late do not constitute malice within the meaning of the statute. Malice requires more egregious conduct than that stated in the facts.
2. **The statute has been misconstrued or does not apply.**
   a. The statute is designed to prohibit a noncustodial parent from improperly interfering with the custodial rights of the custodial parent. Tom's act of detaining his son two weeks longer than the allowed two months was an improper extension of his visitation rights that took place while he was the custodial parent. The statute applies to detentions by noncustodial parents. This case involves a detention by a custodial parent; therefore, the statute does not apply.

PART F

ARGUMENT: Tom's action of returning the son two weeks late after a two-month period constitutes failure to return the child without good cause for a protracted period of time within the meaning of the statute.

COUNTERARGUMENTS: The only difference between Part E and Part F is that Tom has a reason for his failure to return his son for the two-week period. Counterarguments similar to those presented in Part E apply in Part F.

1. **The elements of the statute are not met for the following reasons:**
   a. Tom's return of his son two weeks late after a two-month visitation period does not constitute a "protracted period of time" within the meaning of the statute. A "protracted period of time" as used in the statute is longer than two weeks.

Instructor's note: As noted in the answer to Part E above, two weeks is much longer than one day and more likely to constitute a "protracted period" within the meaning of the statute. As in all the problems of this assignment, statutory or case law would be needed to support the argument that two weeks is not a "protracted period."

   b. The statute requires that the noncustodial parent act with malice. Tom's actions of failing to tell Mary her son's location and returning him two weeks late do not constitute malice within the meaning of the statute. Malice requires more egregious conduct than that stated in the facts.
   c. The statute provides that failure to return the child for a protracted period of time must be without good cause. In this case there is good cause. Tom failed to return his son because his car engine blew up and it took two weeks to fix.
2. **The statute has been misconstrued or does not apply.**
   a. The statute is designed to prohibit a noncustodial parent from improperly interfering with the custodial rights of the custodial parent. Tom's act of detaining his son two weeks longer than the allowed two months was an improper extension of his visitation rights that took place while he was the custodial parent. The statute applies to detentions by noncustodial parents. This case involves a detention by a custodial parent; therefore, the statute does not apply.

SUGGESTED ASSIGNMENT: For each of the parts of this assignment, have the students locate your state law governing custodial interference and answer the questions using that law in lieu of the statute presented in this assignment.

ASSIGNMENT 8

Instructor's note: Of the seven counterarguments or counteranalysis approaches to a legal position based on a court opinion listed in the text, no facts are presented in this assignment which indicate that the following counterarguments are available:

1. Reliance on the court opinion is misplaced because the key facts in the opinion and the key facts of the client's case are different to such a nature or degree that they render the court opinion unusable as precedent. The differences between the key facts of *United States v. Leon* and the fact situation presented in the assignment **affect how the rule of law from the case applies as precedent, not whether it applies.**
2. The court opinion is subject to an interpretation different from that relied upon in support of a legal position. The facts do not raise the question of multiple interpretations of *United States v. Leon*.
3. The opinion relied on presents several possible solutions to the problem, and the one urged by the opposition is not mandatory and is not the best choice. *United States v. Leon* does not present several possible solutions to the problem.
4. There are other equally relevant cases that do not support the position adopted in the case relied on. The problem states that the only court opinion on point is *United States v. Leon*.

PART A

ARGUMENT: The officers executing the warrant were acting in good faith, and the good-faith exception to the exclusionary rule applies—and, therefore, the evidence should not be suppressed.

COUNTERARGUMENTS:

1. **Reliance on *United States v. Leon* is misplaced because the good-faith exception to the exclusionary rule adopted in United States v. Leon does not apply in this case.** The good-faith exception to the exclusionary rule requires that the officers executing the warrant act in the good-faith belief that the warrant is valid.

   In *Leon,* the court emphasized the fact that the error was committed by the magistrate and not the law enforcement officers. In our case, a law enforcement officer was aware the warrant was defective. Officer Jones knew that there was not sufficient probable cause for the issuance of the warrant; therefore, he knew or should have known that the warrant was not valid. His failure to inform the officers executing the warrant that the warrant was defective was an act of bad faith. Although the officers who executed the warrant acted in good faith, the officer who assigned them the task of executing the warrant did not act in good faith. Therefore, the execution was tainted by the bad faith of one of the officers involved in the execution of the warrant, and the good-faith exception does not apply.

2. **The good-faith exception to the exclusionary rule has not been adopted in this state, it has not been universally adopted by the states, and it should not be adopted or followed in this state.** This argument is only available if the law enforcement officers are state officers executing a state search warrant. If the officers are executing a federal warrant, then *United States v. Leon* is mandatory precedent, it must be followed, and this counterargument is not available.

   United States v. Leon is a federal case involving federal law and the execution of a federal search warrant. It is not mandatory precedent in cases involving state officers executing state warrants. Therefore, the argument can be made that the rule adopted in the case should not be adopted by the state court. As noted in the facts, there is no other court opinion on point; therefore, it must be assumed the state court has not addressed the question of a good-faith exception to the exclusionary rule or already adopted the position taken in *United States v. Leon.*

Instructor's note: Students should be informed that, when making this counterargument, they must present reasons why the court should not follow the persuasive precedent. The dissent in *United States v. Leon* and several law review articles present arguments why the opinion should not be followed.

3. **The good-faith exception to the exclusionary rule adopted in *United States v. Leon* does not represent sound public policy and should not be followed.** This counterargument, in effect, is a request to the court to overrule the decision in *Leon,* if this is a federal warrant. This counterargument, therefore, would be available only to the court that issued the opinion because a lower court does not have the power to overturn the decision of a higher court. In this case, the opinion was rendered by the United States Supreme Court, and any request to overturn the decision would have to be presented to that court.

PART B

ARGUMENT: The individuals executing the warrant were not law enforcement officers and according to *Leon* the exclusionary rule is designed only to protect against police misconduct, not misconduct by private citizens. The evidence, therefore, should not be suppressed.

COUNTERARGUMENTS: The counterarguments to the argument in Part B are similar to those presented in Part A.

1. **Reliance on *United States v. Leon* is misplaced because the good-faith exception to the exclusionary rule adopted in *United States v. Leon* does not apply in this case.** But, the exclusionary rule does apply.

   Although a law enforcement officer did not actually execute the warrant, an officer was involved in its execution because Officer Jones delivered the warrant to those who executed it. The private citizens who executed the warrant were trained by the police, were acting at the request of the law enforcement officers, and, therefore, for the purpose of the exclusionary rule were agents of law enforcement and not private citizens. Therefore, the exclusionary rule does apply.

The good-faith exception to the exclusionary rule requires that the officers executing the warrant act in the good-faith belief that the warrant is valid. In *Leon,* the court emphasized the fact that the error was that of the magistrate and not that of law enforcement officers. In our case, a law enforcement officer was aware the warrant was defective. Officer Jones was involved in the execution of the warrant as mentioned above. He knew there was not sufficient probable cause for the issuance of the warrant; therefore, he knew or should have known that the warrant was not valid. His failure to inform those executing the warrant that the warrant was defective was an act of bad faith.

Although the individuals who executed the warrant acted in good faith, the officer who delivered the warrant to them did not act in good faith. Therefore, the execution was tainted by the bad faith of one of the officers involved in its execution and the good-faith exception does not apply.

Instructor's note: In addition to the counterargument presented above that the exclusionary rule does apply, but the good-faith exception does not apply, students should also present counterarguments similar to those presented in Numbers 2 and 3 of Part A above. These arguments address why the good-faith exception presented in *United States v. Leon* should not be adopted or applied.

2. **The good-faith exception to the exclusionary rule has not been adopted in this states, it has not been universally adopted by the states, and it should not be adopted or followed in this state.** This argument is only available if Officer Jones was a state law enforcement officer and the warrant is a state search warrant. If Officer Jones was a federal officer and the warrant was a federal search warrant, then *United States v. Leon* is mandatory precedent, it must be followed, and this counterargument is not available.

   United States v. Leon is a federal case involving federal law and the execution of a federal search warrant. It is not mandatory precedent in cases involving state officers and state warrants. Therefore, the argument can be made that the rule adopted in the case should not be adopted by the state court. As noted in the facts, there is no other court opinion on point; therefore, it must be assumed the state court has not addressed the question of a good-faith exception to the exclusionary rule or already adopted the position taken in *United States v. Leon.*

Instructor's note: Students should be informed that, when making this counterargument, they must present reasons why the court should not follow the persuasive precedent. The dissent in *United States v. Leon* and several law review articles present arguments why the opinion should not be followed.

3. **The good-faith exception to the exclusionary rule adopted in *United States v. Leon* does not represent sound public policy and should not be followed.** This counterargument, in effect, is a request to the court to overrule the decision in *Leon,* if this is a federal warrant. This counterargument, therefore, would be available only to the court that entered the opinion. In this case, the opinion was rendered by the United States Supreme Court and any request to overturn the decision would have to be presented to that court.

ASSIGNMENT 9

Instructor's note: It must be assumed for the purposes of this assignment that the allegations contained in the letter are false. If they are true, an essential element of the statute is missing and Allen does not have a claim for defamation.

PART A

ARGUMENT IN SUPPORT OF THE POSITION THAT TOM DEFAMED ALLEN. Section 41-1-6-9 defines defamation as the intentional publication of a false statement about a person. The statute has been violated by the following acts committed by Tom:

1. The letter contains false statements concerning Allen.
2. The false statements were published. The statute defines publication as communication to a third person. The statements were communicated to the friend, a third person, when Tom gave the letter to the friend.

3. The statute requires that the publication be intentional. Tom's actions were intentional within the meaning of the law.

In the case of *Ender v. Gault,* the court ruled that intentional publication as used in the statute "includes publication that occurs as a result of the gross negligence of the defendant." In that case, the defendant's act of leaving an envelope containing defamatory statements unsealed on the kitchen table, during a party at the plaintiff's house, constituted gross negligence. In the case, a third party opened and read the letter.

The case of *Ender v. Gault* is on point. In both *Gault* and the client's case, the defendants unintentionally allowed a letter to be opened by third party. In both cases, the conduct was careless and negligent and resulted in the publication of the false statements. Tom's act of leaving the letter in the hands of a third party and failing to instruct the party not to open it constituted gross negligence that resulted in the publication of the defamatory statements. Therefore, Tom's actions were intentional within the meaning of the statute.

PART B

COUNTERARGUMENT TO THE ARGUMENT PRESENTED IN PART A THAT TOM DEFAMED ALLEN. It is conceded that the statements were false and communicated to a third party. Tom's actions, however, did not constitute gross negligence and, therefore, were not intentional within the meaning of the statute. There are significant differences between the facts of *Ender v. Gault* and the present case.

In *Gault,* the letter was unsealed and left at a place accessible to several individuals, an open invitation to be read. Gault's actions were clearly grossly negligent as the court stated. In the present case, the letter was sealed with tape and delivered to a friend of Allen with the specific instruction to deliver it to Allen.

These were not grossly negligent acts like the acts in *Gault.* The letter was not open like the letter in *Gault;* it was not left in a place for anyone to read it like in *Gault.* It was reasonable to assume that a friend of Allen would not open a letter directed to Allen that was sealed with tape. One would assume that an instruction not to open the letter was not necessary. Therefore, the holding in *Ender v. Gault* does not support an argument that Tom's actions were grossly negligent and, therefore, intentional within the meaning of the statute.

SUGGESTED ASSIGNMENT: Have the students locate your state law governing defamation and perform the assignment using that law rather than the law presented in this assignment. In many states defamation is governed by common law and there are no defamation statutes. If that is the case in your state, have the students locate the appropriate court opinion(s) and perform the assignment using those opinion(s).

WEB ASSIGNMENT ANSWERS

Instructor's note: When students are performing these assignments, they should be instructed to present all counterarguments that reasonably can be argued given the information included in the assignment.

In Assignment 1 there is no counterargument that the statute relied on has not been adopted in your jurisdiction because the facts state that the applicable statute is Section 51-2-314 of the state criminal code.

The fact that an argument is not likely to succeed, however, does not make it unreasonable.

Also, point out to students that, were this a real case, each counterargument would have to be supported by research.

In Assignment 1, it can be argued that the elements of the statute are not met because Mary is not a merchant within the meaning of the statute. In a real case this counterargument would have to be supported with case law.

ASSIGNMENT 1

1. **The statute has been misconstrued or does not apply.** The statute is designed to govern sales by places of business such as furniture stores. It does not apply to sales that take place at nonbusiness entities such as flea markets.
2. **The elements of the statute are not met.** The statute applies to the sale of goods by merchants and Mary is not a merchant within the meaning of the statute. Sales that take place only twice a month are not sufficient to make an individual a merchant under § 51-2-314.

ASSIGNMENT 2

RELIANCE ON THE COURT OPINION IS MISPLACED—KEY FACT DIFFERENCE. Reliance on the court opinion is misplaced because the key facts in the opinion and the key facts of the client's case are different to such a degree that they render the court opinion unusable as precedent. In *Stewart v. Echo Gas* the court allowed punitive damages because the negligence of the defendant in releasing the vehicle *knowing* it was unsafe and the failure to file the safety checklist amounted to wanton and reckless conduct. The defendant's conduct was wanton and reckless because he acted with knowledge: He released the vehicle knowing it was unsafe and he failed to file the safety check list. In the present case there are no facts indicating that the defendant acted knowingly. There are no facts that the defendant knowingly installed the pole in an improper manner or knowingly failed to inspect and maintain the pole, therefore *Stewart v. Echo Gas* may not be relied upon as precedent.

ASSIGNMENT 3

1. **Reliance on the court opinion is misplaced—Key fact difference.** Reliance on the court opinion is misplaced because the key facts in the opinion and the key facts of the client's case are different to such a degree that they render the court opinion unusable as precedent. In *State v. Wilson* the court refused to grant access to the records after a review of *all* the records and a determination that the files revealed no information favorable to the defense. The *in-camera* review protected the defendant's interest. In the present case, since only half the records were reviewed, the court could not determine whether the files contained information favorable to the defense. *State v. Wilson* does not stand for the proposition that a review of half of the records protects the defendant's interests and therefore it cannot be relied upon as precedent.
2. **Court opinion is subject to a different interpretation.** This is a variation of the first counterargument. If the prosecution is relying on *State v. Wilson,* it is in effect saying that the case stands for the proposition that an *in-camera* review of half of the records protects a defendant's interest in obtaining access to information that would assist the defense. A different interpretation would be that *Wilson* requires a review of all the records to determine if there is any information that would assist the defense. In *Wilson* all the records were reviewed. How could a court know whether there was information that would assist the defense unless all the records were reviewed? Therefore, the prosecution has misinterpreted *Wilson,* and it cannot be relied on as precedent for the prosecution's position.

TEST QUESTIONS AND ANSWERS

TRUE OR FALSE QUESTIONS

Please write a "T" or "F" to the left of each statement.

_____ 1. To determine the strength of a client's case it is necessary to analyze the strength of the opponent's case.

_____ 2. In essence, counteranalysis is the process of discovering and considering the counterargument to a legal position or argument.

_____ 3. Counterargument is an objective evaluation of the strengths and weaknesses of a legal argument.

_____ 4. Under the American Bar Association's Model Rules of Professional Conduct, an attorney has an ethical duty to disclose legal authority adverse to the position of the client that is not disclosed by the opposing counsel.

_____ 5. Under the American Bar Association's Model Rules of Professional Conduct, research and analysis may be complete even though all the legal arguments regarding an issue may not have been explored.

_____ 6. Counteranalysis should be employed in every situation when legal research is conducted.

_____ 7. One way to challenge or attack a legal position or argument based on a court opinion is to show that facts are not present to support each element of the cause of action.

_____ 8. One way to challenge or attack a legal position or argument based on a statute is to show that the statute is not sufficiently broad to permit a construction different from that urged.

_____ 9. A way to challenge or attack a legal position or argument based on a statute is to show that the statute has been misconstrued.

_____10. One way to challenge or attack a legal position or argument based on a statute is to show that the statute relied on as a guide is so functionally different that it cannot be used as a guide to interpret the statute being analyzed.

_____11. One way to challenge or attack a legal position or argument based on a statute is to show that the statute has not been adopted by any other jurisdiction.

_____12. One way to challenge or attack a legal position or argument based on a court opinion is to show that the court opinion relied on violates another legislative act.

_____13. One way to challenge or attack a legal position or argument based on a court opinion is to show that the opinion relied on is not on point because of key fact differences between the opinion and the client's case.

_____14. One way to challenge or attack a legal position or argument based on a court opinion is to show that the opinion relied on is not subject to an interpretation different from the one relied on.

_____15. One way to challenge or attack a legal position or argument based on a court opinion is to show that the opinion relied on is not mandatory precedent and another court opinion allows for other possible positions.

_____16. One way to challenge or attack a legal position or argument based on a court opinion is to show that the court opinion relied on no longer represents sound public policy and, therefore, should not be followed.

_____17. The circumstances of each case will determine which counteranalysis technique(s) to use.

_____18. In a court brief, counteranalysis should be presented at the end of the analysis.

_____19. In an interoffice research memorandum, counteranalysis should be placed after the analysis of each issue.

_____20. When conducting counteranalysis, consider all possible counterarguments, no matter how ridiculous.

TRUE OR FALSE ANSWERS

Answer	Text Section	Answer	Text Section	Answer	Text Section
1. True	I	8. False	VB2	15. True	VC5
2. True	II	9. True	VA3	16. True	VC6
3. False	II	10. True	VB4	17. True	VI
4. True	III	11. False	VB5	18. False	VIIA
5. False	III	12. False	VB6	19. True	VIIB
6. True	IV	13. True	VC1	20. True	VIII
7. False	VB1	14. False	VC3		

Note re. No. 3: Counteranalysis is the objective evaluation of the strengths and weaknesses of a legal argument; counterargument is the opposing argument.

MULTIPLE CHOICE QUESTIONS

Please circle the letter of the **most appropriate** answer.

1. Counteranalysis:
   a. is an exploration of how and why a specific law does or does not apply to the facts of a case.
   b. is the process of anticipating the argument the opponent is likely to raise in response to your analysis of an issue.
   c. is the process of discovering and considering the counterargument to a legal position or argument.
   d. is the same as counterargument.
   e. all of the above
   f. a, b, and c

2. Counteranalysis is important because:
   a. an attorney has an ethical duty to disclose legal authority adverse to the position of the client that is not disclosed by the opposing counsel.
   b. research and analysis are not complete unless all sides of an issue and all legal arguments have been considered.
   c. it is important to locate and disclose adverse authority in order to maintain credibility with your supervisor.
   d. when a legal brief is submitted to a court, if you identify and address adverse authority in the brief, you have an opportunity to soften its impact by discrediting or distinguishing it.
   e. all of the above
   f. a, b, and c
   g. a, b, and d

3. Counteranalysis should be conducted:
   a. whenever the strengths and weakness of a case are being considered.
   b. when preparing an interoffice legal research memorandum.
   c. when you are just thinking about the legal issues in a case.
   d. whenever legal interviews are being conducted.
   e. all of the above
   f. a, b, and c
   g. a and b

4. Which of the following are ways to challenge or attack a legal position or argument based on a statute?
   a. The elements of the statute are not met.
   b. The key facts of the client's case and the facts required by the statute are not sufficiently similar.
   c. The statute is not sufficiently broad to allow an interpretation other than the one relied on.

d. The case relied on to interpret the statute is on point.
   e. all of the above
   f. a, b, and c
   g. b and d

5. Which of the following are ways to challenge or attack a legal position or argument based on a statute?
   a. The statute relied on as a guide does not apply.
   b. The statute is sufficiently broad to allow another interpretation.
   c. The statute has been misconstrued.
   d. The statute has been misapplied.
   e. all of the above
   f. a, b, and c
   g. b, c, and d

6. Which of the following are ways to challenge or attack a legal position or argument based on a statute?
   a. The statute relied on as a guide is so functionally different that it cannot be used as a guide to interpret the statute being analyzed.
   b. The statute relied on has not been adopted in the jurisdiction.
   c. The case relied on to interpret the statute is persuasive authority.
   d. The interpretation of the statute urged by the opposition violates another legislative act.
   e. all of the above
   f. a, b, and c
   g. a, b, and d

7. Which of the following are ways to challenge or attack a legal position or argument based on a court opinion?
   a. The opinion is not on point because of key fact differences.
   b. Reliance on the opinion is misplaced because the principle applied does not apply to the case at hand.
   c. The court opinion is not subject to a different interpretation.
   d. The court opinion is universally followed.
   e. all of the above
   f. a and b
   g. a, b, and d

8. Which of the following are ways to challenge or attack a legal position or argument based on a court opinion?
   a. The statute interpreted in the case does not function differently from the statute in the client's case.
   b. The statute interpreted in the case has been adopted in the jurisdiction.
   c. The statute interpreted in the case does not conflict with a legislative act.
   d. all of the above
   e. a and b
   f. none of the above

9. Which of the following are ways to challenge or attack a legal position or argument based on a court opinion?
   a. The opinion relied on is mandatory precedent.
   b. The opinion relied on allows for other possible solutions.

   c. There are equally relevant cases that do not support the position adopted in the case relied on.
   d. The court opinion relied on no longer represents sound public policy.
   e. a and d
   f. a, b, and c
   g. b, c, and d

10. Counteranalysis is placed:
   a. in the middle of the analysis section of a court brief.
   b. at the beginning of the analysis section of a court brief.
   c. at the beginning of the analysis of each issue in an interoffice research memorandum.
   d. at the end of the analysis of each issue in an interoffice research memorandum.
   e. a and d
   f. b and c
   g. a and c

MULTIPLE CHOICE ANSWERS

Answer	Text Section	Answer	Text Section	Answer	Text Section
1. f	II	5. e	VB	8. f	VC
2. e	III	6. g	VB	9. g	VC
3. f	IV	7. f	VC	10. e	VII
4. a	VB				

CHAPTER 14

Fundamentals of Writing

TEXT ASSIGNMENT ANSWERS

ASSIGNMENT 1

The essential, or actually the minimal, requirements of a well-crafted sentence are a subject and a predicate. In its simplest form, a sentence requires a noun and a verb.

ASSIGNMENT 2

The elements of a well-crafted paragraph are the following:

- a topic sentence,
- the body, and
- a closing sentence.

Each of these elements is not always required in every paragraph. A short paragraph, for example, may not have a closing sentence.

TOPIC SENTENCE. The topic sentence identifies the subject of the paragraph. It introduces the subject and provides the focus of the paragraph. The topic sentence is usually placed at the beginning of the paragraph.

BODY. The body of a paragraph is composed of a sentence or sentences which support or develop the subject introduced by the topic sentence. The sentence(s) should develop the subject clearly and in a logical manner.

CLOSING SENTENCE. A paragraph should end with a closing sentence. The content of the sentence varies according to the subject matter covered in the paragraph. The closing sentence should sum up the topic addressed in the body or apply the subject discussed to the facts of the case.

ASSIGNMENT 3

The difference between active and passive voices is when active voice is used, the subject of the sentence performs the action; when passive voice is used, the subject of the sentence is acted upon.

FOR EXAMPLE   *Active Voice*—The child hit the ball. *Passive Voice*—The ball was hit by the child.

ASSIGNMENT 4

- **Passive Voice**—"The defendant was attacked by the plaintiff at the beginning of the argument."
  Active Voice—"The plaintiff attacked the defendant at the beginning of the argument."
- **Passive Voice**—"It is a requirement of good writing skills that active voice be used."
  Active Voice—"Good writing skills require the use of active voice."

- **Passive Voice**—"Payment must be made by Mr. Smith no later than May 15, 1997."
  Active Voice—"Mr. Smith must make payment no later than May 15, 1997."

ASSIGNMENT 5

A nominalization is a noun created from a verb. Some examples of nominalizations are the following:

Verb	Noun (Nominalization)
determine	determination
realize	realization
possess	possession
important	importance

ASSIGNMENT 6

Legalese refers to terms of art used in the legal profession that are not generally known outside the profession. When a writing is addressed to a lay person, the use of legalese should be avoided or kept to a minimum.

The following are examples of legalese; the legalese is in bold:

"The constitution requires **probable cause** before the police can conduct a search of your residence."

"I **bequeath and devise** my property to my daughter."

"The **aforesaid** party of the first part shall . . ."

ASSIGNMENT 7

The sentence using nonsexist language follows the sentence using sexist language. The changes are in bold.

- "A paralegal may draft a letter to the client informing him of an upcoming hearing." "A paralegal may draft a letter to **the client** informing the client of an upcoming hearing."
- "The lawyer must file his response within thirty days."
  "The lawyer must file **a** response within thirty days."
- "The chairman of the committee conducted a private hearing."
  "The **chairperson** of the committee conducted a private hearing."
- "Each person must bring his records to the conference."
  "Each person must bring **that person's** records to the conference."
- "Everyone must bring his records to the hearing."
  "Everyone must bring **their** records to the hearing."

ASSIGNMENT 8

The proper use of *shall/may, and/or,* and *that/which* is as follows:

- The word **shall** is used to impose a duty that is mandatory. The performance of the duty is not optional.
  The word **may** indicates that the performance of an act is not mandatory. The performance of the act is optional.
- When the word **and** is used in a list of words, all the items listed are included; all are required.
  When **or** is used, all the items listed are not required to be included. Any one or all of the items are included.
  The use of **and/or** creates an ambiguity and is not proper.
- **That** is used to introduce restrictive clauses and **which** is used to introduce nonrestrictive clauses.
  A restrictive clause is a clause that is necessary to the meaning of the sentence.
  A nonrestrictive clause is a clause that is not necessary to the meaning of the sentence.

ASSIGNMENT 9

The following are the basic rules concerning subject-verb agreement, proper verb tense, and noun/pronoun agreement.

SUBJECT-VERB AGREEMENT: The subject and verb should agree in person and number. This means that singular subjects require singular verbs and plural subjects require plural verbs.

The following are some basic rules concerning subject-verb agreement:

1. Two or more subjects joined by *and* usually require a plural verb.
2. Two or more subjects joined by *or* or *nor* require a verb that agrees with the subject closest to the verb.
3. Most indefinite pronouns require singular verbs. Indefinite pronouns are pronouns that do not refer to a specific person or thing, such as *anyone, everybody, nobody, someone, each, something.*
4. Some indefinite pronouns require a verb that matches the noun to which they refer. Some of these pronouns are *all, none, most, some, any,* etc.
5. Collective nouns usually require a singular verb. A collective noun is a noun that refers to a group: *jury, family, crowd, majority,* etc.
6. Nouns that are plural in form but have a singular meaning require a singular verb: *politics, news,* etc.
7. The title of a work takes a singular verb.
8. A relative pronoun requires a verb that agrees with its antecedent. A relative pronoun is a pronoun that refers to another noun in the sentence. *Which, who,* and *that* are examples of relative pronouns. The noun the relative pronoun refers to is called the *antecedent.*

   If the antecedent is singular, the verb should be singular. If the antecedent is plural, the verb should be plural.

VERB TENSE: Verb tense is the time in which a verb's action occurs. Events happening in the present use the present tense; events that occurred in the past use past tense; events that will take place in the future use future tense. Usually sentences and paragraphs are written in the same tense.

The following are some basic guidelines concerning correct verb tense:

1. When presenting your position or legal analysis, use present tense.
2. When addressing a court opinion that has already been decided, use past tense.
3. When discussing a law or rule still in effect, use the present tense.

NOUN-PRONOUN AGREEMENT: Pronouns must agree in number (singular/plural) and gender (feminine/masculine/neuter) with the nouns they refer to, their antecedents. A list of pronouns follows: *I, me, mine, my, we, us, our, ours, you, yours, your, he, him, his, she, her, hers, it, its, they, them, their,* and *theirs.*

There are several guidelines to follow to ensure noun-pronoun agreement.

1. Pronouns must agree with their antecedents. The noun the pronoun refers to is the antecedent.
2. Pronouns that do not refer to a definite person or thing are indefinite pronouns. Indefinite pronouns are usually singular.
3. Antecedents joined by *and* require a plural pronoun.
4. Antecedents joined by *or* or *nor* require a pronoun that agrees in number and gender with the antecedent closest to the pronoun.
5. The number of a pronoun that refers to a collective noun is determined by the function of the collective noun. A collective noun is a noun that refers to a group. If the collective noun functions as a unit, the pronoun is singular.

   If the collective noun does not function as a unit, that is, the members of the collective noun are acting separately and not as a unit, a plural pronoun is required.

ASSIGNMENT 10

Parallel construction means that the items listed are similar in grammatical structure. When a sentence includes a list, group of activities, etc., each of the items must use the same grammatical form; that is, all the items or members of the group should agree in verb tense, number, etc.

ASSIGNMENT 11

A squinting modifier is a modifier located in a position in the sentence that makes it unclear whether it modifies the word that proceeds it or the word that follows it. The following are some examples of squinting modifiers:

"The report that was prepared routinely indicated that the structure was unsafe." (Was the report prepared routinely or did it routinely indicate that the structure was unsafe?)

"Tom stated that he would only lend his cousin cash." (Would Tom lend cash only to his cousin and no one else, or would Tom lend only cash to his cousin?)

"The attorney stated to his client that he would have to pay more attention to the case." (Who would have to pay more attention to the case, the attorney or the client?)

ASSIGNMENT 12

The rules concerning the proper use of commas, colons, semicolons, and apostrophes are as follows:

COMMA: The function of a comma is to separate the parts of a sentence. Some basic rules that apply to commas are the following:

1. Use a comma before a conjunction that joins two main or independent clauses.
2. Set off introductory phrases or clauses with a comma.
3. Use a comma after each item in a series of three or more items, and place a comma before *and* or *or* at the end of the series.
4. Use a comma to avoid a misreading of the subject.
5. Separate coordinate adjectives with a comma. Coordinate adjectives independently modify the same noun. The sequence of coordinating adjectives can be changed without affecting the meaning of the sentence.
6. Set off transitional or interpretive words or phrases with a comma.
7. Set off nonrestrictive clauses with a comma. A nonrestrictive clause is a clause that is not necessary to the meaning of the sentence.
8. Use a comma to set off appositives. Appositives are words that identify or further describe another word.
9. Set off contrasting phrases with a comma or commas.
10. Use commas when required to set off quotations.
11. Place a comma inside the closing quotation, not outside the quotation.
12. Place a comma before and after descriptive titles such as M.D., Ph.D., Esq., etc.
13. Do not use a comma before a parenthesis.
14. Do not use a comma after short prepositional phrases. A prepositional phrase is a phrase consisting of, at a minimum, a preposition and a noun that is the object of the preposition. A short prepositional phrase does not require a comma.

COLON: You should use a colon when you want to introduce or call attention to information that follows, such as lists, conclusions, explanations, quotations, etc. The function of a colon is to introduce what follows. It must be preceded by a main clause that is grammatically complete, that is, a complete sentence.

SEMICOLON: A semicolon is used primarily in two situations:

1. To separate major elements of complex sentences
2. To separate items in a series if the items are long or if one of the items has internal commas

In regard to these situations note the following rules:

1. Use a semicolon to separate main or independent clauses in a sentence that are not joined by a coordinating conjunction. Both main and independent clauses have a subject and a verb. Each could be a separate sentence. A conjunction is a word that is used to connect words, phrases, etc. A coordinating conjunction, such as *and, but,* and *or,* is a conjunction that connects like elements.

2. Use a semicolon when independent clauses are joined by a conjunctive adverb. Some examples of conjunctive adverbs are the following: *therefore, however, furthermore, consequently, likewise, nevertheless,* etc.

3. When a series of items is long or commas are already used in some of the items in the series, use a semicolon to separate the items.

APOSTROPHE: An apostrophe serves to indicate possession or to form a contraction. Some of the basic rules governing the use of apostrophes to indicate possession are the following:

1. Make singular nouns possessive by adding an apostrophe and an *s*. Singular nouns ending in *s* take an apostrophe and an *s* just like any other singular noun.

2. Make plural nouns possessive by adding an apostrophe after the *s*.

3. Use an apostrophe and an *s* after the last word of a compound word or word group.

4. The possessives of personal pronouns do not require an apostrophe.

An apostrophe is also used to form contractions. Contractions are generally not used in formal writing. To make a contraction, use an apostrophe in place of the omitted letter or letters.

FOR EXAMPLE   they're—they are
                   can't—cannot   who's—who is
                   don't—do not   it's—it is

Note the difference between *it's* and *its*. *It's* is the contraction for *it is*. *Its* is the possessive pronoun form for *it*.

ASSIGNMENT 13

1. The statute requires the witnesses to be present when the testator signs the will, and the witnesses must be in the same room with the testator, not in a separate room, and watch the testator sign the will.
   What is wrong: The sentence is too long (thirty-eight words) and it is a run-on sentence. It covers two main ideas: witnesses must be present and how they must witness the signing.
   Correct: The statute requires the witnesses to be present when the testator signs the will. The witnesses must be in the same room with the testator, not in a separate room, and watch the testator sign the will.

2. Mary reached the conclusion that she had made a mistake.
   What is wrong: The sentence uses a nominalization—"reached the conclusion." This weakens the sentence by taking the action away from the actor.
   Correct: Mary concluded that she had made a mistake.

3. A relative pronoun requires a verb which agrees with its antecedent.
   What is wrong: Improper use of which. The clause "which agrees with its antecedent" is a restrictive clause (it is necessary to the meaning of the sentence), and restrictive clauses should be introduced with *that*.
   Correct: A relative pronoun requires a verb that agrees with its antecedent.

4. Either the cousins or Darryl are going to the party.
   What is wrong: Two or more subjects joined by *or* or *nor* require a verb that agrees with the subject closest to the verb. Darryl is closest to the verb, therefore, the verb should be *is*.
   Correct: Either the cousins or Darryl is going to the party. **Or** Either Darryl or the cousins are going to the party.

5. Sara, after giving careful consideration to the matter, reached the conclusion that she should buy the business.
   What is wrong: The verb constructions "giving careful consideration to the matter" and "reached the conclusion" are unnecessarily wordy. (See the superfluous verbs subsection.)
   Correct: Sara carefully considered the matter and concluded that she should buy the business.

6. He decided to thoroughly and completely test the theory.
   What is wrong: The sentence contains a split infinitive—"to thoroughly and completely test."
   Correct: He decided to test the theory thoroughly and completely.
7. Neither the members of the board nor Steve had reached their conclusion.
   What is wrong: Antecedents joined by *or* or *nor* require a pronoun that agrees in number and gender with the antecedent closest to the pronoun. Here the antecedent *Steve* is closest to the pronoun *their;* therefore, the proper pronoun is *his.*
   Correct: Neither the members of the board nor Steve had reached his conclusion. Or Neither Steve nor the members of the board had reached their conclusion.
8. The statute requires stockholder approval for merger but it does not require approval for multiple real estate purchases.
   What is wrong: A comma should be used before a conjunction that joins two main or independent clauses.
   Correct: The statute requires stockholder approval for merger, but it does not require approval for multiple real estate purchases.
9. The key executives, (president, secretary, and treasurer) are required to attend the board meeting.
   What is wrong: A comma is not used before parentheses.
   Correct: The key executives (president, secretary, and treasurer) are required to attend the board meeting.
10. The corporation statute requires: an annual board of directors meeting, an annual shareholder meeting, and the filing of an annual report.
    What is wrong: A colon must be preceded by a main clause that is grammatically complete. "The corporation statute requires" is not a complete sentence.
    Correct: The corporation statute requires the following: an annual board of director meeting, an annual shareholder meeting, and the filing of an annual report.
11. Tom and Pam decided there going to buy stock in the corporation.
    What is wrong: The contraction for they are is *they're* not *there.*
    Correct: Tom and Pam decided they're going to buy stock in the corporation.
12. The law requires a partner to ". . . share partnership profits equally with the other partners. . . ."
    What is wrong: An ellipses is not used at the beginning of a quote.
    Correct: The law requires a partner to "share partnership profits equally with the other partners. . . ."
13. Joseph and Claire decided they were going too there cabin for two weeks.
    What is wrong: *Too* and *there* are the wrong words. *To* and *their* are correct. A computer spell-check will not catch these errors.
    Correct: Joseph and Claire decided they were going to their cabin for two weeks.
14. Fifty five of the partners attended the partnership meeting.
    What is wrong: Hyphens are used for numbers from twenty-one to ninety-nine.
    Correct: Fifty-five of the partners attended the partnership meeting.
15. The law provides that profits should be shared equally, however, the law allows the partners to provide otherwise in the partnership agreement.
    What is wrong: A semicolon is used when independent clauses are joined by a conjunctive adverb.
    Correct: The law provides that profits should be shared equally; however, the law allows the partners to provide otherwise in the partnership agreement.

ASSIGNMENT 14

The correct sentence follows the presentation of the incorrect sentence.

- The court's instructions to the respondent are: to refrain from contacting the plaintiff in person, by telephone, or by mail, to pay monthly child support, and to perform one hundred hours of community service."
  "The court's instructions to the respondent are **the following:** to refrain from contacting the plaintiff in person, by telephone, or by mail; to pay monthly child support; and to perform one hundred hours of community service."

Instructor's note: A colon must be preceded by a main clause that is grammatically complete, that is, a complete sentence. In the incorrect sentence, the colon was not preceded by a complete sentence. A semicolon should be used to separate the items listed because commas are already used in the first item—"person, by telephone, or by mail."

- "The following statutes govern the issue, Section 29-9-516, Section 29-9-517, and Section 29-9-544.
  "The following statutes govern the issue: Section 29-9-516, Section 29-9-517, and Section 29-9-544.

Instructor's note: It is probably more appropriate to use a colon in this sentence in order to draw attention to the material that follows.

ASSIGNMENT 15

The following is a summary of the rules governing the use of quotations, ellipses, brackets, parentheses, hyphens, and dashes.

QUOTATIONS: Use quotation marks to identify and set off quoted material. The guidelines to follow when quoting material are the following:

1. Long quotations are not set off by quotation marks. Instead, they are set off from the rest of the text by a five space indentation from the left and right margins. They are also single spaced. According to the *Bluebook, block quotations* should be used for quotes of 50 words or more.

   Since readers tend to skip over or skim long quotations, use them sparingly and only when the entire language, verbatim, is essential.
2. Place periods and commas inside the quotation marks. Other punctuation, such as semicolons, colons, question marks, and exclamation marks, are placed outside the quotation marks unless they are a part of the quotation.
3. You may use quotation marks to indicate a word is used in a special way or is a special term.
4. When quoting a quote within a quote, use single quotation marks.

ELLIPSES: The function of a series of ellipses is to indicate the omission of part of a quotation. Note the following rules in regard to the use of ellipses:

1. When three ellipses occur at the end of a sentence, add a fourth period for the punctuation to end the sentence.
2. When the omission is at the beginning of a quote, do not use ellipses.
3. If the quote is a phrase or clause, no ellipses are required.

BRACKETS: Brackets usually perform two separate functions:

1. To show changes in or add information to quotations, usually for the purpose of providing clarification to the quotation
2. To indicate an error in the original quote

PARENTHESES: Use parentheses to add to a sentence additional information that is outside the main idea of the sentence or of lesser importance.

   When referring the reader to other cases, attached material, or an appendix, or when providing summary information following a case citation, you may use parentheses.

HYPHENS: A hyphen is required to form compound modifiers and compound nouns. There are numerous words that may or may not require hyphenation. Consult a dictionary when you are unsure whether a word must be hyphenated. Be sure to consult a recently published dictionary. This is an area of the English language that frequently changes.

DASHES: Use a dash in the following situations:

1. To emphasize something
2. To set off lists or briefly summarize material containing commas
3. To show an abrupt change of thought or direction

ASSIGNMENT 16

Instructor's note: The paragraphs with the errors are presented first in each part of this assignment. The errors are highlighted and underlined. The corrected paragraph follows the incorrect paragraph; the correction is in bold and underlined.

The corrected paragraphs in Part A are based on the brief of the appellee in the case of *United States of America v. Rick A Luiz,* an appeal from the United States District Court for the District of New Mexico to the United States Court of Appeals for the Tenth Circuit. The corrected paragraphs in Part B are based on the brief of the appellee in the case of *United States of America v. Leonard Woody,* an appeal from the United States District Court for the District of New Mexico to the United States Court of Appeals for the Tenth Circuit.

PART A

The governments**'** first witness at Bean's sentencing **were** the DEA Task Force Officer Tony Silva. He **testifies** tha**t** in his debriefin**g** Luiz had told him about four **seperate** marijuana "grows" in which Luiz had participated. The first was in 1986 **In** Tress, Texas: this "grow" produced 700 marijuana plants. The second was in 1987 in the Tonto wilderness; **and** it produced **approximatly** 1500 marijuana plants. The third "grow" was in 1988 in Sie**s C**olorado and **they** produced approximately 900 marijuana plants.

The final "gro**w** was in 1991, also at the Sies site.

Before the plants in this **grow** had been **harveted,** a Colorado State Police aircraft was spotted doing a "flyover" of the property. This prompted Luiz to **completely** destroy the crop**,** only fifty two plants were seized. As they were seize**d t**he officers noted that two or three plants were in a single grow site. Approximately 1,000 "grow holes," with sprinkler heads connected to an extensive **irritation** system, were found **another one thousand** uninstalled sprinkler heads, two water tanks and fertilizer also **was** found on the property.

CORRECTED PARAGRAPHS: The government**'s** first witness at Bean's sentencing **was** the DEA Task Force Officer Tony Silva. He **testified** that in his debriefing**,** Luiz had told him about four **separate** marijuana "grows" in which Luiz had participated. The first was in 1986 **in** Tress, Texas**;** this "grow" produced 700 marijuana plants. The second was in 1987 in the Tonto wilderness; it produced **approximately** 1500 marijuana plants. The third "grow" was in 1988 in Sie**s,** Colorado and **it** produced approximately 900 marijuana plants.

The final **"grow"** was in 1991, also at the Sies site.

Before the plants in this **"grow"** had been **harvested,** a Colorado State Police aircraft was spotted doing a "flyover" of the property. This prompted Luiz to destroy the crop**;** only fifty two plants were seized. As they were seize**d,** the officers noted that two or three plants were in a single grow site. Approximately 1,000 "grow holes," with sprinkler heads connected to an extensive **irrigation** system, were found. **Another 1,000** uninstalled sprinkler heads, two water tanks and fertilizer also **were** found on the property.

Instructor's note: In the second sentence of the last paragraph, the word *completely* is redundant and is not included in the corrected paragraph. In many instances, commas were omitted in the incorrect version; they are in bold and underlined in the corrected paragraph.

PART B

The trial court sentenced Smith well within the statutory limits. Therefore, the sentence is legal.

The record **thoroughly,** clearly **and positively** shows that Smith and his attorney **have** ample time to **thoroughly** review **Smiths'** sentence report prior to sentencing. They did so and had: "no problems with it." **It is shown by the record** that Smith never appealed his conviction or sentence. His Section 2255 Motion **were** his first and only attempt to challenge his sentence. **Any objections to the sentence report as submitted were clearly waived by Smith.** The defendant have the responsibility to advise the Court of any claimed errors in the sentence report. His failure to voice any objections **waive** any issue not properly presented. **It has been long held by this court** that "Section 2255 is not available to test the legality of matters which should have been raised on appea**l.** Unless good cause can be shown why a defendant did not appeal or raise a particular issue on appeal; the defendant is barred from raising that issue in a Section 2255 motion.

CORRECTED PARAGRAPHS: The trial court sentenced Smith well within the statutory limits. Therefore, the sentence is legal.

The record clearly shows that Smith and his attorney **had** ample time to review **Smith's** sentence report prior to sentencing. They did so and had "no problems with it." **The record also shows** that Smith never appealed his conviction or sentence. His Section 2255 Motion **was** his first and only attempt to challenge his sentence.

Clearly, Smith waived any objections to the sentence report as submitted. The defendant had the responsibility to advise the Court of any claimed errors in the sentence report. His failure to voice any objections **waived** any issue not properly presented.

This court has long held that "Section 2255 is not available to test the legality of matters which should have been raised on appeal**."** Unless good cause can be shown why a defendant did not appeal or raise a particular issue on appeal, the defendant is barred from raising that issue in a Section 2255 Motion.

Instructor's note: The second paragraph of the incorrect version has been broken into three paragraphs. In the first sentence of the second paragraph the use of the words *thoroughly* and *positively* is redundant. The sentences containing the following were rewritten in active voice:

"It is shown by the record . . ."
"Any objections to the sentence report as submitted were clearly waived by Smith."
"It has been long held by this court . . ."

As in Part A, in many instances commas were omitted in the incorrect version; they are in bold and underlined in the corrected paragraphs.

SUGGESTED ASSIGNMENT: Require students to review and correct the writing assignments of other students. The students should use the guidelines presented in Chapter 14.

WEB ASSIGNMENT ANSWERS

ASSIGNMENT 1

1. John realized that the reasons supporting his argument were few in number.
   What is wrong: *Few in number* is redundant. *Few* is sufficient.
   Correct: John realized that there were few reasons supporting his argument. **Or** John realized that the reasons supporting his argument were few.

2. A member of the board of directors has many duties, and the most important is that he must attend every board meeting.
   What is wrong: The sentence uses sexist language.
   Correct: A member of the board of directors has many duties, and the most important is that the member attends every board meeting.

3. The statute requires that each of the following elements be established: duty, breach, proximate cause, or damages.
   What is wrong: When *or* is used, all the items listed are not required to be included. If the statute requires that each element be established, then *or* is improper.
   Correct: The statute requires that each of the following elements be established: duty, breach, proximate cause, and damages.

4. In the case of *State v. Smith,* decided in 1999, the court holds that the statute requires three steps.
   What is wrong: When addressing a court opinion that has already been decided, use past tense. The verb should be *held.*
   Correct: In the case of *State v. Smith,* decided in 1999, the court held that the statute requires three steps.

5. The board of directors told the president that his responsibilities were to:
   a. attend the monthly board meeting,
   b. improvement of company morale, and
   c. education of new personnel.

What is wrong: The sentence lacks parallel construction.
Correct: The board of directors told the president that his responsibilities were to:
a. attend the monthly board meeting,
b. improve company morale, and
c. educate new personnel.

6. Anybody has the right to vote for the party of their choice.
What is wrong: *Anybody* is an indefinite pronoun. Indefinite pronouns are usually singular, therefore, *his* or *her* is used rather than *their.*
Correct: Anybody has the right to vote for the party of his or her choice.

7. The board of directors, after hours of debate and discussion, reached their decision.
What is wrong: When a collective noun (here *board of directors*) functions as a unit, the pronoun is singular. The use of *their* is incorrect.
Correct: The board of directors, after hours of debate and discussion, reached its decision.

8. The law requires that duty, breach, proximate cause and damages must be established.
What is wrong: A comma should be placed before and at the end of a series. There should be a comma after *proximate cause.*
Correct: The law requires that duty, breach, proximate cause, and damages must be established.

9. The statute requires the witnesses to be present when the testator signs the will; and they must watch the testator sign the will.
What is wrong: A semicolon is used to separate main or independent clauses in a sentence that are not joined by a coordinating conjunction. Here they are joined by the coordinating conjunction *and.*
Correct: The statute requires the witnesses to be present when the testator signs the will, and they must watch the testator sign the will. **OR**
The statute requires the witnesses to be present when the testator signs the will; they must watch the testator sign the will.

10. Although some of the contract is ambiguous, its clear that it requires Mr. Smith to make quarterly payments.
What is wrong: *It's* is the contraction for *it is* not *its.*
Correct: Although some of the contract is ambiguous, it's clear that it requires Mr. Smith to make quarterly payments.

11. The reporter noted that the secretary stated, "I did not keep a record of the transaction".
What is wrong: Periods should be placed inside quotation marks.
Correct: The reporter noted that the secretary stated, "I did not keep a record of the transaction."

12. The defendant acted in self defense when plaintiff attacked him.
What is wrong: *Self-defense* requires a hyphen.
Correct: The defendant acted in self-defense when the plaintiff attacked him.

13. Eric concluded that 25 partners were too many.
What is wrong: Numbers that are composed of one or two words should be spelled out.
Correct: Eric concluded that twenty-five partners were too many.

14. In the Summary the text provided the following information concerning paragraphs, "The second fundamental component of writing is the paragraph. A paragraph is a group of sentences that addresses the same topic. Paragraphs are usually composed of a topic sentence, a sentence or sentences discussing the topic, and a closing sentence. Transition words, sentences, or phrases are used to link paragraphs and provide coherence to the writing."
What is wrong: The quotation is a long quotation (over fifty words) and should be blocked.
Correct: In the Summary the text provided the following information concerning paragraphs:
> The second fundamental component of writing is the paragraph. A paragraph is a group of sentences that addresses the same topic. Paragraphs are usually composed of a topic sentence, a sentence or sentences discussing the topic, and a closing sentence. Transition words, sentences, or phrases are used to link paragraphs and provide coherence to the writing.

15. The contract provides that the party of the first part shall make monthly payments to the party of the second part. Aforesaid payments shall henceforth commence on the first day of May.
What is wrong: The sentences use archaic words—*party of the first part, aforesaid, henceforth.*
Correct: The contract provides that monthly payments shall commence on the first day of May.

ASSIGNMENT 2

Instructor's note: The paragraph with the errors is presented first. The errors are bold and underlined. The corrected paragraph follows the incorrect paragraph; the correction is also bold and underlined.

   In the early morning hours, of December 14, the defendant led police on a highspeed automobile chase through several neighborhoods**,** and on to the freeway. The chase **begun** when the defendant ran a red light in the city limits**,** and was pursued by a member of the city police**, and** the chase ended nearly twenty-five minutes later when defendant unsuccessfully attempted to exit the freeway, causing his automobile to leave the pavement, cut through a wooden fence, and **came** to rest in the backyard of a residence. Defendant then got out of his car and fled from police on foot. After a **30** minute search, police apprehended defendant while he was hiding in a bush. The arresting officer **states** that the defendant was unsteady on his feet**,** and that his eyes **was** bloodshot. The defendant **refuses** to submit **to blood** alcohol test**, and** at trial, an expert trained as a drunk driving enforcement officer **testifies** that the defendant exhibited all the classic signs of someone who was extremely intoxicated.

CORRECTED PARAGRAPH: In the early morning hours of December 14, the defendant led police on a high-speed automobile chase through several neighborhoods and on to the freeway. The chase **began** when the defendant ran a red light in the city **limits and** was pursued by a member of the city police. **The** chase ended nearly twenty-five minutes later when defendant unsuccessfully attempted to exit the freeway, causing his automobile to leave the pavement, cut through a wooden fence, and **come** to rest in the backyard of a residence. Defendant then got out of his car and fled from police on foot. After a **thirty** minute search, police apprehended defendant while he was hiding in a bush. The arresting officer **stated** that the defendant was unsteady on his **feet and** that his eyes **were** bloodshot. The defendant **refused** to submit to **a** blood alcohol **test. At** trial, an expert trained as a drunk driving enforcement officer **testified** that the defendant exhibited all the classic signs of someone who was extremely intoxicated.

TEST QUESTIONS AND ANSWERS

TRUE OR FALSE QUESTIONS

Please write a "T" or "F" to the left of each statement.

_____ 1. The average sentence length should be twenty-five to thirty words.

_____ 2. "The automobile hit the child" is an example of a sentence that is in passive voice.

_____ 3. A paragraph may consist of only one sentence.

_____ 4. Transitional sentences may be placed <u>either</u> at the beginning or end of a paragraph.

_____ 5. A nominalization is a group of related words used to convey information.

_____ 6. The use of legalese is appropriate when communicating with others in the field.

_____ 7. The use of *that* is appropriate when introducing nonrestrictive clauses.

_____ 8. In the sentence "The law requires that there be two witnesses, the signature of the contractor, and that the witnesses must be over the age of majority," the use of *and* means that all the listed items are required.

_____ 9. Two or more subjects joined by *or* require a plural verb.

_____ 10. A squinting modifier is a modifier that does not modify any other part of the sentence.

_____ 11. In regard to noun/pronoun agreement, antecedents joined by *and* require a plural pronoun.

_____ 12. Indefinite pronouns such as *all* are usually plural.

_____ 13. The number of a pronoun that refers to a collective noun is determined by the function of the collective noun.

_____ 14. Place a comma after a conjunction that joins two main or independent clauses.

_____ 15. Use a semicolon when independent clauses are joined by a conjunctive adverb such as *however.*

_____ 16. Commas are placed outside of quotation marks.

_____ 17. Parentheses "( )" are used to indicate an error in a quotation.

_____ 18. Use ellipses to indicate the omission of words at the beginning of a quote.

_____ 19. Use numerals for numbers that are composed of two or more digits.

_____ 20. The use of contractions is not considered acceptable in formal writing.

TRUE OR FALSE ANSWERS

Answer	Text Section	Answer	Text Section	Answer	Text Section
1. False	IA2	8. True	IIIG2	15. True	VB2
2. False	IB2	9. False	IVA2	16. False	VE2
3. True	IIE	10. False	IVE3	17. False	VG
4. True	IID	11. True	IVF3	18. False	VF2
5. False	IIIB	12. False	IVF2	19. False	VB
6. True	IIID	13. True	IVF	20. True	VC
7. False	IIIG3	14. False	VA1		

MULTIPLE CHOICE QUESTIONS

Please circle the letter of the **most appropriate** answer.

1. In regard to sentences:
   a. the subject and verb should be kept as close together as possible.
   b. there are rules governing sentence length.
   c. sentences may be drafted in active or passive voice.
   d. active verbs should be used when possible.
   e. all of the above
   f. a, c, and d
   g. b, c, and d

2. A well-crafted paragraph should include:
   a. a transitional phrase or sentence.
   b. a topic sentence.
   c. the body.
   d. a closing sentence.
   e. all of the above
   f. a, b, and d
   g. b, c, and d

3. Which of the following are examples of sexist language?
   a. spouse
   b. homemaker
   c. draftsman
   d. forbearers
   e. all of the above
   f. none of the above

4. A noun-verb string is:
   a. always composed of redundant words.
   b. often referred to as a nominalization.
   c. never appropriate.
   d. usually in active voice.
   e. all of the above
   f. a, b, and c
   g. None of the above

5. You should use *that* to:
   a. indicate the imposition of a duty that is mandatory.
   b. indicate that all the listed items are not required.
   c. introduce a restrictive clause.
   d. introduce a nonrestrictive clause.
   e. none of the above
   f. a, b, and c

6. In regard to subject-verb agreement:
   a. most indefinite pronouns require plural verbs.
   b. collective nouns usually require plural verbs.
   c. the title of a work takes a singular verb.
   d. a relative pronoun usually requires a plural verb.
   e. all of the above
   f. a, b, and c

7. In regard to verb tense:
   a. when presenting your position or legal analysis, use present tense.
   b. when addressing a court opinion that has already been decided, use past tense.
   c. when discussing a law or rule still in effect, use present tense.
   d. when discussing a statute, use past tense.
   e. all of the above
   f. a, b, and c
   g. a, b, and d

8. A dangling modifier is:
   a. a modifier that does not refer to or modify any part of the sentence.
   b. a modifier located in a position in the sentence that makes it unclear whether it modifies the word that precedes it or the word that follows it.
   c. a modifier that is placed in the wrong location in a sentence.
   d. the same as a split infinitive.

e. all of the above
f. a, b, and c

9. In regard to noun-pronoun agreement:
   a. pronouns must agree with their antecedents.
   b. antecedents joined by *and* require a plural pronoun.
   c. indefinite pronouns are usually plural.
   d. if the collective noun does not function as a unit, a singular pronoun is required.
   e. all of the above
   f. a and b
   g. a, b, and c

10. *Somebody* is an example of:
    a. a collective noun.
    b. a definite pronoun.
    c. an indefinite pronoun.
    d. a reflective pronoun.
    e. none of the above

11. Use a comma:
    a. after a conjunction that joins two main clauses.
    b. to set off interpretative words or phrases.
    c. to set off nonrestrictive clauses.
    d. before and after descriptive titles.
    e. all of the above
    f. a, b, and c
    g. b, c, and d

12. Use a semicolon to:
    a. introduce information that follows, such as a list.
    b. separate major elements of complex sentences.
    c. separate items in a series if the items are long or if one of the items has internal commas.
    d. separate dangling modifiers.

e. all of the above
f. a and c
g. a, b, and c

13. In regard to the use of an apostrophe:
    a. the possessives of personal pronouns do not require apostrophes.
    b. use an apostrophe and an *s* after the last word of a compound word.
    c. make plural nouns possessive by adding an apostrophe after the *s*.
    d. make singular nouns possessive by adding an apostrophe and an *s*.
    e. all of the above
    f. b, c, and d

14. To emphasize something use:
    a. a dash.
    b. a hyphen.
    c. ellipses.
    d. brackets.
    e. None

15. In regard to writing numbers:
    a. spell out numbers composed of one or two words.
    b. use numerals for numbers that are composed of two or more digits.
    c. if there is a list of numbers and one of the items on the list should be written with numerals, spell out all the numbers on the list.
    d. hyphens are used for fractions.
    e. all of the above
    f. a and d
    g. a, b, and c

MULTIPLE CHOICE ANSWERS

Answer	Text Section	Answer	Text Section	Answer	Text Section
1. f	I.	6. c	IVA	11. g	VA
2. e	II	7. f	IV	12. f	VB
3. c	III	8. a	IVE	13. e	VD
4. g	IIIB	9. f	IVF	14. a	VJ
5. c	IIIB3	10. c	IVF	15. a	VIB

CHAPTER 15

The Writing Process for Effective Legal Writing

TEXT ASSIGNMENT ANSWERS

ASSIGNMENT 1

The three stages of the legal writing process presented in the text are the following:

- Prewriting Stage
- Writing Stage
- Postwriting Stage

PREWRITING STAGE. The prewriting stage consists of those steps and activities necessary to become adequately prepared to begin to write. It involves all the activities that should take place prior to the actual writing of the assignment. It consists of three sections:

- the assignment section,
- the constraints section, and
- the organization section.

WRITING STAGE. The writing stage is that stage of the writing process where the legal writing is drafted. It involves converting the material gathered in the prewriting stage into a written product, such as an office memorandum of law.

POSTWRITING STAGE. The postwriting stage is that stage of the writing process where the writing developed in the writing stage is revised and edited. In this stage, the focus is on ensuring the clarity, completeness, and conciseness of the writing. It also involves a focus on narrower concerns such as spelling, punctuation, grammar, etc.

ASSIGNMENT 2

The prewriting stage consists of the following three sections:

1. **Assignment.** This section involves the identification of the type and purpose of the assignment. It requires the writer to address and answer three questions:
   - Is the assignment clearly understood?
   - What type of legal writing is required?
   - Who is the audience?
2. **Constraints.** This section involves the identification and consideration of any constraints placed on the assignment. The text identifies and addresses three major constraints that may affect the performance of an assignment:
   - Time. Time constraints such as deadlines that limit the time allotted for the assignment.
   - Length. Any restriction that governs the length of an assignment.
   - Format. Any rules or guidelines that govern the organization and format of the legal writing.
3. **Organization.** This section involves the organization of the writing assignment. The text emphasizes that organization in the prewriting stage is the key to successful legal writing and focuses on the use of an outline.

ASSIGNMENT 3

The text discusses the following types of legal writing:

- **Law Office Legal Research and Analysis Memorandum.** The law office memorandum is a type of legal writing designed to inform the reader of the results of legal research and analysis. It may be as simple as the identification of the statutory or case law that applies to a legal issue or as complex as the identification of the issues in a case and analysis of the law that applies. It is designed for use in the law office.
- **Correspondence.** There are several types of legal correspondence that a researcher may be required to draft: demand letters, opinion letters, settlement proposals, notices of events such as hearing dates, etc.
- **Court Briefs.** A court brief is a document filed with a court which contains an attorney's legal argument and the legal authority in support of that argument. The text discusses two types of court briefs:
  Trial Court Brief—brief submitted to a court in support of a position taken by an attorney in regard to a legal issue in a case.
  Appellate Court Brief—a formal document filed with an appellate court which presents the legal arguments and authorities in support of the client's position on appeal.

ASSIGNMENT 4

The type of audience is important because legal writing is often intended for different audiences of varying degrees of legal sophistication. The writing may be intended for a judge, an attorney, a lay person familiar with the law and legal writing,or a lay person unfamiliar with the law or legal writing. The goal of legal writing is to clearly communicate information to the reader. To meet this goal it is necessary to identify the type of audience to ensure that the writing is crafted in a manner that meets the needs of the reader and that the reader can understand.

 A legal writing designed to inform a client or other lay person of the legal analysis of an issue is drafted differently from a writing designed to convey the same information to an attorney. The use of legal terminology may not be appropriate for a legal writing intended for the lay person.

ASSIGNMENT 5

Some of the constraints that may affect the performance of an assignment are the following:

- **Time.** Time constraints such as deadlines that may affect the performance of the assignment.
- **Length.** Any restriction that governs the length of an assignment.
- **Format.** Any rules or guidelines that govern the organization and format of the legal writing. These constraints may affect the performance of an assignment in the following ways:
- **Time.** Time constraints such as deadlines require the allocation of time to each stage of the writing process. A failure to allocate time or a failure to stick to the allocation may result in insufficient time to prepare a well-crafted product.

 If there is a deadline and too much time is spent in the prewriting stage, there may not be sufficient time to complete the writing stage.

- **Length.** A restriction that governs the length of an assignment may affect the amount of research material gathered and the organization of the assignment.

If the assignment is limited to 10 pages, the amount of research will be limited to that amount of material necessary to prepare a 10-page writing. Five hundred pages of research would probably be too much. The writing would also have to be organized to allocate sufficient space within the 10 pages for each section of the assignment.

- **Format.** Law offices usually have rules or guidelines that govern the organization and format of most types of legal writing, such as case briefs, office memos, and correspondence. Courts have formal rules governing the format and style of briefs, etc. These format constraints affect the assignment by governing the organization, presentation, and writing of the assignment.

ASSIGNMENT 6

An expanded outline is an outline of the assignment that has been expanded so that it may be integrated into the research and analysis process and provide an organized context within which to place research and ideas.

The creation and elements of an expanded outline for the body of an office legal memorandum are the following:

1. The expanded outline is created by taking several sheets of three-holed or binder paper, or, if a computer is used, by creating separate pages. At the top of the separate pages, the name of each section and subsection of the office legal memorandum format presented in the text is written.
2. Using the office memo format presented in The Use of an Outline section of the text, the expanded outline would consist of separate pages for each of the following sections:

- **Issue**
- **Statement of facts**
- **Analysis—Rule of Law**—Either enacted or common law (separate pages for each rule of law if more than one rule applies).
- **Analysis—Case**—Name, citation, summary of facts showing the case is on point (separate pages for each case if there is more than one case).
- **Analysis—Case**—Rule/Principle/Reasoning applied by the court that is relevant to the client's case (including relevant quotes from the case).
- **Analysis—Application**—Discussion and information concerning how the rule of law presented in the court decision applies in the client's case.
- **Counteranalysis**
- **Conclusion**

ASSIGNMENT 7

An expanded outline is used in the preparation of an office legal memorandum in the following manner. As research is conducted or ideas occur concerning any aspect of the case, they are entered on the appropriate page of the expanded outline.

- **Ideas.** When any idea occurs concerning the assignment, it is entered on the page of the expanded outline that relates to that idea.

Any idea concerning how the issue should be stated is entered on the issue page. Any idea concerning how the rule of law, applied in the case, applies to the client's case is entered on the Analysis—Application page. Any idea concerning how a sentence or sentences should be drafted, such as introductory or transition sentences, would be entered on the appropriate page of the outline.

- **Research.** All relevant research should be entered on the appropriate page as the research is conducted.

FOR EXAMPLE   When the governing rule of law such as a statute is found, it is placed on the rule of law page. When a case on point is found, the information concerning the case is entered on the appropriate case page of the outline. This would include information such as the full citation, pertinent quotes, rule of law or legal principle applied by the court, etc.

If an expanded outline is used correctly, the assignment is organized, all the research and ideas are assembled in the proper place, and many of the sentences are crafted and in place. In effect, a rough draft is prepared.

ASSIGNMENT 8

The following are some of the rules to keep in mind during the writing stage:

- Prepare the writing location. Make sure the work environment is pleasant and physically comfortable. Have available all the resources necessary, such as paper, computer, research materials, etc.
- Write during the time of day when you do your best work.
- Limit interruptions. Legal writing requires focus and concentration. Therefore, select a writing time and environment that allows as much freedom from interruptions and distractions as possible.
- Begin writing, do not procrastinate. Often one of the most difficult steps is beginning. Do not put it off. The longer it is put off, the harder beginning will become. Start writing anything that has to do with the project. Once writing is begun, it gets easier.
- Begin with a part of the assignment you feel most confident about. Writing does not have to take place in the sequence of the outline. Write the easiest material first, especially if you have trouble starting.
- Do not try to make the first draft the final draft. The goal of the first draft should be to translate the research and analysis into organized paragraphs and sentences, not to produce a finished product. Just write the information in rough form. It is much easier to polish a rough draft than to try to make the first draft a finished product.
- Do not begin to write until you are prepared. Do all the research and analysis before beginning. It is much easier to write a rough draft if the prewriting stage is thoroughly completed.
- If you become stuck, move to another part of the assignment. If you are stuck on a particular section, leave it. The mind continues to work on a problem when you are unaware of it. That is why solutions to problems often seem to appear in the morning. Let the subconscious work on the problem while you move on. The solution to the difficulty may become apparent when you return to the problem.
- Establish a timetable. Break the project into logical units and allocate time accordingly. This helps avoid spending too much time on one section of the writing and running out of time. Do not become fanatical about the time schedule, however. It is there as a guide to keep you on track and alert you to the overall time constraints.

ASSIGNMENT 9

The following is a check list for revising and editing:

Revising

- Is the writing well organized? Is it organized in a logical manner? Does each section logically follow the previous section?
- Is it written in a manner the audience will understand? If the writing is addressed to a lay person, is the draft written in plain language the reader will understand?
- Is the writing clear? Does it make sense? Are the sections connected with transition sentences that clearly link the sections and guide the reader from one section to the next?
- Is the writing concise? Are there extra words that can be eliminated? Is it repetitive? If multiple examples are included to illustrate a single point, are all the examples necessary?

- Is the writing complete? Are all the aspects of the assignment covered? If there are multiple issues, is each issue and subissue thoroughly analyzed?
- Are the legal authorities correctly cited? Are all legal citations in the correct form? All legal research sources must be correctly cited. Unless the local court rules or the supervisory attorney's preferences dictate otherwise, proper citation form is governed by *The Bluebook, A Uniform System of Citation.*

Editing

- Be prepared to edit a legal writing several times. It may be necessary to edit a revision several times to catch all the errors.
- Read the document out loud. When you silently read your own draft, the mind may automatically fill in a missing word or correct an error without your knowing it, and you will not catch the error. If possible, have a colleague read it to you.
- Have another person edit the document. Have a colleague whose writing skill you respect edit the document.

ASSIGNMENT 10

The following factors should be kept in mind when engaging in research:

1. **Prepare and use an expanded outline when conducting research.**
2. **Identify the issue first. The first step should be to identify the issue.** The preliminary identification of the issue may be very broad such as "Did negligence occur?" or "Was there a breach of contract when the goods were delivered 10 days late?" This preliminary identification of the issue will usually identify the general area of law to be researched, such as contracts, negligence, etc.
3. **Research issues one at a time.** Thoroughly research to its conclusion one issue before proceeding to the next issue. If you find material on another issue, note a reference to it on the page in the expanded outline for that issue.
4. **Become familiar with the area of law.** If you are unfamiliar with the area of law that applies to the issue, obtain a general overview. Legal encyclopedias and treatises are examples of sources to consult to obtain an overview of an area.
5. **Locate the enacted law that governs the question.** Look first for any enacted law that governs the question, such as a statute or constitutional provision.
6. **Locate the common/case law that may apply.** Locate the relevant common/case law if there is no enacted law that governs or the enacted law is so broadly drafted that case law is required to interpret the enacted law. Mandatory precedent should be located first, then persuasive precedent and secondary authority.
7. **Make sure that the research is current.** Check supplements and Shepardize cases to be sure that the authority located is current.
8. **If you reach a dead end, reanalyze the issue.** If you cannot find any authority, either primary or secondary, chances are the issue is too broadly or too narrowly stated. Restate the issue. If the issue is too broadly stated, restate it in narrower terms. Return to a basic research source for guidance, such as a legal encyclopedia. If the issue is too narrowly framed, restate it in broader terms.

ASSIGNMENT 11

PART A The prewriting stage consists of the following three sections:

- Assignment
- Constraints
- Organization

1. **Assignment.** In this section, the researcher would identify the type and purpose of the assignment. It requires the writer to address and answer three questions:
   - **Is the assignment clearly understood?** In this case the assignment is very clear; the researcher is assigned the task of preparing an office legal memorandum addressing the question of whether Tom can have the property transaction set aside because Mary unduly and improperly influenced his decision.
   - **What type of legal writing is required?** The writing requires the preparation of an office legal memorandum.
   - **Who is the audience?** The assignment is to prepare an office legal memorandum. Therefore, the audience will be an individual trained in the law, and the use of legal terminology, etc., is appropriate.
2. **Constraints.** In this section, the researcher would identify any constraints placed on the assignment. The text identifies and addresses three major constraints that may affect the performance of an assignment:
   - **Time.** In this assignment, there is a 10-day time constraint. Therefore, the researcher must allocate time among research, writing, and editing to ensure there is sufficient time for each stage of the writing process.
   - **Length.** There is a five-page limit to the assignment. The researcher must be sure to not gather excessive material and to organize the writing so that each section of the legal memorandum is allotted sufficient space.
   - **Format.** The writing assignment is the preparation of an office legal memorandum; therefore, the researcher would retrieve the office legal memorandum outline form used by the office.
3. **Organization.** This section involves the organization of the writing assignment. The researcher would create and use an expanded outline. The creation of the expanded outline would be based upon the legal memorandum outline used in the office. The creation and use of the expanded outline is discussed in the answers to Parts B and C of this assignment.

PART B The expanded outline based on the outline presented in the Use of an Outline, Step 2 subsection of the text is as follows.

Instructor's note: The expanded outline should consist of several sheets of three-holed or binder paper, or, if a computer is used, separate computer-generated pages. At the top of the separate pages, the name of each section and subsection of the office legal memorandum format presented in the Use of an Outline, Step 2 subsection should be written.

The expanded outline submitted by the student should consist of separate pages for each of the following sections:

- Issue
- Statement of facts
- Analysis—Rule of Law—Section 96-4-4-1 of the state statutes
- Analysis—Case—*Lorn v. Bell*
- Analysis—Case—Rule/principle/reasoning applied by the court that is relevant to the client's case
- Analysis—Application
- Counteranalysis
- Conclusion
- Recommendation

PART C

Instructor's note: The pages of the expanded outline prepared by the students should contain some or all of the following information:

- **Issue.** Any idea concerning how the issue should be stated should be entered on this page. There may be initial broad statements of the issue, such as "Was the statute violated?" and a completed final statement of the issue, such as "In light of the provisions of the state law governing contracts for the sale of land, Section 96-4-4-1, may a contract be set aside for undue influence when a financial advisor advises a client to sell property at a price below the market price to a friend of the financial advisor?"

- **Statement of facts.** On this page the student should list the facts of the case. This should include most of the facts presented in the assignment. All of the following are key facts: Mary was Tom's stockbroker and financial advisor. Tom owned five acres of property. Mary advised Tom to sell the property to Ana at a price slightly below the market price. She recommended that Tom buy stock with the proceeds. Tom sold the property to Ana. Mary and Ana are very close friends.
- **Analysis—Rule of Law**—Section 96-4-4-1. This page should contain the section number of the statute and the provisions of the statute presented in the assignment.
- **Analysis—Case**—*Lorn v. Bell*. On this page the student should note the case citation and a summary of the facts showing the case is on point. This information is not included in the information included in the assignment.
- **Analysis—Case**—Rule/principle/reasoning applied by the court that is relevant to the client's case. The student should include on this page the court's ruling concerning when undue influence occurs under the statute:
  1. The person influenced is susceptible to undue influence,
  2. The person is influenced to enter the contract,
  3. The opportunity to influence is present,
  4. Undue influence is present, and
  5. The person exercising the undue influence benefits from the undue influence.

  The student should also note on this page that any relevant quote from the court opinion would be included in this section of the outline.
- **Analysis—Application**—On this page the student should include information, comments, or ideas concerning how the rule of law presented in the court decision applies in the client's case. Included here should be some analysis by the student of how the law presented in the assignment applies.

The student may note that, based on the information provided, it appears that the statute applies and the contract should be set aside. Since Mary was Tom's financial advisor, he was susceptible to her influence. Mary did influence his decision, and he did act on her influence. Mary had the opportunity to influence Tom. Mary may have been benefited because her friend Ana was enriched under the agreement.

 FOR EXAMPLE

- **Counteranalysis.** On this page the student should include information, comments, or ideas concerning a counteranalysis of the analysis presented in the analysis section.

In response to an analysis that concludes that the statute applies and the contract may be set aside because of undue influence, the student may note the following counteranalysis on the counteranalysis page: "The counterargument to this analysis is that, although Mary advised Tom to sell the land below market price, this was good and proper advice because the stock market was a better investment. In addition Mary did not benefit from the advice, but rather her friend Ana benefited. The statute, therefore, was not violated."

 FOR EXAMPLE

- **Conclusion.** On this page the student should present any ideas, draft sentences, etc., concerning the conclusion.
- **Recommendation.** On this page the student should include any ideas, draft sentences, etc., concerning the recommendation section of the memo.

The student may note here that it must be determined whether Tom benefited by selling the land. In other words, did he invest in the stock market and come out ahead? Also, it should be determined whether Mary directly benefited in any way. Did Ana give Mary any kind of kickback, etc?

 FOR EXAMPLE

Instructor's note: On each page of the expanded outline the student should include, or make reference to, the fact that any ideas concerning how a sentence or sentences should be drafted, such as introductory, transition, or other sentences, would be entered on the page.

 On the Analysis—Rule of law page, the student may include an introductory sentence such as "The rule of law governing the setting aside of contracts for the sale of land because of undue influence is Section 96-4-4-1."

SUGGESTED ASSIGNMENT: For one or more of the writing assignments you have assigned in this course, require the students to perform Parts A through C of Assignment 11.

ASSIGNMENT 12

PART 1. The prewriting stage consists of the following three sections:

- Assignment
- Constraints
- Organization

1. **Assignment.** In this section, the researcher would identify the type and purpose of the assignment. It requires the writer to address and answer three questions:
   - **Is the assignment clearly understood?** In this case, the assignment is very clear. The researcher is assigned the task of preparing an office memorandum addressing the question of whether there is sufficient evidence to support the charge of bank robbery by use of a "dangerous weapon."
   - **What type of legal writing is required?** The writing requires the preparation of an office memorandum.
   - **Who is the audience?** The assignment is to prepare an office memorandum. Therefore, the audience will be an individual trained in the law and the use of legal terminology, etc., is appropriate.
2. **Constraints.** In this section, the researcher would identify any constraints placed on the assignment. The text identifies and addresses three major constraints that may affect the performance of an assignment:
   - **Time.** In this assignment, there is a seven-day time constraint. Therefore, the researcher must allocate time among research, writing, and editing to ensure there is sufficient time for each stage of the writing process.
   - **Length.** There is a five-page limit to the assignment. The researcher must be sure to not gather excessive material and to organize the writing so that each section of the legal memorandum is allotted sufficient space.
   - **Format.** The writing assignment is the preparation of an office memo; therefore, the researcher would use the standard memo format used by the office.
3. **Organization.** This section involves the organization of the writing assignment. The researcher would create and use an expanded outline. The creation of the expanded outline would be based upon the legal memorandum outline used in the office. The creation and use of the expanded outline is discussed in the answer to Part 2 of this assignment.

PART 2. The expanded outline based on the outline presented in the Use of an Outline, Step 2 subsection of the text is as follows:

Instructor's note: The expanded outline should consist of several sheets of three-holed or binder paper, or, if a computer is used, separate computer-generated pages. At the top of the separate pages, the name of each section and subsection of the office legal memorandum format presented in the Use of an Outline, Step 2 subsection should be written.

The expanded outline submitted by the student should consist of separate pages for each of the following sections:

- Issue
- Statement of facts
- Analysis—Rule of Law—18 U.S.C.§ 2113(a)and (d)
- Analysis—Case—*United States v. Martinez-Jimenez,* 864 F.2d 664 (9th Cir. 1989)
- Analysis—Case—Rule/principle/reasoning applied by the court that is relevant to the client's case
- Analysis—Application
- Counteranalysis
- Conclusion
- Recommendation

Instructor's note: The pages of the expanded outline prepared by the students should contain some or all of the following information:

- **Issue.** Any idea concerning how the issue should be stated should be entered on this page. There may be initial broad statements of the issue, such as "Is there sufficient evidence to support charges of bank robbery by use of a dangerous weapon?" There should be a completed final statement of the issue, such as "Under the federal bank robbery statute, 18 U.S.C.§ 2113 (a) and (d), is there sufficient evidence to support charges of bank robbery with a dangerous weapon when the weapon is a crudely carved wooden replica of a 9mm Barretta handgun, and the teller approached by the robber believed it was a real handgun, but the only other witness did not believe it was real?"
- **Statement of facts.** On this page the student should list the facts of the case. This should include most of the facts presented in the assignment. All of the following are key facts: On January 5 of this year, Mr. Eldon Canter robbed the First State Bank. He entered the bank, approached a teller, pulled out a crudely carved wooden replica of a 9mm Barretta handgun, and robbed the bank. The replica was carved from pine, stained with dark walnut wood stain, and a hole was drilled in the "barrel" to make it look real. The teller, Mr. Canter, approached and believed it was a real Barretta. The teller at the next window was fairly certain that it was fake. No one else observed the replica.
- **Analysis—Rule of Law.** This page should contain the section number of the statute and the provisions of the statute resented in the assignment. 18 U.S.C.§ 2113 (a) and (d).
- **Analysis—Case.** On this page the student should note the case citation and a summary of the facts showing the case is on point. *United States v. Martinez-Jimenez,* 864 F.2d 664 (9th Cir. 1989).
- **Analysis—Case**—Rule/principle/reasoning applied by the court that is relevant to the client's case. The student should include on this page the court's ruling concerning what is a dangerous weapon under the statute and note any relevant quote from the opinion that may be used in the memo such as the following:

  "These cases reflect a policy that the robber's creation of even the appearance of dangerousness is sufficient to subject him to enhanced punishment." *Martinez-Jimenez* at 666. "A robber who carries a toy gun during the commission of a bank robbery creates some of the same risks as those created by one who carries an unloaded or inoperable genuine gun." Id. at 666. The court concluded that:

  > The values of justice, administrability, and deterrence require the rule that a robber's use of a replica or simulated weapon that appears to be a genuine weapon to those present at the scene of the crime, or to those charged with responsibility for responding to the crime, carries the same penalty as the use of a genuine weapon.

- **Analysis—Application.** On this page the student should include information, comments, or ideas concerning how the rule of law presented in the court decision applies in the client's case. Included here should be some analysis by the student of how the law presented in the assignment applies.

FOR EXAMPLE ✓ The student may note that, based on the information provided, it appears that there is sufficient evidence to support the charge that Mr. Canter committed bank robbery by use of a dangerous weapon. Even though in our case the instrumentality was a wooden replica of a handgun rather than a toy replica, the result is the same: In both cases the instrumentality was so sufficiently similar to a real handgun that a witness believed it was real, creating the appearance of dangerousness and the consequent risks.

- **Counteranalysis.** On this page the student should include information, comments, or ideas concerning a counteranalysis of the analysis presented in the previous section.

FOR EXAMPLE ✓ A possible counterargument, however, is that the instrumentality cannot be considered a dangerous weapon if some of the witnesses believe that it is not a dangerous weapon. In *United States v. Martinez-Jimenez,* all the witnesses believed the toy gun was a real handgun. In our case, one witness believed it was fake.

- **Conclusion.** On this page the student should present any ideas, draft sentences, etc., concerning the conclusion.

FOR EXAMPLE ✓ A summary of the statute may be, "The federal bank robbery statute, 18 U.S.C. § 2113(a) and (d), establishes a criminal penalty for bank robbery with a dangerous weapon."

- **Recommendation.** On this page the student should include any ideas, draft sentences, etc., concerning the recommendation section of the memo.

FOR EXAMPLE ✓ Further research should be conducted to determine whether the courts have addressed this issue when some witnesses believe the weapon is fake.

Instructor's note: On each page of the expanded outline the student should include or make reference to the fact that any ideas concerning how a sentence or sentences should be drafted, such as introductory, transition, or other sentences, would be entered on the page.

FOR EXAMPLE ✓ On the Analysis—Rule of Law page, the student may include an introductory sentence such as, "The rule of law governing the bank robbery with a dangerous weapon is 18 U.S.C. § 2113 (a) and (d)."

WEB ASSIGNMENT ANSWERS

ASSIGNMENT 1

PART 1. The prewriting stage consists of the following three sections:

- Assignment
- Constraints
- Organization

1. **Assignment.** In this section, the researcher would identify the type and purpose of the assignment. It requires the writer to address and answer three questions:
   * **Is the assignment clearly understood?** In this case, the assignment is very clear. The researcher is assigned the task of preparing an office memorandum addressing the question of whether the will is admissible under Texas law.
   * **What type of legal writing is required?** The writing requires the preparation of an office memorandum.
   * **Who is the audience?** The assignment is to prepare an office memorandum. Therefore, the audience will be an individual trained in the law, and the use of legal terminology, etc., is appropriate.
2. **Constraints.** In this section, the researcher would identify any constraints placed on the assignment. The text identifies and addresses three major constraints that may affect the performance of an assignment:
   * **Time.** In this assignment, there is a five-day time constraint. Therefore, the researcher must allocate time among research, writing, and editing to ensure there is sufficient time for each stage of the writing process.
   * **Length.** There is a five-page limit to the assignment. The researcher must be sure to not gather excessive material and to organize the writing so that each section of the legal memorandum is allotted sufficient space.
   * **Format.** The writing assignment is the preparation of an office memo; therefore, the researcher would use the standard memorandum format used by the office.
3. **Organization.** This section involves the organization of the writing assignment. The researcher would create and use an expanded outline. The creation of the expanded outline would be based upon the legal memorandum outline used in the office. The creation and use of the expanded outline is discussed in the answer to Part 2 of this assignment.

PART 2. The expanded outline based on the outline presented in the Use of an Outline, Step 2 subsection of the text is as follows:

Instructor's note: The expanded outline should consist of several sheets of three-holed or binder paper, or, if a computer is used, separate computer-generated pages. At the top of the separate pages, the name of each section and subsection of the office legal memorandum format presented in the Use of an Outline, Step 2 subsection should be written.

The expanded outline submitted by the student should consist of separate pages for each of the following sections:

* Issue
* Statement of facts
* Analysis—Rule of Law—Tex. Prob. Code. Ann. Sec. 59, Requisites of a Will (Vernon 1980) and Tex. Prob. Code. Ann. § 60, Exception Pertaining to Holographic Wills (Vernon 1980)
* Analysis—Case—*Dean v. Dickey,* 225 S.W.2d 999 (Civ. App. Tex. 1949)
* Analysis—Case—Rule/principle/reasoning applied by the court that is relevant to the client's case
* Analysis—Application
* Counteranalysis
* Conclusion
* Recommendation

Instructor's note: The pages of the expanded outline prepared by the students should contain some or all of the following information:

* **Issue.** Any idea concerning how the issue should be stated should be entered on this page. There may be initial broad statements of the issue, such as, "Is the will admissible under probate law?" There should be a completed final statement of the issue. For example, "Under Texas Probate Code Sections 59 and 60, is a will entitled to probate if one half of the will is handwritten by the testator, the other half is typewritten, and it is not attested to by subscribing witnesses but is self-proved in accordance with the requirements of Section 60?"
* **Statement of facts.** On this page the student should list the facts of the case. This should include most of the facts presented in the assignment. All of the following are key facts: The first half of the will is written in the

handwriting of Mr. Dixon. The second half of the will is typewritten. The typewritten portion was typed at Mr. Dixon's request by his neighbor, Edgar Mae. Mr. Mae has stated that Mr. Dixon asked him to finish the will because Mr. Dixon was too weak to continue. The will was not attested to by subscribing witnesses, but there is a self-proving affidavit that meets the requirements of Section 60 of the probate code.

- **Analysis—Rule of Law.** This page should contain the section number of the statute and the provisions of the statute presented in the assignment. Tex. Prob. Code. Ann. Sec. 59 Requisites of a Will (Vernon 1980) and Tex. Prob. Code. Ann.§ 60 Exception Pertaining to Holographic Wills (Vernon 1980).
- **Analysis—Case.** On this page the student should note the case citation and a summary of the facts showing the case is on point. *Dean v. Dickey,* 225 S.W.2d 999 (Civ. App. Tex. 1949).
- **Analysis—Case**—Rule/principle/reasoning applied by the court that is relevant to the client's case. The student should include on this page the court's ruling concerning when a will is admissible to probate under the statute and note any relevant quote from the opinion that may be used in the memo, such as the following:

    "In upholding the trial court and rejecting the appellant's contention that the typewritten will was sufficient, the court stated that the statutes, "require that the words 'wholly written' used in these articles be construed to mean wholly written in the handwriting of the testator." *Dean* at 999.

- **Analysis—Application.** On this page the student should include information, comments, or ideas concerning how the rule of law presented in the court decision applies in the client's case. Included here should be some analysis by the student of how the law presented in the assignment applies.

FOR EXAMPLE   It appears that Mr. Dixon's will is not entitled to probate. Mr. Dixon's will was not "wholly written" in the handwriting of the testator; one half of the will was typewritten. Therefore, the exception pertaining to holographic wills in Section 60 does not apply.

- **Counteranalysis.** On this page the student should include information, comments, or ideas concerning a counteranalysis of the analysis presented in the analysis section.

FOR EXAMPLE   A possible counterargument is that since the *Dean* decision is over 45 years old, it may not represent the current thinking of the court and, therefore, should not be followed.

- **Conclusion.** On this page the student should present any ideas, draft sentences, etc., concerning the conclusion.
- **Recommendation.** On this page the student should include any ideas, draft sentences, etc., concerning the recommendation section of the memo.

FOR EXAMPLE   Further case law research in other areas of the law should be conducted to determine if the courts have relaxed the standards in regard to handwritten documents.

Instructor's note: On each page of the expanded outline, the student should include, or make reference to, any ideas concerning how a sentence or sentences should be drafted, such as introductory, transition, or other sentences.

FOR EXAMPLE   On the analysis—rule of law page, the student may include an introductory sentence such as, "The rule of law governing the requisites of a will is Tex. Prob. Code Ann.§§ 59 and 60."

ASSIGNMENT 2

PART 1. The prewriting stage consists of the following three sections:

- Assignment
- Constraints
- Organization

1. **Assignment.** In this section, the researcher would identify the type and purpose of the assignment. It requires the writer to address and answer three questions:
   - **Is the assignment clearly understood?** In this case, the assignment is very clear. The researcher is assigned the task of preparing an office memorandum addressing the question of whether the trial court acted properly when it excused Mr. Eldridge from paying $3,500 in back child support.
   - **What type of legal writing is required?** The writing requires the preparation of an office memorandum.
   - **Who is the audience?** The assignment is to prepare an office memorandum. Therefore, the audience will be an individual trained in the law and the use of legal terminology, etc., is appropriate.
2. **Constraints.** In this section, the researcher would identify any constraints placed on the assignment. The text identifies and addresses three major constraints that may affect the performance of an assignment:
   - **Time.** In this assignment there is a seven-day time constraint. Therefore, the researcher must allocate time among research, writing, and editing to ensure there is sufficient time for each stage of the writing process.
   - **Length.** There is a six-page limit to the assignment. The researcher must be sure to not gather excessive material and to organize the writing so that each section of the legal memorandum is allotted sufficient space.
   - **Format.** The writing assignment is the preparation of an office memo; therefore, the researcher would use the standard memorandum format used by the office.
3. **Organization.** This section involves the organization of the writing assignment. The researcher would create and use an expanded outline. The creation of the expanded outline would be based upon the legal memorandum outline used in the office. The creation and use of the expanded outline is discussed in the answer to Part 2 of this assignment.

PART 2. The expanded outline based on the outline presented in the Use of an Outline, Step 2 subsection of the text is as follows:

Instructor's note: The expanded outline should consist of several sheets of three-holed or binder paper or, if a computer is used, separate computer-generated pages. At the top of the separate pages, the name of each section and subsection of the office legal memorandum format presented in the Use of an Outline, Step 2 subsection should be written.

The expanded outline submitted by the student should consist of separate pages for each of the following sections:

- Issue
- Statement of facts
- Analysis—Rule of Law—Ind. Code § 31-2-11-12
- Analysis—Case—*Cardwell v. Gwaltney,* 556 N.E.2d 953 (Ind. App. 1 Dist. 1990)
- Analysis—Case—Rule/principle/reasoning applied by the court that is relevant to the client's case
- Analysis—Application
- Counteranalysis
- Conclusion
- Recommendation

Instructor's note: The pages of the expanded outline prepared by the students should contain some or all of the following information:

- **Issue.** Any idea concerning how the issue should be stated should be entered on this page. There may be initial broad statements of the issue, such as "Did the trial court properly excuse Mr. Eldridge from paying

$3,500 in back child support?" There should be a completed final statement of the issue, such as "In light of the provisions of Indiana Code §31-2-11-12 governing the modification of delinquent child support payments, may a court retroactively modify a duty to pay delinquent child support payments based upon the fact that the obligor was unemployed during the months the obligations accrued?"

- **Statement of facts.** On this page the student should list the facts of the case. This should include most of the facts presented in the assignment. All of the following are key facts: In January of 1994, Mrs. Eldridge filed a motion with the court seeking an order directing Mr. Eldridge to pay the $7,000 due in delinquent support payments. Mr. Eldridge's response requested that he be excused from having to pay the support obligations that accrued during the 10 months he was unemployed. The court ordered Mr. Eldridge to pay $3,500, one half of the amount due. It excused him from paying the remaining $3,500. The court stated that Mr. Eldridge was excused from paying the full amount because he was unemployed during the months the child support accrued.
- **Analysis—Rule of Law.** This page should contain the section number of the statute and the provisions of the statute presented in the assignment. Ind. Code § 31-2-11-12.
- **Analysis—Case.** On this page the student should note the case citation and a summary of the facts showing the case is on point. *Cardwell v. Gwaltney,* 556 N.E.2d 953 (Ind. App.1 Dist. 1990).
- **Analysis—Case**—Rule/principle/reasoning applied by the court that is relevant to the client's case. The student should include on this page the court's ruling concerning when delinquent support payments may be excused under the statute. The student should also note any relevant quote from the opinion that may be used in the memo, such as the following: The court concluded that the trial court erred in retroactively excusing the support obligation for the time Gwaltney was incarcerated. The court stated, "Even though the trial judge was prompted by equitable concerns when Gwaltney was excused from paying support, the law is that any modification of a support order must act prospectively . . ." *Cardwell* at 954.
- **Analysis—Application.** On this page the student should include information, comments, or ideas concerning how the rule of law presented in the court decision applies in the client's case. Included here should be some analysis by the student of how the law presented in the assignment applies.

FOR EXAMPLE   It appears that the trial court erred in reducing Mr. Eldridge's delinquent child support obligation. The trial court's ruling retroactively modified a delinquent obligation, and under *Cardwell* any modification under the statute must act prospectively.

- **Counteranalysis.** On this page the student should include information, comments, or ideas concerning a counteranalysis of the analysis presented in the analysis section.

FOR EXAMPLE   About the only counterargument may be that the court should reconsider the *Cardwell* ruling and interpret the statute to allow an exception when the obligor, through no fault of his own, is financially unable to pay the support payment.

- **Conclusion.** On this page the student should present any ideas, draft sentences, etc., concerning the conclusion.
- **Recommendation.** On this page the student should include any ideas, draft sentences, etc., concerning the recommendation section of the memo.

FOR EXAMPLE   Research should be conducted to determine if the state supreme court has addressed this or related questions.

Instructor's note: On each page of the expanded outline, the student should include, or make reference to, any ideas concerning how a sentence or sentences should be drafted, such as introductory, transition, or other sentences.

On the analysis—case law page, the student may include an introductory sentence, such as "The court of appeals has addressed the question of back child support payments in the case of *Cardwell v. Gwaltney,* 556 N.E.2d 953 (Ind. App. 1 Dist. 1990).

ASSIGNMENT 3

PART 1. The prewriting stage consists of the following three sections:

- Assignment
- Constraints
- Organization

1. **Assignment.** In this section, the researcher would identify the type and purpose of the assignment. It requires the writer to address and answer three questions:
   - **Is the assignment clearly understood?** In this case, the assignment is very clear. The researcher is assigned the task of preparing an office memorandum addressing the question of whether there is a sufficient basis to support an assault by means of a dangerous weapon charge.
   - **What type of legal writing is required?** The writing requires the preparation of an office memorandum.
   - **Who is the audience?** The assignment is to prepare an office memorandum. Therefore, the audience will be an individual trained in the law, and the use of legal terminology, etc., is appropriate.
2. **Constraints.** In this section, the researcher would identify any constraints placed on the assignment. The text identifies and addresses three major constraints that may affect the performance of an assignment:
   - **Time.** In this assignment, there is a 10 day time constraint. Therefore, the researcher must allocate time among research, writing, and editing to ensure there is sufficient time for each stage of the writing process.
   - **Length.** There is an eight-page limit to the assignment. The researcher must be sure to not gather excessive material and to organize the writing so that each section of the legal memorandum is allotted sufficient space.
   - **Format.** The writing assignment is the preparation of an office memo; therefore, the researcher would use the standard memorandum format used by the office.
3. **Organization.** This section involves the organization of the writing assignment. The researcher would create and use an expanded outline. The creation of the expanded outline would be based upon the legal memorandum outline used in the office. The creation and use of the expanded outline is discussed in the answer to Part 2 of this assignment.

PART 2. The expanded outline based on the outline presented in the Use of an Outline, Step 2 subsection of the text is as follows:

Instructor's note: The expanded outline should consist of several sheets of three-holed or binder paper or, if a computer is used, separate computer-generated pages. At the top of the separate pages, the name of each section and subsection of the office legal memorandum format presented in the Use of an Outline, Step 2 subsection should be written.

The expanded outline submitted by the student should consist of separate pages for each of the following sections:

- Issue
- Statement of facts
- Analysis—Rule of Law—G.L. c. 265 § 15A. Assault and Battery with Dangerous Weapon (State of Massachusetts)
- Analysis—Case—*Commonwealth v. Shea,* 38 Mass. App. Ct. 7, 644 N. W. 2d 244 (1995)
- Analysis—Case—Rule/principle/reasoning applied by the court that is relevant to the client's case
- Analysis—Application
- Counteranalysis
- Conclusion
- Recommendation

Instructor's note: The pages of the expanded outline prepared by the students should contain some or all of the following information:

- **Issue.** Any idea concerning how the issue should be stated should be entered on this page. There may be initial broad statements of the issue, such as "Is there sufficient evidence to support charges of assault with a dangerous weapon?" and a completed final statement of the issue, such as "In light of the provisions of Massachusetts's assault and battery with a dangerous weapon statue, Mass. Gen. Laws c. 265 § 15A(b), can lightning be considered a dangerous weapon?"
- **Statement of facts.** On this page the student should list the facts of the case. This should include most of the facts presented in the assignment. All of the following are key facts: On April 5 of this year, after arguing, Mr. Jones dragged Ms. Steward outside and tied her to a lightning rod attached to their cottage. While tying her to the rod he stated, "I'll fix you, you're gonna fry." A violent electrical storm was taking place at the time. Lightning did not strike the pole while Ms. Steward was tied to it.
- **Analysis—Rule of Law.** This page should contain the section number of the statute and the provisions of the statute presented in the assignment. G.L. c. 265 § 15A. Assault and Battery with Dangerous Weapon (State of Massachusetts).
- **Analysis—Case.** On this page the student should note the case citation and a summary of the facts showing the case is on point. *Commonwealth v. Shea,* 38 Mass. App. Ct. 7, 644 N. W. 2d 244 (1995).
- **Analysis—Case**—Rule/principle/reasoning applied by the court that is relevant to the client's case. The student should include on this page the court's ruling concerning what is a dangerous weapon under the statute, and note any relevant quote from the opinion that may be used in the memo, such as the following: The court discussed other dangerous weapons cases and noted: "The commonality found in those cases is that the object in issue, whether dangerous per se or as used, was an instrumentality which the batterer controlled, either through possession of or authority over it, for use of it in the intentional application of force." *Shea* at 249.
- **Analysis—Application.** On this page the student should include information, comments, or ideas concerning how the rule of law presented in the court decision applies in the client's case. Included here should be some analysis by the student of how the law presented in the assignment applies.

FOR EXAMPLE The lightning in our case was not an instrumentality subject to human control, and, therefore, cannot be considered a deadly weapon under Section 15A.

- **Counteranalysis.** On this page the student should include information, comments, or ideas concerning a counteranalysis of the analysis presented in the analysis section.

FOR EXAMPLE A possible counterargument is that tying someone to a lightning rod involves different risks than throwing someone in the ocean; therefore, *Shea* does not apply.

- **Conclusion.** On this page the student should present any ideas, draft sentences, etc., concerning the conclusion.
- **Recommendation.** on this page the student should include any ideas, draft sentences, etc., concerning the recommendation section of the memo.

FOR EXAMPLE Research should be conducted to determine if this state or other states have addressed the question of whether lightning can be considered a dangerous weapon.

Instructor's note: On each page of the expanded outline the student should include or make reference to any ideas concerning how a sentence or sentences should be drafted, such as introductory, transition, or other sentences.

On the analysis—case law page, the student may include an introductory sentence, such as "A case where the court addressed the question of whether a force of nature can be a deadly weapon is *Commonwealth v. Shea,* 38 Mass. App. Ct. 7, 644 N. W. 2d 244 (1995)."

TEST QUESTIONS AND ANSWERS

TRUE OR FALSE QUESTIONS

Please write a "T" or "F" to the left of each statement.

_____ 1. The vast majority of cases are settled.

_____ 2. One of the reasons writing skills are important is because an individual possessing such skills can produce a finished product in a shorter time than one who does not possess such skills.

_____ 3. It is of primary importance to convey the results of legal research in as few words as possible.

_____ 4. The legal writing process is composed of four stages.

_____ 5. The writing process begins with an identification of the type and purpose of the assignment.

_____ 6. The prewriting stage of the writing process is divided into three sections.

_____ 7. The first section of the prewriting process is preliminary research.

_____ 8. Part of the prewriting stage requires the identification of the audience.

_____ 9. Correspondence is one of the types of legal writing that requires the use of a writing process.

_____10. Legal writing should be crafted in the same manner, whether it is intended for internal or external use.

_____11. Most courts do not have rules governing the format for documents submitted to the court.

_____12. An outline is of greatest value in the writing stage of the legal writing process.

_____13. The basic organizational format for most legal writing is the IRAC format.

_____14. The use of an expanded outline results in the preparation of a rough draft while research is conducted.

_____15. When you begin writing an assignment, it is important to write in the sequence of the outline.

_____16. When writing, it is important not to try to make the first draft the final draft.

_____17. Revising focuses on technical issues such as grammar phrasing.

_____18. Editing focuses on whether the writing is complete.

_____19. One of the general <u>research</u> suggestions mentioned in the book is to prepare an expanded outline.

_____20. When the assignment involves several legal issues, do not attempt to research more than one issue at a time.

TRUE OR FALSE ANSWERS

Answer	Text Section	Answer	Text Section	Answer	Text Section
1. True	I	8. True	IVA1	15. False	IVB
2. True	II	9. True	IVA1	16. True	IVB
3. True	III	10. False	IVA1	17. False	IVC1
4. False	IV	11. False	IVA3	18. False	IVC2
5. True	IVA	12. False	IVA3	19. True	V
6. True	IVA	13. True	IVA3	20. True	V
7. False	IV	14. True	IVA3		

MULTIPLE CHOICE QUESTIONS

Please circle the letter of the **most appropriate** answer.

1. Writing skills are important because:
   a. a job evaluation may be based on writing skills.
   b. good writing skills usually result in the production of more work in less time.
   c. the greater the skill, the greater the quality of the product.
   d. correspondence to a client is less likely to be misunderstood.
   e. all of the above
   f. a, c, and d
   g. b, c, and d

2. The goals of legal writing are:
   a. to clearly convey legal information.
   b. fully address a topic in as few words as possible.
   c. to concisely convey legal information.
   d. to completely convey legal information.
   e. all of the above
   f. a, c, and d

3. The process of legal writing consists of the following stages:
   a. research stage
   b. prewriting stage
   c. writing stage
   d. postwriting stage
   e. all of the above
   f. a, b, and c
   g. b, c, and d

4. The prewriting stage consists of which of the following sections?
   a. research
   b. assignment
   c. constraints
   d. organization
   e. all of the above
   f. a, b, and c
   g. b, c, and d

5. The assignment section of the prewriting stage requires:
   a. a determination of the type of legal writing required.
   b. a determination of the length of the assignment.
   c. a determination of the format of the assignment.
   d. the preparation of an expanded outline.
   e. all of the above
   f. a, b, and c

6. Some of the constraints on legal writing are:
   a. time.
   b. length.
   c. style.
   d. format.
   e. all of the above
   f. a, b, and c
   g. a, b, and d

7. An outline:
   a. provides an organized framework for presenting research.
   b. provides an organized framework for presenting analysis.
   c. is of greatest value in the writing stage.
   d. provides a context in which to place research and ideas.
   e. All of the above
   f. a, b, and d
   g. a and b

8. An outline is integrated into the research and analysis process by:
   a. consulting the local court rule to determine the proper format.
   b. converting the outline to a usable form.
   c. integrating all research, analysis and ideas into the outline.
   d. conducting preliminary research.
   e. all of the above
   f. b and c
   g. b, c, and d

9. An expanded outline:
   a. has a separate page for each section and subsection of the outline.
   b. includes quotes from key cases.
   c. should be kept with you at all times while working on an assignment.
   d. allows the preparation of a rough draft while researching.
   e. all of the above
   f. a and b
   g. a, b, and d

10. Which of the following are guidelines that help the writing process?
    a. Begin writing early in the day when the mind is fresh.
    b. Write in the sequence of the outline.

c. Make the work environment pleasant and physically comfortable.

d. Develop and stick to a fixed timetable.

e. all of the above

f. a, b, and d

11. The revision process requires a determination of whether:

a. the document is well organized.

b. the writing is clear.

c. a new expanded outline is necessary.

d. citations are correct.

e. all of the above.

f. a and b

g. a, b, and d

12. Editing includes a determination of whether:

a. the writing is well organized.

b. the grammar and phrasing are correct.

c. the writing is concise.

d. the writing is complete.

e. all of the above

f. a, c, and d

MULTIPLE CHOICE ANSWERS

Answer	Text Section	Answer	Text Section	Answer	Text Section
1. e	II	5. a	IVA1	9. e	IVA3
2. e	III	6. g	IVA2	10. c	IVB
3. g	IV	7. f	IVA	11. g	IVC
4. g	IVA	8. f	IVA3	12. b	IVC2

CHAPTERS 16 AND 17

Office Legal Memorandum—Assignment to Conclusion

TEXT ASSIGNMENT ANSWERS

ASSIGNMENT 1

NAME AND CITATION OF COURT OPINION. When presenting the case, first identify the case name and citation. The reader should know the name of the case at the beginning of the discussion; this eliminates any possible confusion that may arise as to which case is being discussed.

FACTS OF THE CASE. The next step is to provide sufficient information concerning the facts and rule of law applied in the case to demonstrate that the case is on point. To accomplish this, you must include enough information about the court opinion to demonstrate that the similarity between the key facts and rule of law of the opinion and the client's case is sufficient for the court opinion to govern, or provide guidance, in deciding how the law applies.

RULE OF LAW. The last step when discussing a case that is on point is to identify the rule of law, or legal principle adopted by the court, that applies to the issue being addressed in the office memo.

1. Quote the language of the court whenever practical. Quotes are stronger than paraphrases.
2. When presenting the law, always cite the page of the court opinion where the rule is presented.

ASSIGNMENT 2

PART A. RULE OF LAW. The analysis section begins with the presentation of the rule of law. When presenting the rule of law, paraphrase or quote only the relevant portions of the law.

PART B. RULE OF LAW INTERPRETATION—CASE LAW. The next part of the analysis section is the interpretation of the rule of law. Usually the rule of law that governs the issue being analyzed has some unexpected, unobvious quirk or is so broadly stated that case law must be referenced to determine how it applies. Case law, in effect, provides the link between the rule of law and the issue raised by the facts of the client's case. Court opinions determine and explain how the law is interpreted and applied in specific fact situations.

PART C. APPLICATION OF RULE OF LAW TO CLIENT'S CASE. A critical element of the analysis section is the application of the law to the issue(s) raised by the facts of the client's case. There are two situations that may occur when applying the rule of law to the facts of the case:

1. Case law is not required to determine how the rule of law applies to the issue being analyzed. It is clear from the face of the rule how it applies. In such instances, the rule is simply applied directly to the issue being addressed in the office memo.
2. There is a question of how the rule of law or an element of the rule applies to the issue(s) being analyzed. In such cases, it is necessary to refer to case law for guidance as to how the law applies. Once the case on point is discussed, as addressed in the previous section, the rule of law or legal principle adopted by the court must be applied to the facts of the client's case. This is the next step of the analysis process. It immediately follows the presentation of the rule of law from the case on point.

PART D. COUNTERANALYSIS. The next part of the analysis section is the counteranalysis. The analysis of a legal issue is not complete unless counterarguments to the analysis are explored. The process of addressing the counterarguments is called *counteranalysis*. If rebuttal is necessary, it should follow the counteranalysis. Rebuttal may be required if it is necessary to explain why the counterargument does not apply or to evaluate the merits of the counterargument

ASSIGNMENT 3

The conclusion section should not introduce new information or authorities, nor should it merely repeat the brief answer. It should summarize the conclusions reached in the analysis section. It is recommended that the conclusion be crafted to include a reference to and summary of all the law discussed in the analysis section, both the enacted and case law. Ideally, the conclusion should briefly inform the reader of all the law that applies and how it applies. The reader should be able to obtain from the conclusion a general understanding of the law and its application without having to read the entire memo.

ASSIGNMENT 4

Instructor's note: The format and basic content of the memorandums will be similar to Assignments 5, 6, 7, 9, 10, and 11 presented in the Instructor's Manual. The analysis and conclusion will vary according to state law.

ASSIGNMENT 5

To: Supervisory Attorney
From: Paralegal
Re: *Dixon v. Cary*
          Probate of holographic will

STATEMENT OF ASSIGNMENT

You have asked me to prepare a memorandum addressing the question of whether the will of Thomas Dixon is admissible to probate under Texas law.

ISSUE

Under Texas Probate Code Sections 59 and 60, is a will entitled to probate if one half of the will is handwritten by the testator, the other half is typewritten, and it is not attested to by subscribing witnesses but is self-proved in accordance with the requirements of Section 60?

BRIEF ANSWER

No. Section 60 of the probate code and the state court's interpretation of that section provide that a self-proved holographic will which is not witnessed must be written entirely in the handwriting of the testator.

FACTS

Mary Cary, the sister of Thomas Dixon and the personal representative of his estate, has submitted for probate a holographic will prepared by Mr. Dixon. The first half of the will is written in the handwriting of Mr. Dixon. The second half of the will is typewritten. The typewritten portion was typed at Mr. Dixon's request by his neighbor, Edgar Mae. Mr. Mae has stated that Mr. Dixon asked him to finish the will because Mr. Dixon was too weak to continue. The will was not attested to by subscribing witnesses, but there is a self-proving affidavit that meets the requirements of Section 60 of the probate code.

ANALYSIS

The rule of law governing the attestation of wills is presented in Texas Probate Code Sections 59 and 60. Section 59 provides that every will, "shall be in writing. . . , and shall, if not wholly in the handwriting of the testator, be attested by two (2) or more credible witnesses . . . ." Section 60 provides that "Where the will is written wholly in the handwriting of the testator, the attestation of the subscribing witnesses may be dispensed with. Such a will may be made self-proved at any time during the testator's lifetime by the attachment. . . of an affidavit by the testator. . ." (Vernon 1980). Read together the two statutes require that a will must be attested to by two witnesses unless it is "wholly in the handwriting of the testator."

The statutes, however, do not define what constitutes written "wholly in the handwriting of the testator." Therefore, the statutes do not provide guidance in a situation, such as ours, where one half of the will is written in the testator's handwriting and one half is typewritten at his direction.

The Texas courts have not defined what constitutes "wholly in the handwriting of the testator" as used in Sections 59 and 60. The only case on point is the case of *Dean v. Dickey,* 225 S.W.2d 999 (Tex. Civ. App.1949). In this case the Texas Court of Civil Appeals interpreted the comparable sections of the probate code in effect in 1945. Vernon's Texas Civil Statutes, Article 8283 provided, "Every last will and testament . . . shall, if not wholly written by himself, be attested by two or more credible witnesses. . . ." Article 8284 provided, "Where the will is wholly written by the testator the attestation of the subscribing witnesses may be dispensed with."

In the *Dean* case, the will was typed wholly by the deceased and intended by him to be his last will. It was signed by him and one witness. The trial court denied probate of the will. In upholding the trial court and rejecting the appellant's contention that the typewritten will was sufficient, the court stated that the statutes, "require that the words 'wholly written' used in these articles be construed to mean wholly written in the handwriting of the testator." Id. at _____.

Although the *Dean* case concerned an earlier version of the probate code, in the absence of a more recent case, the interpretation adopted in that case should still apply. The statutes are almost identical in relevant part: the earlier statutes provided "wholly written by" and the current versions read "wholly in the handwriting of." There is no language in the current statutes which indicates that an interpretation different from that adopted in *Dean* is intended.

If the ruling in the *Dean* case is followed and the interpretation applied in that case is applied to our facts, it appears that Mr. Dixon's will is not entitled to probate. Mr. Dixon's will was not "wholly written" in the handwriting of the testator; one half of the will was typewritten. Therefore, the exception pertaining to holographic wills in Section 60 does not apply, the attestation of subscribing witnesses may not be dispensed with, and the will is not entitled to probate because it was not witnessed.

The only possible counterargument is that since the *Dean* decision is over forty-five years old, it may not represent the current thinking of the court and, therefore, should not be followed. This is always a possibility when the precedent case is very old. The holding in *Dean,* however, was based upon the court's concern in ensuring the genuineness of the will, and this concern is equally important today. It has not changed over the years. In addition, the legislature has not amended the statute to evidence a different intent.

CONCLUSION

Sections 59 and 60 of the Texas probate code govern the requirements of the attestation of wills. Section 60 provides that the attestation of subscribing witnesses may be dispensed with when the will is written wholly in the handwriting of the testator. The case of *Dean v. Dickey* provides that a will must be written entirely in the handwriting of the testator before the requirement of subscribing witnesses may be dispensed with; a will typewritten by the testator is not "wholly written" within the meaning of the statute. One half of Mr. Dixon's will was typewritten, therefore, the requirement of subscribing witnesses may not be dispensed with. Since the will was not witnessed, it is not eligible for probate.

RECOMMENDATIONS

Further case law research in other areas of the law should be conducted to determine if the courts have indicated a relaxation of the standards in regard to handwritten documents.

ASSIGNMENT 6

To: Supervisory Attorney
From: Paralegal
Re: *Eldridge v. Eldridge*
        Modification of child support

STATEMENT OF ASSIGNMENT

I have been assigned the task of preparing a memo addressing the question of whether the trial court acted properly when it excused Mr. Eldridge from paying "back" child support in the amount of $3,500.

ISSUE

In light of the provisions of Indiana Code § 31-2-11-12, which governs the modification of delinquent child support payments, may a court retroactively modify a duty to pay delinquent child support payments based upon the fact that the obligor was unemployed during the months the obligations accrued?

BRIEF ANSWER

No. In the case of *Cardwell v. Gwaltney*, the Indiana Court of Appeals ruled that under Section 31-2-11-12 a court may not retroactively modify a support obligation; any modification must act prospectively.

FACTS

Mr. and Mrs. Eldridge were divorced in 1992. In the divorce Mr. Eldridge was ordered to make child support payments in the amount of $700 per month. Mr. Eldridge was unemployed from January through October of 1993. He did not make child support payments during this ten-month period. The child support payments he failed to make totaled $7,000.

In January of 1994, Mrs. Eldridge filed a motion with the court seeking an order directing Mr. Eldridge to pay the $7,000 due in delinquent support payments. Mr. Eldridge responded with a petition to modify his child support obligation. In the petition, he requested that he be excused from having to pay the support obligations that accrued during the ten months he was unemployed. The court ordered Mr. Eldridge to pay $3,500, one half of the amount due. It excused him from paying the remaining $3,500. The court stated that Mr. Eldridge was excused from paying the full amount because he was unemployed during the months the child support accrued.

ANALYSIS

Indiana Code § 31-2-11-12 governs the modification of delinquent child support obligations. Section 31-2-11-12 provides:

(a) Except as provided in subsection (b), a court may not retroactively modify an obligor's duty to pay a delinquent support payment.

(b) A court with jurisdiction over a support order may modify an obligor's duty to pay a support payment that becomes due:

(1) After notice of a petition to modify the support order has been given to each obligee; and

(2) Before a final order concerning the petition for modification is entered.

The statute clearly indicates that a court may not retroactively modify an obligor's duty to pay a delinquent support obligation. The Indiana courts have ruled that a court may not retroactively modify a duty to pay a delinquent support obligation even if the obligor did not have the means to pay when the obligation accrued.

In the case of *Cardwell v. Gwaltney*, 556 N.E.2d 953 (Ind. Ct. App. 1990), Mr. Gwaltney filed a petition requesting that he be absolved from paying the support obligations that accrued during the year he was in prison. He had reached an agreement with his former wife which excused him from paying the support for that year. The trial court approved the agreement. The agreement was opposed by the county attorney because Mr. Gwaltney's former spouse, Ms. Cardwell, had been the recipient of AFDC funds and had assigned her support rights. On appeal the court concluded that the trial court erred in retroactively excusing the support obligation that accrued during the time Gwaltney was incarcerated. The court stated, "Even though the trial judge was prompted by equitable concerns when Gwaltney was excused from paying support, the law is that any modification of a support order must act prospectively. . . ." Id. at _____.

The key facts in our case are substantially the same as those in *Cardwell v. Gwaltney.* In both cases, there were delinquent child support obligations that the obligor did not have the means to pay when they accrued, and the trial court's order retroactively reduced the obligation. In applying the *Cardwell* court's interpretation of Section 31-2-11-12 to our facts, it appears that the trial court erred in reducing Mr. Eldridge's delinquent child support obligation. The trial court's ruling retroactively modified a delinquent obligation, and under *Cardwell* any modification under the statute must act prospectively, not retroactively.

It does not appear that there is any viable counterargument to the analysis presented above. The statutory and case law clearly do not allow retroactive modification of delinquent child support obligations. The argument may be made that the court should reconsider the *Cardwell* ruling and interpret the statute to allow an exception when the obligor, through no fault of his own, was financially unable to pay the support payment when it became due. In *Cardwell,* the court seemed to anticipate this argument when it referred to the commentary to Ind. Child Support Guideline 2:

> An obligor cannot be held in contempt for failure to pay support when he does not have the means to pay, but the obligation accrues and serves as a reimbursement to the custodial parent, or, more likely, to the welfare department if he later acquires the ability to meet his obligation.

Id. at _____.

CONCLUSION

Indiana Code § 31-2-11-12 prohibits the retroactive modification of a delinquent child support obligation. In the case of *Cardwell v. Gwaltney* the Indiana Court of Appeals held that any modification under the statute must act prospectively, not retroactively. The trial court's modification of Mr. Eldridge's delinquent child support obligation acted retroactively and is, therefore, in violation of the statute.

RECOMMENDATIONS

The ruling in *Cardwell* is from the court of appeals. Additional research should be conducted to determine if the Indiana Supreme Court has addressed this or related questions.

ASSIGNMENT 7

To: Supervisory Attorney
From: Paralegal
Re: *Commonwealth v. Jones*
            Assault with a dangerous weapon—lightning

STATEMENT OF ASSIGNMENT

This assignment calls for a determination of whether lightning can be considered a dangerous weapon within the meaning of the state's criminal assault and battery statute.

ISSUE

In light of the provisions of Massachusetts's assault and battery statute, Mass. Gen. Laws c. 265 § 15A(b), can lightning be considered a dangerous weapon?

BRIEF ANSWER

No. In the case of *Commonwealth v. Shea,* the court of appeals determined that in order to be a "dangerous weapon" within the meaning of the statute the instrumentality must be subject to the control of the batterer. Since the lightning in this case was not subject to the control of the batterer, it can not be considered a dangerous weapon.

FACTS

Mr. Sedrick Jones and Ms. Elizabeth Steward live in a cottage on a bluff overlooking the Atlantic ocean. They have been involved in a stormy relationship for the past ten years. On April 5 of this year, after a bout of drinking and arguing, Mr. Jones dragged Ms. Steward outside and tied her to a lightning rod attached to the cottage. While tying her to the rod he stated, "I'll fix you, you're gonna fry." A violent electrical storm was taking place at the time. Lightning did not strike the pole while Ms. Steward was tied to it. In addition to other charges, Mr. Jones was charged with assault and battery with a dangerous weapon. The state contends that lightning is the dangerous weapon.

ANALYSIS

Criminal assault and battery with a dangerous weapon is governed by Mass. Gen. Laws c. 265 Section A. Subsection (b) provides that "Whoever commits assault and battery upon another by means of a dangerous weapon shall be punished by imprisonment in the state prison for not more than ten years. . . ." The statute does not define what constitutes a dangerous weapon nor does it address the question of whether a deadly weapon can be a natural force such as lightning. There is, however, case law which discusses this question.

In the case of *Commonwealth v. Shea,* 38 Mass. App. Ct. 7, 644 N.W.2d 244 (1995), the defendant invited two women to board his boat. Five miles from the shore he stopped the boat, disrobed, made sexual remarks, and advanced toward the women. When they rejected his advances and demanded that he return them to the shore, he threw them off the boat and left them in the water. A jury convicted him of several charges including assault and battery by means of a dangerous weapon (the ocean).

On appeal the court addressed the question of whether the ocean could be considered a dangerous weapon within the meaning of Mass. Gen. Laws c. 265 Section 15A. The court discussed other dangerous weapons cases and noted,

> The commonality found in those cases is that the object in issue, whether dangerous per se or as used, was an instrumentality which the batterer controlled, either through possession of or authority over it, for use of it in the intentional application of force. Because the ocean in its natural state cannot be possessed or controlled, it is not an object or instrumentality capable of use as a weapon for purposes of § 15A.

Id. at _____.

The reasoning the court applied in *Commonwealth v. Shea,* in its determination that the ocean could not be a deadly weapon, can also be applied to lightning. The lightning in our case, just as the ocean in *Commonwealth,* was not an instrumentality subject to human control, and, therefore, cannot be considered a deadly weapon under Section 15A.

A possible counterargument is that lightning is different from the ocean. Mr. Jones's act of tying Ms. Steward to a lightning rod increased the likelihood of her being struck by lightning and is, therefore, different from throwing someone in the ocean. In *Commonwealth,* the court stated, "Our conclusion should not be construed to mean that there can never be criminal liability for causing physical harm to someone by subjecting them to a force of nature." Id. at _____. See the Recommendation section that follows.

This counterargument is weak and can be easily countered. The key to the holding in *Commonwealth* is that the dangerous weapon must be subject to the control of the batterer. The lightning in our case was not subject to the control of Mr. Jones, and, therefore, like the ocean in *Commonwealth,* cannot be a "dangerous weapon" within the meaning of the statute.

CONCLUSION

A criminal penalty is imposed for assault and battery with a dangerous weapon in Mass. Gen. Laws c. 265 Section 15A. In the case of *Commonwealth v. Shea,* the Massachusetts Court of Appeals held that in order to be a "dangerous weapon" the instrumentality must be controlled by the batterer, either through possession of or authority over it. In our case the lightning was not subject to the control of Mr. Jones, and, therefore, cannot be a dangerous weapon within the meaning of the statute.

RECOMMENDATION

Further research should be conducted to determine when there can be criminal liability for causing physical harm to someone by subjecting the individual to a force of nature.

ASSIGNMENT 8

To: Supervisory Attorney
From: Paralegal
Re: *United States v. Eldon Canter*
          Armed bank robbery with a deadly weapon

STATEMENT OF ASSIGNMENT

I have been assigned the task of determining—within the meaning of the federal bank robbery statute—whether a crudely carved wooden replica of a handgun can be considered a "dangerous weapon" when it is used in a bank robbery, and the teller who was approached believed the replica was real.

ISSUE

Under the federal bank robbery statute, 18 U.S.C. § 2113 (a) and (d), is there sufficient evidence to support charges of bank robbery with a dangerous weapon when the weapon is a crudely carved wooden replica of a 9mm Barretta handgun, and the teller approached by the robber believed it was a real handgun, but the only other witness did not believe it was real?

BRIEF ANSWER

Qualified yes. In the case of *United States v. Martinez-Jimenez,* the court held that a dangerous weapon includes a replica if it appears to be a genuine weapon to those present at the scene. In our case the teller being robbed believed the replica was real and another teller, the only other witness, did not believe it was real. If the case is interpreted to provide that it is sufficient if any witness present believed that the replica was a real weapon, then the carved wooden replica was a dangerous weapon within the meaning of the statute.

FACTS

On January 5 of this year, Mr. Eldon Canter robbed the First State Bank. He entered the bank, approached a teller, pulled out a crudely carved wooden replica of a 9mm Barretta handgun, and robbed the bank. The replica was carved from pine, stained with dark walnut wood stain, and a hole was drilled in the "barrel" to make it look real. The teller Mr. Canter approached believed it was a real Barretta. The teller at the next window was fairly certain that it was fake. No one else observed the replica.

ANALYSIS

Mr. Canter is charged with armed bank robbery with a dangerous weapon in violation of 18 U.S.C. Section 2113(a) and (d). The relevant portions of the statute provide:

(a) Whoever, . . . by intimidation, . . . takes . . . any property or money or any other thing of value belonging to . . . a bank. . . .

Shall be fined not more than $5,000 or imprisoned not more than twenty years, or both. (d) Whoever, in committing . . . any offense defined in subsections (a) . . . assaults any person, or puts in jeopardy the life of any person by use of a dangerous weapon or device, shall be fined not more than $10,000 or imprisoned not more than twenty-five years, or both.

The statute does not define what constitutes a "dangerous weapon." Therefore, it is necessary to consult case law to determine how the courts have defined the term in cases where the alleged "dangerous weapon" is not in fact an actual weapon.

A case on point is *United States. v. Martinez-Jimenez,* 864 F.2d 664 (9th Cir. 1989). In this case the defendant robbed a bank with a toy gun that eyewitnesses identified as a dark revolver. The defendant was convicted of armed bank robbery under Section 2113(d).

On appeal the court addressed the question of whether a toy gun is a "dangerous weapon" within the meaning of Section 2113(d). The court noted that "The toy gun did not fit the statutory definition of a firearm under 18 U.S.C. § 921(a)(3). However, it did fall within the meaning of a 'dangerous weapon or device' under Section 2113(d)." Id. at _____. In support of this conclusion, the court referred to other cases where unloaded or inoperable guns were held to be dangerous weapons and stated, "These cases reflect a policy that the robber's creation of even the appearance of dangerousness is sufficient to subject him to enhanced punishment." Id. at _____. The court went on to note that "A robber who carries a toy gun during the commission of a bank robbery creates some of the same risk as those created by one who carries an unloaded or inoperable genuine gun." Id. at _____. The court concluded that:

> The values of justice, administrability, and deterrence require the rule that a robber's use of a replica or simulated weapon that appears to be a genuine weapon to those present at the scene of the crime, or to those charged with responsibility for responding to the crime, carries the same penalty as the use of a genuine weapon.

Id. at _____.

In applying the *United States v. Martinez-Jimenez* holding to our facts, it appears that there is sufficient evidence to support the charge of bank robbery with a dangerous weapon. Even though in our case the instrumentality was a wooden replica of a handgun rather than a toy replica, the result is the same: in both cases the instrumentality was so sufficiently similar to a real handgun that a witness believed it was real, creating the appearance of dangerousness and the consequent risks. As the court noted in its conclusion, the use of a replica or simulated weapon that appears to be genuine subjects the robber to the penalty imposed by Section 2113(d) for use of a dangerous weapon.

A possible counterargument, however, is that the instrumentality cannot be considered a dangerous weapon if some of the witnesses believe that it is not a dangerous weapon. In *United States v. Martinez-Jimenez,* all the witnesses believed the toy gun was a real handgun. The court did not address the question of whether all the witnesses must believe the instrumentality is a real weapon in order for it to be considered a dangerous weapon. It should not, however, make a difference if some of the witnesses do not believe the instrumentality is real. In *United States v. Martinez-Jimenez* the court focused upon the increased risk to the physical security of those present at the scene created by the appearance of dangerousness. Id. at _____. As long as some of the witnesses believe the instrumentality is real, that risk is created. The goal of the court's holding was to eliminate or reduce that risk, and, therefore, the holding should apply whenever the risk is created, even if all the witnesses do not believe the risk is present. See the recommendation section below.

CONCLUSION

The federal bank robbery statute, 18 U.S.C. § 2113(a) and (d), establishes a criminal penalty for bank robbery with a "dangerous weapon." In *United States v. Martinez-Jimenez,* the Ninth Circuit Court of Appeals concluded that a replica that appears to be a genuine weapon to those present at the scene of the crime constitutes a "dangerous weapon" within the meaning of 18 U.S.C. Section 2113(d). In our case, Mr. Cantor used a carved wooden replica of a handgun when he robbed the bank, and the teller he robbed believed it was a real handgun. In light of the holding in *United States v. Martinez-Jimenez,* it appears that there is a sufficient basis to support the charge that he committed bank robbery by use of a "dangerous weapon" in violation of Section 2113(d).

RECOMMENDATION

Additional case law should be researched to determine if there are any cases which hold that all the witnesses must believe the instrumentality is real in order for 18 U.S.C. Section 2113(d) to apply.

ASSIGNMENT 9

To: Supervisory Attorney
From: Paralegal
Re: Mr. Arturo Garcia—child support modification

STATEMENT OF ASSIGNMENT

This assignment addresses two questions:

1. Was Ms. Chavez's act of unilaterally reducing her child support obligation when the oldest child reached the age of majority permissible under New Mexico law?
2. Will a court grant a modification of child support when there is a voluntary change of occupation that substantially reduces the income of the obligor parent?

ISSUES

Issue I

In light of the provisions of the child support statute, NMSA § 40-4-7 (Repl. Pamp. 1994), may the obligor parent unilaterally reduce an undivided child support obligation when one of the children reaches the age of majority and moves out?

Issue II

Under the provisions of the New Mexico Statute governing child support obligations, NMSA § 40-4-11.4 (Repl. Pamp. 1994), will a material change in the financial circumstances of an obligor parent, resulting from a voluntary career change, warrant a reduction in that parent's support obligation when the parent has stated that the change was made because she "can't stand to pay that much money to my ex-husband?"

BRIEF ANSWER

Issue I

No. In the case of *Britton v. Britton,* the New Mexico Supreme Court ruled that modification of support obligations is strictly a matter to be determined by the courts and not by unilateral action of the obligor parent.

Issue II

Qualified no. NMSA Section 40-4-11.4A (Repl. Pamp. 1994) gives a court the authority to modify a child support obligation upon a material and substantial change in circumstances of the obligor parent. In the case of *Wolcott v. Wolcott,* the New Mexico Court of Appeals stated that when a career change is not made in good faith, a reduction in child support is not warranted. If the trial court determines that Ms. Chavez's statement concerning why she changed her occupation is sufficient to constitute bad faith, the court will not reduce her child support obligation.

FACTS

Arturo Garcia and Mary Chavez were granted a divorce in May of 1987. Mr. Garcia was awarded primary custody of the three children from the marriage. Ms. Chavez, a brain surgeon at the time of the divorce, was ordered to pay $3,000 monthly in child support. The child support obligation was undivided; that is, it did not specify a "per child" amount.

Ms. Chavez recently quit her medical practice and enrolled in the legal assistant program at the community college. This career change resulted in a substantial reduction in her income. She has informed several individuals that she quit her practice because she "can't stand to pay that much money" to her ex-husband.

Four months ago when the oldest child turned eighteen and moved out of Mr. Garcia's house, Ms. Chavez reduced the amount of child support she was paying by one third. She did not obtain a court order granting a reduction in her child support obligation. She informed Mr. Garcia that she did not have to pay the full amount because the oldest child had turned eighteen.

Two months ago she reduced her support payment to $500 per month. Again, she did not obtain a court order granting a reduction in the amount she owed. She informed Mr. Garcia, "That's all I can afford to pay now that I'm going to school."

ANALYSIS ISSUE I

Two New Mexico statutes are relevant to questions involving age of majority and child support orders issued by a court. The age of majority is established in NMSA Section 28-6-1 (Repl. Pamp. 1991). This section provides that the age of majority is reached when an individual turns eighteen years old. The statute governing child support obligations is NMSA Section 40-4-7F (Repl. Pamp. 1994) which in relevant part provides "[t]he court may modify and change any order in respect to the . . . maintenance . . . of the children whenever circumstances render such change proper. The district court shall have exclusive jurisdiction of all matters pertaining to the . . . maintenance of the children so long as the children remain minors."

Although NMSA Section 40-4-7F clearly states that the court shall have exclusive jurisdiction over matters concerning the maintenance of children, the statute does not address the specific question of an obligor's power to unilaterally reduce a child support obligation when one of the children reaches the age of majority. This question, however, has been addressed by the New Mexico courts.

In the case of *Britton v. Britton,* 100 N.M. 424, 671 P.2d 1135 (1983), the custodial parent petitioned the court for a judgment for the accrued and unpaid child support arrearages of the obligor parent. The case involved an undivided child support order. The obligor parent had failed to make several child support payments when due. By his actions he had, in effect, unilaterally reduced his support obligations. The trial court entered a final judgement against the obligor parent in the amount of $7,900. He appealed the court's award of arrearages. The state supreme court focused on questions concerning the ambiguity of the original final decree entered by the trial court, the application of the statute of limitations to the collection of accrued arrearages, the Respondent's claim to offset against any arrearages, and other issues. In addressing these questions, the court noted that "[t]he well-established general rule is that an undivided support award directed at more than one child is presumed to continue in force for the full amount until the youngest child reaches majority." Id. at _____. In regard to the obligor parent's failure to meet his child support obligations the court stated:

> Respondent, as the obligor parent, cannot by his actions unilaterally alter the support obligations set forth in the decree. As we stated in our discussion concerning the asserted ambiguity of the decree, Respondent properly should have petitioned to modify the child support terms of the decree in light of this asserted change in circumstances. Modification of support obligations is strictly a matter to be determined by the courts.

Id. at _____.

Although the court addressed different issues in *Britton,* the rules of law and legal principles discussed in the case also apply in our case. Ms. Chavez, the obligor parent, unilaterally reduced the undivided support obligation when the oldest child reached the age of eighteen, the age of majority under NMSA Section 28-6-1A (Repl. Pamp. 1991). She did not petition the court for a modification of the terms of the child support order. As the court noted in *Britton,* a modification of a support obligation is a matter for the courts and cannot be accomplished by the unilateral act of the obligor parent. Therefore, it was not permissible for Ms. Chavez to unilaterally reduce her support payment by one third when the oldest child reached the age of eighteen and moved out.

There does not appear to be any valid counterargument to this analysis. The statute and case law clearly require that any modification of a child support obligation must be made by the court and not by unilateral act of a party. It may be argued that *Britton* does not apply because the facts of the case and the issues the court addressed are somewhat different from those present in our case. Although there are some differences, the cases are fundamentally the same in that in both cases the obligor parent reduced an undivided child support obligation without petitioning the court for an order modifying the terms of the support decree. Therefore, the principles applied in *Britton* should apply in our case.

CONCLUSION ISSUE I

The age of majority in New Mexico is eighteen, NMSA § 28-6-1 (Repl. Pamp. 1991). Under NMSA Section 40-4-7F (Repl. Pamp. 1994), the district court has exclusive jurisdiction over and authority to modify any order pertaining to the maintenance of the children. The court in the *Britton* case stated that an undivided child support order continues until the youngest child reaches majority. The court noted that the modification of a support obligation is strictly a matter for the court and may not be accomplished by the unilateral act of the obligor parent. Ms. Chavez's unilateral act of reducing her child support obligation by one third when her oldest child attained the age of eighteen is clearly not permissible under New Mexico statutory and case law.

ANALYSIS ISSUE II

The relevant rule of law governing the modification of child support orders due to a change in financial circumstances is NMSA Section 40-4-11.4A (Repl. Pamp. 1994). This section provides in relevant part "[a] court may modify a child support obligation upon a showing of material and substantial changes in circumstances subsequent to the adjudication of the pre-existing order." The section does not include provisions which answer the question of when a material change in circumstances resulting from a voluntary career change warrants a reduction in an obligor spouse's support obligation. The New Mexico Court of Appeals, however, has addressed this question.

A case on point is *Wolcott v. Wolcott,* 105 N.M. 608, 735 P.2d 326 (Ct. App. 1987). In this case the husband was a physician specializing in obstetrics and gynecology at the time of the divorce in 1983. In 1985, he closed his office and entered a psychiatric residency program. This career change resulted in a substantial reduction in his income. He unilaterally reduced his child support payments without judicial approval or forewarning his former spouse. Subsequently, he petitioned the trial court for a reduction of his support obligation. The court denied his petition finding that he did not act in good faith when he voluntarily made the career change.

The Court of Appeals upheld the trial court. The court, referring to decisions in other jurisdictions stated:

The common trend in various jurisdictions is that a good faith career change, resulting in a decreased income, may constitute a material change in circumstances that warrants a reduction in a spouse's support obligations. Likewise, where the career change is not made in good faith, a reduction in one's support obligations will not be warranted. (citations omitted)

Id. at _____.

As the court noted in *Wolcott,* where a career change is not made in good faith, a reduction in the support obligation of an obligor parent is not warranted. If *Wolcott* is followed and the trial court determines that Ms. Chavez's career change was not made in good faith, she should not be granted a modification of her child support obligation.

A likely counterargument is that Ms. Chavez's statements that she quit her practice because she could not stand to pay Mr. Garcia "that much money" are insufficient to support a conclusion that the career change was made in bad faith. This argument should not prevail. In *Wolcott,* without any direct evidence or statement from the husband indicating his intent, the court concluded that he was acting in bad faith. The husband's bad faith was inferred from his disregard of financial obligations under the marital settlement, his failure to make full disclosure of his income and assets, and his self-indulgent lifestyle. In our case, Ms. Chavez's statement to several witnesses regarding the reason for her career change is direct evidence clearly indicating that the change was not made in good faith. If *Wolcott* is followed, the trial court has sufficient evidence to find bad faith and deny any petition by Ms. Chavez for a reduction in her support obligation.

CONCLUSION ISSUE II

The New Mexico law governing the modification of child support orders based on a change of circumstances requires a showing of a material and substantial change in circumstances subsequent to the initial court order. NMSA § 40-4-11.4A (Repl. Pamp. 1994). In the *Wolcott* case, the Court of Appeals stated that a reduction in an obligor parent's support obligation is not warranted when a career change is not made in good faith. In our case Ms. Chavez's statement that she quit her practice because she could not stand to pay her ex-husband "that much money" is clear evidence that her career change was not made in good faith. In light of the holding in *Wolcott,* Ms. Chavez is not entitled to a modification of her child support obligation.

RECOMMENDATIONS

Issue I

Since there are differences between the facts and issues discussed in *Britton* and our case, it may be advisable to conduct further research to determine if there is another case which is more on point.

Issue II

Further investigation should be conducted to determine if there is additional evidence indicating that Ms. Chavez's career change was made in bad faith.

ASSIGNMENT 10

To: Supervisory Attorney
From: Paralegal
Re: *Kells v. Simns*
          Implied warranty—fitness for a particular purpose

STATEMENT OF ASSIGNMENT

The purpose of this assignment is to assess the likelihood of our client, Merril Simns, prevailing against a claim of breach of an implied warranty of fitness for a particular purpose in his sale of a riding lawn mower to the plaintiff, Tom Kells.

ISSUE

Under the provisions of the Oregon statute governing implied warranties of fitness for a particular purpose, ORS § 72.3150, does a sale of a riding lawn mower create an implied warranty of fitness for a particular purpose when the buyer tells the seller of his need to mow one-and-a-half acres weekly and the seller, who has no special expertise or other experience with riding mowers, responds that the mower always did a good job when used for mowing an acre?

BRIEF ANSWER

Probably no. An implied warranty of fitness for a particular purpose probably is not created under these circumstances because there is no evidence that the buyer relied on the seller's skill and judgment in selecting the mower for the buyer's purpose, and no evidence that the seller had reason to know of any reliance by the buyer.

FACTS

Merril Simns, our client, has been sued by Tom Kells for breach of an implied warranty of fitness for a particular purpose in the sale of a riding lawn mower. Mr. Simns placed an ad in the Daily Post offering a Ryder 1000 riding lawn mower for sale for $400. In responding to the ad, Mr. Kells told our client that he needed a good riding mower because he needed to mow one-and-a-half acres once a week. Our client replied that the mower had always done a good job for him, even though he had never needed to mow more than one acre. After discussing the terms, Mr. Kells purchased the mower for $300. Mr. Simns has no experience with riding mowers other than his use of the Ryder 1000, nor does he have any special expertise with riding mowers.

One week after the sale, Mr. Kells called our client and informed him that the mower was too small and underpowered for his needs, and requested his money back. Mr. Simns refused. Mr. Kells subsequently filed suit in small claims court alleging breach of an implied warranty of fitness for a particular purpose.

ANALYSIS

The Oregon statute governing implied warranties of fitness for a particular purpose, ORS § 72.3150, states that:

Where the seller at the time of contracting has reason to know any particular purpose for which the goods are required and that the buyer is relying on the seller's skill or judgment to select or furnish suitable goods, there is unless excluded or modified under ORS 72.3610 an implied warranty that the goods shall be fit for such purpose.

This statute has been interpreted by the Oregon courts in a case with some similarities to this one. In *Beam v. Cullett,* 48 Or. App. 47, 615 P.2d 1196 (1980), the court addressed the question of whether an implied warranty of fitness for a particular purpose was created in a sale of a used diesel truck. The court identified four factors for determining whether this type of warranty exists in a transaction:

(1) whether the buyer relies on the seller's skill and judgment to select or furnish suitable goods;

(2) whether the seller at the time of the sale has reason to know of the buyer's purpose;

(3) whether the seller has reason to know that the buyer is relying on the seller's skill and judgment; and

(4) whether the seller possesses superior knowledge and skill with respect to the item sold, for "[t]here can be no justifiable reliance by a buyer who has equal or superior knowledge and skill with respect to the product purchased by him."

Id. at _____.

In *Beam* the buyer told the seller, who was not a dealer in vehicles, of his intended use of the truck. There was no evidence that the buyer justifiably relied on the seller's skill and judgment in selecting the truck for the buyer's purpose and no evidence that the seller had reason to know of any reliance. There also was no evidence that the seller offered to fulfill the stated needs of the buyer. The seller did not have any particular expertise concerning diesel trucks and merely answered the buyer's questions concerning previous repair work done on the truck. Finally, the parties had comparable, limited knowledge of diesel trucks. The court held that under these circumstances no implied warranty of fitness for a particular purpose was created.

Likewise in our case, there is no evidence that Mr. Kells relied on Mr. Simns' skill and judgment and no evidence that Mr. Simns offered the riding mower as suitable for Mr. Kells' needs. While our client knew of Mr. Kells' intended use of the mower, he only stated that the mower had done a good job for him in mowing an acre. Our client had no reason to know that Mr. Kells' might be relying on his skill and judgment in deciding whether to purchase the mower. Further, our client had no special expertise or experience with mowers beyond his use of the Ryder 1000. It appears that both he and Mr. Simns had limited, comparable knowledge of this mower. Under the reasoning of *Beam,* therefore, Mr. Simns' sale of the riding mower to Mr. Kells should not have created an implied warranty of fitness for a particular purpose.

A counterargument to this is that Mr. Simns did have superior knowledge to Mr. Kells on riding mowers. This is a speculative argument at this point for the facts do not indicate whether Mr. Kells had previous experience with riding mowers. Even if Mr. Simns had more knowledge about riding mowers than Mr. Kells, this certainly did not amount to expertise, and there remains no evidence of the necessary reliance factor.

CONCLUSION

ORS § 72.3150 creates an implied warranty of fitness for a particular purpose in the sale of goods when the seller, at the time of the sale, has reason to know the particular purpose for which the goods are required and reason to know that the buyer is relying on the seller's skill or judgment in selecting or furnishing suitable goods. The Oregon Court of Appeals in *Beam v. Cullett* has interpreted this statute to mean that the seller also must have superior knowledge and skill with respect to the item purchased. Given the lack of evidence of reliance by Mr. Kells on Mr. Simns's skill or judgment in the purchase of the riding mower, the lack of evidence that Mr. Simns had any reason to know of any reliance, and the apparent comparable knowledge of the parties to the transaction, the sale in this case should not give rise to an implied warranty of fitness for a particular purpose. Mr. Simns is likely to prevail in the lawsuit.

RECOMMENDATIONS

Further factual research should be conducted to determine whether Mr. Kells had any prior experience with riding mowers, thus making him comparable in knowledge to Mr. Simns. Further research into case law may reveal more information about how the courts determine the comparability of knowledge between a buyer and a seller.

ASSIGNMENT 11

To: Supervisory Attorney
From: Paralegal
Re: *Commonwealth v. Clavel*
        Execution of search warrant—unannounced entry

STATEMENT OF ASSIGNMENT

The purpose of this assignment is to assess the likelihood of our client, Darren Clavel, prevailing on a motion to suppress evidence because of the manner in which the search warrant of his home was executed.

ISSUE

Under the Fourth Amendment's prohibition of unreasonable searches, must evidence be suppressed when police officers executing a search warrant knock on the door of a house, shout "police, open up," wait fifteen seconds, then kick the door open and search the house before the suspect, who is hard of hearing, has the opportunity to reach the door to open it?

BRIEF ANSWER

Yes. Under the Fourth Amendment, absent exigent circumstances, a suspect must be given a reasonable opportunity to surrender his privacy voluntarily. Forcible entry, even after the police announce their identity, is unreasonable and violative of the Fourth Amendment if the occupant of the premises to be searched is not first given this opportunity. Fifteen seconds after a police announcement is not a reasonable opportunity.

FACTS

Our client, Darren Clavel, seeks to suppress evidence seized at his home because of the manner in which the search was executed. Police officers obtained a warrant to search Mr. Clavel's home for drugs. When the officers arrived at his house, they knocked on the door, shouted "police, open up," waited fifteen seconds, then kicked the door open and searched the premises. Mr. Clavel, who is hard of hearing, was inside the house at the time. He heard some noise and was approaching the door to open it when the police kicked it open. The police found a pound of marijuana in the bedroom closet. Mr. Clavel is charged with intent to distribute narcotics.

ANALYSIS

The Fourth Amendment prohibits unreasonable searches and seizures. Under the judicially created exclusionary rule, evidence seized in violation of the Fourth Amendment must be suppressed. The contours of the Fourth Amendment have been developed through case law. A case with factual similarities to ours is *Commonwealth v. DeMichel*, 442 Pa. 553, 277 A.2d 159 (1971). In that case the police executed a search warrant by knocking on the defendant's door, seeing a blind lifted and someone peering out, announcing they were police, waiting five to fifteen seconds, then breaking in the door. Evidence was seized and the defendant was convicted. On appeal the defendant argued that the evidence should have been suppressed due to the illegal execution of the warrant. The Pennsylvania Supreme Court agreed and reversed for a new trial.

The court in *DeMichel* stated that the Fourth Amendment requires police officers to give notice of their identity and announce their purpose prior to executing a search on private premises, absent exigent circumstances. Forcible entry is unreasonable and violative of the Fourth Amendment if the occupant is not first given an adequate opportunity to surrender the premises voluntarily. The court found that the time delay of five to fifteen seconds provided by the police officers was not reasonably sufficient for the defendant to respond. Even if the door was close to the blinds, numerous legitimate reasons can account for an occupant's delay in responding. A five to fifteen second time period was insufficient for the police to reasonably believe the defendant did not intend to open the door.

The court also found that there were no exigent circumstances to dispense with the requirement of providing the defendant a reasonable opportunity to open the door voluntarily. The fact that the evidence in the case could be easily destroyed was insufficient to overcome Fourth Amendment protections; the police must show more than simply a presumption that the evidence will be destroyed because it can be destroyed easily. Finally, the court stated that the fact that the defendant was observed destroying some of the evidence when the police forcibly entered is without significance, for the lawfulness of entry is dependent on what the officers had reason to believe at the time of their entry. A search does not become legal because of what is found.

The reasoning of the court in *DeMichel* applies with equal force to the facts of our case. In our case, as in *DeMichel,* the police provided Mr. Clavel with a very limited time to respond to their announcement at the door. If fifteen seconds was unreasonable in *DeMichel,* it should be equally so in our case, especially since Mr. Clavel had a legitimate reason for the delay in opening the door. The police could not have had time within fifteen seconds to reasonably conclude that Mr. Clavel was refusing to open the door. Nor were there any exigent circumstances to justify the forced entry. Just because drugs can be destroyed does not mean they will be, and there is no evidence that the police had any particular reason to believe that Mr. Clavel would destroy the marijuana while the officers were waiting at the door. Finally, the fact that the officers found marijuana in Mr. Clavel's house does not justify the illegality of the search. Under the reasoning in *DeMichel* the court should suppress the marijuana seized from Mr. Clavel's house as a result of this search.

The counterarguments to this conclusion would be largely fact-based. The police may argue that fifteen seconds was an appropriate waiting time, although they would be hard-pressed to find a justifiable reason for this position. They may argue that there were exigent circumstances for their haste, although there is no evidence of this. As a last resort, the Commonwealth may argue as a matter of policy that the court should modify the exclusionary rule to permit searches under these circumstance, even if the current case law does not support this position.

CONCLUSION

The Fourth Amendment requires that occupants of premises must be allowed a reasonable period of time to voluntarily surrender the premises prior to execution of a search warrant. The court in *Commonwealth v. DeMichel* held that five to fifteen seconds is not a sufficient amount of time between police announcement of their identity and forcible entry, requiring suppression of the evidence seized. Given this precedent, the court should suppress the marijuana seized under similar factual circumstances from Mr. Clavel's home.

RECOMMENDATIONS

Further factual investigation should be conducted to determine whether any other facts exist to support the contentions of the police in their forced entry of Mr. Clavel's home. Also, further research into relevant Fourth Amendment cases may prove helpful in determining what time delays are reasonable in responding to a police announcement at the door of one's home.

ASSIGNMENT 12

To: Supervisory Attorney
From: Paralegal
Re: Mrs. Joyce Helger—probate of copy of lost original will

STATEMENT OF ASSIGNMENT

The purpose of this assignment is to assess the likelihood of the probate court granting a petition for administration of a conformed copy of a will and codicil when the originals cannot be located.

ISSUE

Under Florida case law governing the probate of wills, may conformed copies of a will and codicil be administered in probate when the originals of both cannot be located after the death of the testator?

BRIEF ANSWER

Uncertain. It is difficult to predict whether a court will view conformed copies of a will and codicil as competent and substantial evidence sufficient to overcome the presumption that a will and codicil that were originally in the testator's possession but cannot be located after death were intentionally destroyed by the testator.

FACTS

Mrs. Joyce Helger is our client in the probate of her late husband's estate. Since her husband's sudden death a month ago, Mrs. Helger has been unable to locate the originals of his will and codicil. She knows that her husband prepared a will. She has both a conformed copy of the will, executed December 1, 1991, and a conformed copy of the codicil, executed May 6, 1996. Mrs. Helger thought the law firm that prepared the will kept the original, but the law firm cannot locate the original. The firm's senior partner told Mrs. Helger that the firm does not keep the original of wills or codicils. Mrs. Helger wants to submit the conformed copies of the will and codicil to the probate court for administration.

ANALYSIS

This issue is governed by case law as there are no directly applicable statutes. The general rule of law is a "presumption that a will which was in the possession of the testator prior to death and which cannot be located subsequent to death was destroyed by the testator with the intention of revoking it." In the Estate of Parson, 416 So. 2d 513,_____ (Fla. Dist. Ct. App. 1982). This presumption "may only be overcome by competent and substantial evidence," Id. at _____, and logically applies to both wills and codicils. The court in In re Estate of Kuszmaul, 491 So. 2d 287 (Fla. Dist. Ct. App. 1986), addressed the question of whether a conformed copy of a will found together with an original, properly executed codicil, could be administered in probate. The trial court denied the petition for administration, but the appellate court reversed finding that the presumption of revocation was overcome by competent and substantial evidence.

In Kuszmaul, the court distinguished another case with somewhat similar facts, In re Estate of Baird, 343 So. 2d 41 (Fla. Dist. Ct. App. 1977). In Baird, the court denied probate of an original codicil that was not accompanied by a copy of the will, which were not the same facts as in Kuszmaul. Both the testators in Baird and Kuszmaul showed continuing affection for the beneficiaries of their wills, but the testator in Kuszmaul left additional evidence of intent by writing a letter to one of his beneficiaries after execution of the will which stated that the property devised "would 'someday . . . . be yours.'" Kuszmaul at _____.

The court in Kuszmaul found the facts of the case to be analogous to Will of Herbert, 89 Misc. 2d 340, 391 N.Y.S.2d 351 (1977), which also involved a copy of a will and an original codicil. The Herbert court held that the presumption of revocation was overcome by the fact that the testator kept both the copy of the will and the original codicil in his personal possession, making it unlikely that he intentionally revoked the will. The court in Kuszmaul also noted two relevant Florida statutes. One, Florida Statutes Section 732.5105, states that the execution of a codicil that refers to a previous will has the effect of republishing the will as modified by the codicil, although it is silent on whether it is applicable when the original of the will cannot be found. The other, Florida Statutes Section 732.511, states that even if a will has been revoked, it may be republished and made valid by a codicil that is executed with the formalities required for wills. The codicil in Kuszmaul was executed with the requisite formalities, and the court concluded that the presumption of revocation was overcome.

Our case is more like Kuszmaul and Herbert than like Baird, where only the original codicil, and neither the original nor a copy of the will, was located. In our case Mrs. Helger has a conformed copy of both the executed will and the executed codicil. Both of these documents existed in the Kuszmaul and Herbert cases, although in those cases the codicil was an original. Nonetheless, the reasoning of those cases may apply to our case. Mr. Helger presumably kept the conformed copies of his will and codicil in his possession, which may indicate his intention not to revoke them.

The counterargument is that conformed copies of a will and codicil, alone, do not constitute substantial and competent evidence to overcome the presumption. As neither document is an original, the Kuszmaul and Herbert cases are not on point. Nor are the two Florida statutes referenced above, as they do not indicate whether they are applicable when the original of the will or the codicil cannot be found. The fact that neither can be found suggests that Mr. Helger intended to revoke them, and in fact the conformed copies may not have been in Mr. Helger's possession at the time of his death. We do not know whether the originals were ever in his possession, or where Mrs. Helger found the conformed copies.

There are many unknown facts in our case. We need to do more research in order to assess the likelihood of whether Mrs. Helger will prevail in the probate court. See the Recommendations section below.

CONCLUSION

The courts have developed a presumption that a will that was originally in the testator's possession, but that cannot be located after death, was destroyed by the testator with the intent of revoking it. This presumption may be overcome only by competent and substantial evidence. The courts in Kuszmaul and Herbert held that an original codicil found with a copy of the will is sufficient to overcome the presumption that the will was revoked. In our case, where only copies of both the will and the codicil have been located, it is difficult to predict how likely the probate court would be to administer these documents. We need to conduct more research as recommended below.

RECOMMENDATIONS

We should conduct more case law research into the amount of evidence required to overcome the presumption of revocation when the originals of testamentary documents cannot be found. We also should conduct more factual research. For example, did Mr. Helger ever have the originals of the will and codicil in his possession? Where did Mrs. Helger find the conformed copies? Does the codicil refer to the previous will or attempt to republish it? Was the codicil properly executed? Did Mr. Helger make any statements to his beneficiaries indicating his intent that they would inherit? Would testimony by someone at the law firm that prepared the documents be helpful? Would this testimony be admissible? Are there any other places to search for the originals of the will and codicil?

ASSIGNMENT 13

To: Supervisory Attorney
From: Paralegal
Re: *Mad Dog Review v. Jonesville*
             First Amendment—Freedom of Expression

STATEMENT OF ASSIGNMENT

The purpose of this assignment is to determine if the Jonesville municipal ordinance governing public performances violates the First Amendment.

ISSUE

In light of the freedom of speech protections granted in the First Amendment of the United States Constitution, is a municipal ordinance enforceable which allows a city council to prohibit the public performance of any entertainment which does not comport with local standards of decency or acceptability, and the ordinance does not define the local standards or provide any standards or guidelines that the council must follow?

BRIEF ANSWER

No. The ordinance as drafted violates the First Amendment's guarantee of freedom of speech. In the case of *Atlantic Beach Casino, Inc. v. Morenzoni,* the United States District Court for the District of Rhode Island noted that an ordinance governing licensing of entertainment must contain definite standards which guide the licensing authority. The Jonesville ordinance does not contain any standards.

FACTS

Mad Dog Review is a controversial local rap band. The lyrics of one or its songs, "Mad Dog City Council," describes our city council in explicit terms using "dirty" words and language generally considered obscene. Based upon the language in its songs and specifically in "Mad Dog City Council," the city council of Jonesville banned the group from performing in its community.

The Jonesville city council based its authority to enact the ban on Jonesville Municipal Ordinance § 355-20. The section provides that "The City Council, upon majority vote, may prohibit the public performance of any type of entertainment that does not comport with local standards of decency or acceptability." The ordinance does not define "local standards of decency or acceptability" or provide standards or guidelines that the city council must follow.

ANALYSIS

The First Amendment of the United States Constitution guarantees freedom of speech. The Amendment provides in relevant part "Congress shall make no law . . . abridging the freedom of speech. . . ." The Amendment, however, does not give guidance as to how the freedom of speech protection applies in a specific fact situation such as that presented in our case. Therefore, it is necessary to refer to case law.

The only case on point is *Atlantic Beach Casino, Inc. v. Morenzoni,* 749 F. Supp. 38 (D. R.I. 1990). In this case the plaintiffs scheduled a performance by the group 2 Live Crew. The Westerly Town Council had previously issued the plaintiffs an entertainment license. The Council, concerned about public safety, scheduled a show cause hearing concerning revocation of the plaintiffs' entertainment license. The plaintiffs sought injunctive relief. The Council was acting under the authority granted in Westerly Code of Ordinances Section 17-87. The ordinance provides that "Any license granted under Section 17-84 and 17-88 may be revoked by the Town Council after public hearing for cause shown."

The court noted that the Town Council was engaging in prior restraint by seeking to review and decide in advance whether to allow the performance to go forward. The court stated, "A licensing scheme involving such prior restraint survives constitutional scrutiny only when the law contains 'narrow, objective and definite standards to guide the licensing authority.'" Id. at _____. The court noted that the standards must be explicitly set out in the ordinance. The court stated that the Westerly ordinance left the issuance and revocation of licenses to the unbridled discretion of the Town council. The court commented that the ordinances "do not even approach the necessary level of specificity constitutionally mandated." Id. at _____.

In our case, just as in *Atlantic Beach Casino, Inc. v. Morenzoni,* the ordinance does not have any "narrow, objective or definite standards to guide the licensing authority." Jonesville Municipal Ordinance § 355-20 does not define what constitutes local standards of decency or acceptability or provide any standards or guidelines that the council must follow. If the reasoning applied in *Atlantic Beach Casino, Inc.* is applied in our case, it is clear that the Jonesville Municipal Ordinance is not enforceable because its provisions do not have the necessary level of specificity required by the constitution.

It does not appear that there are any viable counterarguments to the analysis presented above. The municipal ordinance is so broadly constructed and lacking in definite standards and guidelines that it clearly would not pass constitutional scrutiny. *Atlantic Beach Casino, Inc. v. Morenzoni,* however, is a federal district court case. An argument could be made that the question has not been decided by the United States Supreme Court and the district court decision is not mandatory authority and does not have to be followed in this case. This argument is weak because the court in *Atlantic Beach Casino, Inc.* relied heavily on supreme court precedent in reaching its decision.

CONCLUSION

The First Amendment of the Constitution guarantees and protects freedom of speech. In the case of *Atlantic Beach Casino, Inc. v. Morenzoni,* the United States District Court noted that a licensing ordinance governing entertainment must contain definite standards which guide the licensing authority in order to pass constitutional scrutiny. Jonesville Municipal Ordinance § 355-20 does not have any standards or guidelines that the city council must follow. Therefore, the Jonesville Municipal Ordinance is not enforceable because its provisions do not have the necessary level of specificity required by the First Amendment.

RECOMMENDATIONS

Further case law research should be conducted to determine if a higher federal court, such as a circuit court of appeals, has addressed this issue.

WEB ASSIGNMENT ANSWERS

ASSIGNMENT 1

To: Supervisory Attorney
From: Paralegal
Re: *Duran v. Shoptown*

STATEMENT OF ASSIGNMENT

The assignment is to determine the likelihood of Mrs. Duran prevailing on a false imprisonment claim against Shoptown grocery store.

ISSUE

In light of the provisions of the Kan. Stat. Ann. § 21-3424, Criminal Restraint, does false imprisonment occur when an individual is detained for investigation of shoplifting based on the store security person's observation that the individual put an item in the individual's pocket but did not see the individual put it back before leaving the store?

BRIEF ANSWER

No. In the case of *Melia v. Dillon Companies, Inc.,* the Kansas Court of Appeals held that if probable cause exists to believe a person has wrongfully taken merchandise, the merchant's defense under 21-3424(3) includes the right to detain the suspected shoplifter for the purpose of investigation. In our case the security person had probable cause to believe Ms. Duran had taken the item without paying for it, therefore her detention for investigation was not false imprisonment.

FACTS

Janet Duran was shopping at Shoptown, a local grocery store. As she shopped she realized she needed another item, and her hands being full, she put the extra item, nail polish, in her coat pocket. Later she put the polish back. A store security person saw her put the polish in her pocket, but did not see her put it back. When she left the store, the guard stopped her and took her to the manager's office, stating she was being held for shoplifting. The store manager searched her purse and told her to empty her pockets. After she emptied her pockets and the manager searched her purse, the store manager told her she could leave.

ANALYSIS

The Kansas statute governing unlawful restraint is Kan. Stat. Ann. § 21-3424 which provides that "(1) Unlawful restraint is knowingly and without legal authority restraining another so as to interfere substantially with his liberty." Section (3) of the statute establishes when detention by a merchant for shoplifting does not constitute unlawful restraint:

(3) Any merchant, his agent or employee, who has probable cause to believe that a person has actual possession of and (a) has wrongfully taken, or (b) is about to wrongfully take merchandise from a mercantile establishment, may detain such person (a) on the premises or (b) in the immediate vicinity thereof, in a reasonable manner and for a reasonable period of time for the purpose of investigating the circumstances of such possession. Such reasonable detention shall not constitute an arrest nor an unlawful restraint.

The statute does not specifically address the question of whether unlawful restraint occurs when a person is detained based upon an employee's mistaken belief that a customer has pocketed an item and left the store. Kansas case law, however, does provide guidance for interpreting the statute.

A case that is helpful is *Melia v. Dillon Companies, Inc.,* 18 Kan. App. 2d 5, 846 P.2d 257 (1993). In this case Mr. Atkin (Atkin), the head of security for the store, saw Mr. Melia (Melia) leave the store without paying for a pouch of tobacco. Melia was stopped in the parking lot where he stated that he had forgotten to pay for the tobacco. He agreed to reenter the store where he stated he unintentionally left the store without paying. Melia thought he would be allowed to pay for the tobacco, but Atkin informed him that the matter would be treated as a shoplifting offense. Melia was detained until the police arrived. Melia sued the store for false imprisonment and malicious prosecution.

In reviewing the store's appeal of a jury verdict in favor of Melia, the court of appeals addressed the false imprisonment claim. The court noted that "Although 21-3424 is a criminal statute, the merchant's defense set forth in subsection (3) is applicable to civil actions for false imprisonment." *Id* at 259 (referring to *Alvarado v. City of Dodge City,* 238 Kan. 48, 60, 708 P.2d 174 (1985)).

In addressing the detention, the court noted that "probable cause such as may justify a detention exists where the facts and circumstances within the knowledge of the one who is detaining are sufficient to warrant a person of reasonable caution to believe that the person detained has committed an offense." *Id.* at 260. The court noted that Melia concealed the tobacco from view by placing it in his pocked and left the store without paying for it. Based on Atkin's observations of these acts, Atkin had probable cause to believe Melia had wrongfully removed the tobacco. In holding that the trial court erred in denying the store's motion for a directed verdict on the false imprisonment claim the court stated that, "once probable cause exists, the merchant's defense under 21-3424(3) includes the right to reasonably detain a suspected shoplifter for the sole purpose of investigation. . . ." *Id* at 260.

Our case is similar to *Melia.* In our case the store security person observed Ms. Duran place the polish in her pocket and as far as the security person knew she left the store without paying for it. Just as in *Melia,* these observations were sufficient probable cause to believe Ms. Duran had wrongfully removed the polish from the store and sufficient probable cause under 21-3424(3) to detain Ms. Duran for the purpose of investigation. Although Ms. Duran was detained, she was allowed to leave after it was determined that she had not shoplifted the nail polish.

It may be argued that the facts in this case are distinguishable from those in *Melia* because Ms. Duran did not leave the store with the polish and therefore *Melia* is not on point. The principle, however, in both cases is the same. Are there facts and circumstances within the knowledge of the one who is detaining that are sufficient to warrant a person of reasonable caution to believe that the person detained has committed an offense? What the security guard saw was sufficient to warrant a person of reasonable caution to believe that Ms. Duran had taken the polish. Neither the court nor the statute requires that shoplifting in fact take place. All that is required is that probable cause exist. Here, although the security guard was mistaken, based on his observations he had probable cause and therefore was entitled to detain Ms. Duran under Kan. Stat. Ann. 21-3424(3).

CONCLUSION

Kansas statute § 21-3424 defines unlawful restraint and establishes when restraint by merchants for shoplifting does not constitute unlawful restraint. In *Melia v. Dillon Companies, Inc.,* 18 Kan. App. 2d 5, 846 P.2d 257 (1993), the court of appeals held that if probable cause exists, the merchant's defense under 21-3424(3) includes the right to detain a suspected shoplifter for the purpose of investigation. In our case the security person had probable cause to believe Ms. Duran had taken the nail polish, therefore her detention for investigation was not false imprisonment.

RECOMMENDATIONS

The only recommendation would be to search for additional case law that addresses the situation where a security guard's observations are mistaken and an individual is detained upon the mistaken observation.

ASSIGNMENT 2

To: Supervisory Attorney
From: Paralegal
Re: *Frampton v. City*

STATEMENT OF ASSIGNMENT

The assignment is to determine whether law enforcement officers owed a duty of care to Mrs. Frampton and whether their actions are protected by sovereign immunity.

ISSUE

ISSUE I

Under Florida's tort law of negligence, did law enforcement officers owe a duty of care to an individual harmed in an accident caused by a passenger who officers allowed to drive after they arrested the driver for DUI, and the passenger had obviously been drinking but did not appear to the officers to be intoxicated?

ISSUE II

Under the waiver of sovereign immunity statute, Fla. Stat. Ann. § 768.28(1), are the actions of police officers protected by sovereign immunity when an accident is caused by a passenger who officers allowed to drive after they arrested the driver for DUI, and the passenger had obviously been drinking but did not appear to the officers to be intoxicated?

BRIEF ANSWER

ISSUE I

Probably. In the case of *Henderson v. Bowden,* 737 So.2d 532 (Fla 1999) the court held that officers, when directing a passenger to drive after arresting the driver, created a foreseeable risk of harming others that gave rise to a legal duty of care. In *Henderson* the duty of care extended to the passengers, inasmuch as the legal duty arises whenever an action creates a foreseeable risk of harming others, the holding should apply to all "others" placed at risk by the officers conduct, not just passengers.

ISSUE II

No. In the case of *Henderson v. Bowden* the Supreme Court held that the actions of law enforcement officers in regard to detained persons, other than to arrest or detain them, were operational acts not protected by sovereign immunity.

FACTS

On the evening of January 15, city police officers stopped Jerry Myers on suspicion of drunk driving and arrested him for DUI. One passenger, Susan Lane, accompanied Mr. Myers. She had been taking drugs in addition to drinking. Although the officers smelled alcohol on Susan's breath, they did not believe she was intoxicated and did not require her to take a field sobriety test. After determining that she lived only two blocks away, they allowed her to drive the automobile to her house. On the way home she lost control of the vehicle and it swerved into a car driven by our client, Mrs. Frampton, who suffered extensive injuries.

ANALYSIS ISSUE I

Florida's common law provides that four elements must be established to prove a negligence claim: duty, breach of duty, proximate cause, and damages. Florida case law addresses the nature of law enforcement officers' duty when they stop a vehicle.

A case which discusses the officers' duty is *Henderson v. Bowden,* 737 So.2d 532 (Fla 1999). In *Henderson* officers stopped a vehicle for speeding and arrested the driver for DUI. The officers gave Lyons, a passenger, the option of either driving to a nearby Circle K convenience store and calling his parents for a ride home, or having the vehicle impounded. Lyons drove the vehicle to the Circle K, waited a few minutes, then drove away. Lyons subsequently failed to negotiate a turn in the road and collided with a cluster of trees. The passengers in the car were killed.

The officers testified that Lyons insisted he was sober and he did not smell of alcohol. They administered a field sobriety test that indicated Lyons was not impaired. Lyons testified that he repeatedly told the officers that he was intoxicated before they directed him to drive to the Circle K. The parents of the deceased brought a wrongful death action against the officers.

In determining that the officers owed a duty of care to the passengers, the court referred to *McCain v. Florida Power Corp.,* 593 So.2d 500 (Fla.1992) where the court stated that a legal duty arises whenever an action creates a generalized and foreseeable risk of harming others. *Henderson* 737 So.2d at 535 (citing *McCain v. Florida Power Corp.* 593 So.2d 500, 502 (Fla. 1992). The court concluded that the sheriff's deputies "placed the passengers of Lyons' vehicle in danger by directing an intoxicated Lyons to drive to the Circle K and that this direction, more likely than not, created a foreseeable zone of risk, thereby giving rise to a legal duty." *Henderson,* 737 So.2d at 536.

In our case, just as in *Henderson* the officers' conduct of allowing Susan Lane to drive when she smelled of alcohol created a foreseeable risk of harming others and gave rise to a legal duty of care. This is so especially in light of the fact that the officers did not require her to take a field sobriety test.

A counterargument may be raised that *Henderson* does not apply because in *Henderson* the duty of care applied to the passengers of the vehicle who were exposed to the danger by the officers directing an intoxicated passenger to drive. In *Henderson* the victims were passengers and the court does not address the question of whether the duty applies to individuals other than passengers. However, in light of the court's reference to the *McCain* court's standard that a legal duty arises whenever an action creates a foreseeable risk of harming others, the holding should apply to all "others" placed at risk by the officers conduct, not just passengers. If the goal is to prevent harm to "others" there is no reason the "others" should be limited to passengers. See Recommendations on next page.

ANALYSIS ISSUE II

In section 768.28(1) of the Florida Statutes (1997) the state waived sovereign immunity of liability for torts to the extent specified in the act. The section provides:

Actions at law against the state or any of its agencies . . . to recover damages in tort for money damages against the state or its agencies . . . for injury . . . caused by the negligent or wrongful act or omission of any employee of the agency . . . while acting within the scope of the employee's office or employment under circumstances in which the state or such agency or subdivision, if a private person, would be liable to the claimant . . . may be prosecuted subject to the limitation specified in this act.

The section does not address the specific question of whether sovereign immunity is waived in a situation where officers allow a passenger to drive after the driver is arrested and the passenger causes an accident.

The Supreme Court specifically addressed the question in *Henderson v. Bowden,* 737 So.2d 532 (Fla 1999). As noted in Issue I above, in *Henderson* officers stopped a vehicle for speeding. They arrested the driver for DUI. The officers gave Lyons, a passenger, the option of either driving to a nearby Circle K convenience store and calling his parents for a ride home or having the vehicle impounded. Lyons drove the vehicle to the Circle K, waited a few minutes, then drove away. Lyons subsequently failed to negotiate a turn in the road and collided with a cluster of trees, killing the passengers in the car. The officers testified that they believed Lyons was sober.

The court noted that in its opinion in *Kaisner v. Kolb,* 543 So.2d 732 (Fla.1989), it "held that acts by law enforcement officers in respect to persons whom they have detained, other than whether to arrest or detain those persons, were operational acts not protected by sovereign immunity." *Henderson,* 737 So.2d at 537. The court stated that, like *Kaisner,* the case dealt with a situation where officers were alleged to have acted negligently during a roadside detention. The court concluded that the alleged actions of the officers were "not the type of actions insulated from suit and, therefore, not protected by the doctrine of sovereign immunity." *Henderson,* 737 So.2d at 538.

In our case, just as in *Henderson,* the officers allowed the passenger to drive after arresting the driver. Under the holding in *Henderson* such acts are operational acts not protected by sovereign immunity and if *Henderson* is followed, therefore, the city police officers actions are not protected by sovereign immunity.

CONCLUSION ISSUES I AND II

Under Florida common law, duty is one of the elements that must be established to prove negligence. In the case of *Henderson v. Bowden,* 737 So.2d 532 (Fla 1999), the court held that officers, when directing a passenger to drive after arresting the driver, created a foreseeable risk of harming others that gave rise to a legal duty of care. In *Henderson* the duty of care extended to the individuals injured, the passengers of the vehicle driven by the intoxicated driver. If it is determined that this duty of care extends to injured individuals in other vehicles, then in our case the officers owe a duty of care to our client, the driver of the car struck by Ms. Lane's vehicle.

In section 768.28(1) of the Florida Statutes (1997) the state waived sovereign immunity of liability for torts to the extent specified in the act. In *Henderson* the Supreme Court "held that acts by law enforcement officers in respect to persons whom they have detained, other than whether to arrest or detain those persons, were operational acts not protected by sovereign immunity." Id at 537. In our case the actions of the officers in allowing a passenger to drive, after arresting the driver, were "operational acts not protected by sovereign immunity."

RECOMMENDATIONS

We need to conduct additional research to determine whether there are other cases which address the question of the duty of care to nonpassengers.

ASSIGNMENT 3

To: Supervisory Attorney
From: Paralegal
Re: *McKnown v. Grieten*

STATEMENT OF ASSIGNMENT

The assignment is to determine if Mr. Johann Grieten is liable for the automobile accident caused by his daughter Joanne while driving his automobile contrary to his express instructions.

ISSUE

In light of the provisions of the Minnesota statute governing the liability of owners of vehicles, Minn. Stat. Ann. § 170.54, is the owner of a vehicle liable for an accident caused by his daughter when the daughter had permission to drive the vehicle to the mall and home, and the accident occurred when she drove the vehicle again after returning from the mall?

BRIEF ANSWER

Yes. In the case of *Jones v. Fleischhacker,* the Minnesota Supreme Court held that a minor who has parental permission to drive a vehicle is the agent of the parent under Minn. Stat. Ann. § 170.54 even when the minor's use of the vehicle exceeds the initial permission granted by the parent, and therefore the parent is liable for the negligent operation of the vehicle by the minor.

FACTS

Johann Grieten, gave his daughter, Joanne, the car keys and told her to drive to the shopping mall and purchase some paint. He told her, "Go directly to the mall and come directly home. Don't, I repeat, don't go anywhere else. Don't go to your friends house, don't go shopping." She purchased the paint and returned home. Her father was not home when she returned. A friend of Joanne called her and asked her to see a new car her father was going to buy her. As Joanne drove to the dealership to see the car, she failed to yield at a stop sign and collided with Jeffery Mc-Known's car. McKnown is suing Mr. Grieten. Mr. Grieten owns the car his daughter was driving.

ANALYSIS

The Minnesota statute governing the liability of the owner of a vehicle for the negligence of a driver other than the owner is Minn. Stat. Ann. § 170.54. The statute provides that:

> Whenever any motor vehicle shall be operated within this state, by any person other than the owner, with the consent of the owner, express or implied, the operator thereof shall in case of accident, be deemed the agent of the owner of such motor vehicle in the operation thereof.

The statute does not address the liability of a parent owner when a child's use of a vehicle exceeds the consent given by the parent. The Minnesota Supreme Court has addressed this question in the case of *Jones v. Fleischhacker,* 325 N.W.2d 633 (Minn. 1982).

In *Jones* the father, James Fleischhacker, called home to have someone move a vehicle from the garage into the street and move another vehicle from the street into the garage. The son, Ronald, offered to move the vehicles. The father, James, gave Ronald permission to move the vehicles, specifically telling him "I want the GMC taken out of the garage and placed in front of the house and the Travel-All put in the garage. And that's it." In the past Ronald had been expressly forbidden to drive the vehicles by himself. Ronald took the GMC, drove to several of his friends' houses, and while attempting to pass another vehicle at a speed in excess of the speed limit, lost control of the vehicle, and hit a tree. One of his passengers was seriously injured.

The court addressed the question of whether a minor child is deemed to be the agent of the parent when the child, initially given permission by the parent to drive a motor vehicle owned by the parent, violates the parent's express instructions. In addressing the purpose of the statute the court stated that:

> public policy dictates that the statute be accorded the construction that will achieve the purpose of giving to persons injured by the negligent operation of automobiles an approximate certainty of an effective recovery by making the registered owner responsible as well as the possibly or probably irresponsible person whom the owner permits to drive the vehicle.

Jones, 325 N.W.2d at 636. The court went on to note that the statute should be given a liberal construction, "particularly in situations involving minor permittees and sub-permittees." *Id* at 636.

The court held that the trial court erred when it failed to grant the plaintiff's motion for a directed verdict on the issue of whether Ronald was operating the van with permission of the father. In reaching its decision the court noted

> as a matter of law, under section 170.54 there was permission and consent, notwithstanding the efforts of Ronald's father to severely circumscribe that initial permission to the isolated act of moving the van from the garage to the street. "Parents *** cannot with impunity blind themselves to the reality of youthful behavior" in the almost universal proclivity of young people for joyriding.

Jones, 325 N.W.2d at 637 (quoting *Granley,* 288 Minn. At 313, 180 N. W.2d at 192).

If *Jones* is followed Joanne Grieten will be deemed to be the agent of Mr. Grieten under Minn. Stat. § 170.54. In our case just as in *Jones* the minor child was given initial permission to use the vehicle owned by the parent. Just as in *Jones* the child exceeded the permission granted and negligently caused an accident. In the language of the *Jones* court, there was permission and consent, notwithstanding the efforts of Mr. Grieten to circumscribe the initial permission to the act of going directly to the mall and coming directly home.

A counterargument may be raised that *Jones v. Fleischhacker* is not on point because, in *Jones,* the minor was driving the vehicle with permission when he exceeded the permission. In our case, Joanne Grieten did follow the instructions given her; she went to the mall and came directly home. Her act of driving the vehicle again after she returned home was not within the initial permission like the action of the minor in *Jones.* It did not merely exceed the initial permission, it was a separate act for which there was neither permission nor consent, and therefore neither *Jones* nor the act applies.

In light of the court's statement that the statute should be liberally construed in situations involving minor permittees and its quote from *Granley* that parents cannot blind themselves to the reality of youthful behavior such as joy riding, it is likely that *Jones* will be followed. The distinction between our case and *Jones* is a distinction without a difference. In both cases the parent gave the child permission to drive the vehicle. In both cases the parent's initial permission rendered the child an agent of the parent despite the child's independent actions beyond the scope of the permission.

CONCLUSION

Minnesota statute §170.54 provides that when a motor vehicle is operated by a person other than the owner, with the consent of the owner, the operator in case of an accident is deemed the agent of the owner of the vehicle. In *Jones v. Fleischhacker,* 325 N.W.2d 633 (Minn. 1982), the court held that a minor driver will be considered the agent of the parent owner when the minor, given permission to drive the vehicle, drives the vehicle contrary to the express instructions of the parent. In our case Joanne Grieten was given permission by her father, Mr. Grieten, to drive the vehicle and drove it contrary to the express instructions she received. Under the holding in *Jones,* Joanne Grieten is the agent of Mr Grieten under § 170.54, and therefore he is liable for the accident.

RECOMMENDATIONS

None

TEST QUESTIONS AND ANSWERS

TRUE OR FALSE QUESTIONS—*Chapter 16*

Please write a "T" or "F" to the left of each statement.

_____ 1. Correspondence is the type of legal writing most frequently prepared when a law clerk or paralegal engages in legal research and analysis.

_____ 2. The considerations involved in the preparation of office legal memoranda also apply to the preparation of legal analysis documents intended for external use.

_____ 3. An office legal memorandum presents a subjective analysis of the legal arguments in support of the client's case.

_____ 4. An office legal memorandum is often used as a basis for the preparation of a document to be filed with a court.

_____ 5. An office legal memorandum may be used at every stage of the litigation process.

_____ 6. An office legal memorandum is not used to address issues raised on appeal.

_____ 7. Ethical considerations are usually not involved when preparing an assignment intended for internal office use such as an office legal memorandum.

_____ 8. The use of legal terminology is appropriate when drafting an office legal memorandum.

_____ 9. When preparing an office legal memorandum, the most important section of the prewriting stage is determining the constraints on the assignment.

_____10. The brief answer section may not be included in some office legal memorandum formats.

_____11. The components and considerations involved in the preparation of a complex office legal memorandum are not the same as those involved in the preparation of a basic office legal memo.

_____12. Most office legal memoranda begin with the statement of the assignment.

_____13. The heading of an office legal memorandum usually includes information identifying the subject matter of the memo.

_____14. The statement of the assignment section of an office legal memorandum usually includes information identifying the subject of the memo.

_____15. The issue is presented after the heading and before the statement of assignment in an office legal memorandum.

_____16. When the office legal memorandum involves more than one issue, each issue is listed sequentially in the issue section rather than at the beginning of the analysis of each issue.

_____17. If issues are dependent or affected by other issues, they should be listed in chronological order.

_____18. The brief answer section may consist of a one- or two-word answer, such as "yes" or "no."

_____19. In the facts section of an office legal memorandum, the facts may be presented in a combination of chronological and topical order.

_____20. The fact section of an office legal memorandum should be so detailed that any reader who is not familiar with the facts of the case does not have to refer to the case file.

TRUE OR FALSE ANSWERS—*Chapter 16*

Answer	Text Section	Answer	Text Section	Answer	Text Section
1. False	I	8. True	IVA3	15. False	VC
2. True	I	9. False	IVC	16. True	VC
3. False	II	10. True	IVC	17. False	VC4
4. True	III	11. False	IVC	18. False	VD
5. True	III	12. False	VA	19. True	VE3
6. False	III	13. True	VA	20. True	VE2
7. False	III	14. False	VB		

Note: Number 14 is False—This is the Re section of the heading.

TRUE OR FALSE QUESTIONS—*Chapter 17*

Please write a "T" or "F" to the left of each statement.

_____ 1. The analysis section of an office legal memorandum is the most important section.

_____ 2. The analysis section includes the issue, rule of law, analysis, and application of the rule of law to the facts.

_____ 3. The analysis section should begin with the presentation of the case that governs the issue.

_____ 4. The rule of law that governs the issue may be enacted law or a court adopted rule of law.

_____ 5. When introducing statutory law in the analysis section, include only the relevant portions of the law.

_____ 6. When the rule of law involves both general and specific sections, present the specific section first.

_____ 7. When there are multiple rules of law that apply, the citation to each rule must be included when they are presented in the analysis section.

_____ 8. In some instances the rule of law can be directly applied to the facts of the client's case and case law is not required.

_____ 9. If it is clear that the rule of law applies directly to the facts of the client's case, it is not necessary to check the case law.

_____ 10. When presenting case law, begin with a presentation of the facts of the case that demonstrate that the case is on point.

_____ 11. The presentation of the facts in the analysis section of an office legal memorandum is the same as the presentation of the facts in a case brief.

_____ 12. The analysis section must include a discussion of how the law applies to the facts of the client's case.

_____ 13. Counteranalysis should always be included in the analysis section.

_____ 14. There should always be a rebuttal to counteranalysis.

_____ 15. The analysis section includes a miniconclusion.

_____ 16. The conclusion should be crafted so that the reader may obtain from it all the law that applies and how it applies.

_____ 17. In some formats, recommendations are included after the brief answer.

_____ 18. Always use introductory and transitional sentences in the analysis section.

_____ 19. Whenever persuasive authority is presented, you must indicate the reasons for its use.

_____ 20. When there are several cases on point, it is necessary to discuss each case thoroughly.

TRUE OR FALSE ANSWERS—*Chapter 17*

Answer	Text Section		Answer	Text Section		Answer	Text Section
1. True	II		8. True	IIC		15. True	III
2. False	II		9. False	IIC2		16. True	III
3. False	IIB		10. False	IIC3		17. False	IV
4. True	IIB		11. False	IIC3		18. True	V
5. True	IIB2		12. True	IID		19. True	VE
6. False	IIB3		13. True	IIE		20. False	VH
7. True	IIB4		14. False	IIE			

MULTIPLE CHOICE QUESTIONS—*Chapter 16*

Please circle the letter of the **most appropriate** answer.

1. An office legal memorandum:
   a. presents a subjective analysis of the legal arguments in support of the client's position.
   b. contains a summary of the law that applies to the client's facts.
   c. discusses how the law applies to the client's case.
   d. presents an objective legal analysis of the issues raised by the facts of the case.
   e. all of the above
   f. a, b, and c
   g. b, c, and d

2. The major purposes and functions of an office memo are to:
   a. identify and record the law that applies to a specific issue or issues raised by the client's facts.
   b. analyze and explain how the law applies to the issue.
   c. present a subjective analysis of the legal arguments in support of the client's position.
   d. present a conclusion and proposed solution based on the analysis.
   e. all of the above
   f. a, b, and d
   g. a, b, and c

3. An office legal memorandum may be used in a law office:
   a. as a guide to subsequent researchers in the office.
   b. to refresh the memory of an attorney assigned to the case on how the law applies.
   c. as a guide to preparing court documents.
   d. as a guide to the course of action to pursue.
   e. all of the above
   f. a, b, and c
   g. a and d

4. Office legal memoranda are required in which of the following stages of the litigation process?
   a. prior to discovery
   b. during discovery
   c. during trial
   d. on appeal
   e. all of the above
   f. a, b, and c
   g. b and c

5. Which of the following sections may not be included in some office legal memorandum formats?
   a. statement of assignment
   b. issue
   c. brief answer
   d. conclusion
   e. all of the above
   f. a and c
   g. a, c, and d

6. The format of a complex office legal memorandum rarely includes a:
   a. table of contents.
   b. table of authorities.
   c. heading.
   d. brief answer.
   e. a and d
   f. None of the above

7. The heading of an office legal memorandum usually includes:
   a. a statement of the assignment.
   b. a date.
   c. the name of the person preparing the assignment.
   d. information identifying the subject of the memo.
   e. all of the above
   f. a, b, and c
   g. b, c, and d

8. The statement of assignment of an office legal
    memorandum usually includes:
    a. the date.
    b. the name of the person preparing the assignment.
    c. the name of the person for whom the assignment
        is prepared.
    d. case name.
    e. all of the above.
    f. a, b, and d
    g. none of the above

9. In a complex office legal memorandum involving
    several issues:
    a. list each issue at the beginning of the analysis
        section of that issue.
    b. list the issues in logical order.
    c. if the analysis of one issue is dependent on or
        affected by the analysis of another issue, the
        issue that affects the other issue should be
        presented first.
    d. if the issues are dependent on or affected by other
        issues, present the issues in chronological order.
    e. all of the above
    f. a, b, and c
    g. b and c

10. In regard to the brief answer section of an office
    legal memorandum:
    a. it may not be included in some office legal
        memorandum formats.
    b. it may consist of a one-word answer.
    c. it may include reference to information not
        included in the analysis section of the memo.
    d. it is followed by a brief statement of the grounds
        in support of the answer.
    e. all of the above
    f. a and d
    g. a, b, and c

11. The fact section of an office legal memorandum is
    presented after the:
    a. heading and before the issue.
    b. statement of assignment and before the issue.
    c. issue and before the brief answer.
    d. brief answer and before the analysis.

12. The facts in the fact section may be presented in:
    a. chronological order.
    b. topical order.
    c. a combination of chronological and topical.
    d. all of the above
    e. a and b

MULTIPLE CHOICE ANSWERS—*Chapter 16*

Answer	Text Section	Answer	Text Section	Answer	Text Section
1. g	II	5. f	IVC	9. g	VC4
2. f	III	6. g	IVC	10. f	VD
3. e	III	7. g	VA	11. d	Fig-12-4
4. e	III	8. g	VB	12. d	VE3

MULTIPLE CHOICE QUESTIONS—*Chapter 17*

Please circle the letter of the **most appropriate** answer.

1. The recommended format for the analysis section of
    an office legal memorandum includes the:
    a. issue.
    b. rule of law.
    c. application of the law to the client's facts.
    d. conclusion.
    e. all of the above
    f. b and c
    g. b, c, and d

2. The analysis section begins with a presentation of:
    a. the case that is on point.
    b. the rule of law that governs the issue.
    c. a summary of the key facts
    d. the presentation of the issue
    e. all of the above

3. In regard to the presentation of the rule of law in the analysis section:
    a. when there are multiple rules of law that apply, the citation to each rule must be presented.
    b. when the rule of law involves both general and specific sections, the specific section should be presented first.
    c. the rule of law may be paraphrased.
    d. when the law is lengthy, include only the relevant portions.
    e. all of the above
    f. a, c, and d
    g. b and d

4. In regard to case law and the analysis section of an office legal memorandum:
    a. in some instances statutory law can be applied directly to the facts, and case law is not necessary.
    b. in some instances it is not necessary to research case law when a statute clearly applies.
    c. case law links the rule of law and the issue raised by the client's facts.
    d. the analysis section usually begins with the presentation of the case on point.
    e. all of the above
    f. a and c
    g. a, b, and c

5. When presenting case law in the analysis section:
    a. present the facts of the case followed by the citation, then the applicable rule of law adopted by the court.
    b. present the applicable rule of law adopted by the court followed by the citation, then the facts of the case.
    c. present the citation, followed by the applicable rule of law adopted by the court, then the facts of the case.
    d. present the citation followed by the facts of the case, then the applicable rule of law adopted by the court.

6. In regard to the presentation of case law in the analysis section:
    a. include the same amount of factual information in the analysis section as you would in a case brief.
    b. quote language of the court when practical.
    c. the memo flows more smoothly if the applicable rule of law from the case is presented last.
    d. avoid too many quotations.
    e. all of the above
    f. b and c
    g. b, c, and d

7. In regard to counteranalysis:
    a. there may be situations where counteranalysis is not necessary.
    b. analysis is not complete unless there is counteranalysis.
    c. rebuttal is always required when there is counteranalysis.
    d. there may be situations where rebuttal is not required.
    e. a and d
    f. b and c
    g. b and d

8. In regard to the conclusion section:
    a. some law firms do not require a separate conclusion section.
    b. it should not include new information.
    c. it should include a summary of all the law discussed in the analysis section.
    d. a reader should be able to obtain all essential information, such as the applicable law, from the conclusion.
    e. all of the above
    f. a, b, and c
    g. b, c, and d

9. In regard to the recommendation section:
    a. not all law firms require a recommendation section.
    b. in some formats it is included in the analysis section.
    c. recommendations may include what the next step in the case should be.
    d. recommendations may include the identification of additional research that may be necessary.
    e. all of the above
    f. a, c, and d
    g. c and d

10. Some general considerations when preparing the analysis section are:
    a. Always use introductory and transitional sentences.
    b. Always indicate the reasons you are relying on persuasive authority.
    c. When there are several cases on point, discuss each case thoroughly.
    d. In many instances you may not be able to provide a yes or no answer as to how an issue may be resolved.
    e. all of the above
    f. a, b, and c
    g. a, b, and d

MULTIPLE CHOICE ANSWERS—*Chapter 17*

Answer	Text Section	Answer	Text Section	Answer	Text Section
1. f	IIA	5. d	IIC3	8. e	III
2. b	IIB	6. g	IIC	9. f	IV
3. f	IIB	7. g	IIE	10. g	V
4. f	IIC				

CHAPTER 18

External Memoranda—Court Briefs

TEXT ASSIGNMENT ANSWERS

ASSIGNMENT 1

The following discussion describes how to draft the issue, fact statement, point heading, and argument components of a brief.

A. ISSUE. Once the issue is identified, each of its elements (the law, question, and key facts) should be drafted in a persuasive manner.

1. **Law element of the issue.** The law element of the issue should be presented in a persuasive manner.

 FOR EXAMPLE   If the brief supports a prohibitory application of the statute, the presentation of the law component of the issue should emphasize the statute's prohibitory nature. If the brief emphasizes the applicability of the statute, the presentation of the law component of the issue should focus on the statute's applicability.

---

2. **Question element of the issue.** The writer should present the question component of the issue in a persuasive manner that suggests a result. The language used should focus on the result desired.
3. **Fact element of the issue.** Present the key facts of the issue in a manner designed to focus the reader on the facts favorable to the client and persuade the reader to favor the client's position.

B. FACT STATEMENT. A persuasive statement of the facts requires a credible presentation of the facts in a light most favorable to the client's position. This is accomplished by emphasizing favorable facts and deemphasizing or neutralizing unfavorable facts. Some of the techniques to emphasize favorable facts and neutralize unfavorable facts are the following:

1. **Placement.** Readers tend to remember information presented at the beginning and end of a section, and usually the most attention is given to opening and closing sentences. Therefore, introduce the facts favorable to the client's position at the beginning and the end of the fact statement. Present the facts unfavorable to the client's position which you wish to deemphasize in the middle of the section.

   If the fact statement is composed of several paragraphs, place the favorable material at the beginning of the presentation and close with a summary or rephrasing of the favorable key facts. Place the unfavorable facts in the middle of the presentation and mention them only once or as few times as possible.

   Note that the goal is a persuasive presentation of the facts. This goal should not be so rigidly pursued that clarity is lost.
2. **Sentence Length.** Use short sentences to emphasize favorable information and long sentences to deemphasize unfavorable information. Shorter sentences generally draw the attention of the reader, are easier to understand and, therefore, are more powerful. Longer sentences which string together several facts tend to downplay and reduce the impact of each fact.

3. **Active Voice.** Use active voice to emphasize favorable information and passive voice to deemphasize unfavorable information. Active voice draws the attention to and emphasizes the actor. Passive voice draws attention away from and deemphasizes the actor.
4. **Word Choice.** Ideally the words you choose should introduce the client's facts in the most favorable light and the opponent's in the least favorable. You should present the client's position in the most affirmative manner and the opponents in the most questionable. Avoid stating the facts in such a slanted way that your bias is obvious. When in doubt, exercise restraint.

C. POINT HEADING.
A persuasively drafted point heading should focus the reader on the position advocated in the argument. You should draft a point heading in a manner that provides a positive presentation of your position. It should affirmatively and positively characterize the position argued. The discussions above concerning word choice and active voice apply to point headings.

D. ARGUMENT.
The persuasive tone and orientation of the court brief is initially established in the presentation of the issue and fact statements. The persuasive techniques discussed in the previous sections, such as word choice, sentence length, active and passive voices, etc., also apply and should be employed when crafting the argument section of a court brief.

The goal of the argument section is to persuade the court that a position is valid. This is accomplished by a persuasive presentation of the following:

- the law in support of the position,
- the analysis of the law, and
- the argument that the analysis is valid and the opposition's analysis is invalid.

The following is a summary of the techniques to ensure that the argument component of a court brief is presented in a persuasive manner:

1. **Argument—Organization.** The organization of the argument section is similar to that of the office memo: the rule of law is introduced, followed by an interpretation of the law (usually through case law), then an application of the law to the issue raised by the facts of the case. Rather than a separate counteranalysis section, the opposing position is addressed in the presentation of the argument.
   a. **Issue Presentation.** Where there is more than one issue or where there are issues and subissues, discuss the issue supported by the strongest argument first.
   b. **Rule of Law Presentation.** Present the rule of law, whether it is enacted or case law, in a manner that supports your argument. Refer to the section, Law Element of the Issue, above for a discussion of the persuasive presentation of the rule of law.
   c. **Case Presentation.** When introducing case law, discuss the favorable case law first, followed by the unfavorable or opposing case, then a response or rebuttal which emphasizes why the favorable case should be followed. This is similar to the format followed in the fact statement: *the placement of the unfavorable material in the middle of the presentation following the favorable material tends to minimize its importance.*

   The discussion of the case law should emphasize the similarities and applicability of the case relied on to support your position and the dissimilarities and inapplicability of the case relied on by the opposition.
   d. **Argument Order.** When interpreting and applying a rule of law, always introduce your argument first, address the counterargument, then present your response. In addition, spend more time affirmatively stating your position than responding to the opponent's counterargument.
2. **Argument—Word Choice.** A persuasive presentation of the argument should be drafted using forceful, positive, and confident language. Present the opposing position in a manner that deemphasizes its importance or credibility.

ASSIGNMENT 2

Instructor's note: The student's answer to this assignment should be detailed and complete. An extensive detailed answer is presented here.

The components and format of a trial court and appellate court brief are as follows:

TRIAL COURT BRIEFS

The format of a trial brief varies from court to court and jurisdiction to jurisdiction. In many instances, the local court rules establish a required format. Generally, the format and components of a trial court brief consist of some or all of the following:

> **Caption**
> **Table of Contents**
> **Table of Authorities**
> **Preliminary Statement**
> **Question(s) Presented—Issue(s)**
> **Fact Statement**
> **Argument**
> **Conclusion**

CAPTION Every brief submitted to a trial court requires a caption. The format varies from court to court, but the caption usually includes:

- the name of the court,
- the names and status of the parties,
- the file number and type of case—civil or criminal,
- and the title of the document such as BRIEF IN SUPPORT OF MOTION TO DISMISS.

TABLE OF CONTENTS If a table of contents is required, it follows the caption page. The table of contents lists each component of the brief and the page number. If point headings are used in the argument section, they are stated in full in the table of contents. The table allows the reader to quickly locate the various components of the brief.

TABLE OF AUTHORITIES If a table of authorities is required, it is presented after the table of contents page. A table of authorities lists all the law used in the brief and the page on which the law is cited in the brief. This allows the reader to quickly locate where the authority is discussed in the brief. List the case law and enacted law in separate sections. List the case law in alphabetical order by case name.

PRELIMINARY STATEMENT The preliminary statement introduces the procedural posture of the case. It usually includes:

- an identification of the parties,
- the procedural events in the case relevant to the matter the court is addressing,
- a description of the matter being addressed by the court, such as "This matter is before the court on a motion to dismiss the complaint,"
- and the relief sought, such as "This memorandum is submitted in support of the motion to suppress the evidence seized during the search."

QUESTION(S) PRESENTED This section of a brief discusses the legal issue(s) addressed in the brief. The issue should include the rule of law, legal question, and the key facts. When there is more than one issue, list the issues in the order in which they are discussed in the argument section of the brief. An office memorandum identifies the issue(s) objectively. In a trial brief, you should draft the issue(s) in a persuasive manner.

STATEMENT OF FACTS This section is also often referred to as the statement of the case. It corresponds to the statement of facts section of an office memo. Its purpose is to explain the facts of the case. It is different from an office memo in that you should draft it in a persuasive manner designed to introduce the facts in a light that most favors the client's position. The fact section should be accurate, complete, and include background and key facts.

ARGUMENT SECTION   The argument section of a trial brief, like the analysis section of an office memorandum, is the heart of the document. It is unlike the analysis section of an office memo in that it is not an objective legal analysis. It is designed to persuade the court to adopt your interpretation of the law and should be drafted in a persuasive manner. The basic organization and components of the argument section are listed and discussed below:

1. **Summary of Argument**
2. **Point Headings**
3. **Argument**
   a. **Rule of law**
   b. **Case law—(if necessary)—Interpretation of rule of law**
   c. **Application of law to the issue being addressed**
   d. **Discussion of opposing position (similar to counteranalysis in office legal memo)**

This is the format recommended in the text. This format is not necessarily followed in every office, and a different format may be required by local court rule. In some instances, a summary of the argument may not be required, and some local court rules and office formats do not require point headings. This is often the case when the brief is short and involves a single issue. All of the components of the argument section are described here.

1. **Summary of Argument.** The argument section of a trial brief should begin with an introductory paragraph that summarizes the argument. It presents the context of the argument, the issues in the order in which they will be discussed, a summary of the conclusions on each issue, and the major reasons that support each conclusion.

2. **Point Headings.** Point headings are a summary of the position you are asking the court to adopt. They should be drafted persuasively. Point headings are designed to:
   • organize, define, and emphasize the structure of the argument,
   • act as locators—they allow the reader to quickly find specific sections of the argument, and
   • focus the court's attention on the outcome you advocate and provide an outline of your theory.
   In regard to point headings, note the following guidelines:
   a. Place the point headings at the beginning of each section of the argument, and include them in the Table of Contents.
   b. Divide the point headings into major and minor point headings. There should be a major point heading for each issue presented. Use minor headings to introduce significant points supporting the major heading.
   c. Each heading and subheading should be a complete sentence.
   d. Each heading should identify the legal conclusion you want the court to adopt and the basic reasons for the conclusions.
   e. Use minor headings only if there are two or more. The rules of outlining require more than one subheading when subheadings are used. Minor headings present aspects of a major point heading in the context of the specific facts of the case.
   f. Type major headings in all capitals and minor headings in regular type. Minor headings may be underlined. Check the court rules for the proper format.

3. **Argument Format.** The argument section of the trial brief is similar to the analysis section of an office memorandum, and the analysis section of Chapter17 should be referred to when preparing a trial brief. The same basic IRAC format is followed:

>   **Rule of law**
>   **Case law—(if necessary) Interpretation of rule of law**
>   **Name of case**
>   **Facts of case—sufficient to demonstrate case is on point**
>   **Rule or legal principle from case that applies to the issue being addressed**
>   **Application of law to the issue being addressed**
>   **Discussion of opposing position (similar to counteranalysis in office legal memo)**

The major difference between the argument component of an office memorandum and a trial brief is that the trial brief introduces the argument in a persuasive rather than an objective manner. A trial brief is designed to persuade, and you should draft the argument in a persuasive manner.

CONCLUSION The conclusion section of a trial brief requests the specific relief desired. Depending on the complexity of the brief, it may be a single sentence stating the requested relief or a summary of the entire argument.

A single sentence conclusion is appropriate when the trial brief is a simple one-or two-issue brief and the argument section concludes with a summary of the analysis.

When the trial brief is longer and is more complicated, the conclusion may include an overall summary of the law presented in the argument section and end with a request for relief. This type of conclusion is similar to the conclusion section of an office memorandum discussed in Chapter 17, and that section of Chapter 17 should be referred to when preparing this type of conclusion. The conclusion should summarize the argument section and should reflect the persuasive nature of the argument.

APPELLATE COURT BRIEFS

The format of an appellate brief varies from jurisdiction to jurisdiction and is largely governed by the rules of the appellate court. Generally, the format and components of a trial court brief consist of some or all of the following:

> **Cover Page/Title Page**
> **Table of Contents/Index**
> **Table of Authorities**
> **Opinions Below Related Appeals**
> **Jurisdictional Statement**
> **Question(s) Presented—Issue(s)**
> **Statement of the Case/Statement of Facts**
> **Summary of Argument**
> **Argument**
> **Conclusion**

COVER PAGE/TITLE PAGE The title page usually includes the:

- name of the appellate court,
- number assigned to the appeal,
- parties' names and appellate status (appellant or appellee/petitioner or respondent),
- name of the lower court from which the appeal is taken, and
- names and addresses of the attorney(s) submitting the brief.

TABLE OF CONTENTS/INDEX Sometimes referred to as an index, the table of contents lists the major sections of the brief and the page number of each section. The table of contents provides the reader with a reference tool for the location of specific information within the brief. The table includes the point headings and subheadings.

TABLE OF AUTHORITIES The table of authorities lists all the law cited in the brief. The authorities are listed by category, such as constitutional law, statutory law, regulations, case law, etc. The table includes the full citation of the authority and the page number or numbers on which it appears.

OPINIONS BELOW/RELATED APPEALS The brief may include a section which references any prior opinions on the case or related appeals.

JURISDICTIONAL STATEMENT The brief usually includes a separate section which introduces, in a short statement, the subject matter jurisdiction of the appellate court.

Some appellate rules do not require a jurisdictional statement. Some appellate rules require, in addition to the jurisdictional statement, a history of the case and how the matter came before the court.

QUESTIONS PRESENTED This may also be referred to as "Legal Issues" or "Assignment of Error." This section lists the legal issues the party requests the court to consider. State the issues in the order in which they are addressed in the argument section and write them in a persuasive manner.

STATEMENT OF THE CASE/STATEMENT OF FACTS The statement of the case section, often referred to as the statement of facts, is generally similar to the statement of facts section of the trial brief, and the same considerations apply when preparing both.

The statement of the case in an appellate brief, however, differs from the statement of facts in a trial brief in that the statement of the case should also include a summary of the prior proceedings (what happened in the lower court) and appropriate references to the record.

SUMMARY OF ARGUMENT This section may be optional under the appellate court rule. Rule 28 of the Federal Rules of Appellate Procedure states that the argument may be preceded by a summary. The content of the argument summary is the same as that discussed in the Summary of Argument section of the components of a trial brief above—refer to that section.

ARGUMENT SECTION—POINT HEADINGS The considerations involved in preparing point headings are the same for appellate and trial court briefs. Refer to Point Headings in the discussion of the components of a trial brief above.

ARGUMENT SECTION—BODY The argument section of an appellate brief is similar to the argument section of a trial brief. The format is the same as a trial brief. Refer to Argument Format in the discussion of the components of a trial brief above. Present the argument section of an appellate brief in a persuasive manner.

CONCLUSION Prepare the conclusion section of an appellate brief in the same manner as the conclusion of a trial brief. The content, structure, and considerations involved are the same for both. Refer to Conclusion in the discussion of the components of a trial brief above.

ASSIGNMENT 3

Instructor's note: The question component of the issue included in the assignment is listed first followed by the persuasive presentations. More than one persuasive presentation is included in each answer.

A. ". . . should the evidence be suppressed when . . . ?" In the case, the police failed to obtain a search warrant prior to searching a vehicle.

Persuasive Presentations

". . . do the actions of the police require suppression of the evidence when . . . ?"
". . . must the evidence be suppressed when . . .?"
"is evidence admissible when the police. . .?"

B. ". . . did the court err when . . . ?" In the case, the trial court admitted hearsay evidence.

Persuasive Presentations

". . . was it allowable for the trial court . . . ?"
". . . was it permissible for the trial court . . . ?"

C. "Under the Statute of Frauds . . . , is an oral contract valid when . . . ?" Rewrite this portion of the issue using language which focuses on a desired result?"

Persuasive Presentations

"In light of the provisions of the Statute of Frauds . . . , does the statute prohibit the enforcement of an oral contract when . . . ?"
"According to the Statute of Frauds . . . , is an oral contract permissible when . . . ?"

D. "Under the Sale of Goods statutes . . . is a statute enforceable when . . . ?" Rewrite this portion of the issue using language which focuses on a desired result.

Persuasive Presentations

"Under the Sale of Goods statutes . . . , is it permissible to enforce a statute when . . . ?"

ASSIGNMENT 4

Instructor's note: Each issue presented in the assignment is listed first followed by the persuasive presentations.

A. Under the provisions of the exclusionary rule, should evidence be suppressed when law enforcement officers executed a search warrant by unannounced entry because they saw the defendant run into the apartment upon their arrival at the scene?

Persuasive Presentations

"Under the provisions of the exclusionary rule, which requires the suppression of illegally seized evidence, is evidence admissible when law enforcement officers executed a search warrant unannounced because they claim they saw the defendant run into the apartment upon their arrival at the scene?"

"In light of the provisions of the exclusionary rule, must evidence be suppressed when law enforcement officers executed a search warrant unannounced because they saw the defendant run into the apartment upon their arrival at the scene?"

B. Did the district court improperly exercise its discretion when it admitted into evidence photographs of the murder victim?

Persuasive Presentations

"Was the district court's action of admitting into evidence photographs of the murder victim a permissible exercise of its discretion?"

"Did the district court abuse its discretion when it admitted into evidence photographs of the murder victim?"

C. In light of the provisions of the hearsay rule, did the trial court improperly admit into evidence the defendant's statements to his neighbor that he would kill his wife?

Persuasive Presentations

"Under the hearsay rule, which requires the exclusion of hearsay, is it allowable for the trial court to admit into evidence the defendant's statements to his neighbor that he would kill his wife?"

"In light of the provisions of the hearsay rule, was the rule violated when the trial court admitted into evidence the defendant's statements to his neighbor that he would kill his wife?"

D. Does the privileged communications statute allow the admission into evidence of the defendant's threats of physical harm to his spouse?

Peruasive Presentations

"Under the provisions of the privileged communications statute, is evidence required to be excluded when it concerns the defendant's threats of physical harm to his spouse?"

"In light of the provisions of the privileged communications statute, is the admission of evidence prohibited if the evidence is the defendant's threats of physical harm to his spouse?"

ASSIGNMENT 5

Instructor's note: The point headings included in the assignment are listed first, followed by the persuasive presentations.

A. THE EVIDENCE WAS INCORRECTLY SUPPRESSED BY THE TRIAL COURT SINCE THERE WERE SUFFICIENT EXIGENT CIRCUMSTANCES AT THE SCENE.

Persuasive Presentation

"THERE WERE SUFFICIENT EXIGENT CIRCUMSTANCES AT THE SCENE, THEREFORE, THE TRIAL COURT ERRED IN SUPPRESSING THE EVIDENCE."

B. THE DENIAL OF THE DEFENDANT'S MOTION FOR MISTRIAL WAS NOT AN ERROR BY THE TRIAL COURT BECAUSE THE PROSECUTOR'S COMMENT ON THE DEFENDANT'S PRIOR CONVICTION WAS ADMISSIBLE.

Persuasive Presentation

"THE PROSECUTOR'S COMMENT ON THE DEFENDANT'S PRIOR CONVICTION WAS ADMISSIBLE, THEREFORE, THE TRIAL COURT DID NOT ERR IN DENYING THE DEFENDANT'S MOTION FOR MISTRIAL."

C. THE TRIAL COURT'S ALLOWANCE OF THE PEREMPTORY CHALLENGE WAS PROPER. THE CHALLENGE WAS NOT RACIALLY MOTIVATED.

Persuasive Presentation

"AS THE PEREMPTORY CHALLENGE WAS NOT RACIALLY MOTIVATED, THE TRIAL COURT'S ALLOWANCE OF IT WAS PROPER."

D. THE COURT SHOULD NOT GRANT THE DEFENDANT'S MOTION TO DISMISS . . ."

Persuasive Presentation

"THE COURT SHOULD DENY THE DEFENDANT'S MOTION TO DISMISS . . ."

ASSIGNMENT 6

Instructor's note: In each answer, the rule of law included in the assignment is listed first, followed by the persuasive presentations. More than one persuasive presentation is included.

A. "In determining whether an individual has constructive possession, the court decides whether the defendant had knowledge and control of the drugs."

Persuasive Presentation

"In constructive possession cases, the defendant must have knowledge and control of the drugs. The court makes this determination."

"The court determines if the defendant had knowledge and control of the drugs in constructive possession cases."

B. "Under the first part of the test it must be shown that the defendant had knowledge of the presence of the drugs."

Persuasive Presentation

"The first part of the test requires only that the defendant had knowledge of the presence of the drugs."

"Before the requirements of the test are met, it first must be established that the defendant had knowledge of the presence of the drugs."

C. "The court has stated that an arrest has taken place when a reasonable person would not feel free to leave."

Persuasive Presentation

"The court held that an arrest takes place when a reasonable person would not feel free to leave."

"Under the court's holding, an arrest does not take place unless a reasonable person would not feel free to leave."

ASSIGNMENT 7

DISTRICT COURT
STATE OF NEW MEXICO
NO. CIV. 01-388

JANE WHITE
      Plaintiff,
vs.

JEFFERY CALKIN
SAGE RENT-A-CAR INC.
      Defendants,

BRIEF IN SUPPORT OF MOTION TO DISMISS

QUESTION PRESENTED

In light of the provisions of the Mandatory Financial Responsibility Act, NMSA 1978 §§ 66-5-201 to 66-5-239 NMSA 1978, can a claim be stated against a self-insured rental agency for the negligent driving of its lessee?

STATEMENT OF FACTS

Defendant Sage Rent-A-Car Inc. (Sage)lased a vehicle to Defendant, Jeffery Calkin (Calkin). Mr.Calkin was involved in an auto accident with Plaintiff, Jane White, while driving the vehicle. Plaintiff filed suit against Defendants Calkin and Sage, claiming that Calkin's negligence was the cause of the accident. Defendant Sage was self-insured at the time of the accident.

ARGUMENT

This matter came before the court pursuant to defendant Sage's Rule 1-012B(6) motion to dismiss for failure to state a claim. In the case of *Las Luminarias of the N.M. Council v. Isengard,* 92 N.M. 297, 300-301 (Ct. App.1978), the New Mexico Court of Appeals established the standard for the granting of a Rule 1-012B(6) motion. The court stated, "A motion to dismiss a complaint is properly granted only when it appears that the plaintiff cannot recover or be entitled to relief under any state of facts provable under the claim . . ." Therefore, for this motion to be granted it must be shown that plaintiff is not entitled to recover under the facts presented in the complaint.

The New Mexico Mandatory Financial Responsibility Act (MFRA)(66-5-201 to 66-5-239 NMSA 1978) establishes the financial responsibilities of owners of motor vehicles. The act provides that:

No owner shall permit the operation of an uninsured motor vehicle, or a motor vehicle for which evidence of financial responsibility as was affirmed to the department is not currently valid, upon the streets or highways of New Mexico unless the vehicle is specifically exempted from the provisions of the Mandatory Financial Responsibility Act.

NMSA 1978 § 66-5-205A (1998). Plaintiff alleges that this statute requires Sage to carry a motor vehicle insurance policy for all of its vehicles and therefore Sage has a duty to assume responsibility for this accident under the provisions of the MFRA. Complaint at ¶ 36. Plaintiff misreads New Mexico law.

Plaintiff fails to note the actual language of the MFRA which provides that:
Evidence of financial responsibility, when required under the Mandatory
Financial Responsibility Act, may be given by filing:
A. evidence of a motor vehicle insurance policy;
B. a surety bond as provided in Section 66-5-225 NMSA 1978; or
C. a certificate of deposit of money as provided in Section 66-5-226 NMSA 1978.

NMSA 1978 § 66-5-218 (1998). The statute does not mandate the carrying of a vehicle insurance policy. It provides two ways to satisfy the financial responsibility requirement other than by providing evidence of an insurance policy.

Sage satisfied the requirements of the MFRA by filing a surety bond and is self-insured. Because it was self-insured Sage is exempt from the requirements of MFRA:

The following motor vehicles are exempt from the Mandatory Financial Responsibility Act:

. . .

E. a motor vehicle approved as self-insured by the superintendent of insurance pursuant to Section 66-5-207.1 NMSA 1978; . . .

NMSA 1978 §§ 66-5-207207 (1998).

The New Mexico Supreme Court has addressed this question in the case of *Cordova v Wolfel,* 120 N.M. 557, 903 P.2d 1390 (1995). In that case the plaintiff sued the rental company claiming that it was liable for the negligence of its lessee. In upholding the trial court's granting of the rental company's motion for summary judgment, the court noted:

Most authorities agree that self-insurance is not insurance. Insurance is a contract whereby for consideration one party agrees to indemnify or guarantee another party against specified risks. In contrast, self-insurance is a process of risk retention whereby an entity "set[s] aside assets to meet forseeable future losses. A self-insured protects itself from liability; it does not assume the risk of another."

120 N.M. at 559.

In discussing the relationship between the car rental company and its lessees the court stated that the relationship "is one of bailment, and there generally is no common law basis for imposing upon a bailor liability for a bailee's negligent operation of a bailed vehicle." 120 N.M. at 559. The court went on to note that:

The New Mexico legislature has not enacted legislation that would make vehicle lessors generally liable for injuries that result when lessees negligently use their vehicles, and we decline to take that step in the absence of legislative action.

120 N.M. 560.

Clearly, as a matter of law, a claim cannot be stated against defendant Sage and the Court should grant the Motion to Dismiss. Even if the facts stated in the complaint concerning Sage are true, Sage is self-insured and under MFRA section 66-5-207E is exempted from the requirements of the act. As the Supreme Court stated in *Cordova,* a self-insurer does not assume the risk of another and there is no common law basis for imposing upon a leasor liability for the lesee's negligent operation of a bailed vehicle.

Respectfully submitted this _____ day of _____, 2001.

_____

Attorney at law

ASSIGNMENT 8

Instructor's note: The format and basic content of the brief will be similar to the brief in Assignment 7. The analysis and conclusion will vary according to state law.

ASSIGNMENT 9

UNITED STATES COURT OF APPEALS
TENTH CIRCUIT
NO 2002-123

UNITED STATES OF AMERICA
                Plaintiff/Appellee,
      vs.
ARNOLD J. STEWART,
               Defendant/Appellant.

APPEAL FROM THE UNITED STATES DISTRICT COURT
FOR THE DISTRICT OF UTAH

ANSWER BRIEF OF APPELLEE

<u>TABLE OF CONTENTS</u>

TABLE OF STATUTES, CASES, RULES AND OTHER AUTHORITIES

STATUTES:

CASES:

OTHER AUTHORITIES:

PRIOR OR RELATED APPEALS

There are no prior or related appeals in this case.

STATEMENT OF ISSUE PRESENTED FOR REVIEW

This appeal is a review of the trial court's order denying the suppression of evidence and presents the following issue for consideration:

DID STEWART ABANDON HIS EXPECTATION OF PRIVACY IN HIS SUITCASE WHEN HE REQUESTED A PRIVATE CITIZEN TO WATCH IT FOR "JUST A FEW MINUTES" AND FAILED TO CLAIM IT LATER FROM A KNOWN LOCATION?

STATEMENT OF THE CASE

On November 21, 2001, Arnold J. Stewart was indicted by a federal grand jury sitting in the District of Kansas on charges of possession with intent to distribute more than 100 grams of heroin in violation of 21 U.S.C. §§ 841(a)(1)and 841(b)(1)(B). (Doc. at 5). On January 7, 2002, Stewart filed a motion to suppress the physical evidence. (Doc. at 18). On February 14, 2002, the motion was denied. The trial court found:

Under the circumstances, for all intents and purposes the suitcase was abandoned.

The defendant did not express a possessory interest in the suitcase at any time after he learned its location.

Having been abandoned, the defendant had no expectation of privacy in it or its contents.

(Tr. at 40-41). On March 6, 2002 defendant entered a conditional guilty plea, reserving his right to appeal the suppression ruling. (Doc. at 22). On April 27, 2002, the court sentenced Stewart to imprisonment for sixty months, to be followed by a three-year term of supervised release. (Doc. At 55). Stewart filed his notice of appeal on April 29, 2002.

FACTS

On October 15th, 2001, Arnold Stewart arrived at the airport an hour and fifteen minutes prior to his scheduled flight. (Tr. at 6). He was carrying one suitcase that he intended to carry on the flight. (Tr. at 7). His flight was scheduled to leave from gate 9, but he decided to wait at gate 8 because it wasn't so crowded. (Tr. at 8). After a few minutes he decided to get something to eat. (Tr. at 8). He approached Larry Holt who was also waiting at gate 8 and asked him if he would watch his suitcase. (Tr. at 8). Stewart did not know Mr. Holt. (Tr. at 8). Holt asked him how long he would be gone and Stewart replied, "Just a few minutes." (Tr. at 9). Holt said, "Well, ok." (Tr. at 9). Stewart then walked off. (Tr. at 9). Across from where they were seated were several lockers where Stewart could have placed his suitcase. (Tr. 9-10).

Meanwhile, after twenty minutes Mr. Holt became concerned. (Tr. at 41). He thought, "Where is that guy? I wonder if this suitcase contains a bomb." (Tr. at 41). The more he thought about it, the more concerned he became. (Tr. at 41-42). He contacted airport security and expressed his concerns. (Tr. at 42). Approximately a minute later Officer Robert Dwyer arrived. (Tr. at 42). There was no name tag on the suitcase, no airline claim ticket attached, and no evidence of ownership on the exterior. (Tr. at 71). In such situations airport policy is that the suitcase should be immediately inspected, then taken to the security office. (Tr. at 72). Officer Dwyer inspected the suitcase and its contents at the scene. (Tr. at 72). Upon opening the suitcase he found a large bag that contained forty smaller bags of a white powdery substance. (Tr. at 73). The substance was later identified as heroin. (Tr. at 122). The suitcase was taken to the security office and Federal officers were called. (Tr. at 74).

Approximately forty-five minutes after he left, Stewart returned to his seat in the gate area. (Tr. at 13). Holt informed him that he thought Stewart had abandoned the suitcase so he turned it over to airport security. (Tr. at 44). Stewart left the gate area, went to the ticket counter, and asked for information concerning the next flight. (Tr. at 14). The ticket counter is next to the security office. (Tr. at 75). Stewart never entered the office to inquire about the suitcase. (Tr. at 75). He was arrested when he went to the gate area and attempted to board his flight. (Tr. at 91).

SUMMARY OF ARGUMENT

The Fourth Amendment protects individuals from unreasonable searches and seizures. Defendant abandoned any reasonable expectation of privacy in the suitcase when he left it with a stranger and later failed to claim it from its known location.

ARGUMENT

The Fourth Amendment of the United States Constitution protects individuals from unreasonable searches and seizures, and individuals have a reasonable expectation of privacy in their personal possessions. *United States v. Arango,* 912 F.2d 441, 445 (10th Cir. 1990). The Fourth Amendment, however does not provide guidance as to whether an individual loses that expectation when the individual abandons the property. The courts, however, have addressed this question in the case of *United States v. Jones,* 707 F.2d 1169 (10th Cir. 1983).

In *Jones* three armed men robbed a Denver area savings and loan branch. A week later, while responding to a family disturbance call at 3434 High Street, police saw a car bearing the license number observed by a witness at the robbery. Police saw a man carrying a satchel emerge from the back of number 3434. The police ordered him to halt, and the man ran. They found him hiding in the rear of another building. He no longer had the satchel. Shortly thereafter, the police found the satchel lying outside the building where he was hiding. The man, Carless Jones, denied the satchel was his. He was subsequently arrested and indicted on charges of armed robbery of a savings and loan.

Jones filed a motion to suppress the fruits of the search of the satchel claiming the warrantless search violated his Fourth Amendment rights. The trial court held that the search was permissible because Jones had abandoned the satchel and therefore had no legitimate expectation of privacy in it entitling him to Fourth Amendment protection. In denying the motion the court stated, "The test for abandonment is whether an individual has retained any reasonable expectation of privacy in the object." *Jones,* 707 F2d at 1172. The court noted, "When Jones discarded the satchel, he may have hoped that the police would not find it and that he could later retrieve it. However, his ability to recover the satchel depended entirely upon fate and the absence of inquisitive (and acquisitive) passers-by." *Id.* at 1172.

In this case Stewart's actions meet the test for abandonment established in *Jones.* He did not retain a reasonable expectation of privacy in the suitcase. He voluntarily abandoned the suitcase. He had the opportunity to place the suitcase in a coin-operated locker and thereby retain his privacy rights. (Tr. at 9-10) He abandoned those rights when he turned the suitcase over to Holt. He assumed the risk that Holt would not search the suitcase or allow others to search it. He assumed the risk that Holt would not take the suitcase, give it to another, or turn it over to airport security. Just as in *Jones,* his ability to recover the suitcase depended entirely upon fate and the absence of inquisitive or acquisitive passers-by. Just as in *Jones* he never expressed a possessory interest in the suitcase. He did not claim the bag at airport security even though he had been told where the suitcase had been taken. (Tr. at 75).

It may be argued by Stewart that *Jones* is not on point because in *Jones* the satchel was left unattended, and in the present case Stewart left the suitcase in the care of another. However, this is a distinction without a difference. In both cases the property was placed in a position where the ability to recover the property depended entirely upon fate and the absence of inquisitive or acquisitive passers-by. In both cases ownership was not claimed. Therefore, *Jones* is on point, and by his actions Stewart did not retain any reasonable expectation of privacy in the suitcase. The trial court properly applied the law in concluding that Stewart abandoned the suitcase. The trial court was correct as a matter of law when it denied the suppression motion.

CONCLUSION

The trial court properly denied Stewart's suppression motion and this court should affirm the decision.

Respectfully submitted,

_____

United States Attorney

SUGGESTED ASSIGNMENTS: For one or more of the legal memorandum assignments you have assigned in this course, require the students to redraft all or portions of the assignment persuasively. This could include a persuasive drafting of the facts, issue, argument, and conclusion. This could also include the drafting of point headings. A separate assignment could also require that the memo be drafted as a memorandum in support of a motion to be filed with a local court.

WEB ASSIGNMENT ANSWERS

ASSIGNMENT 1

IN THE UNITED STATES DISTRICT COURT
FOR THE DISTRICT OF IDAHO

UNITED STATES OF America,
            Plaintiff,

        vs.   Cr. 2002-122 RJ

DENISE CLEM,
            Defendant.

UNITED STATES' RESPONSE TO DEFENDANT'S

MOTION TO SUPPRESS

QUESTION PRESENTED

Under the Fourth Amendment's prohibition against illegal search and seizure, may drugs be excluded from evidence when they are seized from a trash bag located next to a tree approximately ten feet from defendant's house and twenty feet from the public sidewalk?

STATEMENT OF FACTS

Acting on information provided by an informant, Drug Enforcement Administration agents searched garbage bags at defendant's residence. The bags were located next to a tree approximately ten feet from defendant's house and twenty feet from the public sidewalk. The agents did not have a search warrant. As a result of drugs located in the search, defendant was indicted on charges of possession of heroin. Trash is usually collected by the garbage collectors at the sidewalk. The garbage collectors stated that on occasion they would enter the property and collect bags located next to the tree if they were not running late.

ARGUMENT

The Fourth Amendment prohibits warrantless searches and seizures, but does not address the question of when garbage may be searched without a warrant. The Supreme Court, however, has addressed issues involving warrantless searches of garbage in *California v. Greenwood,* 486 U.S.35, 108 S.Ct. 1625, 100 L.Ed.2d 30 (1988).

In *Greenwood,* the police arranged for garbage collectors to give them Greenwood's garbage after they collected it. The garbage collectors collected the garbage from the curb in front of Greenwood's house where he had placed it for collection. The Court held that the Fourth Amendment does not prohibit the warrantless search and seizure of garbage left for collection outside the curtilage of the home. The Court stated, "The warrantless search and seizure of the garbage bags left at the curb outside the Greenwood house would violate the Fourth Amendment only if respondents manifested a subjective expectation of privacy in their garbage that society accepts as objectively reasonable." 486 U.S. at 39, 108 S.Ct. at 1628-29. The Court concluded that by placing their garbage where they did the respondents "exposed their garbage to the public sufficiently to defeat their claim to Fourth Amendment protection." 486 U.S. at 40, S.Ct. at 1629.

It may be claimed by defendant that *Greenwood* does not apply because in the present case the garbage was not located on a public sidewalk, but on defendant's private property. But the courts have allowed the warrantless search of garbage in situations where the garbage was located on the defendant's property and not placed at the curb, the location where the trash collectors routinely picked it up. A case remarkably similar to the present case is *United States v. Hedrick,* 922 F.2d 396 (CA 7 1991). In *Hedrick* the trash cans were located on a driveway fifty feet south of the house, twenty feet from an unattached garage, twenty-five to thirty feet from the street, and eighteen feet from the public sidewalk. The Court stated, "Therefore, applying the *Greenwood* analysis to garbage within the curtilage, the relevant inquiry is whether the garbage cans were so readily accessible to the public that they exposed the contents to the public for Fourth Amendment purposes." 922 F.2d at 400. In upholding the warrantees search of the garbage at Hedrick's property the Court stated, "Because the distance between the garbage cans and the public sidewalk was relatively short, the garbage was collected by the garbage service from that location, and the garbage cans were clearly visible from the sidewalk, we hold that Hedrick possessed no reasonable expectation of privacy in the garbage." 922 F.2d at 400.

In the present case, just as in *Hedrick,* the garbage was a short distance from the public sidewalk, the garbage was collected at that location, and it was clearly visible from the sidewalk. Just as in *Hedrick,* the motion to suppress the evidence seized from the garbage should be denied because the garbage was so readily accessible to the public that the contents were exposed to the public for Fourth Amendment purposes.

Respectfully submitted,

_____

United States Attorney

ASSIGNMENT 2
ANSWER TO ASSIGNMENT—FOR REVIEW AFTER COMPLETING ASSIGNMENT

COURT OF APPEALS, STATE OF COLORADO

No. 93 CA 1278

THE PEOPLE OF THE STATE OF COLORADO, Plaintiff/Appellee

vs.

GEORGE R. LITCHFIELD, Defendant/Appellant

and,

JAMES BRACKETT, Defendant/Appellant

Appeal from the District Court of Montrose County
Honorable Jerry D. Lincoln, Judge
No.'s 91 CR 55 & 91 CR 56

APPELLANT LITCHFIELD'S BRIEF ON APPEAL

John J. Mitchel, #12430
Attorney for Defendant Litchfield

<u>TABLE OF CONTENTS</u>

TABLE OF STATUTES, CASES, AND OTHER AUTHORITIES

STATEMENT OF ISSUE PRESENTED FOR REVIEW

The defendant was punished by the State of Colorado for possession of marijuana by assessment of a penalty of 2.4 million dollars by the Colorado Department of Revenue. Thereafter, Litchfield was convicted and sentenced for possession of marijuana, resulting in the defendant being subjected twice to punishment for the same conduct, in violation of the U.S. and Colorado constitutions.

STATEMENT OF THE CASE

On May 13, 1991 the defendant was arrested and charged with Possession of More than Eight Ounces of Marijuana with Intent to Sell, 18-18-106(8) CRS (F4) and, Special Offender, 18-18-107 CRS (F2). On May 29, 1991 defendant was assessed by the Colorado Department of Revenue a $240,000.00 tax and a 2.4 million dollar penalty for possession of marijuana, pursuant to section 39-28.7-108 CRS (Vol I, pages 40-42). Defendant moved by written motion to suppress evidence obtained by the police from the unlawful seizure of his vehicle, his person, and search of the vehicle. (Vol.I, pages 12-13). Defendant moved by written motion to dismiss this action on double jeopardy grounds, alleging double punishment for the same conduct. (Vol.I, pages 40-42). The trial court denied defendant's motions to suppress evidence and for dismissal. (Vol.I, pages 66(c)72, Vol.5, pages 1-33). The defendant was tried and convicted on the charge of Possession of More than Eight Ounces of Marijuana with Intent to Sell, 18-18-106(8) CRS after trial to the court on March 22, 1993. Count two was dismissed on the People's motion prior to trial. On June 21, 1993 the defendant was sentenced to five years in the Department of Corrections.

FACTS

On May 13, 1991, shortly after noon (Vol.4, p.67, lines 13-14) Colorado State Patrolman Hoey observed a red Ford Thunderbird travelling north on U.S. Highway 50 in Montrose County, Colorado, about four to five miles north of the town of Montrose, Colorado. (Vol.4, p.40, lines 1-2). Hoey testified that the car "straddled the white painted marks on the highway." (Vol.4, p.41, lines 1(c)2) and "swerved . . . weaved back over to the shoulder, drove off on to the shoulder one time, and then . . . weaved back and forth in the lane." (Ibid, p.42, lines 4-6). Hoey followed the car for about "a mile and a half" (Ibid, lines 22-23), stopped the car for "weaving" (Ibid, p.43, lines 1-2), and met the defendants. Defendant Brackett was the driver (Ibid, p.43, lines 21-25) and defendant Litchfield was in the front passenger seat. (Ibid, p.47, lines 15-22 & p.48, lines 6-9). Hoey had determined at that point that he was going to issue a citation or a warning ticket for weaving. (Ibid, lines 10-14). Brackett gave Hoey a driver's license and he produced a rental contract for a red Mustang, took the latter back, and gave Hoey a rental contract for the Thunderbird. Hoey compared the VIN number on the rental contract with the VIN number on the car, and they matched. (Ibid p.44, lines 1-11). Hoey also found that neither rental agreement produced by Brackett was signed and both documents said the vehicle could not be operated out of Arizona or Nevada. (Ibid, p.45, lines 22-25 & p.46, lines 1-3).

At trial, Hoey testified: "I called in to the State Patrol Office and requested a supervisor, due to the fact that the vehicle was a rental vehicle out of Arizona and the rental papers indicated that it was not to leave the state of Arizona or Nevada. (Vol.5, Transcript of Hearing 3-22-93, page 7, lines 14-17).

Sergeant John Mitchell arrived at Hoey's and the defendants' location and Mitchell said to Hoey that since "the vehicle was supposed to be in Arizona or Nevada and it was in Colorado, that we would seize the vehicle, take it back to the State Patrol office, and contact the rental company to see what they wanted done." (Vol.4, p.47, lines 3-7). According to Hoey, the decision to seize was based on ". . . the fact that the vehicle was not supposed to be out of the state of Nevada or Arizona." (Vol.4, p.62, lines 16-19).

Mitchell said "he was going to search—go through the car and do an inventory pursuant to State Patrol policy for weapons." (Vol.4, lines 21-24). Vehicles.) Mitchell's search proceeded from the passenger compartment, where he detected a musty smell which he could not identify, to the trunk, which he opened with the car keys, where he found several large packages of marijuana. (Vol.4, p.98, lines 1-8). During the social conversation between Hoey, Brackett, and Litchfield, Mitchell said, "You are under arrest. Down on the ground" (Ibid, p.52, lines 18-24). Litchfield's fingerprints were found on one of the packages of marijuana. (Vol.5, Transcript of Hearing 3-22-93, page 14, lines 1-25, page 15, lines 1-17).

On May 29, 1991, before conviction and sentence in the criminal case, the Colorado Department of Revenue penalized the defendant by imposing a tax of $240,000.00 on possession of marijuana at the rate of $100.00 per ounce, and, in addition, the department imposed a penalty of $2,400,000.00 for possession of marijuana, at a rate of ten times the amount of the tax, pursuant to section 39-28.7-108 CRS. (Vol.1, pages 40(c)42). The defendant timely filed an objection in the administrative proceeding, challenging the computation and the legality of the assessment by the Department of Revenue. (Vol.5, Transcript of Hearing 3-10-92, page 3, lines 21-25, page 4, lines 1-25, page 5, lines 1-25, page 6, lines 1-14). The administrative proceeding has not been resolved. The criminal sanction was imposed after the tax and penalty of 2.64 million dollars was assessed.

SUMMARY OF ARGUMENT

The penalty imposed by the state through the Department of Revenue was punishment for possession of marijuana. The subsequent punishment of criminal conviction and sentence to the Department of Corrections violates the double jeopardy clause of Amendment V, U.S. Constitution, and Art. II, Section 18, Constitution of Colorado.

ARGUMENT

The double jeopardy clauses of Amendment V, U.S. Constitution, and Art. II, Section 18, Constitution of Colorado prohibit multiple punishments for the same offense. United States.V Halper, 490 U.S 435, 104 L.Ed.2d 487 (1989). The multiple punishment prohibition applies when the state tries to criminally punish a citizen twice for the same offense. A disproportionately large civil penalty imposed in a subsequent civil proceeding may constitute punishment within the meaning of the double jeopardy rule. Halper, supra. SEE ALSO: In re: Kurth Ranch, 986 F.2d 1308 (CA9, 1993). In In re: Kurth Ranch, the Ninth Circuit Court of Appeals affirmed the district court for the district of Montana ruling that a $100.00 per ounce marijuana tax assessed pursuant to Montana's Dangerous Drug Tax constituted a punishment within the scope of the Fifth Amendment. In Kurth, the defendants were assessed a tax of nearly $865,000.00 for marijuana plants. The ruling applies to the assessment; no payment was required in order to trigger double jeopardy protection. The Kurths administratively challenged the computation and the legality of the assessment. That administrative challenge was suspended pending resolution of the Kurths' criminal charges. The Kurths then pleaded guilty and received sentences in the criminal case.

In this case, the Colorado Department of Revenue assessed the defendant a tax of $240,000.00 on his possession of marijuana at the rate of $100.00 per ounce, just as in Kurth. In addition, the department assessed a penalty of $2,400,000.00 for the possession of marijuana, at the rate of ten times the amount of the tax assessed. After assessment of tax and penalty, the defendant administratively challenged the tax and penalty. After the tax and penalty assessment, the criminal prosecution resulted in conviction and sentence to the Colorado Department of Corrections. At the hearing on defendant's motion to dismiss for violation of double jeopardy protection, the state presented no evidence that would tend to show a rational relationship between the tax and penalty and the actual loss to the state. The government failed to attempt to show that the tax and penalty are anything other than a criminal penalty. The Colorado tax and penalty for possession of marijuana are more onerous than the Montana tax. The Colorado tax and penalty are at least equal to the Montana tax as being the equivalent of criminal penalties, regardless of the legislative label. The first criminal penalty having been assessed against the defendant, the second criminal penalty in the form of criminal conviction and Department of Corrections sentence must be reversed and vacated.

CONCLUSION

The penalty imposed by the state through the Department of Revenue was punishment for possession of marijuana. The subsequent punishment of criminal conviction and sentence to the Department of Corrections violates the double jeopardy clause of the Fifth Amendment, U.S. Constitution, and Art. II, Section 18, Constitution of Colorado. The judgment of conviction should be reversed and this court should order this case dismissed.

Defendant Litchfield adopts all arguments submitted by defendant Brackett in his brief on appeal.

Respectfully submitted this _____ day of _____, 1994.

JOHN J. MITCHEL, #12430
Attorney for Defendant
Litchfield

TEST QUESTIONS AND ANSWERS

TRUE OR FALSE QUESTIONS

Please write a "T" or "F" to the left of each statement.

_____ 1. The fundamental principles that apply to the preparation of office legal memoranda also apply to the preparation of court briefs.

_____ 2. The basic format of a court brief is different from that of an office legal memorandum.

_____ 3. The organizational approach to the legal analysis of an issue in a court brief differs from that of an office legal memorandum.

_____ 4. The major difference between a court brief and an office legal memorandum is the presentation of the format and content.

_____ 5. A court brief is an advocacy document.

_____ 6. Under Rule 3.3(a)(3) of the Model Rules, an attorney has an ethical duty to disclose legal authority adverse to the position of the client that is not disclosed by the opposing counsel.

_____ 7. In a court brief, state the law component of the issue in an objective manner.

_____ 8. In a court brief, the fact component of the issue and the statement of facts should be stated persuasively.

_____ 9. the statement of facts section of a court brief, present the facts unfavorable to the client's position at the end of the statement.

_____10. Use short sentences to emphasize favorable information.

_____11. In the argument section, <u>always</u> follow the counteranalysis with a rebuttal.

_____12. Point headings are a summary of the position advocated in the argument and the counterargument.

_____13. Trial court briefs should consist of a short concise presentation of the law because trial court judges are usually busy.

_____14. Trial court briefs are usually subject to a time constraint.

_____15. Every brief submitted to a trial court requires a caption.

_____16. The argument section of a trial court brief should begin with a preliminary statement.

_____17. The conclusion section of a trial court brief may be as short as a single sentence.

_____18. The individual who opposes the appeal is called the appellee.

_____19. The format and style of an appellate brief is strictly governed by appellate court rules.

_____20. Appellate court rules may establish the type of paper used for the brief.

TRUE OR FALSE ANSWERS

Answer	Text Section	Answer	Text Section	Answer	Text Section
1. True	II	8. True	IIB1&C	15. True	IIIC1
2. False	IIA2	9. False	IIB2	16. False	IIIC7
3. False	IIA3	10. True	IIB2	17. True	IIIC8
4. True	IIB	11. True	IIB3	18. False	IV
5. True	IIB	12. False	IIB3	19. True	IV
6. True	IIB	13. True	IIIA	20. True	IVB
7. False	IIB1	14. True	IIIB		

MULTIPLE CHOICE QUESTIONS

Please circle the letter of the **most appropriate** answer.

1. Court briefs and office legal memoranda are similar in that:
   a. both are written in a persuasive manner.
   b. the basic writing process is the same.
   c. the basic format is the same.
   d. the organizational approach to the legal analysis of an issue is the same.
   e. all of the above
   f. a, b, and c
   g. b, c, and d

2. The basic organizational format of the analysis of an issue in a court brief is the:
   a. rule of law followed by the case law, then the application and conclusion.
   b. issue, followed by the rule of law and case law, then the application and conclusion.
   c. issue followed by the case law and rule of law, then the application and conclusion.
   d. the rule of law followed by the issue and case law, then the application and conclusion.

3. In regard to the presentation of the issue in a court brief, state the:
   a. law component persuasively.
   b. issue component persuasively.
   c. fact component objectively.
   d. fact component persuasively.
   e. a, b, and c
   f. a, b, and d

4. In the statement facts section of a court brief:
   a. include both key and background facts.
   b. place facts unfavorable to the client's position at the end of the fact section.
   c. use short sentences to emphasize unfavorable information.
   d. if the fact section is composed of several paragraphs, place the facts unfavorable to the client's position in the last paragraph.
   e. all of the above
   f. a, c, and d
   g. a and d

5. In the argument section of a court brief:
   a. discuss the issue supported by the strongest argument first.
   b. present the rule of law in an objective manner.
   c. place the law unfavorable to the client's position at the end of the analysis.

   d. always follow the counteranalysis with a rebuttal.
   e. all of the above
   f. a, c, and d
   g. a and d

6. Which of the following are reasons for presenting the issue supported by the strongest argument first in the argument section of a court brief:
   a. First impressions are lasting.
   b. The court is more likely to look more favorably on your weaker arguments.
   c. A judge may not read or give equal attention to an argument presented at the end of the argument section.
   d. Arguments that are weak detract and divert attention from stronger arguments.
   e. all of the above
   f. none of the above
   g. a, b, and d

7. In regard to the persuasive presentation of information in court briefs:
   a. the facts component of the issue should be stated objectively.
   b. the key facts should be stated persuasively in the fact section.
   c. point headings should be presented persuasively.
   d. place unfavorable material at the end of the argument.
   e. all of the above
   f. b and c
   g. a, b, and d

8. Trial court briefs:
   a. are usually subject to time constraints.
   b. are often subject to a required format governed by local rule
   c. always require a caption.
   d. always require a preliminary statement.
   e. all of the above
   f. a, b, and c
   g. b, c, and d

9. In some instances, a trial court brief does not require a:
   a. caption.
   b. table of contents.
   c. table of authorities.
   d. preliminary statement.
   e. all of the above
   f. b and c
   g. b, c, and d

10. The argument section of a trial court brief may include:
    a. a summary of the argument.
    b. a preliminary statement.
    c. point headings.
    d. the legal argument.
    e. all of the above
    f. a, c, and d
    g. a and d

11. Appellate court rules may establish the:
    a. type of paper used.
    b. citation format.
    c. maximum length of the brief.
    d. sections that must be included.
    e. all of the above
    f. b and d
    g. b, c, and d

12. In regard to appellate court briefs:
    a. format <u>and</u> style are strictly governed by appellate court rules.
    b. unlike trial court briefs, appellate court briefs are not drafted persuasively.
    c. they are similar to office legal memoranda in many respects.
    d. they often may include a jurisdictional statement.
    e. all of the above
    f. a, c, and d
    g. b and d

MULTIPLE CHOICE ANSWERS

Answer	Text Section	Answer	Text Section	Answer	Text Section
1. g	IIA	5. g	IIB3	9. g	III
2. a	IIA3	6. e	IIIB3	10. f	IIIC7
3. f	IIB	7. f	IIIB	11. e	IVB
4. a	IIB2	8. f	III	12. f	IIV

CHAPTER 19

Correspondence

TEXT ASSIGNMENT ANSWERS

Instructor's note: The format for the preparation of correspondence varies from office to office. For example, in the sample opinion letter in the text and in the answers to the assignments, each section of the opinion letter is separated by a heading printed in bold and in all capitals. Some office formats do not require the headings. Chapter 19 presents a recommended format; it should be emphasized to students that there are various acceptable formats.

Note: Assignments 6, 7, and 8 require students to read and analyze the facts, statutory law, and case law included in assignments presented in Chapter 17.

ASSIGNMENT 1

The three types of correspondence discussed in this chapter and the purposes of each are as follows:

INFORMATION LETTER. An information letter is a type of correspondence designed to provide information to the reader. The information may be as simple as the date and time of a scheduled court hearing or as complex as a summary of the law involved in the client's case. It is drafted in an objective rather than a persuasive tone.

OPINION LETTER. An opinion letter is a type of correspondence designed to provide the reader with information concerning the law. In addition to a summary of the law, an opinion letter usually provides an objective assessment of the application of the law to the facts of a case and often recommends a course of action. Since it includes a legal opinion or legal advice, an opinion letter constitutes the practice of law and must be signed by an attorney. It is drafted objectively rather than persuasively.

Instructor's note: It should be emphasized to students that an opinion letter constitutes the practice of law and must be signed by an attorney

DEMAND LETTER. A demand letter is a type of correspondence designed to persuade someone to take action favorable to the interests of the client or cease acting in a manner that is detrimental to the client. In other words, it is designed to encourage action or seek relief. It may be as simple as demanding payment on a debt or as complex as requesting that a course of conduct be taken, such as rehiring an employee. In many instances, a demand letter will include a summary of the applicable law in support of the requested action.

ASSIGNMENT 2

The three types of letters differ primarily in the content of the body.

INFORMATION LETTER. The body of an information letter presents general information or at most an objective summary of the research and analysis of the law. It does not include a legal opinion or advice. It also does not include a demand for action or a refraining from action.

OPINION LETTER. In addition to a summary of the law, the body of an opinion letter usually provides an objective assessment of the application of the law to the facts of a case and often recommends a course of action. It constitutes the practice of law and must be signed by an attorney. An opinion letter does not include a demand for action or a refraining from action.

DEMAND LETTER. The body of a demand letter is similar to the body of an opinion letter. It differs in that the presentation of the law and analysis are drafted in a persuasive manner. Unlike an information or opinion letter, a demand letter includes a demand for action or a refraining from action.

ASSIGNMENT 3

Instructor's note: The following is a model opinion letter to be sent to Mrs. Findo. It is drafted in modified block style. The addresses and dates used in the correspondence can be any addresses or dates either you or the student select.

Law Offices of Rita Berdwin

2100 Main Street

Friendly, New Washington, 00065

(200)267-7000 • FAX 267-7001

January 18, 2003

<u>Via Facsimile and U.S. Mail</u>

Mrs. Findo

5501 Glenview Ave.

Friendly, NW 00065

    Re: Whether Mrs. Findo may testify against Mr. Findo in Mr. Findo's criminal trial.

Dear Mrs. Findo:

    On January 1, 2003, we met in my office to discuss the possibility of your testifying against your husband in his upcoming criminal trial. Specifically you wanted to know if you could testify concerning statements your husband made to you prior to his confrontation with Mr. Markum.

    This opinion is based on the facts outlined in the fact section of this letter and the applicable law as of the date of the letter. This letter is solely for your benefit and limited to the facts discussed below. Please contact me if any of the facts are misstated or if you have additional information.

FACTS

    Mr. Findo is charged with assaulting his neighbor, Mr. Markam, with a deadly weapon, a hammer. Prior to the confrontation with Mr. Markham, Mr. Findo stated to you, "Markham is out there building that damn fence again. I'll put a stop to this once and for all." These statements took place in the presence of your children, Tomas age 16 and Alice age 10. You are currently separated from your husband.

ANSWER

    Based upon the above facts and the applicable law, you probably can testify against your husband in the criminal case.

EXPLANATION

The law which governs when a husband or wife may testify against each other is Chapter 735 of the Illinois statutes. The statute provides that a husband and wife may not testify against each other "as to any communication or admission made by either of them to the other . . . during marriage. . . ." The statute prohibits spouses from testifying against each other about statements made to each other while they were married. The state supreme court, however, has established an exception to this statute.

In the case of *People v. Sanders,* the supreme court addressed the question of whether the statute applies when children are present during conversations between a husband and wife. In the case, the conversations took place in front of the spouses' children, ages 8 through 13; the conversations implicated the defendant in a murder.

The court ruled that conversations which take place in the presence of children are not confidential unless the children are too young to understand what is being said. In other words, if a statement is made to a spouse in the presence of children who are old enough to understand it, the spouse can testify about the statement.

The facts in your case are very similar to the facts in *People v. Sanders.* In your case, just as in that case, your husband's statements were made in the presence of your children. In your case, just as in the court case, your children were old enough to understand the statements. Therefore, based on the court's ruling in *People v. Sanders,* it is my opinion that you can testify against your husband concerning the statements he made to you.

I hope this information answers your question. If you have additional information concerning the statements your husband made, or if you have any other questions, please contact me.

Sincerely,

Rita Berdwin

Attorney at Law

RB/wkk

ASSIGNMENT 4
PART A

Instructor's note: The following is a model information letter to be sent to the defendant, David Kent. It is drafted in full block style. The addresses, dates, and names of the attorney, paralegal, or law clerk used in the correspondence can be any address, date, or names either you or the student select.

Law Offices of James Carter

2100 Main Street

Friendly, New Washington, 00065

(200) 267-7000 • FAX 267-7001

April 29, 2003

Mr. David Kent
9100 2nd Street
Friendly, NW 00065

Re: *State v. Kent.* What constitutes an arrest in the state of New Washington, and how the law applies in search warrant situations.

Dear Mr. Kent:

The purpose of this letter is to inform you of what constitutes an arrest in the state of New Washington, and how the law has been interpreted to apply in search warrant situations. The letter focuses on the law governing arrest in a situation similar to your case.

Article II, Section 4 of the state constitution provides that "The right of the people to be secure in their person, . . . against unreasonable searches and seizures shall not be violated. . . ." This means that you cannot be illegally arrested. The constitution does not define what constitutes an arrest or when an arrest takes place. The state supreme court, however, in the case of *State v. Ikard,* has established when an arrest takes place.

In *State v. Ikard,* law enforcement officers were looking for a suspect in an armed robbery. A friend of the suspect was walking down the street. The police stopped him, handcuffed him, and asked him where the suspect was. The court stated that the defendant was under arrest when he was stopped and handcuffed. The court ruled that an arrest takes place when a reasonable person would believe he was not free to leave.

There are exceptions to this rule. One exception is when a person is detained while officers are executing a search warrant. This exception was announced by the court in the case of *State v. Wilson.* In this case, after entering a residence during the execution of a search warrant, an officer held the defendant by the arm and refused to allow him to leave. The court stated that the defendant was not under arrest. The court held that, when law enforcement officers are executing a search warrant for contraband, they have the authority to detain the occupants of the residence while a search is conducted. The detention is not an arrest.

In summary, an arrest takes place when a reasonable person does not believe he is free to leave. When officers are executing a search warrant, the detention of an individual while the residence is being searched is not an arrest.

I hope this correspondence provides the information you requested. If you require additional information, please contact me.

Sincerely,

_____

Tom Smith
Paralegal

TS/wkk

PART B

Instructor's note: The following is a model opinion letter to be sent to the defendant, David Kent. It is drafted in modified block style. The addresses, date, and name of the attorney used in the correspondence can be any address, date, or name either you or the student select. Note that some dates have been added to the facts, such as the date the client came to the law office.

Law Offices of James Carter

2100 Main Street

Friendly, New Washington, 00065

(200) 267-7000 • FAX 267-7001

April 25, 2003

<u>Via Facsimile and U.S. Mail</u>

Mr. David Kent

9100 2nd Street

Friendly, NW 00065

Re: *State v. Kent.* Whether there is sufficient evidence to support the charge of possession of a controlled substance.

Dear Mr. Kent:

On February 1, 2003, we met in my office to discuss the charges filed against you in the case of *State v. Kent.* At that time, you asked for a legal opinion as to whether there is sufficient evidence to support the charge of possession of a controlled substance.

This opinion is based on the facts outlined in the fact section of this letter and the applicable law as of the date of the letter. This letter is solely for your benefit and limited to the facts discussed below. Please contact me if any of the facts are misstated or if you have additional information.

FACTS

On January 7, 2003, police officers executed a search warrant which authorized the search of your apartment for narcotics. The apartment is located on the third floor of an apartment complex. When the police entered the apartment, you were lying on the bed in the bedroom. You were immediately handcuffed, moved to the kitchen, and detained while the search was conducted.

The police found a broken window in the bedroom, and the window screen was pushed out. In the parking lot three stories below the bedroom window, the officers found a bag containing cocaine. The parking lot is a common area of the complex, accessible to the public and all apartment dwellers. There were no witnesses who saw you throw anything out of the apartment window. There were no fingerprints found on the bag or any other evidence linking you to the cocaine. You were later charged with possession of a controlled substance.

ANSWER

Based upon the above facts and the applicable law, there does not appear to be sufficient evidence to support charges of possession of a controlled substance. Without additional evidence, there does not appear to be sufficient evidence to link you to the cocaine.

EXPLANATION

The law which prohibits the possession of cocaine or any controlled substance is Section 95-21-14 of the state criminal code. The statute does not define what is necessary to support charges of possession. The state supreme court, however, has addressed this matter.

In the case of *State v. Bragg,* the court discussed what evidence is necessary to support charges of possession. In this case, the police searched an apartment where Mr. Bragg and several other individuals resided. Narcotics were found in a drawer in the kitchen. Everyone living in the house had access to the kitchen drawer. Only Mr. Bragg was charged with possession. The court held that where an individual does not have actual possession of the drugs, there must be either direct or circumstantial evidence that the defendant had knowledge of and control over the drugs.

In your case there is no evidence that you actually possessed the cocaine. There is no evidence, either direct or circumstantial, that you had knowledge of the presence of the drugs in the parking lot. Also, there is no evidence that you had control over the drugs in the parking lot. There is no evidence that links you to the drugs you were charged with possessing. Therefore, it is my opinion that there is not sufficient evidence to support charges of possession of a controlled substance. Note that if the police have additional evidence, my opinion could change.

I hope this information answers your question. If you have additional information concerning this matter, or if you have any other questions, please contact me.

Sincerely,

_____

James Carter

Attorney at Law

JC/wkk

ASSIGNMENT 5

Instructor's note: The following is a model demand letter to be sent to Mr. Terry Spear, president of Inki Appliances. It is drafted in modified block style. The address of the attorney and date used in the correspondence can be any address or date either you or the student select. Note that some information such as dates and the office file number have been added to the facts.

Law Offices of Alice Black

2100 Main Street

Friendly, New Washington, 00065

(200) 267-7000 • FAX 267-7001

April 25, 2003

<u>Via Facsimile and U.S. Mail</u>

Mr. Terry Spear

President

Inki Appliances, Co.

1001 Maple Drive

Friendly, NW 00065

   Re: Mrs. Tatum

         File No. 97-131

Dear Mr. Spear:

Our office represents Mrs. Tatum in regard to her purchase of a microwave oven from Inki Appliances, Co. The purpose of this letter is to demand that Inki Appliances repair or replace the microwave or refund Mrs. Tatum the purchase price of the defective microwave.

On February 1, 2003, Mrs. Tatum purchased a new microwave from Inki Appliances, Co. One week after Mrs. Tatum purchased the microwave, it quit working. Three days later, on February 11, 2003, she returned it to your store. Since that date, Inki Appliances has refused to repair or replace the microwave and has refused to refund Mrs. Tatum the purchase price.

Section 50-102-314 of the New Washington statutes creates an implied warranty of merchantability for goods sold by merchants. This means that there is a warranty for goods sold by merchants that the goods are merchantable, that is, the goods will work. The warranty of merchantability for the microwave Inki Appliances, Co., sold to Mrs. Tatum was breached because it stopped working after only one week.

In the case of *Smith v. Appliance City,* the New Washington Supreme Court ruled that the seller has three options when an implied warranty is breached: return the purchase price to the buyer, repair the merchandise, or replace the merchandise. Inki Appliances has refused to perform any of these options.

In light of the fact that the warranty of merchantability for the microwave has been breached, we demand that you comply with New Washington law and return the purchase price to Mrs. Tatum, repair the microwave, or replace the microwave. If Inki Appliances does not act in accordance with this letter within thirty days, we will take the appropriate steps necessary to obtain the relief provided by New Washington law.

Please contact us within the time provided to confirm your compliance with the terms of this letter.

Thank you for your consideration of this matter.

Sincerely,

_____

Alice Black

Attorney at Law

AB/wkk

ASSIGNMENT 6

Instructor's note: The following is a model information letter to be sent to Mr. Eldon Canter. It is drafted in full block style. The addresses, dates, and name of the attorney, paralegal, or law clerk used in the correspondence can be any address, dates, and names either you or the student select.

Law Offices of James Carter

2100 Main Street

Friendly, New Washington, 00065

(200) 267-7000 • FAX 267-7001

April 29, 2003

Mr. Eldon Canter

9100 2nd Street

Friendly, NW 00065

Re: *United States v. Eldon Canter.* What constitutes a "dangerous weapon" under the federal bank robbery statutes.

Dear Mr. Canter:

The purpose of this letter is to inform you of the results of our research in regard to what constitutes a "dangerous weapon" under the federal bank robbery statutes. The letter focuses on the question of whether the carved wooden replica of a handgun used in the robbery of the First State Bank can be considered a "dangerous weapon" under the law.

Title 18, Section 2113 (a) and (d) of the United States Code makes it illegal to rob a bank with a dangerous weapon or device. This law does not define what is a "dangerous weapon." The federal courts, however, have addressed this matter.

A court case with facts similar to your case is *United States v. Martinez-Jimenez.* In this case, the defendant robbed a bank with a toy gun that eyewitnesses identified as a dark revolver. The defendant was convicted of armed bank robbery with a "dangerous weapon." The Court stated that the toy gun was a "dangerous weapon" under the law. The Court held that a robber's use of a replica or simulated weapon that appears to be a genuine weapon to the witnesses at the robbery carries the same penalty as the use of a genuine weapon.

In applying the holding in *United States v. Martinez-Jimenez* to the facts of your case, it appears that the carved wooden replica of a handgun used in the robbery of the First State Bank can be considered a "dangerous weapon" under the law. In your case, just as in the *Martinez-Jimenez* case, the wooden replica was so sufficiently similar to a real handgun that a witness believed it was real. As the court noted in its conclusion, the use of a replica or simulated weapon, which appears to be genuine, subjects the robber to the penalty of robbery with a dangerous weapon.

There is one difference between the *Martinez-Jimenez* case and your case. In *Martinez-Jimenez,* all the witnesses believed the toy gun was a real handgun; in your case one witness thought the wooden replica was fake. The Court did not address the question of whether all the witnesses must believe the replica is a real weapon. This should not make a difference, however. In *Martinez-Jimenez,* the Court focused on the increased risk to the physical security of those present at the bank robbery created by the appearance of dangerousness of the fake weapon. As long as some of the witnesses believe the fake weapon is real, that risk is created.

In summary, it appears that the carved wooden replica of a handgun used in the robbery of the First State Bank can be considered a "dangerous weapon" under the federal bank robbery statutes.
I hope this letter answers any question you may have regarding this matter. If you require additional information, please contact me.

Sincerely,

_____

Tom Smith

Paralegal

TS/wkk

ASSIGNMENT 7

Instructor's note: The following is a model opinion letter to be sent to Mrs. Holly Dixon. It is drafted in modified block style. The addresses, dates, and name of the attorney used in the correspondence can be any address, dates, and name either you or the student select.

Law Offices of Rita Berdwin

2100 Main Street

Friendly, Texas, 90065

(200) 267-7000 • FAX 267-7001

January 18, 2003

<u>Via Facsimile and U.S. Mail</u>

Mrs. Holly Dixon

641 Ash Ave.

Friendly, TX 90065

    Re: Whether the holographic will of Thomas Dixon submitted by Mary Cary is admissible to probate under Texas law.

Dear Mrs. Dixon:

    On January 1, 2003, we met in my office to discuss the probate of the will of Thomas Dixon. Specifically, you wanted to know if the half-handwritten, half-typewritten will of Mr. Dixon is admissible to probate under Texas law.

    This opinion is based on the facts outlined in the fact section of this letter and the applicable law as of the date of the letter. This letter is solely for your benefit and limited to the facts discussed below. Please contact me if any of the facts are misstated or if you have additional information.

FACTS

    Mary Cary, the sister of Thomas Dixon and the personal representative of his estate, has submitted for probate a will prepared by Mr. Dixon. The first half of the will is written in the handwriting of Mr. Dixon. The second half of the will is typewritten. The typewritten portion was typed at Mr. Dixon's request by his neighbor, Edgar Mae. Mr. Mae has stated that Mr. Dixon asked him to finish the will because Mr. Dixon was too weak to continue. It was not witnessed by subscribing witnesses, but there is a self-proving affidavit that meets the requirements of Texas law. Therefore, the will was properly signed.

ANSWER

    Based upon the above facts and the applicable law, the will submitted for probate by Mary Cary is probably not eligible for probate. Texas law requires that a will, such as the one submitted by Mrs. Cary, must be entirely hand-written by the deceased. The will in question is half-typewritten and, therefore, is not eligible for probate under Texas Law.

EXPLANATION

    Texas Probate Code Sections 59 and 60 apply to wills that are handwritten by the deceased. These statutes refer to wills written wholly in the handwriting of the deceased and proscribe how such wills must be witnessed. The statutes allow wills that are wholly in the handwriting of the deceased to be probated.

    The statutes provide that handwritten wills are admissible for probate if they are witnessed in the manner as the will prepared by Mr. Dixon. Such wills, however, must be written wholly in the handwriting of the deceased. Sections 59 and 60 of the Texas Probate Code do not define the meaning of "written wholly" in the handwriting of the deceased.

    The Texas Court of Appeals in the case of *Dean v. Dickey,* however, has defined the meaning of "wholly in the handwriting of the deceased." In this case, the will was typed wholly by the deceased. The court held that words "wholly written" as used in the statutes mean wholly written in the handwriting of the testator, not typewritten.

Based upon the decision in *Dean v. Dickey* it appears that the will of Mr. Dixon, submitted by Mrs. Cary, is not entitled to probate. The will was not "wholly written" in the handwriting of Mr. Dixon as required by the court's interpretation of the law. One half was typewritten.

It is possible that the *Dean* case may not be followed by the current Texas courts. The case is over forty-five years old and may not represent the present thinking of the courts. The holding in *Dean,* however, was based upon the court's concern for ensuring the genuineness of the will, and this concern is as equally important today as it was forty-five years ago. This has not changed over the years. In addition, the legislature has not amended the statute to evidence a different intent.

In summary, based on Sections 59 and 60 of the Texas Probate Code and the court's ruling in *Dean v. Dickey,* it is my opinion that the will of Mr. Dixon submitted by Mrs. Cary is not eligible for probate because it was not entirely handwritten by Mr. Dixon.

I hope this information answers your question. If you have additional information concerning this matter, or if you have any other questions, please contact me.

Sincerely,

_____

Rita Berdwin

Attorney at Law

RB/wkk

ASSIGNMENT 8

Instructor's note: The following is a model demand letter to be sent to Mary Chavez. It is drafted in modified block style. Since Ms. Chavez is a brain surgeon, the letter is written in a more sophisticated manner than the other sample letters. In other words, it is assumed that she is capable of understanding correspondence that is technical. The addresses, dates, and name of the attorney in the correspondence can be any addresses, dates, and name either you or the student select. Note that some information such as dates and the office file number have been added to the facts.

Law Offices of James Carter

2100 Main Street

Santa Fe, New Mexico, 87505

(200) 267-7000 • FAX 267-7001

April 2, 2003

Via Facsimile and U.S. Mail

Ms. Mary Chavez

1001 Maple Drive

Santa Fe, NM 87505

   Re: Mr. Arturo Garcia
        File No. 98-147

Dear Ms. Chavez:

Our office represents Mr. Garcia in regard to your failure to meet your child support obligation. The purpose of this letter is to demand that you resume paying the full amount of child support ordered by the court.

Approximately four months ago, your oldest child turned eighteen and moved out of Mr. Garcia's house. At that time, you reduced by one third the amount of child support you were paying. You did not seek or obtain a court order granting a reduction of your support obligation. The support order is undivided in that it does not specify a "per child" amount.

Section 40-4-7F of the New Mexico statutes governs child support obligations in New Mexico. It provides that the district court may modify and change a child support order and "shall have exclusive jurisdiction of all matters" concerning the maintenance of the children so long as the children remain minors. The statute does not address the specific question of a parent's power to unilaterally reduce a child support obligation when one of the children reaches the age of majority. This question, however, has been addressed by the New Mexico courts.

In the case of *Britton v. Britton,* the custodial parent petitioned the court for a judgment for unpaid child support arrearages. The case involved an undivided child support order and a child who had reached the age of majority. The New Mexico Supreme Court noted that "[t]he well-established general rule is that an undivided support award directed at more than one child is presumed to continue in force for the full amount until the youngest child reaches majority." The court stated that a parent cannot unilaterally alter the support order; the parent must petition the court to modify the order.

This letter will serve as formal demand that you resume paying the full child support amount ordered by the court. Your action of reducing your child support obligation by one third without obtaining permission of the court is clearly a violation of New Mexico law. As noted in the Britton case, you cannot reduce your obligation without permission of the court. If you do not act in accordance with this letter within thirty days, we will take the appropriate steps necessary to obtain the relief provided by New Mexico law.

Please contact us within the time provided to confirm your compliance with the terms of this letter.

Thank you for consideration of this matter.

Sincerely,

_____

James Carter

Attorney at Law

JC/wkk

ASSIGNMENT 9

Instructor's note: The following is a model information letter to be sent to Mr. David Keys. It is drafted in full block style. Students may also use modified block.

Law Offices of Alice Black

2100 Main Street

Friendly, New Washington, 00065

(200) 267-7000 • FAX 267-7001

April 29, 2003

Mr. David Keys

761 South Vine Street

Sunnydale, NW 00066

Re: Removal of a member of the board of directors of a corporation.

Dear Mr. Keys:

The purpose of this letter is to inform you of the results of our research in regard to what is required to remove a member of the board of directors of a corporation. The state statute that governs the removal of directors is New Washington Statutes Annotated Section 77-11-22.

The statute provides that at a meeting, called expressly for the purpose of removing directors, any director may be removed by a majority vote of the shares eligible to vote at an election of directors. The statute also provides that a director may be removed with or without cause. That is, there does not have to be a reason to remove a director. In summary, a director may be removed, with or without any stated reason, by majority vote of the eligible shareholders.

I hope this letter answers any question you may have regarding this matter. If you require additional information, please contact me.

Sincerely,

_____

Alice Black

Attorney at Law

AB/wkk

ASSIGNMENT 10

Instructor's note: The format and basic content of the letter will be similar to letter in Assignment 9. The statute will vary according to state law.

ASSIGNMENT 11

Instructor's note: The following is a model information letter to be sent to Mr. Daniel Hope, Vice President, National Insurance Company. It is drafted in full block style. Students may also use modified block.

Law Offices of Alice Black

2100 Main Street

Friendly, New Washington, 00065

(200) 267-7000 • FAX 267-7001

December 14, 2003

Mr. Daniel Hope

Vice President

National Insurance Company

459 Twenty-Second Street

Friendly, NW 00065

   Re: National Insurance Company's duty to defend persons it insures under its automobile insurance policies.

Dear Mr. Hope:

The purpose of this letter is to inform you of the results of our research in regard to National Insurance Company's duty to defend persons it insures under its automobile insurance policies.

There are no state statutes that address this question, but the New Washington courts have established guidelines.

A summary of the relevant New Washington court decisions is as follows:
The obligation to defend an insured against liability must be found in the insuring agreement. *State Farm Ins. Co. v. Peterson,* 56 N. Wash. 38 (1995). The duty to defend is triggered when an injured party's complaint against the insured states facts that bring the case within the coverage of the policy. *Alison v. Lincoln Ins. Co.,* 60 N. Wash. 677 (Ct. App. 2000).

The company may refuse to defend the insured only when the allegations in the complaint are completely outside the insurance policy coverage. *Jamison v. Lincoln Ins. Co.,* 58 N. Wash. 430 (1998). If the allegations against the insured *may* fall within the coverage of the policy, but are potentially excluded by any noncoverage provision in the policy, then the insurer is under a duty to defend the insured. The duty continues until a court finds that the insurer is relieved of the liability under the noncoverage provisions of the policy. *Wilson v. Washington Ins. Co.,* 59 N. Wash. 980 (1999).

If it is determined that the company has unjustifiably failed to defend against claims against its insured, the company is liable for any judgment entered against its insured. In addition, the company may be liable for any reasonable settlement entered into by the insured. *Wrickles v. Washington Ins. Co.,* 61 N. Wash. 104 (Ct. App. 2001).
   In summary, the duty to defend the insured must be found in the insurance policy. The company may refuse to defend only if the claim is completely outside the policy coverage. If there is a question of coverage, the company must defend the insured until the court decides the matter. If the company improperly fails to defend the insured, the company may be liable for the judgment against the insured or settlement by the insured.

I hope this letter answers any question you may have regarding this matter. If you require additional information, please contact me.

Sincerely,

_____

Alice Black

Attorney at Law

AB/wkk

ASSIGNMENT 12

Instructor's note: The following is a model demand letter to be sent to Mr. Karl Sanders. It is drafted in modified block style. Note that some information such as dates and the office file number have been added to the facts.

Law Offices of Alice Black

2100 Main Street

Friendly, New Washington, 00065

(200) 267-7000 • FAX 267-7001

November 1, 2003

<u>Via Facsimile and U.S. Mail</u>

Mr. Karl Sanders

930 North Hardwood Court

Friendly, NW 00065

   Re: Insurance claim from Mr. Karl Sanders for automobile collision with Deborah Anderson.
           File No. 01-206

Dear Mr. Sanders:

    Our office has been retained by Washington Insurance Co. to collect payment from you for damages sustained by their insured, Deborah Anderson, in the above-referenced automobile accident. My client has written to you requesting that you either provide proof of insurance at the time of the accident, or that you pay this claim in full. You have not responded.

    This letter is a demand for payment in the amount of $21,235.00. You may mail your payment in full directly to me. Otherwise, you may contact me to see if we can reach a mutually acceptable agreement for payment of this outstanding debt.

    If I do not receive payment or if you do not contact me by the end of business on December 3, 2003, I will assume that you do not dispute this debt, and I will pursue all the legal remedies available to my client under the law. A lawsuit will be filed in District Court for the full amount of the debt plus interest. I will also request any fees and costs I may incur in the pursuit of the litigation.

Once a judgment is obtained I may take action to have your driver's license and vehicle registration suspended under the New Washington Financial Responsibility Act Section 45-6-124. The act allows a judgment creditor to take action to suspend a debtor's driver's license and vehicle registration for nonpayment of any judgment arising from a motor vehicle accident.

Please be advised that this letter is an attempt to collect a debt and any information you provide will be used for that purpose.

I look forward to hearing from you in regard to this matter. Please do not hesitate to call if you have any questions.

Sincerely,

_____

Alice Black

Attorney at Law

AB/wkk

SUGGESTED ASSIGNMENTS: For one or more of the legal memorandum assignments you have assigned in this course, require the students to draft an information, opinion, or demand letter to be sent to either the client or the opposing party.

WEB ASSIGNMENT ANSWERS

ASSIGNMENT 1

Instructor's note: The following is a model information letter to be sent to Mr. Augustin Alcon. It is drafted in full block style. Students may also use modified block.

Law Offices of Alice Black

2100 Main Street

Friendly, New Washington, 00065

(200) 267-7000 • FAX 267-7001

May 22, 2003

Mr. Augustin Alcon
230 North Second Street
Sunnydale, NW 00066

   Re: The requirements of a valid will.

Dear Mr. Alcon:

The purpose of this letter is to inform you of the results of our research in regard to what is required for a will to be valid. The state statute that governs the validity of wills is New Washington Statutes Annotated Section 15-11-502.

Subsection 1 of the statute provides that for a will to be valid it must be in writing and signed by the person making the will. Under the subsection some other individual may sign if the person making the will asks the individual to sign it. If this is the case the individual must sign in the conscious presence of the person making the will.

The subsection also requires that two persons witness the will. The witnesses must see the person making the will sign it. If they don't see the person sign it, the person making the will must tell the witnesses it is his or her signature or tell the witnesses it is his or her will. All of this must take place in the conscious presence of the person making the will. Also, the witnesses must sign the will within a reasonable time after they witness the signature. They may sign either prior to or after the death of the person making the will.

A will may still be valid even though it doesn't meet the above requirements. Under subsection 2 of the statute, a will is valid if it is signed and written in hand by the person making the will. This type of will does not require witnesses.

I hope this letter answers any question you may have regarding this matter. If you require additional information, please contact me.

Sincerely,

_____

Alice Black

Attorney at Law

AB/wkk

ASSIGNMENT 2

Instructor's note: The following is a model opinion letter to be sent to Mrs. Janet Duran. It is drafted in modified block style.

Law Offices of Alice Black

2100 Main Street

Kansas City, Kansas

(200) 267-7000 • FAX 267-7001

January 18, 2003

Via Facsimile and U.S. Mail

Mrs. Janet Duran

641 Oak Drive

Kansas City, Kansas

Re: Whether there is sufficient evidence to support a false imprisonment claim against Shoptown.

Dear Mrs. Dixon:

We recently met in my office to discuss the possibility of filing a false imprisonment claim against Shoptown for the time they falsely detained you for shoplifting.

This opinion is based on the facts outlined in the fact section of this letter and the applicable law as of the date of the letter. This letter is solely for your benefit and limited to the facts discussed below. Please contact me if any of the facts are misstated or if you have additional information.

FACTS

While shopping at Shoptown you realized you needed another item, and your hands being full, you put the extra item, nail polish, in your coat pocket. Later you put the polish back. A store security person saw you put the polish in your pocket, but did not see you put it back. When you left the store, the guard stopped you and took you to the manager's office. He informed you that you were being held for shoplifting. The store manager searched your purse and told you to empty your pockets. After the search the store manager allowed you to leave.

ANSWER

Based upon the above facts and the applicable law, there is not sufficient evidence to support a claim of false imprisonment claim against Shoptown.

EXPLANATION

The Kansas statute governing unlawful restraint is Kan. Stat. Ann. § 21-3424. Subsection three of that statute provides that a merchant or his employee may detain a customer if there is probable cause to believe that the customer has wrongfully taken merchandise. The merchant may detain a person for a reasonable period of time to investigate the matter. Under the act this detention to investigate is not false imprisonment. The statute, however, does not define what is required for probable cause to believe a customer has wrongfully taken merchandise.

The Kansas Court of Appeals in the case of *Melia v. Dillon Companies, Inc.* discussed what is required for probable cause. In this case Mr. Atkin (Atkin), the head of security for the store, saw Mr. Melia (Melia) leave the store without paying for a pouch of tobacco. Melia was stopped in the parking lot where he stated that he had forgotten to pay for the tobacco. Melia thought he would be allowed to pay for the tobacco, but Atkin informed him that the matter would be treated as a shoplifting offense. Melia was detained until the police arrived. Melia sued the store for false imprisonment.

In addressing the detention, the court noted that probable cause exists when there are facts and circumstances within the knowledge of the one who is detaining sufficient to warrant a person of reasonable caution to believe that the person detained has committed an offense. Neither the court nor the statute requires that a store employee be correct in the belief shoplifting has occurred. All that is required is that probable causes exist.

In your case, the security guard saw you put the nail polish in your pocket and thought you left the store without paying for it. Although he was mistaken, based on his observations he had probable cause to believe shoplifting had occurred and therefore your detention was not false imprisonment. Kan. Stat. Ann. 21-3424(3).

In summary, based on Kan. Stat. Ann. 21-3424(3) and the court's ruling in *Melia v. Dillon Companies, Inc.,* it is my opinion that there is not sufficient evidence to support a claim of false imprisonment against Shoptown.

I hope this information answers your question. I regret that I am not able to provide a more favorable answer. If you have additional information concerning this matter or if you have any other questions, please contact me.

Sincerely,

_____

Alice Black
Attorney at Law

AB/wkk

ASSIGNMENT 3

Instructor's note: The following is a model demand letter to be sent to Mr. Kenneth Anderson, Chairperson Board of Directors, Lodestar Inc. It is drafted in modified block style. Note that some information such as dates and the office file number have been added to the facts.

Law Offices of Alice Black

2100 Main Street

Friendly, New Washington 00065

(200) 267-7000 • FAX 267-7001

April 15, 2003

<u>Via Facsimile and U.S. Mail</u>

Mr. Kenneth Anderson

Chairperson, Board of Directors

Lodestar Inc.

330 Maple Ave.

Friendly, NW 00065

   Re: Ms. Helen Anderson
         File No. 01-206

Dear Mr. Anderson:

Our office represents Ms. Helen Anderson in regard to her position as a stockholder in Lodestar Inc. The purpose of this letter is to demand that you call for the holding of the annual meeting of the shareholders of Lodestar Inc.

In your role as chairperson of the board of directors of Lodestar Inc., it is your duty, under section 2-14 of the corporation's by-laws, to call for the holding of the annual shareholder meeting. For the past two years you have refused to perform this duty. Section 2-14 provides that an annual meeting of the shareholders *shall* be held at the corporate offices on the first Monday of May. The section also provides that the chairperson of the board of directors *shall* call the meeting.

In addition, New Washington Statute Annotated Section 77-11-18B provides that the annual meeting of the shareholders *shall* be held at the time designated in the by-laws of the corporation. The section further provides that if the "annual meeting is not held within any thirteen-month period, the district court may, on the application of any shareholder, order a meeting to be held."

If you do not call for the holding of the annual meeting on the first Monday of next May as required by the corporate by-laws, we will take the appropriate steps necessary to obtain the relief provided by section 77-11-18B.

Please contact us to confirm your compliance with the terms of this letter.

Thank you for your consideration of this matter

Sincerely,

_____

Alice Black

Attorney at Law

AB/wkk

TEST QUESTIONS AND ANSWERS

TRUE OR FALSE QUESTIONS

Please write a "T" or "F" to the left of each statement.

_____ 1. Other than documents submitted to courts, correspondence is the primary form of writing designed for an audience outside the law office.

_____ 2. A header contains the full name and address of the law firm.

_____ 3. The body of legal correspondence is usually composed of four parts.

_____ 4. The reference line may include the case name and number if the correspondence concerns a pending lawsuit.

_____ 5. The closing of legal correspondence usually includes the conclusion.

_____ 6. The initials of the typist are usually included with the initials of the drafter in legal correspondence.

_____ 7. The letterhead of legal correspondence usually includes the firm's fax number.

_____ 8. In full block style everything is flush with the left margin.

_____ 9. In modified block style, the date is centered.

_____10. In modified block style, the signature can be just right of the center of the page or flush left.

_____11. A letter that provides general legal information to a client is referred to as an instruction letter.

_____12. An information letter may include a summary of the law involved in a client's case.

_____13. A paralegal or a law clerk may sign an information letter.

_____14. A paralegal or a law clerk may sign an opinion letter.

_____15. An opinion letter is like an information letter in that it provides information concerning the law.

_____16. The body of an opinion letter usually includes a fact section.

_____17. Although an opinion letter provides a legal opinion, it does not constitute the practice law.

_____18. A demand letter may be designed to persuade someone to take action favorable to the interests of the client.

_____19. An opinion letter is often referred to as an advocacy letter.

_____20. The body of a demand letter may include a facts section.

TRUE OR FALSE ANSWERS

Answer	Text Section	Answer	Text Section	Answer	Text Section
1. True	I	8. False	IIM	15. True	IIIB
2. False	IIA	9. True	IIM	16. True	IIIB
3. False	IIG	10. True	IIM	17. False	IIIB
4. True	IIE	11. False	IIIA	18. True	IIIC
5. False	IIH	12. True	IIIA	19. False	IIIC
6. True	IIJ	13. True	IIIA&B	20. True	IIIC
7. True	IIA	14. False	IIIB		

Note to Instructor re No. 8: The letterhead is centered.

MULTIPLE CHOICE QUESTIONS

Please circle the letter of the **most appropriate** answer.

1. The main categories of legal correspondence that include legal research and analysis are:
   a. information letters.
   b. instruction letters.
   c. opinion letters.
   d. demand letters.
   e. all of the above.
   f. a, c, and d
   g. b, c, and d

2. The recipient's address block should include:
   a. the name of the person to whom the letter is addressed.
   b. the individual's title (if any).
   c. the name of the business (if applicable).
   d. the address.
   e. all of the above
   f. a and c
   g. a, b, and c

3. The body of legal correspondence usually consists of:
   a. an introduction.
   b. a main body.
   c. requests/instructions.
   d. a closing.
   e. all of the above
   f. a, b, and c
   g. a, b, and d

4. Legal correspondence usually includes:
   a. the initials of the drafter.
   b. a reference line.
   c. a salutation.
   d. a method of delivery.
   e. all of the above
   f. b, c, and d
   g. b and c

5. The letterhead of legal correspondence usually:
   a. is placed at the left margin.
   b. is repeated at the top left of every page of the correspondence.
   c. does not include the firm's Web site.
   d. does not include the firm's fax number.
   e. all of the above
   f. a and b
   g. none of the above

6. In modified block style:
   a. the date is flush with the left margin.
   b. the letterhead is flush with the left margin.
   c. the first line of each paragraph is indented.
   d. the date is centered.
   e. a, b, and c
   f. a and c
   g. c and d

7. In full block style:
   a. the date is flush with the left margin.
   b. the letterhead is flush with the left margin.
   c. the first line of each paragraph is indented.
   d. the date is centered.
   e. a, b, and c
   f. a and c
   g. c and d

8. Which of the following are types of legal correspondence mentioned in the text?
   a. letters that confirm an appointment
   b. letters that present a firm's bill
   c. letters that provide general legal information
   d. letters that provide a legal opinion
   e. all of the above
   f. a, c, and d
   g. b, c, and d

9. The body of an opinion letter usually includes which of the following components?
   a. facts
   b. answer
   c. table of authorities
   d. preliminary statement
   e. all of the above
   f. a and b
   g. b, c, and d

10. A demand letter:
    a. may be signed by a paralegal or law clerk.
    b. may include a fact section.
    c. usually includes an answer/conclusion section.
    d. is designed to persuade someone to take action or refrain from action.
    e. all of the above
    f. b, c, and d
    g. b and d

11. A letter that provides the reader with a legal opinion and legal advice is referred to as a (an):
    a. instruction letter.
    b. information letter.
    c. opinion letter.
    d. demand letter.

12. A letter that is intended to persuade someone to take action is referred to as a (an):
    a. instruction letter.
    b. information letter.
    c. opinion letter.
    d. demand letter.

MULTIPLE CHOICE ANSWERS

Answer	Text Section	Answer	Text Section	Answer	Text Section
1. f	I	5. g	IIA	9. f	IIIB
2. e	IID	6. g	IIM	10. g	IIIC
3. f	IIG	7. a	IIM	11. c	IIIB
4. e	II	8. e	III	12. d	IIIC

ISBN 0-7668-5456-6

9 780766 854567

90000

Visit **www.delmarlearning.com** or
www.westlegalstudies.com for your lifelong learning solutions.

For more learning solutions from Thomson:
www.thomson.com/learning

THOMSON
DELMAR LEARNING™